NUMBER ONE IN THE

HORNBLOWER SAGA

The greatest naval adventures of all time!

MR. MIDSHIPMAN HORNBLOWER

C.S. FORESTER

PINNACLE BOOKS • **NEW YORK**

MR. MIDSHIPMAN HORNBLOWER

A Pinnacle Book, published by special arrangement with Little,
Brown and Company.

ISBN: 0-523-42053-6

First printing, August 1974
Second printing, November 1974
Third printing, September 1975
Fourth printing, December 1976
Fifth printing, June 1978
Sixth printing, March 1980
Seventh printing, August 1980
Eighth printing, August 1981
Nineth printing, December 1982

Cover illustration by Bruce Minney

Printed in the United States of America

PINNACLE BOOKS, INC.
1430 Broadway
New York, New York 10018

THE MAST BEGAN TO SLIP . . .

. . . to roll, out towards the end of the yard. All about them were thunderous noises—spars smashing, ropes parting. The guns were still bellowing and everyone below seemed to be yelling and screaming.

The top lurched again. Two of the shrouds parted with the strain, with a noise clearly audible, and as they parted the mast twisted with a jerk.

"The mainyard!" Hornblower screamed to the numbed and foolish Finch. "Jump, damn you!" raved Hornblower. "The shrouds—the yard. Jump!"

The words finally penetrated. Finch nodded. Then he let go of the swivel and seemed to launch himself into the air. The mast rolled again, so that when Hornblower launched himself at the shrouds it was a longer jump. Only his shoulders reached. He swung off, clung, nearly lost his grip, and then he was scrambling along the shrouds. Here was the precious mainyard, and he threw himself across it, his feet feeling for the footrope. He was safe . . .

"Thought we'd lost you," the midshipman on deck told him.

"What has happened?" Hornblower asked, bewildered.

The midshipman stared at him before replying. "We carried her by boarding. Why, man, didn't you see?"

"No, I didn't see it," said Hornblower. "Other matters demanded my attention at that moment."

The Hornblower Saga

Also by C. S. Forester

THE HORNBLOWER COMPANION

Contents

I

HORNBLOWER
and the Even Chance

A January gale was roaring up the Channel, blustering loudly, and bearing on its bosom rain squalls whose big drops rattled loudly on the tarpaulin clothing of those among the officers and men whose duties kept them on deck. So hard and so long had the gale blown that even in the sheltered waters of Spithead the battleship moved uneasily at her anchors, pitching a little in the choppy seas, and snubbing herself against the tautened cables with unexpected jerks. A shore boat was on its way out to her, propelled by oars in the hands of two sturdy women; it danced madly on the steep little waves, now and then putting its nose into one and sending a sheet of spray flying aft. The oarswoman in the bow knew her business, and with rapid glances over her shoulder not only kept the boat on its course but turned the bows into the worst of the waves to keep from capsizing. It slowly drew up along the starboard side of the *Justinian*, and as it approached the main chains the midshipman of the watch hailed it.

"Aye aye," came back the answering hail from the lusty lungs of the woman at the stroke oar; by the curious and ages-old convention of the navy the reply meant that the boat had an officer on board—presumably the huddled figure in the sternsheets looking more like a heap of trash with a boat cloak thrown over it.

That was as much as Mr. Masters, the lieutenant of the watch, could see; he was sheltering as best he could

1

in the lee of the mizzenmast bitts, and in obedience to the order of the midshipman of the watch the boat drew up towards the main chains and passed out of his sight. There was a long delay; apparently the officer had some difficulty in getting up the ship's side. At last the boat reappeared in Masters' field of vision; the women had shoved off and were setting a scrap of lugsail, under which the boat, now without its passenger, went swooping back towards Portsmouth, leaping on the waves like a steeplechaser. As it departed Mr. Masters became aware of the near approach of someone along the quarterdeck; it was the new arrival under the escort of the midshipman of the watch, who, after pointing Masters out, retired to the main chains again. Mr. Masters had served in the navy until his hair was white; he was lucky to have received his commission as lieutenant, and he had long known that he would never receive one as captain, but the knowledge had not greatly embittered him, and he diverted his mind by the study of his fellow men.

So he looked with attention at the approaching figure. It was that of a skinny young man only just leaving boyhood behind, something above middle height, with feet whose adolescent proportions to his size were accentuated by the thinness of his legs and his big half-boots. His gawkiness called attention to his hands and elbows. The newcomer was dressed in a badly fitting uniform which was soaked right through by the spray; a skinny neck stuck out of the high stock, and above the neck was a white bony face. A white face was a rarity on the deck of a ship of war whose crew soon tanned to a deep mahogany, but this face was not merely white; in the hollow cheeks there was a faint shade of green—clearly the newcomer had experienced seasickness in his passage out in the shore boat. Set in the white face were a pair of dark eyes which by contrast looked like holes cut in a sheet of paper; Masters noted with a slight stirring of

2

interest that the eyes, despite their owner's seasickness, were looking about keenly, taking in what were obviously new sights; there was a curiosity and interest there which could not be repressed and which continued to function notwithstanding either seasickness or shyness, and Mr. Masters surmised in his far-fetched fashion that this boy had a vein of caution or foresight in his temperament and was already studying his new surroundings with a view to being prepared for his next experiences. So might Daniel have looked about him at the lions when he first entered their den.

The dark eyes met Masters', and the gawky figure came to a halt, raising a hand self-consciously to the brim of his dripping hat. His mouth opened and tried to say something, but closed again without achieving its object as shyness overcame its owner, but then the newcomer nerved himself afresh and forced himself to say the formal words he had been coached to utter.

"Come aboard, sir."

"Your name?" asked Masters, after waiting for it for a moment.

"H-Horatio Hornblower, sir. Midshipman," stuttered the boy.

"Very good, Mr. Hornblower," said Masters, with the equally formal response. "Did you bring your dunnage aboard with you?"

Hornblower had never heard that word before, but he still had enough of his wits about him to deduce what it meant.

"My sea-chest, sir. It's—it's for'rard, at the entry port."

Hornblower said these things with the barest hesitation; he knew that at sea they said them, that they pronounced the word "forward" like that, and that he had come on board through the "entry port," but it called for a slight effort to utter them himself.

"I'll see that it's sent below," said Masters. "And

3

that's where you'd better go, too. The captain's ashore and the first lieutenant's orders were that he's not to be called on any account before eight bells, so I advise you, Mr. Hornblower, to get out of those wet clothes while you can."

"Yes, sir," said Hornblower; his senses told him, the moment he said it, that he had used an improper expression—the look on Masters' face told him, and he corrected himself (hardly believing that men really said these things off the boards of the stage) before Masters had time to correct him.

"Aye aye, sir," said Hornblower, and as a second afterthought he put his hand to the brim of his hat again.

Masters returned the compliment and turned to one of the shivering messengers cowering in the inadequate shelter of the bulwark. "Boy! Take Mr. Hornblower down to the midshipmen's berth."

"Aye aye, sir."

Hornblower accompanied the boy forward to the main hatchway. Seasickness alone would have made him unsteady on his feet, but twice on the short journey he stumbled like a man tripping over a rope as a sharp gust brought the *Justinian* up against her cables with a jerk. At the hatchway the boy slid down the ladder like an eel over a rock; Hornblower had to brace himself and descend far more gingerly and uncertainly, into the dim light of the lower gundeck and then into the twilight of the 'tween-decks. The smells that entered his nostrils were as strange and as assorted as the noises that assailed his ears. At the foot of each ladder the boy waited for him with a patience whose tolerance was just obvious. After the last descent a few steps—Hornblower had already lost his sense of direction and did not know whether it was aft or forward—took them to a gloomy recess whose shadows were accentuated rather than lightened by a tallow dip spiked onto a bit of copper plate on a table round which were seated half a dozen shirtsleeved

4

men. The boy vanished and left Hornblower standing there, and it was a second or two before the whiskered man at the head of the table looked up at him.

"Speak, thou apparition," said he.

Hornblower felt a wave of nausea overcoming him— the after-effects of his trip in the shore boat were being accentuated by the incredible stuffiness and smelliness of the 'tween-decks. It was very hard to speak, and the fact that he did not know how to phrase what he wanted to say made it harder still.

"My name is Hornblower," he quavered at length.

"What an infernal piece of bad luck for you," said a second man at the table, with a complete absence of sympathy.

At that moment in the roaring world outside the ship the wind veered sharply, heeling the *Justinian* a trifle and swinging her round to snub her at her cables again. To Hornblower it seemed more as if the world had come loose from its fastenings. He reeled where he stood, and although he was shuddering with cold he felt sweat on his face.

"I suppose you have come," said the whiskered man at the head of the table, "to thrust yourself among your betters. Another soft-headed ignoramus come to be a nuisance to those who have to try to teach you your duties. Look at him"—the speaker with a gesture demanded the attention of everyone at the table—"look at him, I say! The King's latest bad bargain. How old are you?"

"S-seventeen, sir," stuttered Hornblower.

"Seventeen!" The disgust in the speaker's voice was only too evident. "You must start at twelve if you ever wish to be a seaman. Seventeen! Do you know the difference between a head and a halliard?"

That drew a laugh from the group, and the quality of the laugh was just noticeable to Hornblower's whirling brain, so that he guessed that whether he said "yes" or

5

"no" he would be equally exposed to ridicule. He groped for a neutral reply.

"That's the first thing I'll look up in Clarke's *Seamanship*," he said.

The ship lurched again at that moment, and he clung onto the table.

"Gentlemen," he began, pathetically, wondering how to say what he had in mind.

"My God!" exclaimed somebody at the table. "He's seasick!"

"Seasick in Spithead!" said somebody else, in a tone in which amazement had as much place as disgust.

But Hornblower ceased to care; he was not really conscious of what was going on round him for some time after that. The nervous excitement of the last few days was as much to blame, perhaps, as the journey in the shore boat and the erratic behaviour of the *Justinian* at her anchors, but it meant for him that he was labelled at once as the midshipman who was seasick in Spithead, and it was only natural that the label added to the natural misery of the loneliness and homesickness which oppressed him during those days when that part of the Channel Fleet which had not succeeded in completing its crews lay at anchor in the lee of the Isle of Wight. An hour in the hammock into which the messman hoisted him enabled him to recover sufficiently to be able to report himself to the first lieutenant; after a few days on board he was able to find his way round the ship without (as happened at first) losing his sense of direction below decks so that he did not know whether he was facing forward or aft. During that period his brother officers ceased to have faces which were mere blurs and came to take on personalities; he came painfully to learn the stations allotted him when the ship was at quarters, when he was on watch, and when hands were summoned for setting or taking in sail. He even came to have an acute enough understanding of his new life to realise that it could have been worse—that destiny might have put him on board a ship ordered immediately to sea instead of one lying at anchor. But it was a poor enough compensation; he was a lonely and unhappy boy. Shyness alone would long have delayed his making friends, but as it happened the midshipmen's berth in the *Justinian* was occupied by men all a good deal older than he; elderly master's mates recruited from the merchant service, and midshipmen in their twenties who through lack of patronage or inability to pass the necessary examination had never succeeded in gaining for themselves commissions as lieutenants. They were inclined, after the first moments of amused interest, to ignore him, and he was glad of it, delighted to shrink into his shell and attract no notice to himself.

For the *Justinian* was not a happy ship during those gloomy January days. Captain Keene—it was when he came aboard that Hornblower first saw the pomp and ceremony that surrounds the captain of a ship of the line—was a sick man, of a melancholy disposition. He had not the fame which enabled some captains to fill their ships with enthusiastic volunteers, and he was devoid of the personality which might have made enthusiasts out of the sullen pressed men whom the press gangs were bringing in from day to day to complete the ship's complement. His officers saw little of him, and did not love what they saw. Hornblower, summoned to his cabin for his first interview, was not impressed—a middle-aged man at a table covered with papers, with the hollow and yellow cheeks of prolonged illness.

"Mr. Hornblower," he said, formally, "I am glad to have this opportunity of welcoming you on board my ship."

"Yes, sir," said Hornblower—that seemed more appropriate to the occasion than "aye aye, sir," and a junior midshipman seemed to be expected to say one or the other on all occasions.

"You are—let me see—seventeen?" Captain Keene picked up the paper which apparently covered Hornblower's brief official career.

"Yes, sir."

"July 4th, 1776," mused Keene, reading Hornblower's date of birth to himself. "Five years to the day before I was posted as captain. I had been six years as lieutenant before you were born."

"Yes, sir," agreed Hornblower—it did not seem the occasion for any further comment.

"A doctor's son—you should have chosen a lord for your father if you wanted to make a career for yourself."

"Yes, sir."

"How far did your education go?"

"I was a Grecian at school, sir."

"So you can construe Xenophon as well as Cicero?"

"Yes, sir. But not very well, sir."

"Better if you knew something about sines and cosines. Better if you could foresee a squall in time to get t'gallants in. We have no use for ablative absolutes in the navy."

"Yes, sir," said Hornblower.

He had only just learned what a topgallant was, but he could have told his captain that his mathematical studies were far advanced. He refrained nevertheless; his instincts combined with his recent experiences urged him not to volunteer unsolicited information.

"Well, obey orders, learn your duties, and no harm can come to you. That will do."

"Thank you, sir," said Hornblower, retiring.

But the captain's last words to him seemed to be contradicted immediately. Harm began to come to Hornblower from that day forth, despite his obedience to orders and diligent study of his duties, and it stemmed from the arrival in the midshipmen's berth of John Simpson as senior warrant officer. Hornblower was sitting at mess with his colleagues when he first saw him—

8

a brawny good-looking man in his thirties, who came in and stood looking at them just as Hornblower had stood a few days before.

"Hullo!" said somebody, not very cordially.

"Cleveland, my bold friend," said the newcomer, "come out from that seat. I am going to resume my place at the head of the table."

"But—"

"Come out, I said," snapped Simpson.

Cleveland moved along with some show of reluctance, and Simpson took his place, and glowered round the table in reply to the curious glances with which everyone regarded him.

"Yes, my sweet brother officers," he said, "I am back in the bosom of the family. And I am not surprised that nobody is pleased. You will all be less pleased by the time I am done with you, I may add."

"But your commission—?" asked somebody, greatly daring.

"My commission?" Simpson leaned forward and tapped the table, staring down the inquisitive people on either side of it. "I'll answer that question this once, and the man who asks it again will wish he had never been born. A board of turnip-headed captains has refused me my commission. It decided that my mathematical knowledge was insufficient to make me a reliable navigator. And so Acting-Lieutenant Simpson is once again Mr. Midshipman Simpson, at your service. At your service. And may the Lord have mercy on your souls."

It did not seem, as the days went by, that the Lord had any mercy at all, for since Simpson's return life in the midshipmen's berth ceased to be one of passive unhappiness and became one of active misery. Simpson had apparently always been an ingenious tyrant, but now, embittered and humilated by his failure to pass his examination for his commission, he was a worse tyrant, and his ingenuity had multiplied itself. He may have been

9

weak in mathematics, but he was diabolically clever at making other people's lives a burden to them. As senior officer in the mess he had wide official powers; as a man with a blistering tongue and a morbid sense of mischief he would have been powerful anyway, even if the *Justinian* had possessed an alert and masterful first lieutenant to keep him in check, and Mr. Clay was neither.

Twice midshipmen rebelled against Simpson's arbitrary authority, and each time Simpson thrashed the rebel, pounding him into insensibility with his huge fists, for Simpson would have made a successful prizefighter. Each time Simpson was left unmarked; each time his opponent's blackened eyes and swollen lips called down the penalty of mast heading and extra duty from the indignant first lieutenant. The mess seethed with impotent rage. Even the toadies and lickspittles among the midshipmen—and naturally there were several—hated the tyrant.

Significantly, it was not his ordinary exactions which roused the greatest resentment—his levying toll upon their sea-chests for clean shirts for himself, his appropriation of the best cuts of the meat served, nor even his taking their coveted issues of spirits. These things could be excused as understandable, the sort of thing they would do themselves if they had the power. But he displayed a whimsical arbitrariness which reminded Hornblower, with his classical education, of the freaks of the Roman emperors. He forced Cleveland to shave the whiskers which were his inordinate pride; he imposed upon Hether the duty of waking up Mackenzie every half hour, day and night, so that neither of them was able to sleep—and there were toadies ready to tell him if Hether ever failed in his task. Early enough he had discovered Hornblower's most vulnerable points, as he had with everyone else. He knew of Hornblower's shyness; at first it was amusing to compel Hornblower to recite verses from Gray's "Elegy in a Country Churchyard" to the assembled mess. The toadies could compel Hornblower to do it; Simpson would

10

lay his dirk-scabbard on the table in front of him with a significant glance, and the toadies would close round Hornblower, who knew that any hesitation on his part would mean that he would be stretched across the table and the dirk-scabbard applied. The flat of the scabbard was painful, the edge of it was agonising, but the pain was nothing to the utter humiliation of it all. And the torment grew worse when Simpson instituted what he aptly called "The Proceedings of the Inquisition," when Hornblower was submitted to a slow and methodical questioning regarding his home life and his boyhood. Every question had to be answered, on pain of the dirk-scabbard; Hornblower could fence and prevaricate, but he had to answer and sooner or later the relentless questioning would draw from him some simple admission which would rouse a peal of laughter from his audience. Heaven knows that in Hornblower's lonely childhood there was nothing to be ashamed of, but boys are odd creatures, especially reticent ones like Hornblower, and are ashamed of things no one else would think twice about. The ordeal would leave him weak and sick; someone less solemn might have clowned his way out of his difficulties and even into popular favour, but Hornblower at seventeen was too ponderous a person to clown. He had to endure the persecution, experiencing all the black misery which only a seventeen year old can experience; he never wept in public, but at night more than once he shed the bitter tears of seventeen. He often thought about death; he often even thought about desertion, but he realised that desertion would lead to something worse than death, and then his mind would revert to death, savouring the thought of suicide. He came to long for death, friendless as he was, and brutally ill-treated, and lonely as only a boy among men—and a very reserved boy—can be. More and more he thought about ending it all the easiest way, hugging the secret thought of it to his friendless bosom.

11

If the ship had only been at sea everyone would have been kept busy enough to be out of mischief; even at anchor an energetic captain and first lieutenant would have kept all hands hard enough at work to obviate abuses, but it was Hornblower's hard luck that the *Justinian* lay at anchor all through that fatal January of 1794 under a sick captain and an inefficient first lieutenant. Even the activities which were at times enforced often worked to Hornblower's disadvantage. There was an occasion when Mr. Bowles the master was holding a class in navigation for his mates and for the midshipmen, and the captain by bad luck happened by and glanced through the results of the problem the class had individually been set to solve. His illness made Keene a man of bitter tongue, and he cherished no liking for Simpson. He took a single glance at Simpson's paper, and chuckled sarcastically.

"Now let us all rejoice," he said. "The sources of the Nile have been discovered at last."

"Pardon, sir?" said Simpson.

"Your ship," said Keene, "as far as I can make out from your illiterate scrawl, Mr. Simpson, is in Central Africa. Let us now see what other *terrae incognitae* have been opened up by the remaining intrepid explorers of this class."

It must have been Fate—it was dramatic enough to be art and not an occurrence in real life; Hornblower knew what was going to happen even as Keene picked up the other papers, including his. The result he had obtained was the only one which was correct; everybody else had added the correction for refraction instead of subtracting it, or had worked out the multiplication wrongly, or had (like Simpson) botched the whole problem.

"Congratulations, Mr. Hornblower," said Keene. "You must be proud to be alone successful among this crowd of intellectual giants. You are half Mr. Simpson's age, I fancy. If you double your attainments while you

12

double your years, you will leave the rest of us far behind. Mr. Bowles, you will be so good as to see that Mr. Simpson pays even further attention to his mathematical studies."

With that he went off along the 'tween-decks with the halting step resulting from his mortal disease, and Hornblower sat with his eyes cast down, unable to meet the glances he knew were being darted at him, and knowing full well what they portended. He longed for death at that moment; he even prayed for it that night.

Within two days Hornblower found himself on shore, and under Simpson's command. The two midshipmen were in charge of a party of seamen, landed to act along with parties from the other ships of the squadron as a press gang. The West India convoy was due to arrive soon; most of the hands would be pressed as soon as the convoy reached the Channel, and the remainder, left to work the ships to an anchorage, would sneak ashore, using every device to conceal themselves and find a safe hiding place. It was the business of the landing parties to cut off this retreat, to lay a cordon along the water-front which would sweep them all up. But the convoy was not yet signalled, and all arrangements were completed.

"All is well with the world," said Simpson.

It was an unusual speech for him, but he was in unusual circumstances. He was sitting in the back room of the Lamb Inn, comfortable in one armchair with his legs on another, in front of a roaring fire and with a pot of beer with gin in it at his elbow.

"Here's to the West India convoy," said Simpson, taking a pull at his beer. "Long may it be delayed."

Simpson was actually genial, activity and beer and a warm fire thawing him into a good humour; it was not time yet for the liquor to make him quarrelsome. Hornblower sat on the other side of the fire and sipped beer without gin in it and studied him, marvelling that for the first time since he had boarded the *Justinian* his unhappiness should have ceased to be active but should have subsided into a dull misery like the dying away of the pain of a throbbing tooth.

"Give us a toast, boy," said Simpson.

"Confusion to Robespierre," said Hornblower, lamely.

The door opened and two more officers came in, one a midshipman while the other wore the single epaulette of a lieutenant—it was Chalk of the *Goliath*, the officer in general charge of the press gangs sent ashore. Even Simpson made room for his superior rank before the fire.

"The convoy is still not signalled," announced Chalk. And then he eyed Hornblower keenly. "I don't think I have the pleasure of your acquaintance."

"Mr. Hornblower—Lieutenant Chalk," introduced Simpson. "Mr. Hornblower is distinguished as the midshipman who was seasick in Spithead."

Hornblower tried not to writhe as Simpson tied that label on him. He imagined that Chalk was merely being polite when he changed the subject.

"Hey, potman! Will you gentlemen join me in a glass? We have a long wait before us, I fear. Your men are all properly posted, Mr. Simpson?"

"Yes, sir."

Chalk was an active man. He paced about the room, stared out of the window at the rain, presented his midshipman—Caldwell—to the other two when the drinks arrived, and obviously fretted at his enforced inactivity.

"A game of cards to pass the time?" he suggested. "Excellent! Hey, potman! Cards and a table and another light."

The table was set before the fire, the chairs arranged, the cards brought in.

"What game shall it be?" asked Chalk, looking round.

He was a lieutenant among three midshipmen, and any suggestion of his was likely to carry a good deal of weight; the other three naturally waited to hear what he had to say.

14

"Vingt-et-un? That is a game for the half-witted. Loo? That is a game for the wealthier half-witted. But whist, now? That would give us all scope for the exercise of our poor talents. Caldwell, there, is acquainted with the rudiments of the game, I know. Mr. Simpson?"

A man like Simpson, with a blind mathematical spot, was not likely to be a good whist player, but he was not likely to know he was a bad one.

"As you wish, sir," said Simpson. He enjoyed gambling, and one game was as good as another for that purpose to his mind.

"Mr. Hornblower?"

"With pleasure, sir."

That was more nearly true than most conventional replies. Hornblower had learned his whist in a good school; ever since the death of his mother he had made a fourth with his father and the parson and the parson's wife. The game was already something of a passion with him. He revelled in the nice calculation of chances, in the varying demands it made upon his boldness or caution. There was even enough warmth in his acceptance to attract a second glance from Chalk, who—a good card player himself—at once detected a fellow spirit.

"Excellent!" he said again. "Then we may as well cut at once for places and partners. What shall be the stakes, gentlemen? A shilling a trick and a guinea on the rub, or is that too great? No? Then we are agreed."

For some time the game proceeded quietly. Hornblower cut first Simpson and then Caldwell as his partner. Only a couple of hands were necessary to show up Simpson as a hopeless whist player, the kind who would always lead an ace when he had one, or a singleton when he had four trumps, but he and Hornblower won the first rubber thanks to overwhelming card strength. But Simpson lost the next in partnership with Chalk, cut Chalk again as partner, and lost again. He gloated over good hands and sighed over poor ones; clearly he was one of those unenlightened people who looked upon whist as a social function, or as a mere crude means, like throwing dice, of arbitrarily transferring money. He never thought of the game either as a social rite or as an intellectual exercise. Moreover, as his losses grew, and as the potman came and went with liquor, he grew restless, and his face was flushed with more than the heat of the fire. He was both a bad loser and a bad drinker, and even Chalk's punctilious good manners were sufficiently strained so that he displayed a hint of relief when the next cut gave him Hornblower as a partner. They won the rubber easily, and another guinea and several shillings were transferred to Hornblower's lean purse; he was now the only winner, and Simpson was the heaviest loser. Hornblower was lost in the pleasure of playing the game again; the only attention he paid to Simpson's writhings and muttered objurgations was to regard them as a distracting nuisance; he even forgot to think of them as danger signals. Momentarily he was oblivious to the fact that he might pay for his present success by future torment.

Once more they cut, and he found himself Chalk's partner again. Two good hands gave them the first game. Then twice, to Simpson's unconcealed triumph, Simpson and Caldwell made a small score, approaching game, and in the next hand an overbold finesse by Hornblower left him and Chalk with the odd trick when their score should have been two tricks greater—Simpson laid his knave on Hornblower's ten with a grin of delight which turned to dismay when he found that he and Caldwell had still only made six tricks; he counted them a second time with annoyance. Hornblower dealt and turned the trump, and Simpson led—an ace as usual, assuring Hornblower of his re-entry. Hornblower had a string of trumps and a good suit of clubs which a single lead might establish. Simpson glanced muttering at his hand; it was extraordinary that he still had not realised the simple truth that the lead of an

16

ace involved leading a second time with the problem no clearer. He made up his mind at last and led again; Hornblower's king took the trick and he instantly led his knave of trumps. To his delight it took the trick; he led again and Chalk's queen gave them another trick. Chalk laid down the ace of trumps and Simpson with a curse played the king. Chalk led clubs of which Hornblower had five to the king queen—it was significant that Chalk should lead them, as it could not be a singleton lead when Hornblower held the remaining trumps. Hornblower's queen took the trick; Caldwell must hold the ace, unless Chalk did. Hornblower led a small one; everyone followed suit, Chalk playing the knave, and Caldwell the ace. Eight clubs had been played, and Hornblower had three more headed by the king and ten—three certain tricks, with the last trumps as re-entries. Caldwell played the queen of diamonds, Hornblower played his singleton, and Chalk produced the ace.

"The rest are mine," said Hornblower, laying down his cards.

"What do you mean?" said Simpson, with the king of diamonds in his hand.

"Five tricks," said Chalk, briskly. "Game and rubber."

"But don't I take another?" persisted Simpson.

"I trump a lead of diamonds or hearts and make three more clubs," explained Hornblower. To him the situation was as simple as two and two, a most ordinary finish to a hand; it was hard for him to realise that foggy-minded players like Simpson could find difficulty in keeping tally of fifty-two cards. Simpson flung down his hand.

"You know too much about the game," he said. "You know the backs of the cards as well as the fronts."

Hornblower gulped. He recognised that this could be a decisive moment if he chose. A second before he had merely been playing cards, and enjoying himself. Now he was faced with an issue of life or death. A torrent of thoughts streamed through his mind. Despite the comfort

17

of his present surroundings he remembered acutely the hideous misery of the life in the *Justinian* to which he must return. This was an opportunity to end that misery one way or the other. He remembered how he had contemplated killing himself, and into the back of his mind stole the germ of the plan upon which he was going to act. His decision crystallised.

"That is an insulting remark, Mr. Simpson," he said. He looked round and met the eyes of Chalk and Caldwell, who were suddenly grave; Simpson was still merely stupid. "For that I shall have to ask satisfaction!"

"Satisfaction?" said Chalk, hastily. "Come, come. Mr. Simpson had a momentary loss of temper. I am sure he will explain."

"I have been accused of cheating at cards," said Hornblower. "That is a hard thing to explain away."

He was trying to behave like a grown man; more than that, he was trying to act like a man consumed with indignation, while actually there was no indignation within him over the point in dispute, for he understood too well the muddled state of mind which had led Simpson to say what he did. But the opportunity had presented itself, he had determined to avail himself of it, and now what he had to do was to play the part convincingly of the man who has received a mortal insult.

"The wine was in and the wit was out," said Chalk, still determined on keeping the peace. "Mr. Simpson was speaking in jest, I am sure. Let's call for another bottle and drink it in friendship."

"With pleasure," said Hornblower, fumbling for the words which would set the dispute beyond reconciliation, "if Mr. Simpson will beg my pardon at once before you two gentlemen, and admit that he spoke without justification and in a manner no gentleman would employ."

He turned and met Simpson's eyes with defiance as he spoke, metaphorically waving a red rag before the bull, who charged with gratifying fury.

"Apologise to *you,* you little whippersnapper!" exploded Simpson, alcohol and outraged dignity speaking simultaneously. "Never this side of Hell."

"You hear that, gentlemen?" said Hornblower. "I have been insulted and Mr. Simpson refuses to apologize while insulting me further. There is only one way now in which satisfaction can be given."

For the next two days, until the West India convoy came in, Hornblower and Simpson, under Chalk's orders, lived the curious life of two duellists forced into each other's society before the affair of honour. Hornblower was careful—as he would have been in any case—to obey every order given him, and Simpson gave them with a certain amount of self-consciousness and awkwardness. It was during those two days that Hornblower elaborated on his original idea. Pacing through the dockyards with his patrol of seamen at his heels he had plenty of time to think the matter over. Viewed coldly—and a boy of seventeen in a mood of black despair can be objective enough on occasions—it was as simple as the calculations of the chances in a problem at whist. Nothing could be worse than his life in the *Justinian,* not even (as he had thought already) death itself. Here was an easy death open to him, with the additional attraction that there was a chance of Simpson dying instead. It was at that moment that Hornblower advanced his idea one step further—a new development and startling even to him, bringing him to a halt so that the patrol behind him bumped into him before they could stop.

"Beg your pardon, sir," said the petty officer.

"No matter," said Hornblower, deep in his thoughts.

He first brought forward his suggestion in conversation with Preston and Danvers, the two master's mates whom he asked to be his seconds as soon as he returned to the *Justinian.*

"We'll act for you, of course," said Preston, looking dubiously at the weedy youth when he made his request.

"How do you want to fight him? As the aggrieved party you have the choice of weapons."

"I've been thinking about it ever since he insulted me," said Hornblower temporising. It was not easy to come out with his idea in bald words, after all.

"Have you any skill with the small-sword?" asked Danvers.

"No," said Hornblower. Truth to tell, he had never even handled one.

"Then it had better be pistols," said Preston.

"Simpson is probably a good shot," said Danvers. "I wouldn't care to stand up before him myself."

"Easy now," said Preston, hastily. "Don't dishearten the man."

"I'm not disheartened," said Hornblower. "I was thinking the same thing myself."

"You're cool enough about it, then," marvelled Danvers.

Hornblower shrugged.

"Maybe I am. I hardly care. But I've thought that we might make the chances more even."

"How?"

"We could make them exactly even," said Hornblower, taking the plunge. "Have two pistols, one loaded and the other empty. Simpson and I would take our choice, without knowing which was which. Then we stand within a yard of each other, and at the word, we fire."

"My God!" said Danvers.

"I don't think that would be legal," said Preston. "It would mean one of you would be killed for certain."

"Killing is the object of duelling," said Hornblower. "If the conditions aren't unfair I don't think any objection can be raised."

"But would you carry it out to the end?" marvelled Danvers.

"Mr. Danvers—" began Hornblower, but Preston interfered.

"We don't want another duel on our hands," he said. "Danvers only meant he wouldn't care to do it himself. We'll discuss it with Cleveland and Hether, and see what they say."

Within an hour the proposed conditions of the duel were known to everyone in the ship. Perhaps it was to Simpson's disadvantage that he had no real friend in the ship, for Cleveland and Hether, his seconds, were not disposed to take too firm a stand regarding the conditions of the duel, and agreed to the terms with only a show of reluctance. The tyrant of the midshipmen's berth was paying the penalty for his tyranny. There was some cynical amusement shown by some of the officers; some of both officers and men eyed Hornblower and Simpson with the curiosity that the prospect of death excites in some minds, as if the two destined opponents were men condemned to the gallows. At noon Lieutenant Masters sent for Hornblower.

"The captain has ordered me to make inquiry into this duel, Mr. Hornblower," he said. "I am instructed to use my best endeavours to compose the quarrel."

"Yes, sir."

"Why insist on this satisfaction, Mr. Hornblower? I understand there were a few hasty words over wine and cards."

"Mr. Simpson accused me of cheating, sir, before witnesses, who were not officers of this ship."

That was the point. The witnesses were not members of the ship's company. If Hornblower had chosen to disregard Simpson's words as the ramblings of a drunken ill-tempered man, they might have passed unnoticed. But as he had taken the stand he did, there could be no hushing it up now, and Hornblower knew it.

"Even so, there can be satisfaction without a duel, Mr. Hornblower."

"If Mr. Simpson will make me a full apology before the same gentlemen, I would be satisfied, sir."

21

Simpson was no coward. He would die rather than submit to such a formal humiliation.

"I see. Now I understand you are insisting on rather unusual conditions for the duel?"

"There are precedents for it, sir. As the insulted party I can choose any conditions which are not unfair."

"You sound like a sea lawyer to me, Mr. Hornblower."

The hint was sufficient to tell Hornblower that he had verged upon being too glib, and he resolved in future to bridle his tongue. He stood silent and waited for Masters to resume the conversation.

"You are determined, then, Mr. Hornblower, to continue with this murderous business?"

"Yes, sir."

"The captain has given me further orders to attend the duel in person, because of the strange conditions on which you insist. I must inform you that I shall request the seconds to arrange for that."

"Yes, sir."

"Very good, then, Mr. Hornblower."

Masters looked at Hornblower as he dismissed him even more keenly than he had done when Hornblower first came on board. He was looking for signs of weakness or wavering—indeed, he was looking for any signs of human feeling at all—but he could detect none. Hornblower had reached a decision, he had weighed all the pros and cons, and his logical mind told him that having decided in cold blood upon a course of action it would be folly to allow himself to be influenced subsequently by untrustworthy emotions. The conditions of the duel on which he was insisting were mathematically advantageous. If he had once considered with favour escaping from Simpson's persecution by a voluntary death it was surely a gain to take an even chance of escaping from it without dying. Similarly if Simpson were (as he almost certainly was) a better swordsman and a better pistol shot than he the even

22

chance was again mathematically advantageous. There was nothing to regret about his recent actions.

All very well; mathematically the conclusions were irrefutable, but Hornblower was surprised to find that mathematics were not everything. Repeatedly during that dreary afternoon and evening Hornblower found himself suddenly gulping with anxiety as the realisation came to him afresh that tomorrow morning he would be risking his life on the spin of a coin. One chance out of two and he would be dead, his consciousness at an end, his flesh cold, and the world, almost unbelievably, would be going on without him. The thought sent a shiver through him despite himself. And he had plenty of time for these reflections, for the convention that forbade him from encountering his destined opponent before the moment of the duel kept him necessarily in isolation, as far as isolation could be found on the crowded decks of the *Justinian*. He slung his hammock that night in a depressed mood, feeling unnaturally tired, and he undressed in the clammy, stuffy dampness of the 'tween-decks feeling more than usually cold. He hugged the blankets round himself, yearning to relax in their warmth, but relaxation would not come. Time after time as he began to drift off to sleep he woke again tense and anxious, full of thoughts of the morrow. He turned over wearily a dozen times, hearing the ship's bell ring out each half hour, feeling a growing contempt at his cowardice. He told himself in the end that it was as well that his fate tomorrow depended upon pure chance, for if he had to rely upon steadiness of hand and eye he would be dead for certain after a night like this.

That conclusion presumably helped him to go to sleep for the last hour or two of the night, for he awoke with a start to find Danvers shaking him.

"Five bells," said Danvers. "Dawn in an hour. Rise and shine!"

Hornblower slid out of his hammock and stood in his

23

shirt; the 'tween-decks was nearly dark and Danvers was almost invisible.

"Number One's letting us have the second cutter," said Danvers. "Masters and Simpson and that lot are going first in the launch. Here's Preston."

Another shadowy figure loomed up in the darkness.

"Hellish cold," said Preston. "The devil of a morning to turn out. Nelson, where's that tea?"

The mess attendant came with it as Hornblower was hauling on his trousers. It maddened Hornblower that he shivered enough in the cold for the cup to clatter in the saucer as he took it. But the tea was grateful, and Hornblower drank it eagerly.

"Give me another cup," he said, and was proud of himself that he could think about tea at that moment.

It was still dark as they went down into the cutter.

"Shove off," said the coxswain, and the boat pushed off from the ship's side. There was a keen cold wind blowing which filled the dipping lug as the cutter headed for the twin lights that marked the jetty.

"I ordered a hackney coach at the George to be waiting for us," said Danvers. "Let's hope it is."

It was there, with the driver sufficiently sober to control his horse moderately well despite his overnight potations. Danvers produced a pocket flask as they settled themselves in with their feet in the straw.

"Take a sip, Hornblower?" he asked, proffering it. "There's no special need for a steady hand this morning."

"No thank you," said Hornblower. His empty stomach revolted at the idea of pouring spirits into it.

"The others will be there before us," commented Preston. "I saw the quarter boat heading back just before we reached the jetty."

The etiquette of the duel demanded that the two opponents should reach the ground separately; but only one boat would be necessary for the return.

24

"The sawbones is with them," said Danvers. "Though God knows what use he thinks he'll be today."

He sniggered, and with overlate politeness tried to cut his snigger off short.

"How are you feeling, Hornblower?" asked Preston.

"Well enough," said Hornblower, forbearing to add that he only felt well enough while this kind of conversation was not being carried on.

The hackney coach levelled itself off as it came over the crest of the hill, and stopped beside the Common. Another coach stood there waiting, its single candle-lamp burning yellow in the growing dawn.

"There they are," said Preston; the faint light revealed a shadowy group standing on frosty turf among the gorse bushes.

Hornblower, as they approached, caught a glimpse of Simpson's face as he stood a little detached from the others. It was pale, and Hornblower noticed that at that moment he swallowed nervously, just as he himself was doing. Masters came towards them, shooting his usual keen inquisitive look at Hornblower as they came together.

"This is the moment," he said, "for this quarrel to be composed. This country is at war. I hope, Mr. Hornblower, that you can be persuaded to save a life for the King's service by not pressing this matter."

Hornblower looked across at Simpson, while Danvers answered for him.

"Has Mr. Simpson offered the proper redress?" asked Danvers.

"Mr. Simpson is willing to acknowledge that he wishes the incident had never taken place."

"That is an unsatisfactory form," said Danvers. "It does not include an apology, and you must agree that an apology is necessary, sir."

"What does your principal say?" persisted Masters.

"It is not for my principal to speak in these circumstances," said Danvers, with a glance at Hornblower, who nodded. All this was as inevitable as the ride in the hangman's cart, and as hideous. There could be no going back now; Hornblower had never thought for one moment that Simpson would apologise, and without an apology the affair must be carried to a bloody conclusion. An even chance that he did not have five minutes longer to live.

"You are determined, then, gentlemen," said Masters. "I shall have to state that fact in my report."

"We are determined," said Preston.

"Then there is nothing for it but to allow this deplorable affair to proceed. I left the pistols in the charge of Doctor Hepplewhite."

He turned and led them towards the other group— Simpson with Hether and Cleveland, and Doctor Hepplewhite standing with a pistol held by the muzzle in each hand. He was a bulky man with the red face of a persistent drinker; he was actually grinning a spirituous grin at that moment, rocking a little on his feet.

"Are the young fools set in their folly?" he asked, but everyone very properly ignored him, having no business to ask such a question at such a moment.

"Now," said Masters. "Here are the pistols, both primed, as you see, but one loaded and the other unloaded, in accordance with the conditions. I have here a guinea which I propose to spin to decide the allocation of the weapons. Now, gentlemen, shall the spin give your principals one pistol each irrevocably—for instance, if the coin shows heads shall Mr. Simpson have this one—or shall the winner of spin have choice of weapons? It is my design to eliminate all possibility of collusion as far as possible."

Hether and Cleveland and Danvers and Preston exchanged dubious glances.

"Let the winner of the spin choose," said Preston at length.

"Very well, gentlemen. Please call, Mr. Hornblower."

"Tails!" said Hornblower as the gold piece spun in the air.

Masters caught it and clapped a hand over it.

"Tails it is," said Masters, lifting his hand and revealing the coin to the grouped seconds. "Please make your choice."

Hepplewhite held out the two pistols to him, death in one hand and life in the other. It was a grim moment. There was only pure chance to direct him; it called for a little effort to force his hand out.

"I'll have this one," he said; as he touched it the weapon seemed icy cold.

"Then now I have done what was required of me," said Masters. "The rest is for you gentlemen to carry out."

"Take this one, Simpson," said Hepplewhite. "And be careful how you handle yours, Mr. Hornblower. You're a public danger."

The man was still grinning, gloating over the fact that someone else was in mortal danger while he himself was in none. Simpson took the pistol Hepplewhite offered him and settled it into his hand; once more his eyes met Hornblower's, but there was neither recognition nor expression in them.

"There are no distances to step out," Danvers was saying. "One spot's as good as another. It's level enough here."

"Very good," said Hether. "Will you stand here, Mr. Simpson?"

Preston beckoned to Hornblower, who walked over. It was not easy to appear brisk and unconcerned. Preston took him by the arm and stood him up in front of Simpson, almost breast to breast—close enough to smell the alcohol on his breath.

"For the last time, gentlemen," said Masters, loudly. "Cannot you be reconciled?"

27

There was no answer from anybody, only deep silence, during which it seemed to Hornblower that the frantic beating of his heart must be clearly audible. The silence was broken by an exclamation from Hether.

"We haven't settled who's to give the word!" he said. "Who's going to?"

"Let's ask Mr. Masters to give it," said Danvers.

Hornblower did not look round. He was looking steadfastly at the grey sky past Simpson's right ear—somehow he could not look him in the face, and he had no idea where Simpson was looking. The end of the world as he knew it was close to him—soon there might be a bullet through his heart.

"I will do it if you are agreed, gentlemen," he heard Masters say.

The grey sky was featureless; for this last look on the world he might as well have been blindfolded. Masters raised his voice again.

"I will say 'one, two, three, fire,' " he announced, "with those intervals. At the last word, gentlemen, you can fire as you will. Are you ready?"

"Yes," came Simpson's voice, almost in Hornblower's ear, it seemed.

"Yes," said Hornblower. He could hear the strain in his own voice.

"One," said Masters, and Hornblower felt at that moment the muzzle of Simpson's pistol against his left ribs, and he raised his own.

It was in that second that he decided he could not kill Simpson even if it were in his power, and he went on lifting his pistol, forcing himself to look to see that it was pressed against the point of Simpson's shoulder. A slight wound would suffice.

"Two," said Masters. "Three. Fire!"

Hornblower pulled his trigger. There was a click and a spurt of smoke from the lock of his pistol. The priming had gone off but no more—his was the unloaded weapon, and he knew what it was to die. A tenth of a second later there was a click and spurt of smoke from Simpson's pistol against his heart. Stiff and still they both stood, slow to realise what had happened.

"A misfire, by God!" said Danvers.

The seconds crowded round them.

"Give me those pistols!" said Masters, taking them from the weak hands that held them. "The loaded one might be hanging fire, and we don't want it to go off now."

"Which was the loaded one?" asked Hether, consumed with curiosity.

"That is something it is better not to know," answered Masters, changing the two pistols rapidly from hand to hand so as to confuse everyone.

"What about a second shot?" asked Danvers, and Masters looked up straight and inflexibly at him.

"There will be no second shot," he said. "Honour is completely satisfied. These two gentlemen have come through this ordeal extremely well. No one can now think little of Mr. Simpson if he expresses his regret for the occurrence, and no one can think little of Mr. Hornblower if he accepts that statement in reparation."

Hepplewhite burst into a roar of laughter.

"Your faces!" he boomed, slapping his thigh. "You ought to see how you all look! Solemn as cows!"

"Mr. Hepplewhite," said Masters. "Your behaviour is indecorous. Gentlemen, our coaches are waiting on the road, the cutter is at the jetty. And I think all of us would be the better for some breakfast; including Mr. Hepplewhite."

That should have been the end of the incident. The excited talk which had gone round the anchored squadron about the unusual duel died away in time, although everyone knew Hornblower's name now, and not as the midshipman who was seasick in Spithead but as the man who was willing to take an even chance in cold blood. But in the *Justinian* herself there was other talk; whispers which were circulated forward and aft.

"Mr. Hornblower has requested permission to speak to you, sir," said Mr. Clay, the first lieutenant, one morning while making his report to the captain.

"Oh, send him in when you go out," said Keene, and sighed.

Ten minutes later a knock on his cabin door ushered in a very angry young man.

"Sir!" began Hornblower.

"I can guess what you're going to say," said Keene.

"Those pistols in the duel I fought with Simpson were not loaded!"

"Hepplewhite blabbed, I suppose," said Keene.

"And it was by your orders, I understand, sir."

"You are quite correct. I gave those orders to Mr. Masters."

"It was unwarrantable liberty, sir!"

That was what Hornblower meant to say, but he stumbled without dignity over the polysyllables.

"Possibly it was," said Keene, patiently, rearranging, as always, the papers on his desk.

The calmness of the admission disconcerted Hornblower, who could only splutter for the next few moments.

"I saved a life for the King's service," went on Keene, when the spluttering died away. "A young life. No one has suffered any harm. On the other hand, both you and Simpson have had your courage amply proved. You both know you can stand fire now, and so does everyone else."

"You have touched my personal honour, sir," said Hornblower, bringing out one of his rehearsed speeches. "For that there can only be one remedy."

"Restrain yourself, please, Mr. Hornblower." Keene shifted himself in his chair with a wince of pain as he prepared to make a speech. "I must remind you of one salutary regulation of the navy, to the effect that no junior officer can challenge his superior to a duel. The reasons for it are obvious—otherwise promotion would be too easy. The mere issuing of a challenge by a junior to a senior is a court-martial offence, Mr. Hornblower."

"Oh!" said Hornblower, feebly.

"Now here is some gratuitous advice," went on Keene. "You have fought one duel and emerged with honour. That is good. Never fight another—that is better. Some people, oddly enough, acquire a taste for duelling, as a tiger acquires a taste for blood. They are never good officers, and never popular ones either."

It was then that Hornblower realised that a great part of the keen excitement with which he had entered the captain's cabin was due to anticipation of the giving of the challenge. There could be a morbid desire for danger —and a morbid desire to occupy momentarily the centre of the stage. Keene was waiting for him to speak, and it was hard to say anything.

"I understand, sir," he said at last.

Keene shifted in his chair again.

"There is another matter I wanted to take up with you, Mr. Hornblower. Captain Pellew of the *Indefatigable* has room for another midshipman. Captain Pellew is partial to a game of whist, and has no good fourth on board. He and I have agreed to consider favourably your application for a transfer should you care to make one. I don't have to point out that any ambitious young officer would jump at the chance of serving in a frigate."

"A frigate!" said Hornblower.

Everybody knew of Pellew's reputation and success. Distinction, promotion, prize money—an officer under Pellew's command could hope for all these. Competition for nomination to the *Indefatigable* must be intense, and this was the chance of a lifetime. Hornblower was on the point of making a glad acceptance, when further considerations restrained him.

"That is very good of you, sir," he said. "I do not know

31

how to thank you. But you accepted me as a midshipman here, and of course, I must stay with you."

The drawn, apprehensive face relaxed into a smile.

"Not many men would have said that," said Keene. "But I am going to insist on your accepting the offer. I shall not live very much longer to appreciate your loyalty. And this ship is not the place for you—this ship with her useless captain (don't interrupt me) and her worn-out first lieutenant and her old midshipmen. You should be where there may be speedy opportunities of advancement. I have the good of the service in mind, Mr. Hornblower, when I suggest you accept Captain Pellew's invitation—and it might be less disturbing for me if you did."

"Aye aye, sir," said Hornblower.

II

HORNBLOWER

and the Cargo of Rice

The wolf was in among the sheep. The tossing grey water of the Bay of Biscay was dotted with white sails as far as the eye could see, and although a strong breeze was blowing every vessel was under perilously heavy canvas. Every ship but one was trying to escape; the exception was His Majesty's frigate *Indefatigable,* Captain Sir Edward Pellew. Farther out in the Atlantic, hundreds of miles away, a great battle was being fought, where the ships of the line were thrashing out the question as to whether England or France should wield the weapon of the sea power; here in the Bay the convoy which the French ships were intended to escort was exposed to the attack of a ship of prey at liberty to capture any ship she could overhaul. She had come surging up from leeward, cutting off all chance of escape in that direction, and the clumsy merchant ships were forced to beat to windward; they were all filled with the food which revolutionary France (her economy disordered by the convulsion through which she was passing) was awaiting so anxiously, and their crews were all anxious to escape confinement in an English prison. Ship after ship was overhauled; a shot or two, and the new-fangled tricolour came fluttering down from the gaff, and a prize crew was hurriedly sent on board to conduct the captive to an English port while the frigate dashed after fresh prey.

On the quarterdeck of the *Indefatigable* Pellew fumed over each necessary delay. The convoy, each ship as close to the wind as she would lie, and under all the sail she could carry, was slowly scattering, spreading farther and farther with the passing minutes, and some of these would find safety in mere dispersion if any time was wasted. Pellew did not wait to pick up his boat; at each surrender he merely ordered away an officer and an armed guard, and the moment the prize crew was on its way he filled his main topsail again and hurried off after the next victim. The brig they were pursuing at the moment was slow to surrender. The long nine-pounders in the *Indefatigable*'s bows bellowed out more than once; on that heaving sea it was not so easy to aim accurately and the brig continued on her course hoping for some miracle to save her.

"Very well," snapped Pellew. "He has asked for it. Let him have it."

The gunlayers at the bow chasers changed their point of aim, firing at the ship instead of across her bows.

"Not into the hull, damn it," shouted Pellew—one shot had struck the brig perilously close to her waterline. "Cripple her."

The next shot by luck or by judgment was given better elevation. The slings of the fore topsail yard were shot away, the reefed sail came down, the yard hanging lopsidedly, and the brig came up into the wind for the *Indefatigable* to heave-to close beside her, her broadside ready to fire into her. Under that threat her flag came down.

"What brig's that?" shouted Pellew through his megaphone.

"*Marie Galante* of Bordeaux," translated the officer beside Pellew as the French captain made reply. "Twenty four days out from New Orleans with rice."

"Rice!" said Pellew. "That'll sell for a pretty penny when we get her home. Two hundred tons, I should say. Twelve of a crew at most. She'll need a prize crew of four, a midshipman's command."

He looked round him as though for inspiration before giving his next order.

"Mr. Hornblower!"

"Sir!"

"Take four men of the cutter's crew and board that brig. Mr. Soames will give you our position. Take her into any English port you can make, and report there for orders."

"Aye aye, sir."

Hornblower was at his station at the starboard quarter-deck carronades—which was perhaps how he had caught Pellew's eye—his dirk at his side and a pistol in his belt. It was a moment for fast thinking, for anyone could see Pellew's impatience. With the *Indefatigable* cleared for action, his sea-chest would be part of the surgeon's operating table down below, so that there was no chance of getting anything out of it. He would have to leave just as he was. The cutter was even now clawing up to a position on the *Indefatigable*'s quarter, so he ran to the ship's side and hailed her, trying to make his voice sound as big and as manly as he could, and at the word of the lieutenant in command she turned her bows in towards the frigate.

"Here's our latitude and longitude, Mr. Hornblower," said Soames the master, handing a scrap of paper to him.

"Thank you," said Hornblower, shoving it into his pocket.

He scrambled awkwardly into the mizzen chains and looked down into the cutter. Ship and boat were pitching together, almost bows on to the sea, and the distance between them looked appallingly great; the bearded seaman standing in the bows could only just reach up to the chains with his long boat hook. Hornblower hesitated for a long second; he knew he was ungainly and awkward—book learning was of no use when it came to jumping into a boat—but he had to make the leap, for Pellew was fuming behind him and the eyes of the boat's crew and of the whole ship's company were on him. Better to jump and hurt himself, better to jump and make an exhibition of himself, than to delay the ship. Waiting was certain fail-

35

ure, while he still had a choice if he jumped. Perhaps at a word from Pellew the *Indefatigable*'s helmsman allowed the ship's head to fall off from the sea a little. A somewhat diagonal wave lifted the *Indefatigable*'s stern and then passed on, so that the cutter's bows rose as the ship's stern sank a trifle. Hornblower braced himself and leaped. His feet reached the gunwale and he tottered there for one indescribable second. A seaman grabbed the breast of his jacket and he fell forward rather than backward. Not even the stout arm of the seaman, fully extended, could hold him up, and he pitched head foremost, legs in the air, upon the hands on the second thwart. He cannoned onto their bodies, knocking the breath out of his own against their muscular shoulders, and finally struggled into an upright position.

"I'm sorry," he gasped to the men who had broken his fall.

"Never you mind, sir," said the nearest one, a real tarry sailor, tattooed and pigtailed. "You're only a featherweight."

The lieutenant in command was looking at him from the sternsheets.

"Would you go to the brig, please, sir?" he asked, and the lieutenant bawled an order and the cutter swung round as Hornblower made his way aft.

It was a pleasant surprise not to be received with the broad grins of tolerantly concealed amusement. Boarding a small boat from a big frigate in even a moderate sea was no easy matter; probably every man on board had arrived head first at some time or other, and it was not in the tradition of the service, as understood in the *Indefatigable,* to laugh at a man who did his best without shirking.

"Are you taking charge of the brig?" asked the lieutenant.

"Yes, sir. The captain told me to take four of your men."

"They had better be topmen, then," said the lieutenant,

casting his eyes aloft at the rigging of the brig. The fore topsail yard was hanging precariously, and the jib halliard had slacked off so that the sail was flapping thunderously in the wind. "Do you know these men, or shall I pick 'em for you?"

"I'd be obliged if you would, sir."

The lieutenant shouted four names, and four men replied.

"Keep 'em away from drink and they'll be all right," said the lieutenant. "Watch the French crew. They'll recapture the ship and have you in a French gaol before you can say 'Jack Robinson' if you don't."

"Aye aye, sir," said Hornblower.

The cutter surged alongside the brig, white water creaming between the two vessels. The tattooed sailor hastily concluded a bargain with another man on his thwart and pocketed a lump of tobacco—the men were leaving their possessions behind just like Hornblower— and sprang for the main chains. Another man followed him, and they stood and waited while Hornblower with difficulty made his way forward along the plunging boat. He stood, balancing precariously, on the forward thwart. The main chains of the brig were far lower than the mizzen chains of the *Indefatigable,* but this time he had to jump upwards. One of the seamen steadied him with an arm on his shoulder.

"Wait for it, sir," he said. "Get ready. Now jump, sir."

Hornblower hurled himself, all arms and legs, like a leaping frog, at the main chains. His hands reached the shrouds, but his knee slipped off, and the brig, rolling, lowered him thigh deep into the sea as the shrouds slipped through his hands. But the waiting seamen grabbed his wrists and hauled him on board, and two more seamen followed him. He led the way onto the deck.

The first sight to meet his eyes was a man seated on the hatch cover, his head thrown back, holding to his mouth a bottle, the bottom pointing straight up to the sky. He was one of a large group all sitting round the hatch cover; there were more bottles in evidence; one was passed by one man to another as he looked, and as he approached a roll of the ship brought an empty bottle rolling past his toes to clatter into the scuppers. Another of the group, with white hair blowing in the wind, rose to welcome him, and stood for a moment with waving arms and rolling eyes, bracing himself as though to say something of immense importance and seeking earnestly for the right words to use.

"Goddam English," was what he finally said, and, having said it, he sat down with a bump on the hatch cover and from a seated position proceeded to lie down and compose himself to sleep with his head on his arms.

"They've made the best of their time, sir, by the Holy," said the seaman at Hornblower's elbow.

"Wish we were as happy," said another.

A case still a quarter full of bottles, each elaborately sealed, stood on the deck beside the hatch cover, and the seaman picked out a bottle to look at it curiously. Hornblower did not need to remember the lieutenant's warnings; on his shore excursions with press gangs he had already had experience of the British seaman's tendency to drink. His boarding party would be as drunk as the Frenchmen in half an hour if he allowed it. A frightful mental picture of himself drifting in the Bay of Biscay with a disabled ship and a drunken crew, rose in his mind and filled him with anxiety.

"Put that down," he ordered.

The urgency of the situation made his seventeen-year-old voice crack like a fourteen-year-old's, and the seaman hesitated, holding the bottle in his hand.

"Put it down, d'ye hear?" said Hornblower, desperate with worry. This was his first independent command; conditions were absolutely novel, and excitement brought out all the passion of his mercurial temperament, while at the same time the more calculating part of his mind told him that if he were not obeyed now he never would be. His pistol was in his belt, and he put his hand on the butt, and it is conceivable that he would have drawn it and used it (if the priming had not got wet, he said to himself bitterly when he thought about the incident later on) but the seaman with one more glance at him put the bottle back into the case. The incident was closed, and it was time for the next step.

"Take these men for'rard," he said, giving the obvious order. "Throw 'em into the forecastle."

"Aye aye, sir."

Most of the Frenchmen could still walk, but three were dragged by their collars while the British herded the others before them.

"Come alongee," said one of the seamen. "Thisa waya."

He evidently believed a Frenchman would understand him better if he spoke like that. The Frenchman who had greeted their arrival, now awakened and suddenly realising he was being dragged forward, broke away and turned back to Hornblower.

"I officer," he said, pointing to himself. "I not go wit' zem."

"Take him away!" said Hornblower. In his tense condition he could not stop to debate trifles.

He dragged the case of bottles down to the ship's side and pitched them overboard two at a time—obviously it was wine of some special vintage which the Frenchmen had decided to drink before the English could get their hands on it, but that weighed not at all with Hornblower, for a British seaman could get drunk on vintage claret as easily as upon service rum. The task was finished before the last of the Frenchmen disappeared into the forecastle, and Hornblower had time to look about him. The strong breeze blew confusingly round his ears, and the ceaseless thunder of the flapping jib made it hard to think as he looked at the ruin aloft. Every sail was flat aback, the brig was moving jerkily, gathering sternway for a space before

39

her untended rudder threw her round to spill the wind and bring her up again like a jibbing horse. His mathematical mind had already had plenty of experience with a well-handled ship, with the delicate adjustment between after sails and headsails. Here the balance had been disturbed, and Hornblower was at work on the problem of forces acting on plane surfaces when his men came trooping back to him. One thing at least was certain, and that was that the precariously hanging fore topsail yard would tear itself free to do all sorts of unforeseeable damage if it were tossed about much more. The ship must be properly hove-to, and Hornblower could guess how to set about it, and he formulated the order in his mind just in time to avoid any appearance of hesitation.

"Brace the after yards to larboard," he said. "Man the braces, men."

They obeyed him, while he himself went gingerly to the wheel; he had served a few tricks as helmsman, learning his professional duties under Pellew's orders, but he did not feel happy about it. The spokes felt foreign to his fingers as he took hold; he spun the wheel experimentally but timidly. But it was easy. With the after yards braced round the brig rode more comfortably at once, and the spokes told their own story to his sensitive fingers as the ship became a thing of logical construction again. Hornblower's mind completed the solution of the problem of the effect of the rudder at the same time as his senses solved it empirically. The wheel could be safely lashed, he knew, in these conditions, and he slipped the becket over the spoke and stepped away from the wheel, with the *Marie Galante* riding comfortably and taking the seas on her starboard bow.

The seaman took his competence gratifyingly for granted, but Hornblower, looking at the tangle on the foremast, had not the remotest idea of how to deal with the next problem. He was not even sure about what was wrong. But the hands under his orders were seamen of

40

vast experience, who must have dealt with similar emergencies a score of times. The first—indeed the only—thing to do was to delegate his responsibility.

"Who's the oldest seaman among you?" he demanded —his determination not to quaver made him curt.

"Matthews, sir," said someone at length, indicating with his thumb the pigtailed and tattooed seaman upon whom he had fallen in the cutter.

"Very well, then. I'll rate you petty officer, Matthews. Get to work at once and clear that raffle away for'rard. I'll be busy here aft."

It was a nervous moment for Hornblower, but Matthews put his knuckles to his forehead.

"Aye aye, sir," he said, quite as a matter of course.

"Get that jib in first, before it flogs itself to pieces," said Hornblower, greatly emboldened.

"Aye aye, sir."

"Carry on, then."

The seamen turned to go forward, and Hornblower walked aft. He took the telescope from its becket on the poop, and swept the horizon. There were a few sails in sight; the nearest ones he could recognise as prizes, which, with all sail set that they could carry, were heading for England as fast as they could go. Far away to windward he could see the *Indefatigable's* topsails as she clawed after the rest of the convoy—she had already overhauled and captured all the slower and less weatherly vessels so that each succeeding chase would be longer. Soon he would be alone on this wide sea, three hundred miles from England. Three hundred miles—two days with a fair wind; but how long if the wind turned foul?

He replaced the telescope; the men were already hard at work forward, so he went below and looked round the neat cabins of the officers, two single ones for the captain and the mate, presumably, and a double one for the bosun and the cook or the carpenter. He found the lazarette, identifying it by the miscellaneous stores within it;

41

the door was swinging to and fro with a bunch of keys dangling. The French captain, faced with the loss of all he possessed, had not even troubled to lock the door again after taking out the case of wine. Hornblower locked the door and put the keys in his pocket, and felt suddenly lonely—his first experience of the loneliness of the man in command at sea. He went on deck again, and at sight of him Matthews hurried aft and knuckled his forehead.

"Beg pardon, sir, but we'll have to use the jeers to sling that yard again."

"Very good."

"We'll need more hands than we have, sir. Can I put some o' they Frenchies to work?"

"If you think you can. If any of them are sober enough."

"I think I can, sir. Drunk or sober."

"Very good."

It was at that moment that Hornblower remembered with bitter self-reproach that the priming of his pistol was probably wet, and he had not scorn enough for himself at having put his trust in a pistol without repriming after evolutions in a small boat. While Matthews went forward he dashed below again. There was a case of pistols which he remembered having seen in the captain's cabin, with a powder flask and bullet bag hanging beside it. He loaded both weapons and reprimed his own, and came on deck again with three pistols in his belt just as his men appeared from the forecastle herding half a dozen Frenchmen. He posed himself in the poop, straddling with his hands behind his back, trying to adopt an air of magnificent indifference and understanding. With the jeers taking the weight of yard and sail, an hour's hard work resulted in the yard being slung again and the sail reset.

When the work was advancing towards completion Hornblower came to himself again to remember that in a few minutes he would have to set a course, and he dashed below again to set out the chart and the dividers and par-

42

allel rulers. From his pocket he extracted the crumpled scrap of paper with his position on it—he had thrust it in there so carelessly a little while back, at a time when the immediate problem before him was to transfer himself from the *Indefatigable* to the cutter. It made him unhappy to think how cavalierly he had treated that scrap of paper then; he began to feel that life in the navy, although it seemed to move from one crisis to another, was really one continuous crisis, that even while dealing with one emergency it was necessary to be making plans to deal with the next. He bent over the chart, plotted his position, and laid off his course. It was a queer uncomfortable feeling to think that what had up to this moment been an academic exercise conducted under the reassuring supervision of Mr. Soames was now something on which hinged his life and his reputation. He checked his working, decided on his course, and wrote it down on a scrap of paper for fear he should forget it.

So when the fore topsail yard was reslung, and the prisoners herded back into the forecastle, and Matthews looked to him for further orders, he was ready.

"We'll square away," he said. "Matthews, send a man to the wheel."

He himself gave a hand at the braces; the wind had moderated and he felt his men could handle the brig under her present sail.

"What course, sir?" asked the man at the wheel, and Hornblower dived into his pocket for his scrap of paper.

"Nor'east by north," he said, reading it out.

"Nor'east by north, sir," said the helmsman, and the *Marie Galante,* running free, set her course for England.

Night was closing in by now, and all round the circle of the horizon there was not a sail in sight. There must be plenty of ships just over the horizon, he knew, but that did not do much to ease his feeling of loneliness as darkness came on. There was so much to do, so much to bear in mind, and all the responsibility lay on his unaccustomed shoulders. The prisoners had to be battened down in the forecastle, a watch had to be set—there was even the trivial matter of hunting up flint and steel to light the binnacle lamp. A hand forward as a lookout, who could also keep an eye on the prisoners below; a hand aft at the wheel. Two hands snatching some sleep—knowing that to get in any sail would be an all-hands job—a hasty meal of water from the scuttlebutt and of biscuit from the cabin stores in the lazarette—a constant eye to be kept on the weather. Hornblower paced the deck in the darkness.

"Why don't you get some sleep, sir?" asked the man at the wheel.

"I will, later on, Hunter," said Hornblower, trying not to allow his tone to reveal the fact that such a thing had never occurred to him.

He knew it was sensible advice, and he actually tried to follow it, retiring below to fling himself down on the captain's cot, but of course he could not sleep. When he heard the lookout bawling down the companionway to rouse the other two hands to relieve the watch (they were asleep in the next cabin to him) he could not prevent himself from getting up again and coming on deck to see that all was well. With Matthews in charge he felt he should not be anxious, and he drove himself below again, but he had hardly fallen onto the cot again when a new thought brought him to his feet again, his skin cold with anxiety, and a prodigious self-contempt vying with the anxiety for first place in his emotions. He rushed on deck and walked forward to where Matthews was squatting by the knightheads.

"Nothing has been done to see if the brig is taking in any water," he said—he had hurriedly worked out the wording of that sentence during his walk forward, so as to cast no aspersion on Matthews and yet at the same time, for the sake of discipline, attributing no blame to himself.

"That's so, sir," said Matthews.

"One of those shots fired by the *Indefatigable* hulled her," went on Hornblower. "What damage did it do?"

"I don't rightly know, sir," said Matthews. "I was in the cutter at the time."

"We must look as soon as it's light," said Hornblower. "And we'd better sound the well now."

Those were brave words; during his rapid course in seamanship aboard the *Indefatigable* Hornblower had had a little instruction everywhere, working under the orders of every head of department in rotation. Once he had been with the carpenter when he sounded the well—whether he could find the well in this ship and sound it he did not know.

"Aye aye, sir," said Matthews, without hesitation, and strolled aft to the pump. "You'll need a light, sir. I'll get one."

When he came back with the lantern he shone it on the coiled sounding line hanging beside the pump, so that Hornblower recognized it at once. He lifted it down, inserted the three-foot weighted rod into the aperture of the well, and then remembered in time to take it out again and make sure it was dry. Then he let it drop, paying out the line until he felt the rod strike the ship's bottom with a satisfactory thud. He hauled out the line again, and Matthews held the lantern as Hornblower with some trepidation brought out the timber to examine it.

"Not a drop, sir!" said Matthews. "Dry as yesterday's pannikin."

Hornblower was agreeably surprised. Any ship he had ever heard of leaked to a certain extent; even in the well-found *Indefatigable* pumping had been necessary every day. He did not know whether this dryness was a remarkable phenomenon or a very remarkable one. He wanted to be both noncommittal and imperturbable.

"H'm," was the comment he eventually produced. "Very good, Matthews. Coil that line again."

The knowledge that the *Marie Galante* was making no

45

water at all might have encouraged him to sleep, if the wind had not chosen to veer steadily and strengthen itself somewhat, soon after he retired again. It was Matthews who came down and pounded on his door with the unwelcome news.

"We can't keep the course you set much longer, sir," concluded Matthews. "And the wind's coming gusty-like."

"Very good, I'll be up. Call all hands," said Hornblower, with a testiness that might have been the result of a sudden awakening if it had not really disguised his inner quaverings.

With such a small crew he dared not run the slightest risk of being taken by surprise by the weather. Nothing could be done in a hurry, as he soon found. He had to take the wheel while his four hands laboured at reefing topsails and snugging the brig down, and the task took half the night, and by the time it was finished it was quite plain that with the wind veering northerly the *Marie Galante* could not steer northeast by north any longer. Hornblower gave up the wheel and went below to the chart, but what he saw there only confirmed the pessimistic decision he had already reached by mental calculation. As close to the wind as they could lie on this tack they could not weather Ushant. Short-handed as he was he did not dare continue in the hope that the wind might back; all his reading and all his instruction had warned him of the terrors of a lee shore. There was nothing for it but to go about; he returned to the deck with a heavy heart.

"All hands wear ship," he said, trying to bellow the order in the manner of Mr. Bolton, the third lieutenant of the *Indefatigable*.

They brought the brig safely round, and she took up her new course, close hauled on the starboard tack. Now she was heading away from the dangerous shores of France, without a doubt, but she was heading nearly as directly away from the friendly shores of England— gone was all hope of an easy two days' run to England;

46

gone was any hope of sleep that night for Hornblower.

During the year before he joined the navy Hornblower had attended classes given by a penniless French *émigré* in French, music, and dancing. Early enough the wretched *émigré* had found that Hornblower had no ear for music whatever, which made it almost impossible to teach him to dance, and so he had endeavoured to earn his fee by concentrating on French. A good deal of what he had taught Hornblower had found a permanent resting place in Hornblower's tenacious memory. He had never thought it would be of much use to him, but he discovered the contrary when the French captain at dawn insisted on an interview with him. The Frenchman had a little English, but it was a pleasant surprise to Hornblower to find that they actually could get along better in French, as soon as he could fight down his shyness sufficiently to produce the halting words.

The captain drank thirstily from the scuttlebutt; his cheeks were of course unshaven and he wore a bleary look after twelve hours in a crowded forecastle where he had been battened down three parts drunk.

"My men are hungry," said the captain; he did not look hungry himself.'

"Mine also," said Hornblower. "I also."

It was natural when one spoke French to gesticulate, to indicate his men with a wave of the hand and himself with a tap on the chest.

"I have a cook," said the captain.

It took some time to arrange the terms of a truce. The Frenchmen were to be allowed on deck, the cook was to provide food for everyone on board, and while these amenities were permitted, until noon, the French would make no attempt to take the ship.

"Good," said the captain at length, and when Hornblower had given the necessary orders permitting the release of the crew he shouted for the cook and entered into an urgent discussion regarding dinner. Soon smoke was issuing satisfactorily from the galley chimney.

Then the captain looked up at the grey sky, at the close reefed topsails, and glanced into the binnacle at the compass.

"A fowl wind for England," he remarked.

"Yes," said Hornblower, shortly. He did not want this Frenchman to guess at his trepidation and bitterness.

The captain seemed to be feeling the motion of the brig under his feet with attention.

"She rides a little heavily, does she not?" he said.

"Perhaps," said Hornblower. He was not familiar with the *Marie Galante* nor with ships at all, and he had no opinion on the subject, but he was not going to reveal his ignorance.

"Does she leak?" asked the captain.

"There is no water in her," said Hornblower.

"Ah!" said the captain. "But you would find none in the well. We are carrying a cargo of rice, you must remember."

"Yes," said Hornblower.

He found it very hard at that moment to remain outwardly unperturbed, as his mind grasped the implications of what was being said to him. Rice would absorb every drop of water taken in by the ship, so that no leak would be apparent on sounding the well—and yet every drop of water taken in would deprive her of that much buoyancy, all the same.

"One shot from your cursed frigate struck us in the hull," said the captain. "Of course you have investigated the damage?"

"Of course," said Hornblower, lying bravely.

But as soon as he could he had a private conversation with Matthews on the point, and Matthews instantly looked grave.

"Where did the shot hit her, sir?" he asked.

"Somewhere on the port side, for'rard, I should judge."

48

He and Matthews craned their necks over the ship's side.

"Can't see nothin', sir," said Matthews. "Lower me over the side in a bowline and I'll see what I can find, sir."

Hornblower was about to agree and then changed his mind.

"I'll go over the side myself," he said.

He could not analyse the motives which impelled him to say that. Partly he wanted to see things with his own eyes; partly he was influenced by the doctrine that he should never give an order he was not prepared to carry out himself—but mostly it must have been the desire to impose a penance on himself for his negligence.

Matthews and Carson put a bowline round him and lowered him over. He found himself dangling against the ship's side, with the sea bubbling just below him; as the ship pitched the sea came up to meet him, and he was wet to the waist in the first five seconds; and as the ship rolled he was alternately swung away from the side and bumped against it. The men with the line walked steadily aft, giving him the chance to examine the whole side of the brig above water, and there was not a shot hole to be seen. He said as much to Matthews when they hauled him on deck.

"Then it's below the waterline, sir," said Matthews, saying just what was in Hornblower's mind. "You're sure the shot hit her, sir?"

"Yes, I'm sure," snapped Hornblower.

Lack of sleep and worry and a sense of guilt were all shortening his temper, and he had to speak sharply or break down in tears. But he had already decided on the next move—he had made up his mind about that while they were hauling him up.

"We'll heave her to on the other tack and try again," he said.

On the other tack the ship would incline over to the other side, and the shot hole, if there was one, would not be so deeply submerged. Hornblower stood with the water dripping from his clothes as they wore the brig round; the wind was keen and cold, but he was shivering with expectancy rather than cold. The heeling of the brig laid him much more definitely against the side, and they lowered him until his legs were scraping over the marine growths which she carried there between wind and water. Then they walked aft with him, dragging him along the side of the ship, and just abaft the foremast he found what he was seeking.

"Avast, there!" he yelled up to the deck, mastering the sick despair that he felt. The motion of the bowline along the ship ceased. "Lower away! Another two feet!"

Now he was waist-deep in the water, and when the brig swayed the water closed briefly over his head, like a momentary death. Here it was, two feet below the waterline even with the brig hove-to on this tack—a splintered, jagged hole, square rather than round, and a foot across. As the sea boiled round him Hornblower even fancied he could hear it bubbling into the ship, but that might be pure fancy.

He hailed the deck for them to haul him up again, and they stood eagerly listening for what he had to say.

"Two feet below the waterline, sir?" said Matthews. "She was close hauled and heeling right over, of course, when we hit her. But her bows must have lifted just as we fired. And of course she's lower in the water now."

That was the point. Whatever they did now, however much they heeled her, that hole would be under water. And on the other tack it would be far under water, with much additional pressure; yet on the present tack they were headed for France. And the more water they took in, the lower the brig would settle, and the greater would be the pressure forcing water in through the hole. Something must be done to plug the leak, and Hornblower's reading of the manuals of seamanship told him what it was.

"We must fother a sail and get it over that hole," he announced. "Call those Frenchmen over."

To fother a sail was to make something like a vast hairy doormat out of it, by threading innumerable lengths of half-unravelled line through it. When this was done the sail was lowered below the ship's bottom and placed against the hole. The inward pressure would then force the hairy mass so tightly against the hole that the entrance of water would be made at least much more difficult.

The Frenchmen were not quick to help in the task; it was no longer their ship, and they were heading for an English prison, so that even with their lives at stake they were somewhat apathetic. It took time to get out a new topgallant sail—Hornblower felt that the stouter the canvas the better—and to set a party to work cutting lengths of line, threading them through, and unravelling them. The French captain looked at them squatting on the deck all at work.

"Five years I spent in a prison hulk in Portsmouth during the last war," he said. "Five years."

"Yes," said Hornblower.

He might have felt sympathy, but he was not only preoccupied with his own problems but he was numb with cold. He not only had every intention if possible of escorting the French captain to England and to prison again but he also at that very moment intended to go below and appropriate some of his spare clothing.

Down below it seemed to Hornblower as if the noises all about him—the creaks and groans of a wooden ship at sea—were more pronounced than usual. The brig was riding easily enough, hove-to, and yet the bulkheads down below were cracking and creaking as if the brig were racking herself to pieces in a storm. He dismissed the notion as a product of his overstimulated imagination, but by the time he had towelled himself into something like warmth and put on the captain's best suit it recurred to him; the brig was groaning as if in stress.

He came on deck again to see how the working party was progressing. He had hardly been on deck two minutes when one of the Frenchmen, reaching back for another length of line, stopped in his movement to stare at the deck. He picked at a deck seam, looked up and caught Hornblower's eye, and called to him. Hornblower made no pretence of understanding the words; the gestures explained themselves. The deck seam was opening a little; the pitch was bulging out of it. Hornblower looked at the phenomenon without understanding it—only a foot or two of the seam was open, and the rest of the deck seemed solid enough. No! Now that his attention was called to it, and he looked further, there were one or two other places in the deck where the pitch had risen in ridges from out of the seams. It was something beyond his limited experience, even beyond his extensive reading. But the French captain was at his side staring at the deck too.

"My God!" he said. "The rice! The rice!"

The French word *"riz"* that he used was unknown to Hornblower, but he stamped his foot on the deck and pointed down through it.

"The cargo!" he said in explanation. "It—it grows bigger."

Matthews was with them now, and without knowing a word of French he understood.

"Didn't I hear this brig was full of rice, sir?" he asked.

"Yes."

"That's it, then. The water's got into it and it's swelling."

So it would. Dry rice soaked in water would double or treble its volume. The cargo was swelling and bursting the seams of the ship open. Hornblower remembered the unnatural creaks and groans below. It was a black moment; he looked round at the unfriendly sea for inspiration and support, and found neither. Several seconds passed before he was ready to speak, and ready to maintain the dignity of a naval officer in face of difficulties.

"The sooner we get that sail over that hole the better, then," he said. It was too much to be expected that his voice should sound quite natural. "Hurry those Frenchmen up."

He turned to pace the deck, so as to allow his feelings to subside and to set his thoughts running in an orderly fashion again, but the French captain was at his elbow, voluble as a Job's comforter.

"I said I thought the ship was riding heavily," he said. "She is lower in the water."

"Go to the devil," said Hornblower, in English—he could not think up the French for that phrase.

Even as he stood he felt a sudden sharp shock beneath his feet, as if someone had hit the deck underneath them with a mallet. The ship was springing apart bit by bit.

"Hurry with that sail!" he yelled, turning back to the working party, and then was angry with himself because the tone of his voice must have betrayed undignified agitation.

At last an area five feet square of the sail was fothered, lines were rove through the grommets, and the working party hurried forward to work the sail under the brig and drag it aft to the hole. Hornblower was taking off his clothes, not out of regard for the captain's property but so as to keep them dry for himself.

"I'll go over and see that it's in place," he said. "Matthews, get a bowline ready for me."

Naked and wet, it seemed to him as if the wind blew clear through him; rubbing against the ship's side as she rolled he lost a good deal of skin, and the waves passing down the ship smacked at him with a boisterous lack of consideration. But he saw the fothered sail placed against the hole, and with intense satisfaction he saw the hairy mass suck into position, dimpling over the hole to form a deep hollow so that he could be sure that the hole was plugged solid. They hauled him up again when he hailed, and awaited his orders; he stood naked, stupid with cold and fatigue and lack of sleep, struggling to form his next decision.

"Lay her on the starboard tack," he said at length.

If the brig were going to sink, it hardly mattered if it were one hundred or two hundred miles from the French coast; if she were to stay afloat he wanted to be well clear of that lee shore and the chance of recapture. The shot hole with its fothered sail would be deeper under water to increase the risk, but it seemed to be the best chance. The French captain saw them making preparations to wear the brig round, and turned upon Hornblower with voluble protests. With this wind they could make Bordeaux easily on the other tack. Hornblower was risking all their lives, he said. Into Hornblower's numb mind crept, uninvited, the translation of something he had previously wanted to say. He could use it now.

"*Allez au diable,*" he snapped, as he put the French-man's stout woolen shirt on over his head.

When his head emerged the Frenchman was still protesting volubly, so violently indeed that a new doubt came into Hornblower's mind. A word to Matthews sent him round the French prisoners to search for weapons. There was nothing to be found except the sailors' knives, but as a matter of precaution Hornblower had them all impounded, and when he had dressed he went to special trouble with his three pistols, drawing the charges from them and reloading and repriming afresh. Three pistols in his belt looked piratical, as though he were still young enough to be playing imaginative games, but Hornblower felt in his bones that there might be a time when the Frenchmen might try to rise against their captors, and three pistols would not be too many against twelve desperate men who had makeshift weapons ready to hand, belaying pins and the like.

Matthews was awaiting him with a long face.

"Sir," he said. "Begging your pardon, but I don't like

the looks of it. Straight, I don't. I don't like the feel of her. She's settlin' down and she's openin' up, I'm certain sure. Beg your pardon, sir, for saying so."

Down below Hornblower had heard the fabric of the ship continuing to crack and complain; up here the deck seams were gaping more widely. There was a very likely explanation; the swelling of the rice must have forced open the ship's seams below water, so that plugging the shot hole would have only eliminated what would be by now only a minor leak. Water must still be pouring in, the cargo still swelling, opening up the ship like an overblown flower. Ships were built to withstand blows from without, and there was nothing about their construction to resist an outward pressure. Wider and wider would gape the seams, and faster and faster the sea would gain access to the cargo.

"Look'ee there, sir!" said Matthews suddenly.

In the broad light of day a small grey shape was hurrying along the weather scuppers; another one followed it and another after that. Rats! Something convulsive must be going on down below to bring them on deck in daytime, from out of their comfortable nests among the unlimited food of the cargo. The pressure must be enormous. Hornblower felt another small shock beneath his feet at that moment, as something further parted beneath them. But there was one more card to play, one last line of defence that he could think of.

"I'll jettison the cargo," said Hornblower. He had never uttered that word in his life, but he had read it. "Get the prisoners and we'll start."

The battened-down hatch cover was domed upwards curiously and significantly; as the wedges were knocked out one plank tore loose at one end with a crash, pointing diagonally upwards, and as the working party lifted off the cover a brown form followed it upwards—a bag of rice, forced out by the underlying pressure until it jammed in the hatchway.

"Tail onto those tackles and sway it up," said Hornblower.

Bag by bag the rice was hauled up from the hold; sometimes the bags split, allowing a torrent of rice to pour onto the deck, but that did not matter. Another section of the working party swept rice and bags to the lee side and into the ever-hungry sea. After the first three bags the difficulties increased, for the cargo was so tightly jammed below that it called for enormous force to tear each bag out of its position. Two men had to go down the hatchway to pry the bags loose and adjust the slings. There was a momentary hesitation on the part of the two Frenchmen to whom Hornblower pointed—the bags might not all be jammed and the hold of a tossing ship was a dangerous place wherein a roll might bury them alive —but Hornblower had no thought at that moment for other people's human fears. He scowled at the brief check and they hastened to lower themselves down the hatchway. The labour was enormous as it went on hour after hour; the men at the tackles were dripping with sweat and drooping with fatigue, but they had to relieve periodically the men below, for the bags had jammed themselves in tiers, pressed hard against the ship's bottom below and the deck beams above, and when the bags immediately below the hatchway had been swayed up the surrounding ones had to be pried loose, out of each tier. Then when a small clearance had been made in the neighborhood of the hatchway, and they were getting deeper down into the hold, they made the inevitable discovery. The lower tiers of bags had been wetted, their contents had swelled, and the bags had burst. The lower half of the hold was packed solid with damp rice which could only be got out with shovels and a hoist. The still intact bags of the upper tiers, farther away from the hatchway, were still jammed tight, calling for much labour to free them and to manhandle them under the hatchway to be hoisted out.

Hornblower, facing the problem, was distracted by a touch on his elbow when Matthews came up to speak to him.

"It ain't no go, sir," said Matthews. "She's lower in the water an' settlin' fast."

Hornblower walked to the ship's side with him and looked over. There could be no doubt about it. He had been over the side himself and could remember the height of the waterline, and he had for a more exact guide the level of the fothered sail under the ship's bottom. The brig was a full six inches lower in the water—and this after fifty tons of rice at least had been hoisted out and flung over the side. The brig must be leaking like a basket, with water pouring in through the gaping seams to be sucked up immediately by the thirsty rice.

Hornblower's left hand was hurting him, and he looked down to discover that he was gripping the rail with it so tightly as to cause him pain, without knowing he was doing so. He released his grip and looked about him, at the afternoon sun, at the tossing sea. He did not want to give in and admit defeat. The French captain came up to him.

"This is folly," he said. "Madness, sir. My men are overcome by fatigue."

Over by the hatchway, Hornblower saw, Hunter was driving the French seamen to their work with a rope's end which he was using furiously. There was not much more work to be got out of the Frenchmen; and at that moment the *Marie Galante* rose heavily to a wave and wallowed down the farther side. Even his inexperience could detect the sluggishness and ominous deadness of her movements. The brig had not much longer to float, and there was a good deal to do.

"I shall make preparations for abandoning the ship, Matthews," he said.

He poked his chin upwards as he spoke; he would not allow either a Frenchman or a seaman to guess at his despair.

"Aye aye, sir," said Matthews.

The *Marie Galante* carried a boat on chocks abaft the mainmast; at Matthews' summons the men abandoned their work on the cargo and hurried to the business of putting food and water in her.

"Beggin' your pardon, sir," said Hunter aside to Hornblower, "but you ought to see you have warm clothes, sir. I been in an open boat ten days once, sir."

"Thank you, Hunter," said Hornblower.

There was much to think of. Navigating instruments, charts, compass—would he be able to get a good observation with his sextant in a tossing little boat? Common prudence dictated that they should have all the food and water with them that the boat could carry; but—Hornblower eyed the wretched craft dubiously—seventeen men would fill it to overflowing anyway. He would have to leave much to the judgment of the French captain and of Matthews.

The tackles were manned and the boat was swayed up from the chocks and lowered into the water in the tiny lee afforded on the lee quarter. The *Marie Galante* put her nose into a wave, refusing to rise to it; green water came over the starboard bow and poured aft along the deck before a sullen wallow on the part of the brig sent it into the scuppers. There was not much time to spare—a rending crash from below told that the cargo was still swelling and forcing the bulkheads. There was a panic among the Frenchmen, who began to tumble down into the boat with loud cries. The French captain took one look at Hornblower and then followed them; two of the British seamen were already over the side fending off the boat.

"Go along," said Hornblower to Matthews and Carson, who still lingered. He was the captain; it was his place to leave the ship last.

So waterlogged was the brig now that it was not at all difficult to step down into the boat from the deck; the

British seamen were in the sternsheets and made room for him.

"Take the tiller, Matthews," said Hornblower; he did not feel he was competent to handle that overloaded boat. "Shove off, there!"

The boat and the brig parted company; the *Marie Galante,* with her helm lashed, poked her nose into the wind and hung there. She had acquired a sudden list, with the starboard side scuppers nearly under water. Another wave broke over her deck, pouring up to the open hatchway. Now she righted herself, her deck nearly level with the sea, and then she sank, on an even keel, the water closing over her, her masts slowly disappearing. For an instant her sails even gleamed under the green water.

"She's gone," said Matthews.

Hornblower watched the disappearance of his first command. The *Marie Galante* had been entrusted to him to bring into port, and he had failed, failed on his first independent mission. He looked very hard at the setting sun, hoping no one would notice the tears that were filling his eyes.

III

HORNBLOWER
and the Penalty of Failure

Daylight crept over the tossing waters of the Bay of Biscay to reveal a small boat riding on its wide expanses. It was a very crowded boat; in the bows huddled the French crew of the sunken brig *Marie Galante,* amidships sat the captain and his mate, and in the sternsheets sat Midshipman Horatio Hornblower and the four English seamen who had once constituted the prize crew of the brig. Hornblower was seasick, for his delicate stomach, having painfully accustomed itself to the motion of the *Indefatigable,* rebelled at the antics of the small boat as she pitched jerkily to her sea-anchor. He was cold and weary as well as seasick after his second night without sleep—he had been vomiting spasmodically all through the hours of darkness, and in the depression which seasickness brings he had thought gloomily about the loss of the *Marie Galante*. If he had only remembered earlier to plug that shot hole! Excuses came to his mind only to be discarded. There had been so much to do, and so few men to do it with—the French crew to guard, the damage aloft to repair, the course to set. The absorbent qualities of the cargo of rice which the *Marie Galante* carried had deceived him when he had remembered to sound the well. All this might be true, but the fact remained that he had lost his ship, his first command. In his own eyes there was no excuse for his failure.

The French crew had wakened with the dawn and were

chattering like a nest of magpies; Matthews and Carson beside him were moving stiffly to ease their aching joints.

"Breakfast, sir?" said Matthews.

It was like the games Hornblower had played as a lonely little boy, when he had sat in the empty pig-trough and pretended he was cast away in an open boat. Then he had parcelled out the bit of bread or whatever it was which he had obtained from the kitchen into a dozen rations, counting them carefully, each one to last a day. But a small boy's eager appetite had made those days very short, not more than five minutes long; after standing up in the pig-trough and shading his eyes and looking round the horizon for the succour that he could not discover, he would sit down again, tell himself that the life of a castaway was hard, and then decide that another night had passed and that it was time to eat another ration from his dwindling supply. So here under Hornblower's eye the French captain and mate served out a biscuit of hard bread to each person in the boat, and filled the pannikin for each man in turn from the water breakers under the thwarts. But Hornblower, when he sat in the pig-trough, despite his vivid imagination, never thought of this hideous seasickness, of the cold and the cramps, nor of how his skinny posterior would ache with its constant pressure against the hard timbers of the sternshects; nor, in the sublime self-confidence of childhood, had he ever thought how heavy could be the burden of responsibility on the shoulders of a senior naval officer aged seventeen.

He dragged himself back from the memories of that recent childhood to face the present situation. The grey sky, as far as his inexperienced eye could tell, bore no presage of deterioration in the weather. He wetted his finger and held it up, looking in the boat's compass to gauge the direction of the wind.

"Backing westerly a little, sir," said Matthews, who had been copying his movements.

"That's so," agreed Hornblower, hurriedly going through in his mind his recent lessons in boxing the compass. His course to weather Ushant was nor'east by north, he knew, and the boat close hauled would not lie closer than eight points off the wind—he had lain-to to the sea-anchor all night because the wind had been coming from too far north to enable him to steer for England. But now the wind had backed. Eight points from nor'east by north was nor'west by west, and the wind was even more westerly than that. Close hauled he could weather Ushant and even have a margin for contingencies, to keep him clear of the lee shore which the seamanship books and his own common sense told him was so dangerous.

"We'll make sail, Matthews," he said; his hand was still grasping the biscuit which his rebellious stomach refused to accept.

"Aye aye, sir."

A shout to the Frenchmen crowded in the bows drew their attention; in the circumstances it hardly needed Hornblower's halting French to direct them to carry out the obvious task of getting in the sea-anchor. But it was not too easy, with the boat so crowded and hardly a foot of freeboard. The mast was already stepped, and the lug sail bent ready to hoist. Two Frenchmen, balancing precariously, tailed onto the halliard and the sail rose up the mast.

"Hunter, take the sheet," said Hornblower. "Matthews, take the tiller. Keep her close hauled on the port tack."

"Close hauled on the port tack, sir."

The French captain had watched the proceedings with intense interest from his seat amidships. He had not understood the last, decisive order, but he grasped its meaning quickly enough when the boat came round and steadied on the port tack, heading for England. He stood up, spluttering angry protests.

"The wind is fair for Bordeaux," he said, gesticulating

with clenched fists. "We could be there by tomorrow. Why do we go north?"

"We go to England," said Hornblower.

"But—but—it will take us a week! A week even if the wind stays fair. This boat—it is too crowded. We cannot endure a storm. It is madness."

Hornblower had guessed at the moment the captain stood up what he was going to say, and he hardly bothered to translate the expostulations to himself. He was too tired and too seasick to enter into an argument in a foreign language. He ignored the captain. Not for anything on earth would he turn the boat's head towards France. His naval career had only just begun, and even if it were to be blighted on account of the loss of the *Marie Galante* he had no intention of rotting for years in a French prison.

"Sir!" said the French captain.

The mate who shared the captain's thwart was protesting too, and now they turned to their crew behind them and told them what was going on. An angry movement stirred the crowd.

"Sir!" said the captain again. "I insist that you head towards Bordeaux."

He showed signs of advancing upon them; one of the crew behind him began to pull the boat hook clear, and it would be a dangerous weapon. Hornblower pulled one of the pistols from his belt and pointed it at the captain, who, with the muzzle four feet from his breast, fell back before the gesture. Without taking his eyes off him Hornblower took a second pistol with his left hand.

"Take this, Matthews," he said.

"Aye aye, sir," said Matthews, obeying, and then, after a respectful pause, "Beggin' your pardon, sir, but hadn't you better cock your pistol, sir?"

"Yes," said Hornblower, exasperated at his own forgetfulness.

He drew the hammer back with a click, and the men—

63

acing sound made more acute still the French captain's sense of his own danger, with a cocked and loaded pistol pointed at his stomach in a heaving boat. He waved his hands desperately.

"Please," he said, "point it some other way, sir."

He drew farther back, huddling against the men behind him.

"Hey, avast there, you," shouted Matthews loudly; a French sailor was trying to let go the halliard unobserved.

"Shoot any man who looks dangerous, Matthews," said Hornblower.

He was so intent on enforcing his will upon these men, so desperately anxious to retain his liberty, that his face was contracted into a beast-like scowl. No one looking at him could doubt his determination for a moment. He would allow no human life to come between him and his decisions. There was still a third pistol in his belt, and the Frenchmen could guess that if they tried a rush a quarter of them at least would meet their deaths before they overpowered the Englishmen, and the French captain knew he would be the first to die. His expressive hands, waving out from his sides—he could not take his eyes from the pistol —told his men to make no further resistance. Their murmurings died away, and the captain began to plead.

"Five years I was in an English prison during the last war," he said. "Let us reach an agreement. Let us go to France. When we reach the shore—anywhere you choose, sir—we will land and you can continue on your journey. Or we can all land, and I will use all my influence to have you and your men sent back to England under cartel, without exchange or ransom. I swear I will."

"No," said Hornblower.

England was far easier to reach from here than from the French Biscay coast; as for the other suggestion, Hornblower knew enough about the new government washed up by the revolution in France to be sure that they would never part with prisoners on the representation of a merchant captain. And trained seamen were scarce in France; it was his duty to keep these dozen from returning.

"No," he said again, in reply to the captain's fresh protests.

"Shall I clout 'im on the jaw, sir?" asked Hunter, at Hornblower's side.

"No," said Hornblower again, but the Frenchman saw the gesture and guessed at the meaning of the words, and subsided into sullen silence.

But he was roused again at the sight of Hornblower's pistol on his knee, still pointed at him. A sleepy finger might press that trigger.

"Sir," he said, "put that pistol away, I beg of you. It is dangerous."

Hornblower's eye was cold and unsympathetic.

"Put it away, please. I will do nothing to interfere with your command of this boat. I promise you that."

"Do you swear it?"

"I swear it."

"And these others?"

The captain looked round at his crew with voluble explanations, and grudgingly they agreed.

"They swear it too."

"Very well, then."

Hornblower started to replace the pistol in his belt, and remembered to put it on half-cock in time to save himself from shooting himself in the stomach. Everyone in the boat relaxed into apathy. The boat was rising and swooping rhythmically now, a far more comfortable motion than when it had jerked to a sea-anchor, and Hornblower's stomach lost some of its resentment. He had been two nights without sleep. His head lowered on his chest, and then he leaned sideways against Hunter, and slept peacefully, while the boat, with the wind nearly abeam, headed steadily for England. He was awakened late in the day when Matthews, cramped and weary, was compelled to surrender the tiller to Carson, and after that they kept watch and watch, a hand at the sheet and a hand at the tiller and the others trying to rest. Hornblower took his turn at the sheet, but he would not trust himself with the tiller, especially when night fell; he knew he had not the knack of keeping the boat on her course by the feel of the wind on his cheek and the tiller in his hand.

It was not until long after breakfast the next day—almost noon, in fact—that they sighted the sail. It was a Frenchman who saw it first, and his excited cry roused them all. There were three square topsails coming up over the horizon on their weather bow, nearing them so rapidly on a converging course that each time the boat rose on a wave a considerably greater area of canvas was visible.

"What do you think she is, Matthews?" asked Hornblower, while the boat buzzed with the Frenchmen's excitement.

"I can't tell, sir, but I don't like the looks of her," said Matthews doubtfully. "She ought to have her t'gallants set in this breeze—and her courses too, an' she hasn't. An' I don't like the cut of her jib, sir. She—she might be a Frenchie to me, sir."

Any ship travelling for peaceful purposes would naturally have all possible sail set. This ship had not. Hence she was engaged in some belligerent design, but there were more chances that she was British than that she was French, even here in the Bay. Hornblower took a long look at her: a smallish vessel, although ship-rigged. Flush-decked, with a look of speed about her—her hull was visible at intervals now, with a line of gunports.

"She looks French all over to me, sir," said Hunter. "Privateer, seemly."

"Stand by to jibe," said Hornblower.

They brought the boat round before the wind, heading directly away from the ship. But in war as in the jungle, to fly is to invite pursuit and attack. The ship set courses and topgallants and came tearing down upon them, passed them at half a cable's length and then hove-to having cut off their escape. The ship's rail was lined with a curious crowd—a large crew for a vessel that size. A hail came across the water to the boat, and the words were French. The English seamen subsided into curses, while the French captain cheerfully stood up and replied, and the French crew brought the boat alongside the ship.

A handsome young man in a plum-coloured coat with a lace stock greeted Hornblower when he stepped on the deck.

"Welcome, sir, to the *Pique*," he said in French. "I am Captain Neuville, of this privateer. And you are—?"

"Midshipman Hornblower, of His Britannic Majesty's Ship *Indefatigable*," growled Hornblower.

"You seem to be in an evil humour," said Neuville. "Please do not be so distressed at the fortunes of war. You will be accommodated in this ship, until we return to port, with every comfort possible at sea. I beg of you to consider yourself quite at home. For instance, those pistols in your belt must discommode you more than a little. Permit me to relieve you of their weight."

He took the pistols neatly from Hornblower's belt as he spoke, looked Hornblower keenly over, and then went on.

"That dirk that you wear at your side, sir. Would you oblige me by the loan of it? I assure you that I will return it to you when we part company. But while you are on board here I fear that your impetuous youth might lead you into some rash act while you are wearing a weapon which a credulous mind might believe to be lethal. A thousand thanks. And now might I show you the berth that is being prepared for you?"

With a courteous bow he led the way below. Two decks down, presumably at the level of a foot or two below the waterline, was a wide bare 'tween-decks, dimly lighted and scantily ventilated by the hatchways.

"Our slave deck," explained Neuville, carelessly.

"Slave deck?" asked Hornblower.

"Yes. It is here that the slaves were confined during the middle passage."

Much was clear to Hornblower at once. A slave ship could be readily converted into a privateer. She would already be armed with plenty of guns to defend herself against treacherous attacks while making her purchases in the African rivers; she was faster than the average merchant ship both because of the lack of need of hold space and because with a highly perishable cargo such as slaves speed was a desirable quality, and she was constructed to carry large numbers of men and the great quantities of food and water necessary to keep them supplied while at sea in search of prizes.

"Our market in San Domingo has been closed to us by recent events, of which you must have heard, sir," went on Neuville, "and so that the *Pique* could continue to return dividends to me I have converted her into a privateer. Moreover, seeing that the activities of the Committee of Public Safety at present make Paris a more unhealthy spot even than the West Coast of Africa, I decided to take command of my vessel myself. To say nothing of the fact that a certain resolution and hardihood are necessary to make a privateer a profitable investment."

Neuville's face hardened for a moment into an expression of the grimmest determination, and then softened at once into its previous meaningless politeness.

"This door in this bulkhead," he continued, "leads to the quarters I have set aside for captured officers. Here, as you see, is your cot. Please make yourself at home here. Should this ship go into action—as I trust she will frequently do—the hatches above will be battened down. But expect on those occasions you will of course be at liberty to move about the ship at your will. Yet I suppose I had better add that any harebrained attempt on the part of prisoners to interfere with the working or wellbeing of this ship would be deeply resented by the crew. They serve on shares, you understand, and are risking their lives and their liberty. I would not be surprised if any rash person who endangered their dividends and freedom were dropped over the side into the sea."

Hornblower forced himself to reply; he would not reveal that he was almost struck dumb by the calculating callousness of this last speech.

"I understand," he said.

"Excellent! Now is there anything further you may need, sir?"

Hornblower looked round the bare quarters in which he was to suffer lonely confinement, lit by a dim glimmer of light from a swaying slush lamp.

"Could I have something to read?" he asked.

Neuville thought for a moment.

"I fear there are only professional books," he said. "But I can let you have Grandjean's *Principles of Navigation,* and Lebrun's *Handbook on Seamanship* and some similar volumes, if you think you can understand the French in which they are written."

"I'll try," said Hornblower.

Probably it was as well that Hornblower was provided with the materials for such strenuous mental exercise. The effort of reading French and of studying his profession at one and the same time kept his mind busy during the dreary days while the *Pique* cruised in search of prizes. Most of the time the Frenchmen ignored him—he had to force himself upon Neuville once to protest against the employment of his four British seamen on the menial work of pumping out the ship, but he had to retire worsted from the argument, if argument it could be called, when Neuville icily refused to discuss the question. Hornblower went back to his quarters with burning cheeks and red ears, and, as ever, when he was mentally disturbed, the thought of his guilt returned to him with new force.

If only he had plugged that shot hole sooner! A clearer-headed officer, he told himself, would have done so. He had lost his ship, the *Indefatigable's* precious prize, and there was no health in him. Sometimes he made himself review the situation calmly. Professionally, he might not—probably would not—suffer for his negligence. A midshipman with only four for a prize crew, put on board a two hundred ton brig that had been subjected to considerable firing from a frigate's guns, would not be seriously blamed when she sank under him. But Hornblower knew at the same time that he was at least partly at fault. If it was ignorance—there was no excuse for ignorance. If he had allowed his multiple cares to distract him from the business of plugging the shot hole immediately, that was incompetence, and there was no excuse for incompetence. When he thought along those lines he was overwhelmed by waves of despair and of self-contempt, and there was no one to comfort him. The day of his birthday, when he looked at himself at the vast age of eighteen, was the worst of all. Eighteen and a discredited prisoner in the hands of a French privateersman! His self-respect was at its lowest ebb.

The *Pique* was seeking her prey in the most frequented waters in the world, the approaches to the Channel, and there could be no more vivid demonstration of the vastness of the ocean than the fact that she cruised day after day without glimpsing a sail. She maintained a triangular course, reaching to the northwest, tacking to the south, running under easy sail northeasterly again, with lookouts at every masthead, with nothing to see but the tossing waste of water—until the morning when a high-pitched yell from the fore topgallant masthead attracted the attention of everybody on deck, including Hornblower, standing lonely in the waist. Neuville, by the wheel, bellowed a question to the lookout, and Hornblower, thanks to his recent studies, could translate the answer. There was a sail visible to windward, and next moment the lookout reported that it had altered course and was running down towards them.

That meant a great deal. In wartime any merchant ship would be suspicious of strangers and would give them as wide a berth as possible; and especially when she was to windward and therefore far safer. Only someone prepared to fight or possessed of a perfectly morbid curiosity would abandon a windward position. A wild and unreasonable hope filled Hornblower's breast; a ship of war at sea— thanks to England's maritime mastery—would be far more probably English than French. And this was the cruising ground of the *Indefatigable,* his own ship, stationed there specially to fulfill the double function of looking out for French commerce-destroyers and intercepting French blockade-runners. A hundred miles from here she had put him and his prize crew on board the *Marie Galante.* It was a thousand to one, he exaggerated despairingly to himself, against any ship sighted being the *Indefatigable.* But—hope reasserted itself—the fact that she was coming down to investigate reduced the odds to ten to one at most. Less than ten to one.

He looked over at Neuville, trying to think his thoughts. The *Pique* was fast and handy, and there was a clear avenue of escape to leeward. The fact that the stranger had altered course towards them was a suspicious circumstance, but it was known that Indiamen, the richest prizes of all, had sometimes traded on the similarity of their appearance to that of ships of the line, and, by showing a bold front, had scared dangerous enemies away. That would be a temptation to a man eager to make a prize. At Neuville's orders all sail was set, ready for instant flight or pursuit, and, close-hauled, the *Pique* stood towards the

71

stranger. It was not long before Hornblower, on the deck, caught a glimpse of a gleam of white, like a tiny grain of rice, far away on the horizon as the *Pique* lifted on a swell. Here came Matthews, red-faced and excited, running aft to Hornblower's side.

"That's the old *Indefatigable,* sir," he said. "I swear it!"

He sprang onto the rail, holding on by the shrouds, and stared under his hand.

"Yes! There she is, sir! She's loosing her royals now, sir. We'll be back on board of her in time for grog!"

A French petty officer reached up and dragged Matthews by the seat of his trousers from his perch, and with a blow and a kick drove him forward again, while a moment later Neuville was shouting the orders that wore the ship round to head away directly from the *Indefatigable.* Neuville beckoned Hornblower over to his side.

"Your late ship, I understand, Mr. Hornblower?"

"Yes."

"What is her best point of sailing?"

Hornblower's eyes met Neuville's.

"Do not look so noble," said Neuville, smiling with thin lips. "I could undoubtedly induce you to give me the information. I know of ways. But it is unnecessary, fortunately for you. There is no ship on earth—especially none of His Britannic Majesty's clumsy frigates—that can outsail the *Pique* running before the wind. You will soon see that."

He strolled to the taffrail and looked aft long and earnestly through his glass, but no more earnestly than did Hornblower with his naked eye.

"You see?" said Neuville, proffering the glass.

Hornblower took it, but more to catch a closer glimpse of his ship than to confirm his observations. He was homesick, desperately homesick, at that moment, for the *Indefatigable.* But there could be no denying that she was being left fast behind. Her top gallants were out of sight again now, and only her royals were visible.

"Two hours and we shall have run her mastheads under," said Neuville, taking back the telescope and shutting it with a snap.

He left Hornblower standing sorrowful at the taffrail while he turned to berate the helmsman for not steering a steadier course; Hornblower heard the explosive words without listening to them, the wind blowing into his face and ruffling his hair over his ears, and the wake of the ship's passage boiling below him. So might Adam have looked back at Eden; Hornblower remembered the stuffy dark midshipmen's berth, the smells and the creakings, the bitter cold nights, turning out in response to the call for all hands, the weevily bread and the wooden beef, and he yearned for them all, with the sick feeling of hopeless longing. Liberty was vanishing over the horizon. Yet it was not these personal feelings that drove him below in search of action. They may have quickened his wits, but it was a sense of duty which inspired him.

The slave deck was deserted as usual, with all hands at quarters. Beyond the bulkhead stood his cot with the books upon it and the slush lamp swaying above it. There was nothing there to give him any inspiration. There was another locked door in the after bulkhead. That opened into some kind of boatswain's store; twice he had seen it unlocked and paint and similar supplies brought out from it. Paint! That gave him an idea; he looked from the door up to the slush lamp and back again, and as he stepped forward he took his claspknife out of his pocket. But before very long he recoiled again, sneering at himself. The door was not panelled, but was made of two solid slabs of wood, with the crossbeams on the inside. There was the keyhole of the lock, but it presented no point of attack. It would take him hours and hours to cut through that door with his knife, at a time when minutes were precious.

73

His heart was beating feverishly—but no more feverishly than his mind was working—as he looked round again. He reached up to the lamp and shook it; nearly full. There was a moment when he stood hesitating, nerving himself, and then he threw himself into action. With a ruthless hand he tore the pages out of Grandjean's *Principles de la Navigation,* crumpling them up in small quantities into little loose balls, which he laid at the foot of the door. He threw off his uniform coat and dragged his blue woollen jersey over his head; his long powerful fingers tore it across and plucked eagerly at it to unravel it. After starting some loose threads he would not waste more time on it, and dropped the garment onto the paper and looked round again. The mattress of the cot! It was stuffed with straw, by God! A slash of his knife tore open the ticking, and he scooped the stuff out by the armful; constant pressure had almost solidified it, but he shook it and handled it so that it bulked out far larger in a mass on the deck nearly up to his waist. That would give him the intense blaze he wanted. He stood still, compelling himself to think clearly and logically—it was impetuosity and lack of thought which had occasioned the loss of the *Marie Galante,* and now he had wasted time on his jersey. He worked out the successive steps to take. He made a long spill out of a page of the *Manuel de Matelotage,* and lighted it at the lamp. Then he poured out the grease—the lamp was hot and the grease liquid—over his balls of paper, over the deck, over the base of the door. A touch from his taper lighted one ball, the flame travelled quickly. He was committed now. He piled the straw upon the flames, and in a sudden access of insane strength he tore the cot from its fastenings, smashing it as he did so, and piled the fragments on the straw. Already the flames were racing through the straw. He dropped the lamp upon the pile, grabbed his coat, and walked out. He thought of closing the door, but decided against it—the more air the better. He wriggled into his coat and ran up the ladder.

On the deck he forced himself to lounge nonchalantly against the rail, putting his shaking hands into his pockets. His excitement made him weak, nor was it lessened as he waited. Every minute before the fire could be discovered was important. A French officer said something to him with a triumphant laugh and pointed aft over the taffrail, presumably speaking about leaving the *Indefatigable* behind. Hornblower smiled bleakly at him; that was the first gesture that occurred to him, and then he thought that a smile was out of place, and he tried to assume a sullen scowl. The wind was blowing briskly, so that the *Pique* could only just carry all plain sail; Hornblower felt it on his cheeks, which were burning. Everyone on deck seemed unnaturally busy and preoccupied; Neuville was watching the helmsman with occasional glances aloft to see that every sail was doing its work; the men were at the guns, two hands and a petty officer heaving the log. God, how much longer would he have?

Look there! The coaming of the after hatchway appeared distorted, wavering in the shimmering air. Hot air must be coming up through it. And was that, or was it not, the ghost of a wreath of smoke? It was! In that moment the alarm was given. A loud cry, a rush of feet, an instant bustle, the loud beating of a drum, highpitched shouts— *"Au feu! Au feu!"*

The four elements of Aristotle, thought Hornblower, insanely, earth, air, water, and fire, were the constant enemies of the seaman, but the lee shore, the gale, and the wave, were none of them as feared in wooden ships as fire. Timbers many years old, and coated thick with paint, burnt fiercely and readily. Sails and tarry rigging would burn like fireworks. And within the ship were tons and tons of gunpowder waiting its chance to blast the seaman into fragments. Hornblower watched the fire parties flinging themselves into their work, the pumps being dragged over the decks, the hoses rigged. Someone came racing aft with a message for Neuville, presumably to report the site of the fire. Neuville heard him, and darted a glance at Hornblower against the rail before he hurled orders back at the messenger. The smoke coming up through the after hatchway was dense now; at Neuville's orders the after guard flung themselves down the opening through the smoke. And there was more smoke, and more smoke; smoke caught up by the following wind and blown forward in wisps—smoke must be pouring out of the sides of the ship at the waterline.

Neuville took a stride towards Hornblower, his face working with rage, but a cry from the helmsman checked him. The helmsman, unable to take his hands from the wheel, pointed with his foot to the cabin skylight. There was a flickering of flame below it. A side pane fell in as they watched, and a rush of flame came through the opening. That store of paint, Hornblower calculated—he was calmer now, with a calm that would astonish him later, when he came to look back on it—must be immediately under the cabin, and blazing fiercely. Neuville looked round him, at the sea and the sky, and put his hands to his head in a furious gesture. For the first time in his life Hornblower saw a man literally tearing his hair. But his nerve held. A shout brought up another portable pump; four men set to work on the handles, and the clank-clank, clank-clank made an accompaniment that blended with the roar of the fire. A thin jet of water was squirted down the gaping skylight. More men formed a bucket chain, drawing water from the sea and passing it from hand to hand to pour in the skylight, but those buckets of water were less effective even than the stream from the pumps. From below came the dull thud of an explosion, and Hornblower caught his breath as he expected the ship to be blown to pieces. But no further explosion followed; either a gun had been set off by the flames or a cask had burst violently in the heat. And then the bucket line suddenly disintegrated; beneath the feet of one of the men a seam had gaped in a broad red smile from which came a rush of flame. Some officer had seized Neuville by the arm, and was arguing with him vehemently, and Hornblower could see Neuville yield in despair. Hands were scurrying aloft to get in the fore topsail and fore course, and other hands went to the main braces. Over went the wheel, and the *Pique* came up into the wind.

The change was dramatic, although at first more apparent than real; with the wind blowing in the opposite direction the roar of the fire did not come so clearly to the ears of those forward of it. But it was an immense gain, all the same; the flames, which had started in the steerage in the farthest after part of the ship, no longer were blown forward, but were turned back upon timber already half consumed. Yet the after part of the deck was fully alight; the helmsman was driven from the wheel, and in a flash the flames took hold of the driver and consumed it utterly— one moment the sail was there, and the next there were only charred fragments hanging from the gaff. But, head to wind, the other sails did not catch and a mizzen trysail hurriedly set kept the ship bows on.

It was then that Hornblower, looking forward, saw the *Indefatigable* again. She was tearing down towards them with all sail set; as the *Pique* lifted he could see the white bow wave foaming under her bowsprit. There was no question about surrender, for under the menace of that row of guns no ship of the *Pique*'s force, even if uninjured, could resist. A cable's length to windward the *Indefatigable* rounded-to, and she was hoisting out her boats before even she was fully round. Pellew had seen the smoke, and had deduced the reason for the *Pique*'s heaving-to, and had made his preparations as he came up. Longboat and launch had each a pump in their bows where sometimes they carried a carronade; they dropped down to the stern of the *Pique* to cast their jets of water up into the flaming stern without more ado. Two gigs full of men ran straight aft to join in the battle with the flames, but Bolton, the third lieutenant, lingered for a moment as he caught Hornblower's eyes.

"Good God, it's you!" he exclaimed. "What are you doing here?"

Yet he did not stay for an answer. He picked out Neuville as the captain of the *Pique,* strode aft to receive his surrender, cast his eyes aloft to see that all was well there, and then took up the task of combatting the fire. The flames were overcome in time, more because they had consumed everything within reach of them than for any other reason; the *Pique* was burnt from the taffrail forward for some feet of her length right to the water's edge, so that she presented a strange spectacle when viewed from the deck of the *Indefatigable.* Nevertheless, she was in no immediate danger; given even moderate good fortune and a little hard work she could be sailed to England to be repaired and sent to sea again.

But it was not her salvage that was important, but rather the fact that she was no longer in French hands, would no longer be available to prey on English commerce. That was the point that Sir Edward Pellew made in conversation with Hornblower, when the latter came on board to report himself. Hornblower had begun, at Pellew's order, by recounting what had happened to him from the time he had been sent as prize master on board the *Marie Galante.* As Hornblower had expected—perhaps as he had even feared—Pellew had passed lightly over the loss of the brig. She had been damaged by gunfire before surrendering, and no one now could establish whether the damage was small or great. Pellew did not give the matter a second thought. Hornblower had tried to save her and had been unsuccessful with his tiny crew

78

—and at that moment the *Indefatigable* could not spare him a larger crew. He did not hold Hornblower culpable. Once again, it was more important that France should be deprived of the *Marie Galante*'s cargo than that England should benefit by it. The situation was exactly parallel to that of the salvaging of the *Pique*.

"It was lucky she caught fire like that," commented Pellew, looking across to where the *Pique* lay, still hove-to with the boats clustering about her but with only the thinnest trail of smoke drifting from her stern. "She was running clean away from us, and would have been out of sight in an hour. Have you any idea how it happened, Mr. Hornblower?"

Hornblower was naturally expecting that question and was ready for it. Now was the time to answer truthfully and modestly, to receive the praise he deserved, a mention in the Gazette, perhaps even appointment as acting-lieutenant. But Pellew did not know the full details of the loss of the brig, and might make a false estimate of them even if he did.

"No, sir," said Hornblower. "I think it must have been spontaneous combustion in the paint locker. I can't account for it otherwise."

He alone knew of his remissness in plugging that shot hole, he alone could decide on his punishment, and this was what he had chosen. This alone could re-establish him in his own eyes, and when the words were spoken he felt enormous relief, and not one single twinge of regret.

"It was fortunate, all the same," mused Pellew.

IV

HORNBLOWER
and the Man Who Felt Queer

This time the wolf was prowling round outside the sheep fold. H.M. Frigate *Indefatigable* had chased the French corvette *Papillon* into the mouth of the Gironde, and was seeking a way of attacking her where she lay anchored in the stream under the protection of the batteries at the mouth. Captain Pellew took his ship into shoal water as far as he dared, until in fact the batteries fired warning shots to make him keep his distance, and he stared long and keenly through his glass at the corvette. Then he shut his telescope and turned on his heel to give the order that worked the *Indefatigable* away from the dangerous lee shore—out of sight of land, in fact. His departure might lull the French into a sense of security which, he hoped, would prove unjustified. For he had no intention of leaving them undisturbed. If the corvette could be captured or sunk not only would she be unavailable for raids on British commerce but also the French would be forced to increase their coastal defences at this point and lessen the effort that could be put out elsewhere. War is a matter of savage blow and counter blow, and even a forty gun frigate could strike shrewd blows if shrewdly handled.

Midshipman Hornblower was walking the lee side of the quarterdeck, as became his lowly station as the junior officer of the watch, in the afternoon, when Midshipman Kennedy approached him. Kennedy took off his hat with a flourish and bowed low as his dancing master had once taught him, left foot advanced, hat down by the right knee. Hornblower entered into the spirit of the game, laid his hat against his stomach, and bent himself in the middle three times in quick succession. Thanks to his physical awkwardness he could parody ceremonial solemnity almost without trying.

"Most grave and reverend signor," said Kennedy. "I bear the compliments of Captain Sir Ed'ard Pellew, who humbly solicits Your Gravity's attendance at dinner at eight bells in the afternoon watch."

"My respects to Sir Edward," replied Hornblower, bowing to his knees at the mention of the name, "and I shall condescend to make a brief appearance."

"I am sure the captain will be both relieved and delighted," said Kennedy. "I will convey him my felicitations along with your most flattering acceptance."

Both hats flourished with even greater elaboration than before, but at that moment both young men noticed Mr. Bolton, the officer of the watch, looking at them from the windward side, and they hurriedly put their hats on and assumed attitudes more consonant with the dignity of officers holding their warrants from King George.

"What's in the captain's mind?" asked Hornblower.

Kennedy laid one finger alongside his nose.

"If I knew that I should rate a couple of epaulettes," he said. "Something's brewing, and I suppose one of these days we shall know what it is. Until then all that we little victims can do is to play unconscious of our doom. Meanwhile, be careful not to let the ship fall overboard."

There was no sign of anything brewing while dinner was being eaten in the great cabin of the *Indefatigable*. Pellew was a courtly host at the head of the table. Conversation flowed freely and along indifferent channels among the senior officers present—the two lieutenants, Eccles and Chadd, and the sailing master, Soames. Hornblower and the other junior officer—Mallory, a midshipman of over two years' seniority—kept silent, as midshipmen should, thereby being able to devote their undivided attention to the food, so vastly superior to what was served in the midshipmen's berth.

"A glass of wine with you, Mr. Hornblower," said Pellew, raising his glass.

Hornblower tried to bow gracefully in his seat while raising his glass. He sipped cautiously, for he had early found that he had a weak head and he disliked feeling drunk.

The table was cleared and there was a brief moment of expectancy as the company awaited Pellew's next move.

"Now, Mr. Soames," said Pellew, "let us have that chart."

It was a map of the mouth of the Gironde with the soundings; somebody had pencilled in the positions of the shore batteries.

"The *Papillon*," said Sir Edward (he did not condescend to pronounce it French-fashion), "lies just here. Mr. Soames took the bearings."

He indicated a pencilled cross on the chart, far up the channel.

"You gentlemen," went on Pellew, "are going in with the boats to fetch her out."

So that was it. A cutting-out expedition.

"Mr. Eccles will be in general command. I will ask him to tell you his plan."

The grey-haired first lieutenant with the surprisingly young blue eyes looked round at the others.

"I shall have the launch," he said, "and Mr. Soames the cutter. Mr. Chadd and Mr. Mallory will command the first and second gigs. And Mr. Hornblower will command the jolly boat. Each of the boats except Mr. Hornblower's will have a junior officer second in command."

That would not be necessary for the jolly boat with its crew of seven. The launch and cutter would carry from thirty to forty men each, and the gigs twenty each; it was a large force that was being despatched, nearly half the ship's company.

"She's a ship of war," explained Eccles, reading their thoughts. "No merchantman. Ten guns a side, and full of men."

Nearer two hundred men than a hundred, certainly—plentiful opposition for a hundred and twenty British seamen.

"But we will be attacking her by night and taking her by surprise," said Eccles, reading their thoughts again.

"Surprise," put in Pellew, "is more than half the battle, as you know, gentlemen—please pardon the interruption, Mr. Eccles."

"At the moment," went on Eccles, "we are out of sight of land. We are about to stand in again. We have never hung about this part of the coast, and the Frogs'll think we've gone for good. We'll make the land after nightfall, stand in as far as possible, and then the boats will go in. High water tomorrow morning is at 4:50; dawn is at 5:30. The attack will be delivered at 4:30 so that the watch below will have had time to get to sleep. The launch will attack on the starboard quarter, and the cutter on the larboard quarter. Mr. Mallory's gig will attack on the larboard bow, and Mr. Chadd's on the starboard bow. Mr. Chadd will be responsible for cutting the corvette's cable as soon as he has mastered the forecastle, and the other boats' crews have at least reached the quarterdeck."

Eccles looked round at the other three commanders of the large boats, and they nodded understanding. Then he went on.

"Mr. Hornblower with the jolly boat will wait until the attack has gained a foothold on the deck. He will then board at the main chains, either to starboard or larboard as he sees fit, and he will at once ascend the main rigging, paying no attention to whatever fighting is going on on deck. He will see to it that the main topsail is loosed and he will sheet it home on receipt of further orders. I myself, or Mr. Soames in the event of my being killed or wounded, will send two hands to the wheel and will attend to steering the corvette as soon as she is under weigh. The tide will take us out, and the *Indefatigable* will be awaiting us just out of gunshot from the shore batteries."

"Any comments, gentlemen?" asked Pellew.

That was the moment when Hornblower should have spoken up—the only moment when he could. Eccles' orders had set in motion sick feelings of apprehension in his stomach. Hornblower was no main-topman, and Hornblower knew it. He hated heights, and he hated going aloft. He knew he had none of the monkeylike agility and self-confidence of the good seaman. He was unsure of himself aloft in the dark even in the *Indefatigable,* and he was utterly appalled at the thought of going aloft in an entirely strange ship and finding his way among strange rigging. He felt himself quite unfitted for the duty assigned to him, and he should have raised a protest at once on account of his unfitness. But he let the opportunity pass, for he was overcome by the matter-of-fact way in which the other officers accepted the plan. He looked round at the unmoved faces; nobody was paying any attention to him, and he jibbed at making himself conspicuous. He swallowed; he even got as far as opening his mouth, but still no one looked at him and his protest died stillborn.

"Very well, then, gentlemen," said Pellew. "I think you had better go into the details, Mr. Eccles."

Then it was too late. Eccles, with the chart before him, was pointing out the course to be taken through the shoals and mudbanks of the Gironde, and expatiating on the position of the shore batteries and on the influence of the lighthouse of Cordouan upon the distance to which the *Indefatigable* could approach in daylight. Hornblower listened, trying to concentrate despite his apprehensions. Eccles finished his remarks and Pellew closed the meeting.

"Since you all know your duties, gentlemen, I think you should start your preparations. The sun is about to set and you will find you have plenty to do."

The boats' crews had to be told off; it was necessary to see that the men were armed, and the boats were provisioned in case of emergency. Every man had to be instructed in the duties expected of him. And Hornblower had to rehearse himself in ascending the main shrouds and laying out along the main topsail yard. He did it twice, forcing himself to make the difficult climb up the futtock shrouds, which, projecting outwards from the mainmast, made it necessary to climb several feet while hanging back downwards, locking fingers and toes into the ratlines. He could just manage it, moving slowly and carefully although clumsily. He stood on the foot rope and worked his way out to the yard-arm—the foot rope was attached along the yard so as to hang nearly four feet below it. The principle was to set his feet on the rope with his arms over the yard, then, holding the yard in his armpits, to shuffle sideways along the foot rope to cast off the gaskets and loose the sail. Twice Hornblower made the whole journey, battling with the disquiet of his stomach at the thought of the hundred-foot drop below him. Finally, gulping with nervousness, he transferred his grip to the brace and forced himself to slide down it to the deck—that would be his best route when the time came to sheet the topsail home. It was a long perilous descent; Hornblower told himself—as indeed he had said to himself when he had first seen men go aloft—that similar feats in a circus at home would be received with "ohs" and "ahs" of appreciation. He was by no means satisfied with himself even when he reached the deck, and at the back of his mind was a vivid mental picture of his missing his hold, when the time came for him to repeat the performance in the *Papillon,* and falling headlong to the deck—a second or two of frightful fear while rushing through the air, and then a shattering crash. And the success of the attack hinged on him, as much as on anyone—if the topsail were not promptly set to give the corvette steerage way she would run aground on one of the innumerable shoals in the river mouth to be ignominiously recaptured, and half the crew of the *Indefatigable* would be dead or prisoners.

In the waist the jolly boat's crew was formed up for his inspection. He saw to it that the oars were properly muffled, that each man had pistol and cutlass, and made sure that every pistol was at half-cock so that there was no fear of a premature shot giving warning of the attack. He allocated duties to each man in the loosing of the topsail, laying stress on the possibility that casualties might necessitate unrehearsed changes in the scheme.

"I will mount the rigging first," said Hornblower.

That had to be the case. He had to lead—it was expected of him. More than that; if he had given any other order it would have excited comment—and contempt.

"Jackson," went on Hornblower, addressing the coxswain, "you will quit the boat last and take command if I fall."

"Aye aye, sir."

It was usual to use the poetic expression "fall" for "die," and it was only after Hornblower had uttered the word that he thought about its horrible real meaning in the present circumstances.

"Is that all understood?" asked Hornblower harshly; it was his mental stress that was making his voice grate so.

Everyone nodded except one man.

"Begging your pardon, sir," said Hales, the young man who pulled stroke oar. "I'm feeling a bit queer-like."

Hales was a lightly built young fellow of swarthy countenance. He put his hand to his forehead with a vague gesture as he spoke.

86

"You're not the only one to feel queer," snapped Hornblower.

The other men chuckled. The thought of running the gauntlet of the shore batteries, of boarding an armed corvette in the teeth of opposition, might well raise apprehension in the breast of a coward. Most of the men detailed for the expedition must have felt qualms to some extent.

"I don't mean that, sir," said Hales indignantly. " 'Course I don't."

But Hornblower and the others paid him no attention.

"You just keep your mouth shut," growled Jackson. There could be nothing but contempt for a man who announced himself sick after being told off on a dangerous duty. Hornblower felt sympathy as well as contempt. He himself had been too much of a coward even to give voice to his apprehensions—too much afraid of what people would say about him.

"Dismiss," said Hornblower. "I'll pass the word for all of you when you are wanted."

There were some hours yet to wait while the *Indefatigable* crept inshore, with the lead going steadily and Pellew himself attending to the course of the frigate. Hornblower, despite his nervousness and his miserable apprehension, yet found time to appreciate the superb seamanship displayed as Pellew brought the big frigate in through these tricky waters on that dark night. His interest was so caught by the procedure that the little tremblings which had been assailing him ceased to manifest themselves; Hornblower was of the type that would continue to observe and to learn on his deathbed. By the time the *Indefatigable* had reached the point off the mouth of the river where it was desirable to launch the boats Hornblower had learned a good deal about the practical application of the principles of coastwise navigation, and a good deal about the organisation of a cutting-out expedition—and by self-analysis he had learned even more about the psychology of a raiding party before a raid.

He had mastered himself to all outside appearance by the time he went down into the jolly boat as she heaved on the inky-black water, and he gave the command to shove off in a quiet steady voice. Hornblower took the tiller—the feel of that solid bar of wood was reassuring, and it was old habit now to sit in the sternsheets with hand and elbow upon it, and the men began to pull slowly after the dark shapes of the four big boats; there was plenty of time and the flowing tide would take them up the estuary. That was just as well, for on one side of them lay the batteries of St. Dye, and inside the estuary on the other side was the fortress of Blaye; forty big guns trained to sweep the channel, and none of the five boats—certainly not the jolly boat—could withstand a single shot from one of them.

He kept his eyes attentively on the cutter ahead of him. Soames had the dreadful responsibility of taking the boats up the channel, while all he had to do was to follow in her wake—all, except to loose that main topsail. Hornblower found himself shivering again.

Hales, the man who had said he felt queer, was pulling stroke oar; Hornblower could just see his dark form moving rhythmically backward and forward at each slow stroke. After a single glance Hornblower paid him no more attention, and was staring after the cutter when a sudden commotion brought his mind back into the boat. Someone had missed his stroke; someone had thrown all six oars into confusion as a result. There was even a slight clatter.

"Mind what you're doing, blast you, Hales," whispered Jackson, the coxswain, with desperate urgency.

For answer there was a sudden cry from Hales, loud but fortunately not too loud, and Hales pitched forward against Hornblower's and Jackson's legs, kicking and writhing.

"The bastard's having a fit," growled Jackson.

The kicking and writing went on. Across the water through the darkness came a sharp scornful whisper.

"Mr. Hornblower," said the voice—it was Eccles putting a world of exasperation into his *sotto voce* question, "cannot you keep your men quiet?"

Eccles had brought the launch round almost alongside the jolly boat to say this to him, and the desperate need for silence was dramatically demonstrated by the absence of any of the usual blasphemy; Hornblower could picture the cutting reprimand that would be administered to him tomorrow publicly on the quarterdeck. He opened his mouth to make an explanation, but he fortunately realised that raiders in open boats did not make explanations when under the guns of the fortress of Blaye.

"Aye aye, sir," was all he whispered back, and the launch continued on its mission of shepherding the flotilla in the tracks of the cutter.

"Take his oar, Jackson," he whispered furiously to the coxswain, and he stooped and with his own hands dragged the writing figure towards him and out of Jackson's way.

"You might try pouring water on 'im, sir," suggested Jackson hoarsely, as he moved to the after thwart. "There's the baler 'andy."

Seawater was the seaman's cure for every ill, his panacea; seeing how often sailors had not merely wet jackets but wet bedding as well they should never have a day's illness. But Hornblower let the sick man lie. His struggles were coming to an end, and Hornblower wished to make no noise with the baler. The lives of more than a hundred men depended on silence. Now that they were well into the actual estuary they were within easy reach of cannon shot from the shore—and a single cannon shot would rouse the crew of the *Papillon,* ready to man the bulwarks to beat off the attack, ready to drop cannon balls into the boats alongside, ready to shatter approaching boats with a tempest of grape.

Silently the boats glided up the estuary; Soames in the cutter was setting a slow pace, with only an occasional stroke at the oars to maintain steerage way. Presumably he knew very well what he was doing; the channel he had selected was an obscure one between mudbanks, impracticable for anything except small boats, and he had a twenty foot pole with him with which to take the soundings—quicker and much more silent than using the lead. Minutes were passing fast, and yet the night was still utterly dark, with no hint of approaching dawn. Strain his eyes as he would, Hornblower could not be sure that he could see the flat shores on either side of him. It would call for sharp eyes on the lands to detect the little boats being carried up by the tide.

Hales at his feet stirred and then stirred again. His hand feeling round in the darkness, found Hornblower's ankle and apparently examined it with curiosity. He muttered something, the words dragging out into a moan.

"Shut up!" whispered Hornblower, trying like the saint of old, to make a tongue of his whole body, that he might express the urgency of the occasion without making a sound audible at any distance. Hales set his elbow on Hornblower's knee and levered himself up into a sitting position, and then levered himself further until he was standing, swaying with bent knees and supporting himself against Hornblower.

"Sit down, damn you!" whispered Hornblower, shaking with fury and anxiety.

"Where's Mary?" asked Hales in a conversational tone.

"Shut up!"

"Mary!" said Hales, lurching against him. "Mary!"

Each successive word was louder. Hornblower felt instinctively that Hales would soon be speaking in a loud voice, that he might even soon be shouting. Old recollections of conversations with his doctor father stirred at the back of his mind; he remembered that persons emerging from epileptic fits were not responsible for their actions, and might be, and often were, dangerous.

"Mary!" said Hales again.

Victory and the lives of a hundred men depended on silencing Hales, and silencing him instantly. Hornblower thought of the pistol in his belt, and of using the butt, but there was another weapon more conveniently to his hand. He unshipped the tiller, a three foot bar of solid oak, and he swung it with all the venom and fury of despair. The tiller crashed down on Hales' head, and Hales, an unuttered word cut short in his throat, fell silent in the bottom of the boat. There was no sound from the boat's crew, save for something like a sigh from Jackson, whether approving or disapproving Hornblower neither knew nor cared. He had done his duty, and he was certain of it. He had struck down a helpless idiot; most probably he had killed him, but the surprise upon which the success of the expedition depended had not been imperilled. He reshipped the tiller and resumed the silent task of keeping in the wake of the gigs.

Far away ahead—in the darkness it was impossible to estimate the distance—there was a nucleus of greater darkness, close on the surface of the black water. It might be the corvette. A dozen more silent strokes, and Hornblower was sure of it. Soames had done a magnificent job of pilotage, leading the boats straight to that objective. The cutter and launch were diverging now from the two gigs. The four boats were separating in readiness to launch their simultaneous converging attack.

"Easy!" whispered Hornblower, and the jolly boat's crew ceased to pull.

Hornblower had his orders. He had to wait until the attack had gained a foothold on the deck. His hand clenched convulsively on the tiller; the excitement of dealing with Hales had driven the thought of having to ascend strange

91

rigging in the darkness clear out of his head, and now it recurred with redoubled urgency. Hornblower was afraid.

Although he could see the corvette, the boats had vanished from his sight, had passed out of his field of vision. The corvette rode to her anchor, her spars just visible against the night sky—that was where he had to climb! She seemed to tower up hugely. Close by the corvette he saw a splash in the dark water—the boats were closing in fast and someone's stroke had been a little careless. At the same moment came a shout from the corvette's deck, and when the shout was repeated it was echoed a hundred fold from the boats rushing alongside. The yelling was lusty and prolonged, of set purpose. A sleeping enemy would be bewildered by the din, and the progress of the shouting would tell each boat's crew of the extent of the success of the others. The British seamen were yelling like madmen. A flash and a bang from the corvette's deck told of the firing of the first shot; soon pistols were popping and muskets banging from several points of the deck.

"Give way!" said Hornblower. He uttered the order as if it had been torn from him by the rack.

The jolly boat moved forward, while Hornblower fought down his feelings and tried to make out what was going on on board. He could see no reason for choosing either side of the corvette in preference to the other, and the larboard side was the nearer, and so he steered the boat to the larboard main chains. So interested was he in what he was doing that he only remembered in the nick of time to give the order "in oars." He put the tiller over and the boat swirled round and the bowman hooked on. From the deck just above came a noise exactly like a tinker hammering on a cooking pot—Hornblower noted the curious noise as he stood up in the sternsheets. He felt the cutlass at his side and the pistol in his belt, and then he sprang for the chains. With a mad leap he reached them and hauled himself up. The shrouds came into his hands,

92

his feet found the ratlines beneath them, and he began to climb. As his head cleared the bulwark and he could see the deck the flash of a pistol shot illuminated the scene momentarily, fixing the struggle on the deck in a static moment, like a picture. Before and below him a British seaman was fighting a furious cutlass-duel with a French officer, and he realised with vague astonishment that the kettle-mending noise he had heard was the sound of cutlass against cutlass—that clash of steel against steel that poets wrote about. So much for romance.

The realisation carried him far up the shrouds. At his elbow he felt the futtock shrouds and he transferred himself to them, hanging back downward with his toes hooked into the ratlines and his hands clinging like death. That only lasted for two or three desperate seconds, and then he hauled himself onto the topmast shrouds and began the final ascent, his lungs bursting with the effort. Here was the topsail yard, and Hornblower flung himself across it and felt with his feet for the footrope. Merciful God! There was no footrope—his feet searching in the darkness met only unresisting air. A hundred feet above the deck he hung, squirming and kicking like a baby held up at arm's length in its father's hands. There was no footrope; it may have been with this very situation in mind that the Frenchmen had removed it. There was no footrope, so that he could not make his way out to the yard-arm. Yet the gaskets must be cast off and the sail loosed—everything depended on that. Hornblower had seen daredevil seamen run out along the yards, standing upright, as though walking a tightrope. That was the only way to reach the yard-arm now.

For a moment he could not breathe as his weak flesh revolted against the thought of walking along the yard above the black abyss. This was fear, the fear that stripped a man of his manhood, turning his bowels to water and his limbs to paper. Yet his furiously active mind continued to work. He had been resolute enough in dealing with Hales. Where he personally was not involved he had been brave enough; he had not hesitated to strike down the wretched epileptic with all the strength of his arm. That was the poor sort of courage he was capable of displaying. In the simple vulgar matter of physical bravery he was utterly wanting. This was cowardice, the sort of thing that men spoke about behind their hands to other men. He could not bear the thought of that in himself—it was worse (awful though the alternative might be) than the thought of falling through the night to the deck. With a gasp he brought his knee up onto the yard, heaving himself up until he stood upright. He felt the rounded, canvas-covered timber under his feet, and his instincts told him not to dally there for a moment.

"Come on, men!" he yelled, and he dashed out along the yard.

It was twenty feet to the yard-arm, and he covered the distance in a few frantic strides. Utterly reckless by now, he put his hands down on the yard, clasped it, and laid his body across it again, his hands seeking the gaskets. A thump on the yard told him that Oldroyd, who had been detailed to come after him, had followed him out along the yard—he had six feet less to go. There could be no doubt that the other members of the jolly boat's crew were on the yard, and that Clough had led the way to the starboard yard-arm. It was obvious from the rapidity with which the sail came loose. Here was the brace beside him. Without any thought of danger now, for he was delirious with excitement and triumph, he grasped it with both hands and jerked himself off the yard. His waving legs found the rope and twined about it, and he let himself slide down it.

Fool that he was! Would he never learn sense and prudence? Would he never remember that vigilance and precaution must never be relaxed? He had allowed himself to

94

slide so fast that the rope seared his hands, and when he tried to tighten his grip so as to slow down his progress it caused him such agony that he had to relax it again and slide on down the rope stripping the skin from his hands as though peeling off a glove. His feet reached the deck and he momentarily forgot the pain as he looked around him.

There was the faintest grey light beginning to show now, and there were no sounds of battle. It had been a well worked surprise—a hundred men flung suddenly on the deck of the corvette had swept away the anchor watch and mastered the vessel in a single rush before the watch below could come up to offer any resistance. Chadd's stentorian voice came pealing from the forecastle.

"Cable's cut, sir!"

Then Eccles bellowed from aft.

"Mr. Hornblower!"

"Sir!" yelled Hornblower.

"Man the halliards!"

A rush of men came to help—not only his own boat's crew but every man of initiative and spirit. Halliards, sheets and braces; the sail was trimmed round and was drawing full in the light southerly air, and the *Papillon* swung round to go down with the first of the ebb. Dawn was coming up fast, with a trifle of mist on the surface of the water.

Over the starboard quarter came a sullen bellowing roar and then the misty air was torn by a series of infernal screams, supernaturally loud. The first cannon balls Hornblower had ever heard were passing him by.

"Mr. Chadd! Set the headsails! Loose the fore tops'l. Get aloft, some of you, and set the mizzen tops'l."

From the port bow came another salvo—Blaye was firing at them from one side, St. Dye from the other, now they could guess what had happened on board the *Papillon*. But the corvette was moving fast with wind and tide, and it would be no easy matter to cripple her in the half-light. It had been a very near-run thing; a few seconds' delay could have been fatal. Only one shot from the next salvo passed within hearing, and its passage was marked by a loud snap overhead.

"Mr. Mallory, get that fore-stay spliced!"

"Aye aye, sir!"

It was light enough to look round the deck now; he could see Eccles at the break of the poop, directing the handling of the corvette, and Soames beside the wheel conning her down the channel. Two groups of red-coated marines, with bayonets fixed, stood guard over the hatchways. There were four or five men lying on the deck in curiously abandoned attitudes. Dead men; Hornblower could look at them with the callousness of youth. But there was a wounded man, too, crouched groaning over his shattered thigh—Hornblower could not look at him as disinterestedly, and he was glad, maybe only for his own sake, when at that moment a seaman asked for and received permission from Mallory to leave his duties and attend to him.

"Stand by to go about!" shouted Eccles from the poop; the corvette had reached the tip of the middle ground shoal and was about to make the turn that would carry her into the open sea.

The men came running to the braces, and Hornblower tailed on along with them. But the first contact with the harsh rope gave him such pain that he almost cried out. His hands were like raw meat, and fresh-killed at that, for blood was running from them. Now that his attention was called to them they smarted unbearably.

The headsail sheets came over, and the corvette went handily about.

"There's the old *Indy!*" shouted somebody.

The *Indefatigable* was plainly visible now, lying-to just out of shot from the shore batteries, ready to rendezvous

96

with her prize. Somebody cheered, and the cheering was taken up by everyone, even while the last shots from St. Dye, fired at extreme range, pitched sullenly into the water alongside. Hornblower had gingerly extracted his handkerchief from his pocket and was trying to wrap it round his hand.

"Can I help you with that, sir?" asked Jackson.

Jackson shook his head as he looked at the raw surface.

"You was careless, sir. You ought to 'a gone down 'and over 'and," he said, when Hornblower explained to him how the injury had been caused. "Very careless, you was, beggin' your pardon for saying so, sir. But you young gennelmen often is. You don't 'ave no thought for your necks, nor your 'ides, sir."

Hornblower looked up at the main topsail yard high above his head, and remembered how he had walked along that slender stick of timber out to the yard-arm in the dark. At the recollection of it, even here with the solid deck under his feet, he shuddered a little.

"Sorry, sir. Didn't mean to 'urt you," said Jackson, tying the knot. "There, that's done, as good as I can do it, sir."

"Thank you, Jackson," said Hornblower.

"We got to report the jolly boat as lost, sir," went on Jackson.

"Lost?"

"She ain't towing alongside, sir. You see, we didn't leave no boatkeeper in 'er. Wells, 'e was to be boatkeeper, you remember, sir. But I sent 'im up the rigging a'ead o' me, seeing that 'Ales couldn't go. We wasn't too many for the job. So the jolly boat must 'a come adrift, sir, when the ship went about."

"What about Hales, then?" asked Hornblower.

" 'E was still in the boat, sir."

Hornblower looked back up the estuary of the Gironde. Somewhere up there the jolly boat was drifting about, and

97

lying in it was Hales, probably dead, possibly alive. In either case the French would find him, surely enough, but a cold wave of regret extinguished the warm feeling of triumph in Hornblower's bosom when he thought about Hales back there. If it had not been for Hales he would never have nerved himself (so at least he thought) to run out to the main topsail yard-arm; he would at this moment be ruined and branded as a coward instead of basking in the satisfaction of having capably done his duty.

Jackson saw the bleak look in his face.

"Don't you take on so, sir," he said. "They won't 'old the loss of the jolly boat agin you, not the captain and Mr. Eccles, they won't."

"I wasn't thinking about the jolly boat," said Hornblower. "I was thinking about Hales."

"Oh, 'im?" said Jackson. "Don't you fret about 'im, sir. 'E wouldn't never 'ave made no seaman, not no 'ow."

V

HORNBLOWER
and the Man Who Saw God

Winter had come to the Bay of Biscay. With the passing of the Equinox the gales began to increase in violence, adding infinitely to the labours and dangers of the British navy watching over the coast of France; easterly gales, bitter cold, which the storm-tossed ships had to endure as best they could, when the spray froze on the rigging and the labouring hulls leaked like baskets; westerly gales, when the ships had to claw their way to safety from a lee shore and make a risky compromise between gaining sufficient sea-room and maintaining a position from which they could pounce on any French vessel venturing out of harbour. We speak about the storm-tossed ships. But those ships were full of storm-tossed men, who week by week and month by month had to endure the continued cold and the continual wet, the salt provisions, the endless toil, the boredom and misery of life in the blockading fleet. Even in the frigates, the eyes and claws of the blockaders, boredom had to be endured, the boredom of long periods with the hatches battened down, with the deck seams above dripping water on the men below, long nights and short days, broken sleep and yet not enough to do.

Even in the *Indefatigable* there was a feeling of restlessness in the air, and even a mere midshipman like Hornblower could be aware of it as he was looking over the men of his division before the captain's regular weekly inspection.

"What's the matter with your face, Styles?" he asked.

"Boils, sir. Awful bad."

On Styles' cheeks and lips there were half a dozen dabs of sticking plaster.

"Have you done anything about them?"

"Surgeon's mate, sir, 'e give me plaister for 'em, an' 'e says they'll soon come right, sir."

"Very well."

Now was there, or was there not, something strained about the expressions on the faces of the men on either side of Styles? Did they look like men smiling secretly to themselves? Laughing up their sleeves? Hornblower did not want to be an object of derision; it was bad for discipline—and it was worse for discipline if the men shared some secret unknown to their officers. He glanced sharply along the line again. Styles was standing like a block of wood, with no expression at all on his swarthy face; the black ringlets over his ears were properly combed, and no fault could be found with him. But Hornblower sensed that the recent conversation was a source of amusement to the rest of his division, and he did not like it.

After divisions he tackled Mr. Low the surgeon, in the gun room.

"Boils?" said Low. "Of course the men have boils. Salt pork and split peas for nine weeks on end—what d'you expect but boils? Boils—gurry sores—blains—all the plagues of Egypt."

"On their faces?"

"That's one locality for boils. You'll find out others from your own personal experience."

"Does your mate attend to them?" persisted Hornblower.

"Of course."

"What's he like?"

"Muggridge?"

"Is that his name?"

"He's a good surgeon's mate. Get him to compound a black draught for you and you'll see. In fact, I'd prescribe one for you—you seem in a mighty bad temper, young man."

Mr. Low finished his glass of rum and pounded on the table for the steward. Hornblower realised that he was lucky to have found Low sober enough to give him even this much information, and turned away to go aloft so as to brood over the question in the solitude of the mizzen top. This was his new station in action; when the men were not at their quarters a man might find a little blessed solitude there—something hard to find in the crowded *Indefatigable*. Bundled up in his pea-jacket, Hornblower sat in the mizzen top; over his head the mizzen topmast drew erratic circles against the grey sky; beside him the topmast shrouds sang their high-pitched note in the blustering gale, and below him the life of the ship went on as she rolled and pitched, standing to the northward under close reefed topsails. At eight bells she would wear to the southward again on her incessant patrol. Until that time Hornblower was free to meditate on the boils on Styles' face and the covert grins on the faces of the other men of the division.

Two hands appeared on the stout wooden barricade surrounding the top, and as Hornblower looked up with annoyance at having his meditations interrupted a head appeared above them. It was Finch, another man in Hornblower's division, who also had his station in action here in the mizzen top. He was a frail little man with wispy hair and pale blue eyes and a foolish smile, which lit up his face when, after betraying some disappointment at finding the mizzen top already occupied, he recognised Hornblower.

"Beg pardon, sir," he said. "I didn't know as how you was up here."

Finch was hanging on uncomfortably, back downwards,

101

in the act of transferring himself from the futtock shrouds in the top, and each roll threatened to shake him loose.

"Oh, come here if you want to," said Hornblower, cursing himself for his softheartedness. A taut officer, he felt, would have told Finch to go back whence he came and not bother him.

"Thank 'ee, sir. Thank 'ee," said Finch, bringing his leg over the barricade and allowing the ship's roll to drop him into the top.

He crouched down to peer under the foot of the mizzen topsail forward to the mainmast head, and then turned back to smile disarmingly at Hornblower like a child caught in moderate mischief. Hornblower knew that Finch was a little weak in the head—the all-embracing press swept up idiots and landsmen to help man the fleet—although he was a trained seaman who could land, reef, and steer. That smile betrayed him.

"It's better up here than down below, sir," said Finch, apologetically.

"You're right," said Hornblower with a disinterested intonation which would discourage conversation.

He turned away to ignore Finch, settled his back again comfortably, and allowed the steady swing of the top to mesmerize him into dreamy thought that might deal with his problem. Yet it was not easy, for Finch was as restless almost as a squirrel in a cage, peering forward, changing his position, and so continually breaking in on Hornblower's train of thought, wasting the minutes of his precious half hour of freedom.

"What the devil's the matter with you, Finch?" he rasped at last, patience quite exhausted.

"The Devil, sir?" said Finch. "It isn't the Devil. He's not up here, begging your pardon, sir."

That weak mysterious grin again, like a mischievous child. A great depth of secrets lay in those strange blue

102

eyes. Finch peered under the topsail again; it was a gesture like a baby's playing peep-bo.

"There!" said Finch. "I saw him that time, sir. God's come back to the maintop, sir."

"God?"

"Aye indeed, sir. Sometimes He's in the maintop. More often than not, sir. I saw Him that time, with His beard all a-blowing in the wind. 'Tis only from here that you can see Him, sir."

What could be said to a man with that sort of delusion? Hornblower racked his brains for an answer, and found none. Finch seemed to have forgotten his presence, and was playing peep-bo again under the foot of the mizzen topsail.

"There He is!" said Finch to himself. "There He is again! God's in the maintop, and the Devil's in the cable tier."

"Very appropriate," said Hornblower cynically, but to himself. He had no thought of laughing at Finch's delusions.

"The Devil's in the cable tier during the dogwatches," said Finch again to no one at all. "God stays in the maintop for ever."

"A curious timetable," was Hornblower's *sotto voce* comment.

From down on the deck below came the first stroke of eight bells, and at the same moment the pipes of the bosun's mates began to twitter, and the bellow of Waldron the bosun made itself heard.

"Turn out the watch below! All hands wear ship! All hands! All hands! You, master-at-arms, take the name of the last man up the hatchway. All hands!"

The interval of peace, short as it was, and broken by Finch's disturbing presence, was at an end. Hornblower dived over the barricade and gripped the futtock shrouds; not for him was the easy descent through the lubber's

103

hole, not when the first lieutenant might see him and reprimand him for unseamanlike behaviour. Finch waited for him to quit the top, but even with this length start Hornblower was easily outpaced in the descent to the deck, for Finch, like the skilled seaman he was, ran down the shrouds as lightly as a monkey. Then the thought of Finch's curious illusions was temporarily submerged in the business of laying the ship on her new course.

But later in the day Hornblower's mind reverted inevitably to the odd things Finch had been saying. There could be no doubt that Finch firmly believed he saw what he said he saw. Both his words and his expression made that certain. He had spoken about God's beard—it was a pity that he had not spared a few words to describe the Devil in the cable tier. Horns, cloven hoof, and pitchfork? Hornblower wondered. And why was the Devil only loose in the cable tier during the dogwatches? Strange that he should keep to a timetable. Hornblower caught his breath as the sudden thought came to him that perhaps there might be some worldly explanation. The Devil might well be loose in the cable tier in a metaphorical fashion during the dogwatches. Devil's work might be going on there. Hornblower had to decide on what was his duty; and he had to decide further on what was expedient. He could report his suspicions to Eccles, the first lieutenant; but after a year of service Hornblower was under no illusions about what might happen to a junior midshipman who worried a first lieutenant with unfounded suspicions. It would be better to see for himself first, as far as that went. But he did not know what he would find—if he should find anything at all—and he did not know how he should deal with it if he found anything. Much worse than that, he did not know if he would be able to deal with it in officerlike fashion. He could make a fool of himself. He might mishandle whatever situation he found, and bring down obloquy and derision upon his head, and he might imperil the discipline of the ship—weaken the slender thread of allegiance that bound officers and men together, the discipline which kept three hundred men at the bidding of their captain suffering untold hardship without demur; which made them ready to face death at the word of command. When eight bells told the end of the afternoon watch and the beginning of the first dogwatch it was with trepidation that Hornblower went below to put a candle in a lantern and made his way forward to the cable tier.

It was dark down here, stuffy, odorous, and as the ship heaved and rolled he found himself stumbling over the various obstacles that impeded his progress. Yet forward there was a faint light, a murmur of voices. Hornblower choked down his fear that perhaps mutiny was being planned. He put his hand over the horn window of the lantern, so as to obscure its light, and crept forward. Two lanterns swung from the low deck beams, and crouching under them were a score or more of men—more than that, even—and the buzz of their talk came loudly but indistinguishably to Hornblower's ears. Then the buzz increased to a roar, and someone in the centre of the circle rose suddenly to as near his full height as the deck beams allowed. He was shaking himself violently from side to side for no apparent reason; his face was away from Hornblower, who saw with a gasp that his hands were tied behind him. The men roared again, like spectators at a prizefight, and the man with his hands tied swung round so that Hornblower could see his face. It was Styles, the man who suffered from boils; Hornblower knew him at once. But that was not what made the most impression on Hornblower. Clinging to the man's face, weird in the shifting meagre light, was a grey writhing shape, and it was to shake this off that Styles was flinging himself about so violently. It was a rat; Hornblower's stomach turned over with horror.

With a wild jerk of his head Styles broke the grip of

105

the rat's teeth and flung the creature down, and then instantly plunged down on his knees, with his hands still bound behind him, to pursue it with his own teeth.

"Time!" roared a voice at that moment—the voice of Partridge, bosun's mate. Hornblower had been roused by it often enough to recognise it at once.

"Five dead," said another voice. "Pay all bets of evens or better."

Hornblower plunged forward. Part of the cable had been coiled down to make a rat pit ten feet across in which knelt Styles with dead and living rats about his knees. Partridge squatted beside the ring with a sandglass —used for timing the casting of the log—in front of him.

"Six dead," protested someone. "That un's dead."

"No, he ain't."

" 'Is back's broken. 'E's a dead 'un."

" 'E ain't a dead 'un," said Partridge.

The man who had protested looked up at that moment, and caught sight of Hornblower, and his words died away unspoken; at his silence the others followed his glance and stiffened into rigidity, and Hornblower stepped forward. He was still wondering what he should do; he was still fighting down the nausea excited by the horrible things he had seen. Desperately, he mastered his horror, and, thinking fast, took his stand on discipline.

"Who's in charge here?" he demanded.

He ran his eye round the circle. Petty officers and second-class warrant officers, mainly; bosun's mates, carpenter's mates. Muggridge, the surgeon's mate—his presence explained much. But his own position was not easy. A midshipman of scant service depended for his authority on board largely on the force of his own personality. He was only a warrant officer himself; when all was said and done a midshipman was much less important to the ship's economy—and was far more easily replaced—than, say,

106

Washburn the cooper's mate over there, who knew all about the making and storage of the ship's water barrels.

"Who's in charge here?" he demanded again, and once more received no direct reply.

"We ain't on watch," said a voice in the background.

Hornblower by now had mastered his horror; his indignation still flared within him but he could appear outwardly calm.

"No, you're not on watch," he said coldly. "You're gambling."

"Gambling, Mr. Hornblower?" he said. "That's a very serious charge. Just a gentlemanly competition. You'll find it hard to sub—substantiate any charges of gambling."

Muggridge had been drinking, quite obviously, following perhaps the example of the head of his department. There was brandy to be got in the medical stores. A surge of wrath made Hornblower tremble; the effort necessary to keep himself standing stock still was almost too much for him. But the rise in internal pressure brought him inspiration.

"Mr. Muggridge," he said icily, "I advise you not to say too much. There are other charges possible, Mr. Muggridge. A member of His Majesty's forces can be charged with rendering himself unfit for service, Mr. Muggridge. And similarly there might be charges of aiding and abetting which might include *you*. I should consult the Articles of War if I were you, Mr. Muggridge. The punishment for such an offence is flogging round the fleet, I believe."

Hornblower pointed to Styles, with the blood streaming from his bitten face, and gave more force to his argument by the gesture. He had met the men's arguments with a more effective one along the same lines; they had taken up a legalistic defence and he had legalistically beaten it down. He had the upper hand now and could give vent to his moral indignation.

107

"I could bring charges against every one of you," he roared. "You could be court-martialled—disrated—flogged—every man Jack of you. By God, one more look like that from you, Partridge, and I'll do it. You'd all be in irons five minutes after I spoke to Mr. Eccles. I'll have no more of these filthy games. Let those rats loose, there, you, Oldroyd, and you, Lewis. Styles, get your face plastered up again. You, Partridge, takes these men and coil this cable down properly again before Mr. Waldron sees it. I'll keep my eye on all of you in future. The next hint I have of misbehaviour and you'll all be at the gratings. I've said it and by God I mean it!"

Hornblower was surprised both at his own volubility and at his self-possession. He had not known himself capable of carrying off matters with such a high hand. He sought about in his mind for a final salvo with which to make his retirement dignified, and it came to him as he turned away so that he turned back to deliver it.

"After this I want to see you in the dogwatches skylarking on deck, not skulking in the cable tiers like a lot of Frenchmen."

That was the sort of speech to be expected of a pompous old captain, not a junior midshipman, but it served to give dignity to his retirement. There was a feverish buzz of voices as he left the group. Hornblower went up on deck, under the cheerless grey sky dark with premature night, to walk the deck to keep himself warm while the *Indefatigable* slashed her way to windward in the teeth of a roaring westerly, the spray flying in sheets over her bows, the straining seams leaking and her fabric groaning; the end of a day like all the preceding ones and the predecessor probably of innumerable more.

Yet the days passed, and with them came at last a break in the monotony. In the sombre dawn a hoarse bellow from the lookout turned every eye to windward, to where a dull blotch on the horizon marked the presence of a ship. The watch came running to the braces as the *Indefatigable* was laid as close to the wind as she would lie. Captain Pellew came on deck with a pea-jacket over his nightshirt, his wigless head comical in a pink nightcap; he trained his glass on the strange sail—a dozen glasses were pointing in that direction. Hornblower, looking through the glass reserved for the junior officer of the watch, saw the grey rectangle split into three, saw the three grow narrow, and then broaden again to coalesce into a single rectangle again.

"She's gone about," said Pellew. "Hands 'bout ship!"

Round came the *Indefatigable* on the other tack; the watch raced aloft to shake out a reef from the topsails while from the deck the officers looked up at the straining canvas to calculate the chances of the gale which howled round their ears splitting the sails or carrying away a spar. The *Indefatigable* lay over until it was hard to keep one's footing on the streaming deck; everyone without immediate duties clung to the weather rail and peered at the other ship.

"Fore and main topmasts exactly equal," said Lieutenant Bolton to Hornblower, his telescope to his eye. "Topsails white as milady's fingers. She's a Frenchie all right."

The sails of British ships were darkened with long service in all weathers; when a French ship escaped from harbour to run the blockade her spotless unweathered canvas disclosed her nationality without real need to take into consideration less obvious technical characteristics.

"We're weathering on her," said Hornblower; his eye was aching with staring through the glass, and his arms even were weary with holding the telescope to his eye, but in the excitement of the chase he could not relax.

"Not as much as I'd like," growled Bolton.

"Hands to the mainbrace!" roared Pellew at that moment.

It was a matter of the most vital concern to trim the

109

sails so as to lie as close as possible to the wind; a hundred yards gained to windward would count as much as a mile gained in a stern chase. Pellew was looking up at the sails, back at the fleeting wake, across at the French ship, gauging the strength of the wind, estimating the strain on the rigging, doing everything that a lifetime of experience could suggest to close the gap between the two ships. Pellew's next order sent all hands to run out the guns on the weather side; that would in part counteract the heel and give the *Indefatigable* more grip upon the water.

"Now we're walking up to her," said Bolton with grudging optimism.

"Beat to quarters!" shouted Pellew.

The ship had been expecting that order. The roar of the marine bandsmen's drums echoed through the ship; the pipes twittered as the bosun's mates repeated the order, and the men ran in disciplined fashion to their duties. Hornblower, jumping for the weather mizzen shrouds, saw the eager grins on half a dozen faces—battle and the imminent possibility of death were a welcome change from the eternal monotony of the blockade. Up in the mizzen top he looked over his men. They were uncovering the locks of their muskets and looking to the priming; satisfied with their readiness for action Hornblower turned his attention to the swivel gun. He took the tarpaulin from the breech and the tompion from the muzzle, cast off the lashings which secured it, and saw that the swivel moved freely in the socket and the trunnions freely in the crotch. A jerk of the lanyard showed him that the lock was sparking well and there was no need for a new flint. Finch came climbing into the top with the canvas belt over his shoulder containing the charges for the gun; the bags of musket balls lay handy in a garland fixed to the barricade. Finch rammed home a cartridge down the short muzzle; Hornblower had ready a bag of balls to ram down onto it. Then he took a priming-quill and forced it down the touchhole, feeling sensitively to make sure the sharp point pierced the thin serge bag of the cartridge. Priming-quill and flintlock were necessary up here in the top, where no slow match or port-fire could be used with the danger of uncontrollable fire so great in the sails and the rigging. Yet musketry and swivel-gun fire from the tops were an important tactical consideration. With the ships laid yard-arm to yard-arm Hornblower's men could clear the hostile quarterdeck where centred the brains and control of the enemy.

"Stop that, Finch!" said Hornblower irritably; turning, he had caught sight of him peering up at the maintop and at this moment of tension Finch's delusions annoyed him.

"Beg your pardon, sir," said Finch, resuming his duties.

But a moment later Hornblower heard Finch whispering to himself.

"Mr. Bracegirdle's there," whispered Finch. "An' Old-royd's there, an' all those others. But *He's* there too, so He is."

"Hands wear ship!" came the shouted order from the deck below.

The old *Indefatigable* was spinning round on her heel, the yards groaning as the braces swung them round. The French ship had made a bold attempt to rake her enemy as she clawed up to her, but Pellew's prompt handling defeated the plan. Now the ships were broadside to broadside, running free before the wind at long cannon shot.

"Just look at 'im!" roared Douglas, one of the musket men in the top. "Twenty guns a side. Looks brave enough, doesn't he?"

Standing beside Douglas Hornblower could look down on the Frenchman's deck, her guns run out with the guns' crews clustering round them, officers in white breeches and blue coats walking up and down, the spray flying from her bows as she drove headlong before the wind.

111

"She'll look braver still when we take her into Plymouth Sound," said the seaman on the far side of Hornblower.

The *Indefatigable* was slightly the faster ship; an occasional touch of starboard helm was working her in closer to the enemy, into decisive range, without allowing the Frenchman to headreach upon her. Hornblower was impressed by the silence on both sides; he had always understood that the French were likely to open fire at long range and to squander ineffectively the first carefully loaded broadside.

"When's he goin' to fire?" asked Douglas, echoing Hornblower's thoughts.

"In his own good time," piped Finch.

The gap of tossing water between the two ships was growing narrower. Hornblower swung the swivel gun round and looked along the sights. He could aim well enough at the Frenchman's quarterdeck, but it was much too long a range for a bag of musket balls—in any case he dared not open fire until Pellew gave permission.

"Them's the men for us!" said Douglas, pointing to the Frenchman's mizzen top.

It looked as if there were soldiers up there, judging by the blue uniforms and the crossbelts; the French often eked out their scanty crews of trained seamen by shipping soldiers; in the British navy the marines were never employed aloft. The French soldiers saw the gesture and shook their fists, and a young officer among them drew his sword and brandished it over his head. With the ships parallel to each other like this the French mizzen top would be Hornblower's particular objective should he decide on trying to silence the firing there instead of sweeping the quarterdeck. He gazed curiously at the men it was his duty to kill. So interested was he that the bang of a cannon took him by surprise; before he could look down the rest of the Frenchman's broadside had gone off in straggling fashion, and a moment later the *Indefatigable* lurched as all her guns went off together. The wind blew the smoke forward, so that in the mizzen top they were not troubled by it at all. Hornblower's glance showed him dead men flung about on the *Indefatigable*'s deck, dead men falling on the Frenchman's deck. Still the range was too great—very long musket shot, his eye told him.

"They're shootin' at us, sir," said Herbert.

"Let 'em," said Hornblower.

No musket fired from a heaving masthead at that range could possibly score a hit; that was obvious—so obvious that even Hornblower, madly excited as he was, could not help but be aware of it, and his certainty was apparent in his tone. It was interesting to see how the two calm words steadied the men. Down below the guns were roaring away continuously, and the ships were nearing each other fast.

"Open fire now, men!" said Hornblower. "Finch!"

He stared down the short length of the swivel gun. In the coarse V of the notch on the muzzle he could see the Frenchman's wheel, the two quartermasters standing behind it, the two officers beside it. He jerked the lanyard. A tenth of a second's delay, and then the gun roared out. He was conscious, before the smoke whirled round him, of the firing-quill, blown from the touchhole, flying past his temple; Finch was already sponging out the gun. The musket balls must have spread badly; only one of the helmsmen was down and someone else was already running to take his place. At that moment the whole top lurched frightfully; Hornblower felt it but he could not explain it. There was too much happening at once. The solid timbers under his feet jarred him as he stood—perhaps a shot had hit the mizzen mast. Finch was ramming in the cartridge; something struck the breech of the gun a heavy blow and left a bright splash of metal there—a musket bullet from the Frenchman's mizzen top. Hornblower tried to keep his head; he took out another sharp-

113

ened quill and coaxed it down into the touchhole. It had to be done purposefully and yet gently; a quill broken off in the touchhole was likely to be a maddening nuisance. He felt the point of the quill pierce the cartridge; Finch rammed home the wad on top of the musket balls. A bullet struck the barricade beside him as Hornblower trained the gun down, but he gave it no thought. Surely the top was swaying more even than the heavy sea justified? No matter. He had a clear shot at the enemy's quarterdeck. He tugged at the lanyard. He saw men fall. He actually saw the spokes of the wheel spin round as it was left untended. Then the two ships came together with a shattering crash and his world dissolved into a chaos compared with which what had gone before was orderly.

The mast was falling. The top swung round in a dizzy arc so that only his fortunate grip on the swivel saved him from being flung out like a stone from a sling. It wheeled round. With the shrouds on one side shot away and two cannon balls in its heart the mast tottered and rolled. Then the tug of the mizzen stays inclined it forward, the tug of the other shrouds inclined it to starboard, and the wind in the mizzen topsail took charge when the back stays parted. The mast crashed forward; the topmast caught against the mainyard and the whole structure hung there before it could dissolve into its constituent parts. The severed butt-end of the mast must be resting on the deck for the moment; mast and topmast were still united at the cap and the trestle-trees into one continuous length, although why the topmast had not snapped at the cap was hard to say. With the lower end of the mast resting precariously on the deck, and the topmast resting against the mainyard Hornblower and Finch still had a chance of life, but the ship's motion, another shot from the Frenchman, or the parting of the over-strained material could all end that chance. The mast could slip outwards, the topmast could break, the butt-end of the mast could slip along the

114

deck—they had to save themselves if they could before any one of these imminent events occurred. The main topmast and everything above it was involved in the general ruin. It too had fallen and was dangling, sails, spars and ropes in one frightful tangle. The mizzen topsail had torn itself free. Hornblower's eyes met Finch's; Finch and he were clinging to the swivel gun, and there was no one else in the steeply inclined top.

The starboard side mizzen topmast shrouds still survived; they, as well as the topmast, were resting across the mainyard, strained taut as fiddle strings, the mainyard tightening them just as the bridge tightens the strings of a fiddle. But along those shrouds lay the only way to safety —a sloping path from the peril of the top to the comparative safety of the mainyard.

The mast began to slip, to roll, out towards the end of the yard. Even if the mainyard held, the mizzen mast would soon fall into the sea alongside. All about them were thunderous noises—spars smashing, ropes parting; the guns were still bellowing and everyone below seemed to be yelling and screaming.

The top lurched again, frightfully. Two of the shrouds parted with the strain, with a noise clearly audible through the other din, and as they parted the mast twisted with a jerk, swinging round further the mizzen top, the swivel gun, and the two wretched beings who clung to it. Finch's staring blue eyes rolled with the movement of the top. Later Hornblower knew that the whole period of the fall of the mast was no longer than a few seconds, but at this time it seemed as if he had at least long minutes in which to think. Like Finch's, his eyes stared round him, saw the chance of safety.

"The mainyard!" he screamed.

Finch's face bore its foolish smile. Although instinct or training kept him gripping the swivel gun he seemingly had no fear, no desire to gain the safety of the mainyard.

"Finch, you fool!" yelled Hornblower.

He locked a desperate knee round the swivel so as to free a hand with which to gesticulate, but still Finch made no move.

"Jump, damn you!" raved Hornblower. "The shrouds—the yard. Jump!"

Finch only smiled.

"Jump and get to the maintop! Oh, Christ—!" Inspiration came in that frightful moment. "The maintop! God's there, Finch! Go along to God, quick!"

Those words penetrated into Finch's addled brain. He nodded with sublime unworldliness. Then he let go of the swivel and seemed to launch himself into the air like a frog. His body fell across the mizzen topmast shrouds and he began to scramble along them. The mast rolled again, that when Hornblower launched himself at the shrouds it was a longer jump. Only his shoulders reached the outermost shroud. He swung off, clung, nearly lost his grip, but regained it as a counterlurch of the leaning mast came to his assistance. Then he was scrambling along the shrouds, mad with panic. Here was the precious mainyard, and he threw himself across it, grappling its welcome solidity with his body, his feet feeling for the footrope. He was safe and steady on the yard just as the outward roll of the *Indefatigable* gave the balancing spars their final impetus, and the mizzen topmast parted company from the broken mizzen mast and the whole wreck fell down into the sea longside. Hornblower shuffled along the yard, whither Finch had preceded him, to be received with rapture in the maintop by Midshipman Bracegirdle. Bracegirdle was not God, but as Hornblower leaned across the breastwork of the maintop he thought to himself that if he had not spoken about God being in the maintop Finch would never have made that leap.

"Thought we'd lost you," said Bracegirdle, helping him

116

in and thumping him on the back. "Midshipman Horn-blower, our flying angel."

Finch was in the top, too, smiling his fool's smile and surrounded by the crew of the top. Everything seemed mad and exhilarating. It was a shock to remember that they were in the midst of a battle, and yet the firing had ceased, and even the yelling had almost died away. He staggered to the side of the top—strange how difficult it was to walk—and looked over. Bracegirdle came with him. Foreshortened by the height he could make out a crowd of figures on the Frenchman's deck. Those check shirts must surely be worn by British sailors. Surely that was Eccles, the *Indefatigable*'s first lieutenant, on the quarterdeck with a speaking trumpet.

"What has happened?" he asked Bracegirdle, bewildered.

"What has happened?" Bracegirdle stared for a moment before he understood. "We carried her by boarding. Eccles and the boarders were over the ship's side the moment we touched. Why, man, didn't you see?"

"No, I didn't see it," said Hornblower. He forced himself to joke. "Other matters demanded my attention at that moment."

He remembered how the mizzen top had lurched and swung, and he felt suddenly sick. But he did not want Bracegirdle to see it.

"I must go on deck and report," he said.

The descent of the main shrouds was a slow, ticklish business, for neither his hands nor his feet seemed to wish to go where he tried to place them. Even when he reached the deck he still felt insecure. Bolton was on the quarterdeck supervising the clearing away of the wreck of the mizzen mast. He gave a start of surprise as Hornblower approached.

"I thought you were overside with Davy Jones," he

said. He glanced aloft. "You reached the mainyard in time?"

"Yes, sir."

"Excellent. I think you're born to be hanged, Hornblower." Bolton turned away to bellow at the men. " 'Vast heaving, there! Clynes, get down into the chains with that tackle! Steady, now, or you'll lose it."

He watched the labours of the men for some moments before he turned back to Hornblower.

"No more trouble with the men for a couple of months," he said. "We'll work 'em 'till they drop, refitting. Prize crew will leave us shorthanded, to say nothing of our butcher's bill. It'll be a long time before they want something new. It'll be a long time for you, too, I fancy, Hornblower."

"Yes, sir," said Hornblower.

VI

HORNBLOWER

the Frogs, and the Lobsters

"They're coming," said Midshipman Kennedy.

Midshipman Hornblower's unmusical ear caught the raucous sounds of a military band, and soon, with a gleam of scarlet and white and gold, the head of the column came round the corner. The hot sunshine was reflected from the brass instruments; behind them the regimental colour flapped from its staff, borne proudly by an ensign with the colour guard round him. Two mounted officers rode behind the colour, and after them came the long red serpent of the half-battalion, the fixed bayonets flashing in the sun, while all the children of Plymouth, still not sated with military pomp, ran along with them.

The sailors standing ready on the quay looked at the soldiers marching up curiously, with something of pity and something of contempt mingled with their curiosity. The rigid drill, the heavy clothing, the iron discipline, the dull routine of the soldier were in sharp contrast with the far more flexible conditions in which the sailor lived. The sailors watched as the band ended with a flourish, and one of the mounted officers wheeled his horse to face the column. A shouted order turned every man to face the quay side, the movements being made so exactly together that five hundred boot-heels made a single sound. A huge sergeant-major, his sash gleaming on his chest, and the silver mounting of his cane winking in the sun, dressed the already perfect line. A third order brought down every musket-butt to earth.

"Unfix—bayonets!" roared the mounted officer, uttering the first words Hornblower had understood.

Hornblower positively goggled at the ensuing formalities, as the fuglemen strode their three paces forward, all exactly to time like marionettes worked by the same strings, turned their heads to look down the line, and gave the time for detaching the bayonets, for sheathing them, and for returning the muskets to the men's sides. The fuglemen fell back into their places, exactly to time again as far as Hornblower could see, but not exactly enough apparently, as the sergeant-major bellowed his discontent and brought the fuglemen out and sent them back again.

"I'd like to see him laying aloft on a stormy night," muttered Kennedy. "D'ye think he could take the main tops'l earring?"

"These Lobsters!" said Midshipman Bracegirdle.

The scarlet lines stood rigid, all five companies, the sergeants with their halberds indicating the intervals—from halberd to halberd the line of faces dipped down and then up again, with the men exactly sized off, the tallest men at the flanks and the shortest men in the centre of each company. Not a finger moved, not an eyebrow twitched. Down every back hung rigidly a powdered pigtail.

The mounted officer trotted down the line to where the naval party waited, and Lieutenant Bolton, in command, stepped forward with his hand to his hat brim.

"My men are ready to embark, sir," said the army officer. "The baggage will be here immediately."

"Aye aye, major," said Bolton—the army title and the navy reply in strange contrast.

"It would be better to address me as 'my lord,' " said the major.

120

"Aye aye, sir—my lord," replied Bolton, caught quite off his balance.

His Lordship, the Earl of Edrington, Major commanding this wing of the 43rd Foot, was a heavily built young man in his early twenties. He was a fine soldierly figure in his well-fitting uniform, and mounted on a magnificent charger, but he seemed a little young for his present responsible command. But the practice of the purchase of commissions was likely to put very young men in high command, and the army seemed satisfied with the system.

"The French auxiliaries have their orders to report here," went on Lord Edrington. "I suppose arrangements have been made for their transport as well?"

"Yes, my lord."

"Not one of the beggars can speak English, as far as I can make out. Have you got an officer to interpret?"

"Yes, sir. Mr. Hornblower!"

"Sir!"

"You will attend the embarkation of the French troops."

"Aye aye, sir."

More military music—Hornblower's tone-deaf ear distinguished it as making a thinner noise than the British infantry band—heralded the arrival of the Frenchmen farther down the quay by a side road, and Hornblower hastened there. This was the Royal, Christian, and Catholic French army, or a detachment of it at least—a battalion of the force raised by the *émigré* French nobles to fight against the Revolution. There was the white flag with the golden lilies at the head of the column, and a group of mounted officers to whom Hornblower touched his hat. One of them acknowledged his salute.

"The Marquis of Pouzauges, Brigadier General in the service of His Most Christian Majesty Louis XVII," said this individual in French by way of introduction. He

121

wore a glittering white uniform with a blue ribbon across it.

Stumbling over the French words, Hornblower introduced himself as an aspirant of His Britannic Majesty's Marine, deputed to arrange the embarkation of French troops.

"Very good," said Pouzauges. "We are ready."

Hornblower looked down the French column. The men were standing in all attitudes, gazing about them. They were all well enough dressed, in blue uniforms which Hornblower guessed had been supplied by the British government, but the white crossbelts were already dirty, the metalwork tarnished, the arms dull. Yet doubtless they could fight.

"Those are the transports allotted to your men, sir," said Hornblower pointing. "The *Sophia* will take three hundred, and the *Dumbarton*—that one over there—will take two hundred and fifty. Here at the quay are the lighters to ferry the men out."

"Give the orders, M. de Moncoutant," said Pouzauges to one of the officers beside him.

The hired baggage carts had now come creaking up along the column, piled high with the men's kits, and the column broke into chattering swarms as the men hunted up their possessions. It was some time before the men were reassembled, each with his own kit-bag, and then there arose the question of detailing a fatigue party to deal with the regimental baggage; the men who were given the task yielded up their bags with obvious reluctance to their comrades, clearly in despair of ever seeing any of the contents again. Hornblower was still giving out information.

"All horses must go to the *Sophia*," he said. "She has accommodation for six chargers. The regimental baggage—"

He broke off short, for his eye had been caught by a singular jumble of apparatus lying in one of the carts.

"What is that, if you please?" he asked curiosity overpowering him.

"That, sir," said Pouzauges, "is a guillotine."

"A guillotine?"

Hornblower had read much lately about this instrument. The Red Revolutionaries had set one up in Paris and kept it hard at work. The King of France, Louis XVI himself, had died under it. He did not expect to find one in the train of a counter-revolutionary army.

"Yes," said Pouzauges, "we take it with us to France. It is in my mind to give those anarchists a taste of their own medicine."

Hornblower did not have to make reply, fortunately, as a bellow from Bolton interrupted the conversation.

"What the hell's all this delay for, Mr. Hornblower? D'you want us to miss the tide?"

It was of course typical of life in any service that Hornblower should be reprimanded for the time wasted by the inefficiency of the French arrangements—that was the sort of thing he had already come to expect, and he had already learned that it was better to submit silently to reprimand than to offer excuses. He addressed himself again to the task of getting the French aboard their transports. It was a weary midshipman who at last reported himself to Bolton with his tally sheets and the news that the last Frenchman and horse and pieces of baggage were safely aboard, and he was greeted with the order to get his things together quickly and transfer them and himself to the *Sophia* where his services as interpreter were still needed.

The convoy dropped quickly down Plymouth Sound, rounded the Eddystone, and headed down channel, with H.M.S. *Indefatigable* flying her distinguishing pendant, the two gunbrigs which had been ordered to assist in convoying the expedition, and the four transports—a small enough force, it seemed to Hornblower, with which to attempt the overthrow of the French Republic. There were only eleven hundred infantry; the half-battalion of the 43rd and the weak battalion of Frenchmen (if they could be called that, seeing that many of them were soldiers of fortune of all nations) and although Hornblower had enough sense not to try to judge the Frenchmen as they lay in rows in the dark and stinking 'tween-decks in the agonies of seasickness he was puzzled that anyone could expect results from such a small force. His historical reading had told him of many small raids, in many wars, launched against the shores of France, and, although he knew that they had once been described by an opposition statesman as "breaking windows with guineas" he had been inclined to approve of them in principle, as bringing about a dissipation of the French strength—until now, when he found himself part of such an expedition.

So it was with relief that he heard from Pouzauges that the troops he had seen did not constitute the whole of the force to be employed—were indeed only a minor fraction of it. A little pale with seasickness, but manfully combating it, Pouzauges laid out a map on the cabin table and explained the plan.

"The Christian Army," explained Pouzauges, "will land here, at Quiberon. They sailed from Portsmouth—these English names are hard to pronounce—the day before we left Plymouth. There are five thousand men under the Baron de Charette. They will march on Vannes and Rennes."

"And what is your regiment to do?" asked Hornblower.

Pouzauges pointed to the map again.

"Here is the town of Muzillac," he said. "Twenty leagues from Quiberon. Here the main road from the south crosses the river Marais, where the tide ceases to flow. It is only a little river, as you see, but its banks are

124

marshy, and the road passes it not only by a bridge but by a long causeway. The rebel armies are to the south, and on their northward march must come by Muzillac. We shall be there. We shall destroy the bridge and defend the crossing, delaying the rebels long enough to enable M. de Charette to raise all Brittany. He will soon have twenty thousand men in arms, the rebels will come back to their allegiance, and we shall march on Paris to restore His Most Christian Majesty to the throne."

So that was the plan. Hornblower was infected with the Frenchmen's enthusiasm. Certainly the road passed within ten miles of the coast, and there, in the broad estuary of the Vilaine, it should be possible to land a small force and seize Muzillac. There should be no difficulty about defending a causeway, such as Pouzauges described, for a day or two against even a large force. That would afford Charette every chance.

"My friend M. de Moncoutant here," went on Pouzauges, "is Lord of Muzillac. The people there will welcome him."

"Most of them will," said Moncoutant, his grey eyes narrowing. "Some will be sorry to see me. But I shall be glad of the encounter."

Western France, the Vendée and Brittany, had long been in a turmoil, and the population there, under the leadership of the nobility, had risen in arms more than once against the Paris government. But every rebellion had ended in defeat; the Royalist force now being convoyed to France was composed of the fragments of the defeated armies—a final cast of the dice, and a desperate one. Regarded in that light, the plan did not seem so sound.

It was a grey morning—a morning of grey sky and grey rocks—when the convoy rounded Belle Ile and stood in towards the estuary of the Vilaine river. Far to the north-ward were to be seen white topsails in Quiberon Bay—

Hornblower, from the deck of the *Sophia,* saw signals pass back and forth from the *Indefatigable* as she reported her arrival to the senior officer of the main expedition there. It was a proof of the mobility and ubiquity of naval power that it could take advantage of the configuration of the land so that two blows could be struck almost in sight of each other from the sea yet separated by forty miles of roads on land. Hornblower raked the forbidding shore with his glass, re-read the orders for the captain of the *Sophia,* and stared again at the shore. He could distinguish the narrow mouth of the Marais river and the strip of mud where the troops were to land. The lead was going in the chains as the *Sophia* crept towards her allotted anchorage, and the ship was rolling uneasily; these waters, sheltered though they were, were a bedlam of conflicting currents that could make a choppy sea even in a calm. Then the anchor cable rumbled out through the hawsehole and the *Sophia* swung to the current while the crew set to work hoisting out the boats.

"France, dear beautiful France," said Pouzauges at Hornblower's side.

A hail came over the water from the *Indefatigable.*

"Mr. Hornblower!"

"Sir!" yelled Hornblower back through the captain's megaphone.

"You will go on shore with the French troops and stay with them until you receive further orders."

"Aye aye, sir."

So that was the way in which he was to set foot on foreign soil for the first time in his life.

Pouzauges' men were now pouring up from below; it was a slow and exasperating business getting them down the ship's side into the waiting boats. Hornblower wondered idly regarding what was happening on shore at this moment—without doubt mounted messengers were galloping north and south with the news of the arrival of the expedition, and soon the French Revolutionary generals would be parading their men and marching them hurriedly towards this place; it was well that the important strategic point that had to be seized was less than ten miles inland. He turned back to his duties; as soon as the men were ashore he would have to see that the baggage and reserve ammunition were landed, as well as the horses, now standing miserably in improvised stalls forward of the mainmast.

The first boats had left the ship's side; Hornblower watched the men stagger up the shore through mud and water, the French on the left and the red-coated British infantry on the right. There were some fishermen's cottages in sight up the beach, and Hornblower saw advance parties go forward to seize them; at least the landing had been effected without a single shot being fired. He came on shore with the ammunition, to find Bolton in charge of the beach.

"Get those ammunition boxes well above high water mark," said Bolton. "We can't send 'em forward until the Lobsters have found us some carts for 'em. And we'll need horses for those guns too."

At that moment Bolton's working party was engaged in manhandling two six-pounder guns in field carriages up the beach; they were to be manned by seamen and drawn by horses commandeered by the landing party, for it was in the old tradition that a British expeditionary force should always be thrown on shore dependent for military necessities on the countryside. Pouzauges and his staff were waiting impatiently for their chargers, and mounted them the moment they had been coaxed out of the boats onto the beach.

"Forward for France!" shouted Pouzauges, drawing his sword and raising the hilt to his lips.

Moncoutant and the others clattered forward to head the advancing infantry, while Pouzauges lingered to exchange a few words with Lord Edrington. The British infantry was drawn up in a rigid scarlet line; farther inland occasional red dots marked where the light company had been thrown forward as pickets. Hornblower could not hear the conversation, but he noticed that Bolton was drawn into it, and finally Bolton called him over.

"You must go forward with the Frogs, Hornblower," he said.

"I'll give you a horse," added Edrington. "Take that one—the roan. I've got to have someone I can trust along with them. Keep your eye on them and let me know the moment they get up to any monkey tricks—God knows what they'll do next."

"Here's the rest of your stores coming ashore," said Bolton. "I'll send 'em up as soon as you send some carts back to me. What the hell's *that?*"

"That's a portable guillotine, sir," said Hornblower. "Part of the French baggage."

All three turned and looked at Pouzauges, sitting his horse impatiently during this conversation which he did not understand. He knew what they were referring to, all the same.

"That's the first thing to be sent to Muzillac," he said to Hornblower. "Will you have the goodness to tell these gentlemen so?"

Hornblower translated.

"I'll send the guns and a load of ammunition first," said Bolton. "But I'll see he gets it soon. Now off you go."

Hornblower dubiously approached the roan horse. All he knew about riding he had learned in farmyards, but he got his foot up into the stirrup and climbed into the saddle, grabbing nervously at the reins as the animal started to move off. It seemed as far down to the ground from there as it did from the main topgallant yard. Pouzauges wheeled his horse about and started up the beach, and the roan followed its example, with Hornblower hanging on desperately, spattered by the mud thrown up by the French horse's heels.

From the fishing hamlet a muddy lane, bordered by green turf banks, led inland, and Pouzauges trotted smartly along it, Hornblower jolting behind him. They covered three or four miles before they overtook the rear of the French infantry, marching rapidly through the mud, and Pouzauges pulled his horse to a walk. When the column climbed a slight undulation they could see the white banner far ahead. Over the banks Hornblower could see rocky fields; out on the left there was a small farmhouse of grey stone. A blue-uniformed soldier was leading away a white horse pulling a cart, while two or three more soldiers were holding back the farmer's frantic wife. So the expeditionary force had secured some of its necessary transport. In another field a soldier was prodding a cow along with his bayonet—Hornblower could not imagine with what motive. Twice he heard distant musket shots to which no one seemed to pay any attention. Then, coming down the road, they encountered two soldiers leading bony horses towards the beach; the jests hurled at them by the marching column had set the men's faces in broad grins. But a little way farther on Hornblower saw a plough standing lonely in a little field, and a grey bundle lying near it. The bundle was a dead man.

Over on their right was the marshy river valley, and it was not long before Hornblower could see, far ahead, the bridge and the causeway which they had been sent to seize. The lane they were following came down a slight incline into the town, passing between a few grey cottages before emerging into the highroad along which there lay the town. There was a grey stone church, there was a building that could easily be identified as an inn and posting house with soldiers swarming round it, a slight broadening of the highroad, with an avenue of trees, which Hornblower assumed must be the central square of the

129

town. A few faces peered from upper windows, but otherwise the houses were shut and there were no civilians to be seen except two women hastily shuttering their shops. Pouzauges reined up his horse in the square and began issuing orders. Already the horses were being led out of the post-house, and groups of men were bustling to and fro on seemingly urgent errands. In obedience to Pouzauges one officer called his men together—he had to expostulate and gesticulate before he succeeded—and started towards the bridge. Another party started along the highway in the opposite direction to guard against a possible surprise attack from there. A crowd of men squatted in the square devouring the bread that was brought out from one of the shops after its door had been beaten in, and two or three times civilians were dragged up to Pouzauges and at his orders were hurried away again to the town jail. The seizure of the town of Muzillac was complete.

Pouzauges seemed to think so, too, after an interval, for with a glance at Hornblower he turned his horse and trotted towards the causeway. The town ended before the road entered the marshes, and in a bit of waste ground beside the road the party sent out in this direction had already lighted a fire, and the men were gathered round it, toasting on their bayonets chunks of meat cut from a cow whose half-flayed corpse lay beside the fire. Farther on, where the causeway became the bridge over the river, a sentry sat sunning himself with his musket leaning against the parapet of the bridge at his back. Everything was peaceful enough. Pouzauges trotted as far as the crown of the bridge with Hornblower beside him, and looked over the country on the farther side. There was no sign of any enemy, and when they returned there was a mounted red-coated soldier waiting for them—Lord Edrington.

"I've come to see for myself," he said. "The position

looks strong enough in all conscience here. Once you have the guns posted you should be able to hold this bridge until you can blow up the arch. But there's a ford, passable at low water, half a mile lower down. That is where I shall station myself—if we lose the ford they can turn the whole position and cut us off from the shore. Tell this gentleman—what's his name?—what I said."

Hornblower translated as well as he could, and stood by as interpreter while the two commanders pointed here and there and settled their respective duties.

"That's settled, then," said Edrington at length. "Don't forget, Mr. Hornblower, that I must be kept informed of every development."

He nodded to them and wheeled his horse and trotted off. As he left a cart approached from the direction of Muzillac, while behind it a loud clanking heralded the arrival of the two six-pounders, each drawn painfully by a couple of horses led by seamen. Sitting up on the front of the cart was Midshipman Bracegirdle, who saluted Hornblower with a broad grin.

"From quarterdeck to dung cart is but a step," he announced, swinging himself down. "From midshipman to captain of artillery."

He looked along the causeway and then around him.

"Put the guns over there and they'll sweep the whole length," suggested Hornblower.

"Exactly," said Bracegirdle.

Under his orders the guns were wheeled off the road and pointed along the causeway, and the dung cart was unloaded of its contents, a tarpaulin spread on the ground, the gunpowder cartridges laid on it and covered with another tarpaulin. The shot and the bags of grape were piled beside the guns, the seamen working with a will under the stimulus of their novel surroundings.

"Poverty brings strange bedfellows," said Bracegirdle.

131

"And wars strange duties. Have you ever blown up a bridge?"

"Never," said Hornblower.

"Neither have I. Come, and let us do it. May I offer you a place in my carriage?"

Hornblower climbed up into the cart with Bracegirdle, and two seamen led the plodding horse along the causeway to the bridge. There they halted and looked down at the muddy water—running swiftly with the ebb—craning their heads over the parapet to look at the solid stone construction.

"It is the keystone of the arch which we should blow out," said Bracegirdle.

That was the proverbial recipe for the destruction of a bridge, but as Hornblower looked from the bridge to Bracegirdle and back again the idea did not seem easy to execute. Gunpowder exploded upwards and had to be held in on all sides—how was that to be done under the arch of the bridge?

"What about the pier?" he asked, tentatively.

"We can but look and see," said Bracegirdle and turned to the seaman by the cart. "Hannay, bring a rope."

They fastened the rope to the parapet and slid down it to a precarious foothold on the slippery ledge round the base of the pier, the river gurgling at their feet.

"That seems to be the solution," said Bracegirdle, crouching almost double under the arch.

Time slipped by fast as they made their preparations; a working party had to be brought from the guard of the bridge, picks and crowbars had to be found or extemporised, and some of the huge blocks with which the pier was built had to be picked out at the shoulder of the arch. Two kegs of gunpowder, lowered gingerly from above, had to be thrust into the holes so formed, a length of slow match put in at each bunghole, and led to the ex-

132

terior while the kegs were tamped into their caves with all the stones and earth that could be crammed into them. It was almost twilight under the arch when the work was finished, the working party made laboriously to climb the rope up to the bridge, and Bracegirdle and Hornblower were left to look at each other again.

"I'll fire the fuses," said Bracegirdle. "You go next, sir."

It was not a matter for much argument. Bracegirdle was under orders to destroy the bridge, and Hornblower addressed himself to climbing up the rope while Bracegirdle took his tinderbox from his pocket. Once on the roadway of the bridge Hornblower sent away the cart and waited. It was only two or three minutes before Bracegirdle appeared, frantically climbing the rope and hurling himself over the parapet.

"Run!" was all that was said.

Together they scurried down the bridge and halted breathless to crouch by the abutment of the causeway. Then came a dull explosion, a tremor of the earth under their feet, and a cloud of smoke.

"Let's come and see," said Bracegirdle.

They retraced their steps towards where the bridge was still shrouded in smoke and dust.

"Only partly—" began Bracegirdle as they neared the scene and the dust cleared away.

And at that moment there was a second explosion which made them stagger as they stood. A lump of the roadbed hit the parapet beside them and burst like a shell, spattering them with fragments. There was a rumble and a clatter as the arch subsided into the river.

"That must have been the second keg going off," said Bracegirdle, wiping his face. "We should have remembered the fuses were likely to be of different lengths. Two promising careers might have ended suddenly if we had been any nearer."

"At any rate, the bridge is gone," said Hornblower.

"All's well that ends well," said Bracegirdle.

Seventy pounds of gunpowder had done their work. The bridge was cut clear across, leaving a ragged gap several feet wide, beyond which the roadway reached out toward the gap from the farther pier as a witness to the toughness of the mortar. Beneath their feet as they peered over they could see the river bed almost choked with lumps of stone.

"We'll need no more than an anchor watch tonight," said Bracegirdle.

Hornblower looked round to where the roan horse was tethered; he was tempted to return to Muzillac on foot, leading the animal, but shame forbade. He climbed with an effort into the saddle and headed the animal back up the road; ahead of him the sky was beginning to turn red with the approach of sunset.

He entered the main street of the town and rounded the slight bend to the central square, to see something that made him, without his own volition, tug at his reins and halt his horse. The square was full of people, townsfolk and soldiers, and in the centre of the square a tall narrow rectangle reached upwards towards the sky with a glittering blade at its upper end. The blade fell with a reverberating thump, and the little group of men round the base of the rectangle dragged something to one side and added it to the heap already there. The portable guillotine was at work.

Hornblower sat sick and horrified—this was worse than any flogging at the gratings. He was about to urge his horse forward when a strange sound caught his ear. A man was singing, loud and clear, and out from a building at the side of the square emerged a little procession. In front walked a big man with dark curly hair, wearing a white shirt and dark breeches. At either side and behind him walked soldiers. It was this man who was singing;

the tune meant nothing to Hornblower, but he could hear the words distinctly—it was one of the verses of the French revolutionary song, echoes of which had penetrated even across the channel.

"Oh, sacred love of the Fatherland—" sang the man in the white shirt, and when the civilians in the square heard what he was singing, there was a rustle among them and they dropped to the knees, their heads bowed and their hands crossed upon their breasts.

The executioners were winding the blade up again, and the man in the white shirt followed its rise with his eyes while he still sang without a tremor in his voice. The blade reached the top, and the singing ceased at last as the executioners fell on the man with the white shirt and led him to the guillotine. Then the blade fell with another echoing crash.

It seemed that this was to be the last execution, for the soldiers began to push the civilians back towards their homes, and Hornblower urged his horse forward through the dissolving crowd. He was nearly thrown from his saddle when the animal plunged sideways, snorting furiously —it had scented the horrid heap that lay beside the guillotine. At the side of the square was a house with a balcony, and Hornblower looked up at it in time to see Pouzauges still standing there, wearing his white uniform and blue ribbon, his staff about him and his hands on the rail. There were sentries at the door, and to one of them Hornblower handed over his horse as he entered; Pouzauges was just descending the stairs.

"Good evening, sir," said Pouzauges with perfect courtesy. "I am glad you have found your way to headquarters. I trust it was without trouble? We are about to dine and will enjoy your company. You have your horse, I suppose? M. de Villers here will give orders for it to be looked after, I am sure."

It was all hard to believe. It was hard to believe that

this polished gentleman had ordered the butchery that had just ended; it was hard to believe that the elegant young men with whom he sat at dinner were staking their lives on the overthrow of a barbarous but lusty young republic. But it was equally hard to believe, when he climbed into a four-poster bed that night, that he, Midshipman Horatio Hornblower, was in imminent deadly peril himself.

Outside in the street women wailed as the headless corpses, the harvest of the executions, were carried away, and he thought he would never sleep, but youth and fatigue had their way, and he slept for most of the night, although he awoke with the feeling that he had just been fighting off a nightmare. Everything was strange to him in the darkness, and it was several moments before he could account for the strangeness. He was in a bed and not—as he had spent the preceding three hundred nights—in a hammock; and the bed was steady as a rock instead of swaying about with the lively motion of a frigate. The stuffiness about him was the stuffiness of bed curtains, and not the stuffiness of the midshipmen's berth with its compound smell of stale humanity and stale bilgewater. He was on shore, in a house, in a bed, and everything about him was dead quiet, unnaturally so to a man accustomed to the innumerable noises of a wooden ship at sea.

Of course; he was in a house in the town of Muzillac in Brittany. He was sleeping in the headquarters of Brigadier General the Marquis de Pouzauges, commanding the French troops who constituted part of this expedition, which was itself part of a larger force invading Revolutionary France in the Royalist cause. Hornblower felt a quickening of the pulse, a faint sick feeling of insecurity, as he realized afresh that he was now in France, ten miles from the sea and the *Indefatigable* with only a rabble of Frenchmen—half of them mercenaries only

136

nominally Frenchmen at that—around him to preserve him from death or captivity. He regretted his knowledge of French—if he had had none he would not be here, and good fortune might even have put him among the British half-battalion of the 43rd guarding the ford a mile away.

It was partly the thought of the British troops which roused him out of bed. It was his duty to see that liaison was kept up with them, and the situation might have changed while he slept. He drew aside the bed curtains and stepped down to the floor; as his legs took the weight of his body they protested furiously—all the riding he had done yesterday had left every muscle and joint aching so that he could hardly walk. But he hobbled in the darkness over to the window, found the latch of the shutters, and pushed them open. A three-quarter moon was shining down into the empty street of the town, and looking down he could see the three-cornered hat of the sentry posted outside, and the bayonet reflecting the moonlight. Returning from the window, he found his coat and his shoes and put them on, belted his cutlass about him, and then he crept downstairs as quietly as he could. In the room off the entrance hall a tallow dip guttered on the table, and beside it a French sergeant slept with his head on his arms, lightly, for he raised his head as Hornblower paused in the doorway. On the floor of the room the rest of the guard off duty were snoring stertorously, huddled together like pigs in a sty, their muskets stacked against the wall.

Hornblower nodded to the sergeant, opened the front door, and stepped out into the street. His lungs expanded gratefully as he breathed in the clean night air—morning air, rather, for there to the east the sky was assuming a lighter tinge—and the sentry, catching sight of the British naval officer, came clumsily to attention. In the square there still stood the gaunt harsh framework of the guillotine reaching up to the moonlit sky, and round it

137

the black patch of the blood of its victims. Hornblower wondered who they were, who it could have been that the Royalists should seize and kill at such short notice, and he decided that they must have been petty officials of the Revolutionary government—the mayor and the customs officer and so on—if they were not merely men against whom the *émigrés* had cherished grudges since the days of the revolution itself. It was a savage, merciless world, and at the moment he was very much alone in it, lonely, depressed, and unhappy.

He was distracted from these thoughts by the sergeant of the guard emerging from the door with a file of men; the sentry in the street was relieved, and the party went on round the house to relieve the others. Then across the street, he saw four drummers appear from another house, with a sergeant commanding them. They formed into a line, their drumsticks poised high before their faces, and then at a word from the sergeant, the eight drumsticks fell together with a crash, and the drummers proceeded to march slowly along the street beating out a jerky exhilarating rhythm. At the first corner, they stopped, and the drums rolled long and menacingly, and then they marched on again, beating out the previous rhythm. They were beating to arms, calling the men to their duties from their billets, and Hornblower, tone-deaf but highly sensitive to rhythm, thought it was fine music, real music. He turned back to headquarters with his depression fallen away from him. The sergeant of the guard came marching back with the relieved sentries; the first of the awakened soldiers were beginning to appear sleepily in the streets, and then, with a clatter of hoofs, a mounted messenger came riding up to headquarters, and the day was begun.

A pale young French officer read the note which the messenger brought, and politely handed it to Hornblower to read; he had to puzzle over it for a space—he was not accustomed to handwritten French—but its meaning became clear to him at length. It implied no new development; the main expeditionary force, landed yesterday at Quiberon, would move forward this morning on Vannes and Rennes while the subsidiary force to which Hornblower was attached must maintain its position at Muzillac guarding its flank. The Marquis de Pouzauges, immaculate in his white uniform and blue ribbon, appeared at that moment, read the note without comment, and turned to Hornblower with a polite invitation to breakfast.

They went back to the big kitchen with its copper cooking pans glittering on the walls, and a silent woman brought them coffee and bread. She might be a patriotic Frenchwoman and an enthusiastic counter-revolutionary, but she showed no signs of it. Her feelings, of course, might easily have been influenced by the fact that this horde of men had taken over her house and were eating her food and sleeping in her rooms without payment. Maybe some of the horses and waggons seized for the use of the army were hers too—and maybe some of the people who had died under the guillotine last night were her friends. But she brought coffee, and the staff, standing about in the big kitchen with their spurs clinking, began to breakfast. Hornblower took his cup and a piece of bread—for four months before this his only bread had been ship's biscuit—and sipped at the stuff. He was not sure if he liked it; he had only tasted coffee three or four times before. But the second time he raised his cup to his lips, he did not sip; before he could do so, the distant boom of a cannon made him lower his cup and stand stock still. The cannon shot was repeated, and again, and then it was echoed by a sharper, nearer note—Midshipman Bracegirdle's six-pounders on the causeway.

In the kitchen there was instant stir and bustle. Somebody knocked a cup over and sent a river of black liquid swirling across the table. Somebody else managed to catch his spurs together so that he stumbled into somebody else's arms. Everyone seemed to be speaking at once. Hornblower was as excited as the rest of them; he wanted to rush out and see what was happening, but he thought at that moment of the disciplined calm which he had seen in H.M.S. *Indefatigable* as she went into action. He was not of this breed of Frenchmen, and to prove it he made himself put his cup to his lips again and drink calmly. Already most of the staff had dashed out of the kitchen shouting for their horses. It would take time to saddle up; he met Pouzauges' eye as the latter strode up and down the kitchen, and he drained his cup—a trifle too hot for comfort, but he felt it was a good gesture. There was bread to eat, and he made himself bite and chew and swallow, although he had no appetite; if he was to be in the field all day, he could not tell when he would get his next meal, and so he crammed a half loaf into his pocket.

The horses were being brought into the yard and saddled; the excitement had infected them, and they plunged and sidled about amid the curses of the officers. Pouzauges leapt up into his saddle and clattered away with the rest of the staff behind him, leaving behind only a single soldier holding Hornblower's roan. That was as it had better be—Hornblower knew that he would not keep his seat for half a minute if the horse took it into his head to plunge or rear. He walked slowly out to the animal, which was calmer now when the groom petted him, and climbed with infinite slowness and precaution into the saddle. With a pull at the bit he checked the brute's exuberance and walked it sedately into the street and towards the bridge in the wake of the galloping staff. It was better to make sure of arriving by keeping his horse down to a walk than to gallop and be thrown. The guns were still booming and he could see the puffs of smoke from

140

Bracegirdle's six-pounders. On his left, the sun was rising in a clear sky.

At the bridge the situation seemed obvious enough. Where the arch had been blown up a few skirmishers on either side were firing at each other across the gap, and, at the far end of the causeway, across the Marais, a cloud of smoke revealed the presence of a hostile battery firing slowly and at extreme range. Beside the causeway on this side were Bracegirdle's two six-pounders, almost perfectly covered by a dip in the ground. Bracegirdle, with his cutlass belted round him, was standing between the guns which his party of seamen were working, and he waved his hand lightheartedly at Hornblower when he caught sight of him. A dark column of infantry appeared on the distant causeway. Bang—bang went Bracegirdle's guns. Hornblower's horse plunged at the noise, distracting him, but when he had time to look again, the column had disappeared. Then suddenly the causeway parapet near him flew into splinters; something hit the roadbed beside his horse's feet a tremendous blow and passed on with a roar —that was the closest so far in his life that a cannon shot had missed him. He lost a stirrup during the resultant struggle with his horse, and deemed it wiser, as soon as he regained moderate control, to dismount and lead the animal off the causeway towards the guns. Bracegirdle met him with a grin.

"No chance of their crossing here," he said. "At least, not if the Frogs stick to their work, and it looks as if they're willing to. The gap's within grapeshot range; they'll never bridge it. Can't think what they're burning powder for."

"Testing our strength, I suppose," said Hornblower, with an air of infinite military wisdom.

He would have been shaking with excitement if he had allowed his body to take charge. He did not know if he were being stiltedly unnatural, but even if he were that

141

was better than to display excitement. There was something strangely pleasant, in a nightmare fashion, in standing here posing as a hardened veteran with cannon balls howling overhead; Bracegirdle seemed happy and smiling and quite master of himself, and Hornblower looked sharply at him, wondering if this were as much a pose as his own. He could not tell.

"Here they come again," said Bracegirdle. "Oh, only skirmishers."

A few scattered men were running out along the causeway to the bridge. At long musket range they fell to the ground and began spasmodic firing; already there were some dead men lying over there and the skirmishers took cover behind the corpses. On this side of the gap the skirmishers, better sheltered, fired back at them.

"They haven't a chance, here at any rate," said Bracegirdle. "And look there."

The main body of the Royalist force, summoned from the town, was marching up along the road. While they watched it, a cannon shot from the other side struck the head of the column and ploughed into it—Hornblower saw dead men flung this way and that, and the column wavered. Pouzauges came riding up and yelled orders, and the column, leaving its dead and wounded on the road, changed direction and took shelter in the marshy fields beside the causeway.

With nearly all the Royalist force assembled, it seemed indeed as if it would be utterly impossible for the Revolutionaries to force a crossing here.

"I'd better report on this to the Lobsters," said Hornblower.

"There was firing down that way at dawn," agreed Bracegirdle.

Skirting the wide marsh here ran a narrow path through the lush grass, leading to the ford which the 43rd were guarding. Hornblower led his horse onto the path before

142

he mounted; he felt he would be more sure in that way of persuading the horse to take that direction. It was not long before he saw a dot of scarlet on the river-bank— pickets thrown out from the main body to watch against any unlikely attempt to cross the marshes and stream round the British flank. Then he saw the cottage that indicated the site of the ford; in the field beside it was a wide patch of scarlet indicating where the main body was waiting for developments. At this point the marsh narrowed where a ridge of slightly higher ground approached the water; a company of redcoats was drawn up here with Lord Edrington on horseback beside them. Hornblower rode up and made his report, somewhat jerkily as his horse moved restlessly under him.

"No serious attack, you say?" asked Edrington.

"No sign of one when I left, sir."

"Indeed?" Edrington stared across the river. "And here it's the same story. No attempt to cross the ford in force. Why should they show their hand and then not attack?"

"I thought they were burning powder unnecessarily, sir," said Hornblower.

"They're not fools," snapped Edrington, with another penetrating look across the river. "At any rate, there's no harm in assuming they are not."

He turned his horse and cantered back to the main body and gave an order to a captain who scrambled to his feet to receive it. The captain bellowed an order, and his company stood up and fell into line, rigid and motionless. Two further orders turned them to the right and marched them off in file, every man in step, every musket sloped at the same angle. Edrington watched them go.

"No harm in having a flank guard," he said.

The sound of a cannon across the water recalled them to the river; on the other side of the marsh a column of troops could be seen marching rapidly along the bank.

143

"That's the same column coming back, sir," said the company commander. "That or another just like it."

"Marching about and firing random shots," said Edrington. "Mr. Hornblower, have the *émigré* troops any flank guard out towards Quiberon?"

"Towards Quiberon, sir?" said Hornblower, taken aback.

"Damn it, can't you hear a plain question? Is there, or is there not?"

"I don't know, sir," confessed Hornblower, miserably.

There were five thousand *émigré* troops at Quiberon, and it seemed quite unnecessary to keep a guard out in that direction.

"Then present my compliments to the French *émigré* general, and suggest he post a strong detachment up the road, if he has not done so."

"Aye aye, sir."

Hornblower turned his horse's head back up the path towards the bridge. The sun was shining strongly now over the deserted fields. He could still hear the occasional thud of a cannon shot, but overhead a lark was singing in the blue sky. Then as he headed up the last low ridge towards Muzillac and the bridge he heard a sudden irregular outburst of firing; he fancied he heard screams and shouts, and what he saw, as he topped the rise, made him snatch at his reins and drag his horse to a halt. The fields before him were covered with fugitives in blue uniforms with white crossbelts, all running madly towards him. In among the fugitives were galloping horsemen, whirling sabres that flashed in the sunshine. Farther out to the left a whole column of horsemen were trotting fast across the fields, and farther back the sun glittered on lines of bayonets moving rapidly from the highroad towards the sea.

There could be no doubt of what had happened; during those sick seconds when he sat and stared, Hornblower realised the truth; the Revolutionaries had pushed in a force between Quiberon and Muzillac, and, keeping the *émigrés* occupied by demonstrations from across the river, had rushed down and brought off a complete surprise by this attack from an unexpected quarter. Heaven only knew what had happened at Quiberon—but this was no time to think about that. Hornblower dragged his horse's head round and kicked his heels into the brute's sides, urging him frantically back up the path towards the British. He bounced and rolled in his saddle, clinging on madly, consumed with fear lest he lose his seat and be captured by the pursuing French.

At the clatter of hoofs every eye turned towards him when he reached the British post. Edrington was there, standing with his horse's bridle over his arm.

"The French!" yelled Hornblower hoarsely, pointing back. "They're coming!"

"I expected nothing else," said Edrington.

He shouted an order before he put his foot in the stirrup to mount. The main body of the 43rd was standing in line by the time he was in the saddle. His adjutant went galloping off to recall the company from the water's edge.

"The French are in force, horse, foot, and guns, I suppose?" asked Edrington.

"Horse and foot at least, sir," gasped Hornblower, trying to keep his head clear. "I saw no guns."

"And the *émigrés* are running like rabbits?"

"Yes, sir."

"Here come the first of them."

Over the nearest ridge a few blue uniforms made their appearance, their wearers still running while stumbling with fatigue.

"I suppose we must cover their retreat, although they're not worth saving," said Edrington. "Look there!"

The company he had sent out as a flank guard was in sight on the crest of a slight slope: it was formed into a

145

tiny square, red against the green, and as they watched they saw a mob of horsemen flood up the hill towards it and break into an eddy around it.

"Just as well I had them posted there," remarked Edrington calmly. "Ah, here comes Mayne's company."

The force from the ford came marching up. Harsh orders were shouted. Two companies wheeled round while the sergeant-major with his sabre and his silver-headed cane regulated the pace and the alignment as if the men were on the barrack square.

"I would suggest you stay by me, Mr. Hornblower," said Edrington.

He moved his horse up into the interval between the two columns, and Hornblower followed him dumbly. Another order, and the force began to march steadily across the valley, the sergeants calling the step and the sergeant-major watching the intervals. All round them now were fleeing *emigre* soldiers, most of them in the last stages of exhaustion—Hornblower noticed more than one of them fall down on the ground gasping and incapable of further movement. And then over the low slope to the right appeared a line of plumes, a line of sabres—a regiment of cavalry trotting rapidly forward. Hornblower saw the sabres lifted, saw the horses break into a gallop, heard the yells of the charging men. The redcoats around him halted; another shouted order, another slow, deliberate movement, and the half-battalion was in a square with the mounted officers in the centre and the colours waving over their heads. The charging horsemen were less than a hundred yards away. Some officer with a deep voice began giving orders, intoning them as if at some solemn ceremony. The first order brought the muskets from the men's shoulders, and the second was answered by a simultaneous click of opened priming pans. The third order brought the muskets to the present along one face of the square.

"Too high!" said the sergeant-major. "Lower, there, Number Seven."

The charging horsemen were only thirty yards away; Hornblower saw the leading men, their cloaks flying from their shoulders, leaning along their horses' necks with their sabres pointed forward at the full stretch of their arms.

"Fire!" said the deep voice.

In reply came a single sharp explosion as every musket went off at once. The smoke swirled round the square and disappeared. Where Hornblower had been looking, there were now a score of horses and men on the ground, some struggling in agony, some lying still. The cavalry regiment split like a torrent encountering a rock and hurtled harmlessly past the other faces of the square.

"Well enough," said Edrington.

The deep voice was intoning again; like marionettes all on the same string the company that had fired now reloaded, every man biting out his bullet at the same instant, every man ramming home his charge, every man spitting his bullet into his musket barrel with the same instantaneous inclination of the head. Edrington looked keenly at the cavalry collecting together in a disorderly mob down the valley.

"The Forty-Third will advance!" he ordered.

With solemn ritual the square opened up again into two columns and continued its interrupted march. The detached company came marching up to join them from out of a ring of dead men and horses. Someone raised a cheer.

"Silence in the ranks!" bellowed the sergeant-major. "Sergeant, take that man's name."

But Hornblower noticed how the sergeant-major was eyeing keenly the distance between the columns; it had to be maintained exactly so that a company wheeling back filled it to make the square.

"Here they come again," said Edrington.

The cavalry were forming for a new charge, but the square was ready for them. Now the horses were blown and the men were less enthusiastic. It was not a solid wall of horses that came down on them, but isolated groups, rushing first at one face and then at another, and pulling up or swerving aside as they reached the line of bayonets. The attacks were too feeble to meet with company volleys; at the word of command sections here and there gave fire to the more determined groups. Hornblower saw one man—an officer, judging by his gold lace—rein up before the bayonets and pull out a pistol. Before he could discharge it, half a dozen muskets went off together; the officer's face became a horrible bloody mask, and he and his horse fell together to the ground. Then all at once, the cavalry wheeled off, like starlings over a field, and the march could be resumed.

"No discipline about these Frogs, not on either side," said Edrington.

The march was headed for the sea, for the blessed shelter of the *Indefatigable,* but it seemed to Hornblower as if the pace were intolerably slow. The men were marching at the parade step, with agonising deliberation, while all round them and far ahead of them the fugitive *émigrés* poured in a broad stream towards safety. Looking back, Hornblower saw the fields full of marching columns—hurrying swarms, rather—of Revolutionary infantry in hot pursuit of them.

"Once let men run, and you can't do anything else with them," commented Edrington, following Hornblower's gaze.

Shouts and shots over to the flank caught their attention. Trotting over the fields, leaping wildly at the bumps, came a cart drawn by a lean horse. Someone in a seaman's frock and trousers was holding the reins; other seamen were visible over the sides firing muskets at the horsemen hovering about them. It was Bracegirdle with his dung

148

cart; he might have lost his guns but he had saved his men. The pursuers dropped away as the cart neared the columns; Bracegirdle, standing up in the cart, caught sight of Hornblower on his horse and waved to him excitedly.

"Boadicea and her chariot!" he yelled.

"I'll thank you, sir," shouted Edrington with lungs of brass, "to go on and prepare for our embarkation."

"Aye aye, sir!"

The lean horse trotted on with the cart lurching after it and the grinning seamen clinging on to the sides. At the other flank appeared a swarm of infantry, a mad, gesticulating crowd, half running to cut off the 43rd's retreat. Edrington swept his glance round the fields.

"The Forty-Third will form line!" he shouted.

Like some ponderous machine, well oiled, the half-battalion fronted towards the swarm; the columns became lines, each man moving into his position like a brick laid on a wall.

"The Forty-Third will advance!"

The scarlet line swept forward, slowly, inexorably. The swarm hastened to meet it, officers to the front waving their swords and calling on their men to follow.

"Make ready!"

Every musket came down together; the priming pans clicked.

"Present!"

Up came the muskets, and the swarm hesitated before that fearful menace. Individuals tried to get back into the crowd to cover themselves from the volley with the bodies of their comrades.

"Fire!"

A crashing volley; Hornblower, looking over the heads of the British infantry from his point of vantage on horse-back, saw the whole face of the swarm go down in swathes. Still the red line moved forward, at each deliberate step a shouted order brought a machinelike response

149

as the men reloaded; five hundred mouths spat in five hundred bullets, five hundred right arms raised five hundred ramrods at once. When the muskets came to the present the red line was at the swathe of dead and wounded, for the swarm had withdrawn before the advance, and shrank back still further at the threat of the volley. The volley was fired; the advance went on. Another volley; another advance. Now the swarm was shredding away. Now men were running from it. Now every man had turned tail and fled from that frightful musketry. The hillside was black with fugitives as it had been when the *émigrés* were fleeing.

"Halt!"

The advance ceased; the line became a double column, and the retreat began again.

"Very creditable," remarked Edrington.

Hornblower's horse was trying jerkily to pick its way over a carpet of dead and wounded, and he was so busy keeping his seat, and his brain was in such a whirl, that he did not immediately realise that they had topped the last rise so that before them lay the glittering waters of the estuary. There were the ships riding at anchor, and there, blessed sight, were the boats swarming towards the shore. The strip of muddy beach was packed solid with *émigrés*. It was high time, for already the boldest of the Revolutionary infantry were hovering round the columns, taking long shots into them. Here and there a man fell.

"Close up!" snapped the sergeants, and the files marched on stolidly, leaving the wounded and dead behind them.

The adjutant's horse suddenly snorted and plunged, and then fell first to its knees, and, kicking, to its side, while the freckle-faced adjutant freed his feet from the stirrups and flung himself out of the saddle just in time to escape being pinned underneath.

150

"Are you hit, Stanley?" asked Edrington.

"No, my lord. All safe and sound," said the adjutant, brushing at his scarlet coat.

"You won't have to foot it far," said Edrington. "No need to throw out skirmishers to drive those fellows off. This is where we must make our stand."

He looked about him, at the fishermen's cottages above the beach, the panic-stricken *émigrés* at the water's edge, and the masses of Revolutionary infantry coming up in pursuit, leaving small enough time for preparation. Some of the redcoats poured into the cottages, appearing a moment later at the windows; it was fortunate that the fishing hamlet guarded one flank of the gap down to the beach while the other was guarded by a steep and inaccessible headland on whose summit a small block of redcoats established themselves. In the gap between the two points the remaining four companies formed a long line just sheltered by the crest of the beach.

The boats of the squadron were already loading with *émigrés* among the small breakers below. Hornblower heard the crack of a single pistol shot; he could guess that some officer down there was enforcing his orders in the only possible way to prevent the fear-driven men from pouring into the boats and swamping them. As if in answer came the roar of cannon on the other side. A battery of artillery had unlimbered just out of musket range and was firing at the British position, while all about it gathered the massed battalions of the Revolutionary infantry. The cannon balls howled close overhead.

"Let them fire away," said Edrington. "The longer the better."

The artillery could do little harm to the British in the fold of ground that protected them, and the Revolutionary commander must have realised that as well as the necessity for wasting no time. Over there the drums began to roll—a noise of indescribable menace—and then the columns surged forward. So close were they already that Hornblower could see the features of the officers in the lead, waving their hats and swords.

"Forty-Third, make ready!" said Edrington, and the priming pans clicked as one. "Seven paces forward—march!"

One—two—three—seven paces, painstakingly taken, took the line to the little crest.

"Present! Fire!"

A volley nothing could withstand. The columns halted, swayed, received another smashing volley, and another, and fell back in ruin.

"Excellent!" said Edrington.

The battery boomed again; a file of two redcoat soldiers was tossed back like dolls, to lie in a horrible bloody mass close beside Hornblower's horse's feet.

"Close up!" said a sergeant, and the men on either side had filled the gap.

"Forty-Third, seven paces back—march!"

The line was below the crest again, as the red-coated marionettes withdrew in steady time. Hornblower could not remember later whether it was twice or three times more that the Revolutionary masses came on again, each time to be dashed back by that disciplined musketry. But the sun was nearly setting in the ocean behind him when he looked back to see the beach almost cleared and Bracegirdle plodding up to them to report.

"I can spare one company now," said Edrington in reply but not taking his eyes off the French masses. "After they are on board, have every boat ready and waiting."

One company filed off; another attack was beaten back —after the preceding failures it was not pressed home with anything like the dash and fire of the earlier ones. Now the battery was turning its attention to the headland on the flank, and sending its balls among the redcoats there, while a battalion of French moved over to the attack at that point. "That gives us time," said Edrington. "Captain Griffin, you can march the men off. Colour party, remain here."

Down the beach went the centre companies to the waiting boats, while the colours still waved to mark their old position, visible over the crest to the French. The company in the cottages came out, formed up, and marched down as well. Edrington trotted across to the foot of the little headland; he watched the French forming for the attack and the infantry wading out to the boats.

"Now, grenadiers!" he yelled, suddenly. "Run for it! Colour party!"

Down the steep seaward face of the headland came the last company, running, sliding, and stumbling. A musket, clumsily handled, went off unexpectedly. The last man came down the slope as the colour party reached the water's edge and began to climb into a boat with its precious burden. A wild yell went up from the French, and their whole mass came rushing towards the evacuated position.

"Now, sir," said Edrington, turning his horse seawards.

Hornblower fell from his saddle as his horse splashed into the shallows. He let go of the reins and plunged out, waist deep, shoulder deep, to where the longboat lay on its oars with its four-pounder gun in its bows and Bracegirdle beside it to haul him in. He looked up in time to see a curious incident: Edrington had reached the *Indefatigable*'s gig, still holding his horse's reins. With the French pouring down the beach towards them, he turned and took a musket from the nearest soldier, pressed the muzzle to the horse's head, and fired. The horse fell in its death agony in the shallows; only Hornblower's roan remained as prize to the Revolutionaries.

"Back water!" said Bracegirdle, and the longboat backed away from the beach; Hornblower lay in the eyes of the boat feeling as if he had not the strength to move

153

a limb, and the beach was covered with shouting, gesticulating Frenchmen, lit redly by the sunset.

"One moment," said Bracegirdle, reaching for the lanyard of the four-pounder, and tugging at it smartly.

The gun roared out in Hornblower's ear, and the charge cut a swathe of destruction on the beach.

"That was canister," said Bracegirdle. "Eighty-four balls. Easy, port! Give way, starboard!"

The longboat turned, away from the beach and towards the welcoming ships. Hornblower looked back at the darkening coast of France. This was the end of an incident; his country's attempt to overturn the revolution had met with a bloody repulse. Newspapers in Paris would exult; the Gazette in London would give the incident five cold lines. Clairvoyant, Hornblower could foresee that in a year's time, the world would hardly remember the incident. In twenty years, it would be entirely forgotten. Yet those headless corpses up there in Muzillac; those shattered redcoats; those Frenchmen caught in the four-pounder's blast of canister—they were all as dead as if it had been a day in which history had been changed. And he was just as weary. And in his pocket there was still the bread he had put there that morning and forgotten all about.

VII

HORNBLOWER
and the Spanish Galleys

The old *Indefatigable* was lying at anchor in the Bay of Cadiz at the time when Spain made peace with France. Hornblower happened to be midshipman of the watch, and it was he who called the attention of Lieutenant Chadd to the approach of the eight-oared pinnace, with the red and yellow of Spain drooping at the stern. Chadd's glass made out gleam of gold on epaulette and cocked hat, and he bellowed the order for sideboys and marine guard to give the traditional honours to a captain in an allied service. Pellew, hurriedly warned, was at the gangway to meet his visitor, and it was at the gangway that the entire interview took place. The Spaniard, making a low bow with his hat across his stomach, offered a sealed envelope to the Englishman.

"Here, Mr. Hornblower," said Pellew, holding the letter unopened, "speak French to this fellow. Ask him to come below for a glass of wine."

But the Spaniard, with a further bow, declined the refreshment, and, with another bow, requested that Pellew open the letter immediately. Pellew broke the seal and read the contents, struggling with the French which he could read to a small extent although he could not speak it at all. He handed it to Hornblower.

"This means the Dagoes have made peace, doesn't it?"

Hornblower struggled through twelve lines of compliments addressed by His Excellency the Duke of Belchite

155

(Grandee of the First Class, with eighteen other titles ending with Captain-General of Andalusia) to the Most Gallant Ship-Captain Sir Edward Pellew, Knight of the Bath. The second paragraph was short and contained only a brief intimation of peace. The third paragraph was as long as the first, and repeated its phraseology almost word for word in a ponderous farewell.

"That's all, sir," said Hornblower.

But the Spanish captain had a verbal message with which to supplement the written one.

"Please tell your captain," he said, in his lisping Spanish-French, "that now as a neutral power, Spain must enforce her rights. You have already been at anchor here for twenty-four hours. Six hours from now——" The Spaniard took a gold watch from his pocket and glanced at it——"if you are within range of the batteries at Puntales there they will be given orders to fire on you."

Hornblower could only translate the brutal message without any attempt at softening it, and Pellew listened, white with anger despite his tan.

"Tell him——" he began, and then mastered his rage. "Damme if I'll let him see he has made me angry."

He put his hat across his stomach and bowed in as faithful an imitation of the Spaniard's courtliness as he could manage, before he turned to Hornblower.

"Tell him I have received his message with pleasure. Tell him I much regret that circumstances are separating him from me, and that I hope I shall always enjoy his personal friendship whatever the relations between our countries. Tell him—oh, you can tell him that sort of thing I want said, can't you, Hornblower? Let's see him over the side with dignity. Sideboys! Bosun's mates! Drummers!"

Hornblower poured out compliments to the best of his ability, and at every phrase the two captains exchanged bows, the Spaniard withdrawing a pace at each bow and

Pellew following him up, not to be outdone in courtesy. The drums beat a ruffle, the marines presented arms, the pipes shrilled and twittered until the Spaniard's head had descended to the level of the maindeck, when Pellew stiffened up, clapped his hat on his head, and swung round on his first lieutenant.

"Mr. Eccles, I want to be under weigh within the hour, if you please."

Then he stamped down below to regain his equanimity in private.

Hands were aloft loosing sail ready to sheet home, while the clank of the capstan told how other men were heaving the cable short, and Hornblower was standing on the port-side gangway with Mr. Wales the carpenter, looking over at the white houses of one of the most beautiful cities in Europe.

"I've been ashore there twicet," said Wales. "The wine's good—vino, they calls it—if you happens to like that kind o' muck. But don't you ever try that brandy, Mr. Hornblower. Poison, it is, rank poison. Hello! We're going to have an escort, I see."

Two long sharp prows had emerged from the inner bay, and were pointing towards the *Indefatigable*. Hornblower could not restrain himself from giving a cry of surprise as he followed Wales' gaze. The vessels approaching were galleys; along each side of them the oars were lifting and falling rhythmically, catching the sunlight as they feathered. The effect, as a hundred oars swung like one, was perfectly beautiful. Hornblower remembered a line in a Latin poet which he had translated as a schoolboy, and recalled his surprise when he discovered that to a Roman the "white wings" of a ship of war were her oars. Now the simile was plain; even a gull in flight, which Hornblower had always looked upon until now as displaying the perfection of motion, was not more beautiful than those galleys. They lay low in the

157

water, immensely long for their beam. Neither the sails nor the lateen yards were set on the low raking masts. The bows blazed with gilding while the waters of the bay foamed round them as they headed into the teeth of the gentle breeze with the Spanish red and gold streaming aft from the masthead. Up—forward—down—went the oars with unchanging rhythm, the blades not varying an inch in their distance apart during the whole of the stroke. From the bows of each two long guns looked straight forward in the direction the galleys pointed.

"Twenty-four-pounders," said Wales. "If they catch you in a calm, they'll knock you to pieces. Lie off on your quarter where you can't bring a gun to bear and rake you till you strike. An' then God help you—better a Turkish prison than a Spanish one."

In a line-ahead that might have been drawn with a ruler and measured with a chain the galleys passed close along the port side of the *Indefatigable* and went ahead of her. As they passed the roll of the drum and the call of the pipes summoned the crew of the *Indefatigable* to attention out of compliment to the flag and the commission pendant going by, while the galley's officers returned the salute.

"It don't seem right, somehow," muttered Wales under his breath, "to salute 'em like they was a frigate."

Level with the *Indefatigable*'s bowsprit the leader backed her starboard-side oars, and spun like a top, despite her length and narrow beam, across the frigate's bows. The gentle wind blew straight to the frigate from the galley, and then from her consort as the latter followed; and a foul stench came back on the air and assailed Hornblower's nostrils, and not Hornblower's alone, clearly, for it brought forth cries of disgust from all the men on deck.

"They all stink like that," explained Wales. "Four men to the oar an' fifty oars. Two hundred galley slaves,

158

that is. All chained to their benches. When you goes aboard one of them as a slave you're chained to your bench, an' you're never unchained until they drop you overside. Sometimes when the hands aren't busy they'll hose out the bilge, but that doesn't happen often, bein' Dagoes an' not many of 'em."

Hornblower as always sought exact information.

"How many, Mr. Wales?"

"Thirty, mebbe. Enough to hand the sails if they're making a passage. Or to man the guns—they strike the yards and sails, like now, before they goes into action, Mr. Hornblower," said Wales, pontifical as usual, and with that slight emphasis on the "Mister" inevitable when a warrant officer of sixty with no hope of further promotion addressed a warrant officer of eighteen (his nominal equal in rank) who might some day be an admiral. "So you see how it is. With no more than thirty of a crew an' two hundred slaves they daren't let 'em loose, not ever."

The galleys had turned again, and were now passing down the *Indefatigable*'s starboard side. The beat of the oars had slowed very noticeably, and Hornblower had ample time to observe the vessel closely, the low forecastle and high poop with the gangway connecting them along the whole length of the galley; upon that gangway walked a man with a whip. The rowers were invisible below the bulwarks, the oars being worked through holes in the sides closed, as far as Hornblower could see, with sheets of leather round the oar-looms to keep out the sea. On the poop stood two men at the tiller and a small group of officers, their gold lace flashing in the sunshine. Save for the gold lace and the twenty-four-pounder bow chasers Hornblower was looking at exactly the same sort of vessel as the ancients used to fight their battles. Polybius and Thucydides wrote about galleys almost identical with these—for that matter it was not much

159

more than two hundred years since the galleys had fought their last great battle at Lepanto against the Turks. But those battles had been fought with hundreds of galleys a side.

"How many do they have in commission now?" asked Hornblower.

"A dozen, mebbe—not that I knows for sure, o' course. Carthagena's their usual station, beyond the Gut."

Wales, as Hornblower understood, meant by this through the Strait of Gibraltar in the Mediterranean.

"Too frail for the Atlantic," Hornblower commented.

It was easy to deduce the reasons for the survival of this small number—the innate conservatism of the Spaniards would account for it to a large extent. Then there was the point that condemnation to the galleys was one way of disposing of criminals. And when all was said and done a galley might still be useful in a calm—merchant ships becalmed while trying to pass the Strait of Gibraltar might be snapped up by galleys pushing out from Cadiz or Carthagena. And at the very lowest estimate there might be some employment for galleys to tow vessels in and out of harbour with the wind unfavourable.

"Mr. Hornblower!" said Eccles. "My respects to the captain, and we're ready to get under weigh."

Hornblower dived below with his message.

"My compliments to Mr. Eccles," said Pellew, looking up from his desk, "and I'll be on deck immediately."

There was just enough of a southerly breeze to enable the *Indefatigable* to weather the point in safety. With her anchor catted she braced round her yards and began to steal seaward; in the disciplined stillness which prevailed the sound of the ripple of water under her cutwater was clearly to be heard—a musical note which told nothing, in its innocence, of the savagery and danger of the world of the sea into which she was entering. Creeping along under her topsail the *Indefatigable* made no more than three knots, and the galleys came surging past her again, oars beating their fastest rhythm, as if the galleys were boasting of their independence of the elements. Their gilt flashed in the sun as they overtook to windward, and once again their foul stench offended the nostrils of the men of the *Indefatigable*.

"I'd be obliged if they'd keep to leeward of us," muttered Pellew, watching them through his glass. "But I suppose that's not Spanish courtesy. Mr. Cutler!"

"Sir!" said the gunner.

"You may commence the salute."

"Aye aye, sir."

The forward carronade on the lee side roared out the first of its compliments, and the fort of Puntales began its reply. The sound of the salute rolled round the beautiful bay; nation was speaking to nation in all courtesy.

"The next time we hear those guns they'll be shotted, I fancy," said Pellew, gazing across at Puntales and the flag of Spain flying above it.

Indeed, the tide of war was turning against England. Nation after nation had retired from the contest against France, some worsted by arms, and some by the diplomacy of the vigorous young republic. To any thinking mind it was obvious that once the step from war to neutrality had been taken, the next step would be easy, from neutrality to war on the other side. Hornblower could foresee, close at hand, a time when all Europe would be arrayed in hostility to England, when she would be battling for her life against the rejuvenescent power of France and the malignity of the whole world.

"Set sail, please, Mr. Eccles," said Pellew.

Two hundred trained pairs of legs raced aloft; two hundred trained pairs of arms let loose the canvas, and the *Indefatigable* doubled her speed, heeling slightly to the gentle breeze. Now she was meeting the long Atlantic

161

swell. So were the galleys; as the *Indefatigable* overtook them, Hornblower could see the leader put her nose into a long roller so that a cloud of spray broke over her forecastle. That was asking too much of such frail craft. Back went one bank of oars; forward went the other. The galleys rolled hideously for a moment in the trough of the sea before they completed their turn and headed back for the safe waters of Cadiz Bay. Someone forward in the *Indefatigable* began to boo, and the cry was instantly taken up through the ship. A storm of boos and whistles and catcalls pursued the galleys, the men monentarily quite out of hand while Pellew spluttered with rage on the quarterdeck and the petty officers strove in vain to take the names of the offenders. It was an ominous farewell to Spain.

Ominous indeed. It was not long before Captain Pellew gave the news to the ship that Spain had completed her change-over; with the treasure convoy safely in she had declared war against England; the revolutionary republic had won the alliance of the most decayed monarchy in Europe. British resources were now stretched to the utmost; there was another thousand miles of coast to watch, another fleet to blockade, another horde of privateers to guard against, and far fewer harbours in which to take refuge and from which to draw the fresh water and the meagre stores which enabled the hard-worked crews to remain at sea. It was then that friendship had to be cultivated with the half-savage Barbary States, and the insolence of the Deys and the Sultans had to be tolerated so that North Africa could provide the skinny bullocks and the barley grain to feed the British garrisons in the Mediterranean—all of them beleaguered on land—and the ships which kept open the way to them. Oran, Tetuan, Algiers wallowed in unwontedly honest prosperity with the influx of British gold.

It was a day of glassy calm in the Strait of Gibraltar.

The sea was like a silver shield, the sky like a bowl of sapphire, with the mountains of Africa on the one hand, the mountains of Spain on the other as dark serrations on the horizon. It was not a comfortable situation for the *Indefatigable,* but that was not because of the blazing sun which softened the pitch in the deck seams. There is almost always a slight current setting inwards into the Mediterranean from the Atlantic, and the prevailing winds blow in the same direction. In a calm like this it was not unusual for a ship to be carried far through the Straits, past the Rock of Gibraltar, and then to have to beat for days and even weeks to make Gibraltar Bay. So that Pellew was not unnaturally anxious about his convoy of grain ships from Oran. Gibraltar had to be revictualled —Spain had already marched an army up for the siege— and he dared not risk being carried past his destination. His orders to his reluctant convoy had been enforced by flag and gun signals, for no shorthanded merchant ship relished the prospect of the labour Pellew wished to be executed. The *Indefatigable* no less than her convoy had lowered boats and the helpless ships were now all in tow. That was backbreaking, exhausting labour, the men at the oars tugging and straining, dragging the oar blades through the water, while the towlines tightened and bucked with superhuman perversity and the ships sheered freakishly from side to side. It was less than a mile an hour that the ships made in this fashion, at the cost of the complete exhaustion of the boats' crews, but at least it postponed the time when the Gibraltar current would carry them to leeward, and similarly gave more chance for the longed-for southerly wind—two hours of a southerly wind was all they wished for—to waft them up to the Mole.

Down in the *Indefatigable*'s longboat and cutter the men tugging at their oars were so stupefied with their toil that they did not hear the commotion in the ship. They

163

were just tugging and straining, under the pitiless sky, living through their two hours' spell of misery, but they were roused by the voice of the captain himself, hailing them from the forecastle.

"Mr. Bolton! Mr. Chadd! Cast off there, if you please. You'd better come and arm your men at once. Here come our friends from Cadiz."

Back on the quarterdeck, Pellew looked through his glass at the hazy horizon; he could make out from here by now what had first been reported from the masthead.

"They're heading straight for us," he said.

The two galleys were on their way from Cadiz; presumably a fast horseman from the lookout point at Tarifa had brought them the news of this golden opportunity, of the flat calm and the scattered and helpless convoy. This was the moment for galleys to justify their continued existence. They could capture and at least burn, although they could not hope to carry off, the unfortunate merchant ships while the *Indefatigable* lay helpless hardly out of cannon's range. Pellew looked round at the two merchant ships and the three brigs; one of them was within half a mile of him and might be covered by his gunfire, but the others—a mile and a half, two miles away—had no such protection.

"Pistols and cutlasses, my lads!" he said to the men pouring up from overside. "Clap onto that stay tackle now. Smartly with that carronade, Mr. Cutler!"

The *Indefatigable* had been in too many expeditions where minutes counted to waste any time over these preparations. The boats' crews seized their arms, the six-pounder carronades were lowered into the bows of the cutter and longboat, and soon the boats, crowded with armed men, and provisioned against sudden emergency, were pulling away to meet the galleys.

"What the devil d'you think you're doing, Mr. Hornblower?"

Pellew had just caught sight of Hornblower in the act of swinging out the jolly boat which was his special charge. He wondered what his midshipman thought he could achieve against a war-galley with a twelve-foot boat and a crew of six.

"We can pull to one of the convoy and reinforce the crew, sir," said Hornblower.

"Oh, very well then, carry on. I'll trust to your good sense even though that's a broken reed."

"Good on you, sir!" said Jackson ecstatically, as the jolly boat shoved off from the frigate. "Good on you! No one else wouldn't never have thought of that."

Jackson, the coxswain of the jolly boat, obviously thought that Hornblower had no intention of carrying out his suggestion to reinforce the crew of one of the merchant ships.

"Those stinking Dagoes," said stroke oar, between his teeth.

Hornblower was conscious of the presence in his crew of the same feeling of violent hostility toward the Spanish galleys as he felt within himself. In a fleeting moment of analysis, he attributed it to the circumstances in which they had first made the galley's acquaintance, as well as to the stench which the galleys trailed after them. He had never known this feeling of personal hatred before; when previously he had fought it had been as a servant of the King, not out of personal animosity. Yet here he was gripping the tiller under the scorching sky and leaning forward in his eagerness to be at actual grips with this enemy.

The longboat and cutter had a long start of them, and even though they were manned by crews who had already served a spell at the oars they were skimming over the water at such a speed that the jolly boat with all the advantage of the glassy-smooth water only caught slowly up to them. Overside the sea was of the bluest, deepest blue until the oar blades churned it white. Ahead of them the vessels of the convoy lay scattered where the sudden calm had caught them, and just beyond them Hornblower caught sight of the flash of oar blades as the galleys came sweeping down on their prey. Longboat and cutter were diverging in an endeavour to cover as many vessels as possible, and the gig was still far astern. There would hardly be time to board a ship even if Hornblower should wish to. He put the tiller over to incline his course after the cutter; one of the galleys at that moment abruptly made its appearance in the gap between two of the merchant ships. Hornblower saw the cutter swing round to point her six-pounder carronade at the advancing bows.

"Pull, you men! Pull!" he shrieked, mad with excitement.

He could not imagine what was going to happen, but he wanted to be in the fray. That six-pounder popgun was grossly inaccurate at any range longer than musket shot. It would serve to hurl a mass of grape into a crowd of men, but its ball would have small effect on the strengthened bows of a war galley.

"Pull!" shrieked Hornblower again. He was nearly up to them, wide on the cutter's quarter.

The carronade boomed out. Hornblower thought he saw the splinters fly from the galley's bow, but the shot had no more effect of deterring her than a peashooter could stop a charging bull. The galley turned a little, getting exactly into line, and then her oars' beat quickened. She was coming down to ram, like the Greeks at Salamis.

"Pull!" shrieked Hornblower.

Instinctively, he gave the tiller a touch to take the jolly boat out into a flanking position.

"Easy!"

The jolly boat's oars stilled, as their way carried them past the cutter. Hornblower could see Soames standing up in the sternsheets looking at the death which was cleaving the blue water towards him. Bow to bow the cutter might

166

have stood a chance, but too late the cutter tried to evade the blow altogether. Hornblower saw her turn, presenting her vulnerable side to the galley's stem. That was all he could see, for the next moment the galley herself hid from him the final act of the tragedy. The jolly boat's starboard side oars only just cleared the galley's starboard oars as she swept by. Hornblower heard a shriek and a crash, saw the galley's forward motion almost cease at the collision. He was mad with the lust of fighting, quite insane, and his mind was working with the rapidity of insanity.

"Give way, port!" he yelled, and the jolly boat swung round under the galley's stern. "Give way all!"

The jolly boat leaped after the galley like a terrier after a bull.

"Grapple them, damn you, Jackson!"

Jackson shouted an oath in reply, as he leaped forward, seemingly hurdling the men at the oars without breaking their stroke. In the bows Jackson seized the boat's grapnel on its long line and flung it hard and true. It caught somewhere in the elaborate gilt rail on the galley's quarter. Jackson hauled on the line, the oars tugged madly in the effort to carry the jolly boat up to the galley's stern. At that moment Hornblower saw it, the sight which would long haunt his dreams—up from under the galley's stern came the shattered forepart of the cutter, still with men clinging to it who had survived the long passage under the whole length of the galley which had overrun them. There were straining faces, empurpled faces, faces already relaxing in death. But in a moment it was past and gone, and Hornblower felt the jerk transmitted through the line to the jolly boat as the galley leaped forward.

"I can't hold her!" shouted Jackson.

"Take a turn round the cleat, you fool!"

The galley was towing the jolly boat now, dragging her along at the end of a twenty-foot line close on her quarter, just clear of the arc of her rudder. The white water bubbled all around her, her bows were cocked up with the strain. It was a mad moment, as though they had harpooned a whale. Someone came running aft on the Spaniard's poop, knife in hand to cut the line.

"Shoot him, Jackson!" shrieked Hornblower again.

Jackson's pistol cracked, and the Spaniard fell to the deck out of sight—a good shot. Despite his fighting madness, despite the turmoil of rushing water and glaring sun, Hornblower tried to think out his next move. Inclination and commonsense alike told him that the best plan was to close with the enemy despite the odds.

"Pull up to them, there!" he shouted—everyone in the boat was shouting and yelling. The man in the bows of the jolly boat faced forward and took the grapnel line and began to haul in on it, but the speed of the boat through the water made any progress difficult, and after a yard or so had been gained the difficulty became insurmountable, for the grapnel was caught in the poop rail ten or eleven feet above water, and the angle of pull became progressively steeper as the jolly boat neared the stern of the galley. The boat's bow cocked higher out of the water than ever.

"Belay!" said Hornblower, and then, his voice rising again, "Out pistols, lads!"

A row of four or five swarthy faces had appeared at the stern of the galley. Muskets were pointing into the jolly boat, and there was a brief but furious exchange of shots. One man fell groaning into the bottom of the jolly boat, but the row of faces disappeared. Standing up precariously in the swaying sternsheets, Hornblower could still see nothing of the galley's poop deck save for the tops of two heads, belonging, it was clear, to the men at the tiller.

"Reload," he said to his men, remembering by a miracle to give the order. The ramrods went down the pistol barrels.

"Do that carefully if you ever want to see Pompey again," said Hornblower.

He was shaking with excitement and mad with fury of fighting, and it was the automatic, drilled part of him which was giving these levelheaded orders. His higher faculties were quite negatived by his lust for blood. He was seeing things through a pink mist—that was how he remembered it when he looked back upon it later. There was a sudden crash of glass. Someone had thrust a musket barrel through the big stern window of the galley's after cabin. Luckily having thrust it through he had to recover himself to take aim. An irregular volley of pistols almost coincided with the report of the musket. Where the Spaniard's bullet went no one knew; but the Spaniard fell back from the window.

"By God! That's our way!" screamed Hornblower, and then, steadying himself, "Reload."

As the bullets were being spat into the barrels he stood up. His unused pistols were still in his belt; his cutlass was at his side.

"Come aft, here," he said to stroke oar; the jolly boat would stand no more weight in the bows than she had already. "And you, too."

Hornblower poised himself on the thwarts, eyeing the grapnel line and the cabin window.

"Bring 'em after me one at a time, Jackson," he said.

Then he braced himself and flung himself at the grapnel line. His feet grazed the water as the line sagged, but using all his clumsy strength his arms carried him upwards. Here was the shattered window at his side; he swung up his feet, kicked out a big remaining piece of the pane, and then shot his feet through and then the rest of himself. He came down on the deck of the cabin with a thud; it was dark in here compared with the blinding sun outside. As he got to his feet, he trod on something which gave out a cry of pain—the wounded Spaniard, evidently—and the hand with which he drew his cutlass was sticky with blood. Spanish blood. Rising, he hit his head a thunderous crash on the deck beams above, for the little cabin was very low, hardly more than five feet, and so severe was the blow that his senses almost left him. But before him was the cabin door and he reeled out through it, cutlass in hand. Over his head he heard a stamping of feet, and shots were fired behind him and above him—a further exchange, he presumed, between the jolly boat and the galley's stern rail. The cabin door opened into a low half-deck, and Hornblower reeled along it out into the sunshine again. He was on the tiny strip of maindeck at the break of the poop. Before him stretched the narrow gangway between the two sets of rowers; he could look down at these latter—two seas of bearded faces, mops of hair and lean sunburned bodies, swinging rhythmically back and forward to the beat of the oars.

That was all the impression he could form of them at the moment. At the far end of the gangway at the break of the forecastle stood the overseer with his whip; he was shouting words in rhythmic succession to the slaves— Spanish numbers, perhaps, to give them the time. There were three or four men on the forecastle; below them the half-doors through the forecastle bulkhead were hooked open, through which Hornblower could see the two big guns illuminated by the light through the port holes out of which they were run almost at the water level. The guns' crews were standing by the guns, but numerically they were far fewer than two twenty-four-pounders would demand. Hornblower remembered Wales' estimate of no more than thirty for a galley's crew. The men of one gun at least had been called aft to defend the poop against the jolly boat's attack.

A step behind him made him leap with anxiety and he swung round with his cutlass ready to meet Jackson stumbling out of the half-deck, cutlass in hand.

"Nigh on cracked my nut," said Jackson.

He was speaking thickly like a drunken man, and his words were chorused by further shots fired from the poop at the level of the top of their heads.

"Oldroyd's comin' next," said Jackson. "Franklin's dead."

On either side of them a companion ladder mounted to the poop deck. It seemed logical, mathematical, that they should each go up one but Hornblower thought better of it.

"Come along," he said, and headed for the starboard ladder, and, with Oldroyd putting in an appearance at that moment, he yelled to him to follow.

The hand ropes of the ladder were of twisted red and yellow cord—he even could notice that as he rushed up the ladder, pistol in hand and cutlass in the other. After the first step, his eye was above deck level. There were more than a dozen men crowded on the tiny poop, but two were lying dead, and one was groaning with his back to the rail, and two stood by the tiller. The others were looking over the rail at the jolly boat. Hornblower was still insane with fighting madness. He must have leaped up the final two or three steps with a bound like a stag's, and he was screaming like a maniac as he flung himself at the Spaniards. His pistol went off apparently without his willing it, but the face of the man a yard away dissolved into bloody ruin, and Hornblower dropped the weapon and snatched the second, his thumb going to the hammer as he whirled his cutlass down with a crash on the sword which the next Spaniard raised as a feeble guard. He struck and struck and struck with a lunatic's strength. Here was Jackson beside him shouting hoarsely and striking out right and left.

"Kill 'em! Kill 'em!" shouted Jackson.

Hornblower saw Jackson's cutlass flash down on the head of the defenceless man at the tiller. Then out of the

171

tail of his eye he saw another sword threaten him as he battered with his cutlass at the man before him, but his pistol saved him as he fired automatically again. Another pistol went off beside him—Oldroyd's, he supposed —and then the fight on the poop was over. By what miracle of ineptitude the Spaniards had allowed the attack to take them by surprise Hornblower never could discover. Perhaps they were ignorant of the wounding of the man in the cabin, and had relied on him to defend that route; perhaps it had never occurred to them that three men could be so utterly desperate as to attack a dozen; perhaps they never realised that three men had made the perilous passage of the grapnel line; perhaps—most probably—in the mad excitement of it all, they simply lost their heads, for five minutes could hardly have elapsed altogether from the time the jolly boat hooked on until the poop was cleared. Two or three Spaniards ran down the companion to the maindeck, and forward along the gangway between the rows of slaves. One was caught against the rail and made a gesture of surrender, but Jackson's hand was already at his throat. Jackson was a man of immense physical strength; he bent the Spaniard back over the rail, farther and farther, and then caught him by the thigh with his other hand and heaved him over. He fell with a shriek before Hornblower could interpose. The poop deck was covered with writhing men, like the bottom of a boat filled with flapping fish. One man was getting to his knees when Jackson and Oldroyd seized him. They swung him up to toss him over the rail.

"Stop that!" said Hornblower, and quite callously they dropped him again with a crash on the bloody planks.

Jackson and Oldroyd were like drunken men, unsteady on their feet, glazed of eye and stertorous of breath; Hornblower was just coming out of his insane fit. He stepped forward to the break of the poop, wiping the sweat out of his eyes while trying to wipe away the red mist that tinged his vision. Forward by the forecastle were gathered the rest of the Spaniards, a large group of them; as Hornblower came forward, one of them fired a musket at him but the ball went wide. Down below him the rowers were still swinging rhythmically, forward and back, forward and back, the hairy heads and the naked bodies moving in time to the oars; in time to the voice of the overseer, too, for the latter was still standing on the gangway (the rest of the Spaniards were clustered behind him) calling the time—*"Seis, siete, ocho."*

"Stop!" bellowed Hornblower.

He walked to the starboard side to be in full view of the starboard-side rowers. He held up his hand and bellowed again. A hairy face or two was raised, but the oars still swung.

"Uno, dos, tres," said the overseer.

Jackson appeared at Hornblower's elbow, and levelled a pistol to shoot the nearest rower.

"Oh, belay that!" said Hornblower testily. He knew he was sick of killings now. "Find my pistols and reload them."

He stood at the top of the companion like a man in a dream—in a nightmare. The galley slaves went on swinging and pulling; his dozen enemies were still clustered at the break of the forecastle thirty yards away; behind him the wounded Spaniards groaned away their lives. Another appeal to the rowers was as much ignored as the preceding ones. Oldroyd must have had the clearest head or have recovered himself quickest.

"I'll haul down his colours, sir, shall I?" he said.

Hornblower woke from his dream. On a staff above the taffrail fluttered the yellow and red.

"Yes, haul 'em down at once," he said.

Now his mind was clear, and now his horizon was no longer bounded by the narrow limits of the galley. He

173

looked about him, over the blue, blue sea. There were the merchant ships; over there lay the *Indefatigable*. Behind him boiled the white wake of the galley—a curved wake. Not until that moment did he realise that he was in control of the tiller, and that for the last three minutes the galley had been cutting over the blue seas unsteered.

"Take the tiller, Oldroyd," he ordered.

Was that a galley disappearing into the hazy distance? It must be, and far in its wake was the longboat. And there, on the port bow, was the gig, resting on her oars—Hornblower could see little figures standing waving in bow and stern, and it dawned upon him that this was in acknowledgment of the hauling down of the Spanish colours. Another musket banged off forward, and the rail close at his hip was struck a tremendous blow which sent gilded splinters flying in the sunlight. But he had all his wits about him again, and he ran back over the dying men; at the after end of the poop he was out of sight of the gangway and safe from shot. He could still see the gig on the port bow.

"Starboard your helm, Oldroyd."

The galley turned slowly—her narrow length made her unhandy if the rudder were not assisted by the oars—but soon the bow was about to obscure the gig.

"Midships!"

Amazing that there, leaping in the white water that boiled under the galley's stern, was the jolly boat with one live man and two dead men still aboard.

"Where are the others, Bromley?" yelled Jackson.

Bromley pointed overside. They had been shot from the taffrail at the moment that Hornblower and the others were preparing to attack the poop.

"Why in hell don't you come aboard?"

Bromley took hold of his left arm with his right; the limb was clearly useless. There was no reinforcement to be obtained here, and yet full possession must be taken

174

of the galley. Otherwise it was even conceivable that they would be carried off to Algeciras; even if they were masters of the rudder the man who controlled the oars dictated the course of the ship if he willed. There was only one course left to try.

Now that his fighting madness had ebbed away, Hornblower was in a sombre mood. He did not care what happened to him; hope and fear had alike deserted him, along with his previous exalted condition. It might be resignation that possessed him now. His mind, still calculating, told him that with only one thing left to do to achieve victory he must attempt it, and the flat, dead condition of his spirits enabled him to carry the attempt through like an automaton, unwavering and emotionless. He walked forward to the poop rail again; the Spaniards were still clustered at the far end of the gangway, with the overseer still giving the time to the oars. They looked up at him as he stood there. With the utmost care and attention he sheathed his cutlass, which he had held in his hand up to that moment. He noticed the blood on his coat and on his hands as he did so. Slowly, he settled the sheathed weapon at his side.

"My pistols, Jackson," he said.

Jackson handed him his pistols and with the same callous care, he thrust them into his belt. He turned back to Oldroyd, the Spaniards watching every movement fascinated.

"Stay by the tiller, Oldroyd. Jackson, follow me. Do nothing without my orders."

With the sun pouring down on his face, he strode down the companion ladder, walked to the gangway, and approached the Spaniards along it. On either side of him the hairy heads and naked bodies of the galley slaves still swung with the oars. He neared the Spaniards; swords and muskets and pistols were handled nervously, but every eye was on his face. Behind him Jackson coughed.

175

Two yards only from the group, Hornblower halted and swept them with his glance. Then, with a gesture, he indicated the whole of the group except the overseer; and then pointed to the forecastle.

"Get for'rard, all of you," he said.

They stood staring at him, although they must have understood the gesture.

"Get for'rard," said Hornblower with a wave of his hand and a tap of his foot on the gangway.

There was only one man who seemed likely to demur actively, and Hornblower had it in mind to snatch a pistol from his belt and shoot him on the spot. But the pistol might misfire, the shot might rouse the Spaniards out of their fascinated dream. He stared the man down.

"Get for'rard, I say."

They began to move, they began to shamble off. Hornblower watched them go. Now his emotions were returning to him, and his heart was thumping madly in his chest so that it was hard to control himself. Yet he must not be precipitate. He had to wait until the others were well clear before he could address himself to the overseer.

"Stop those men," he said.

He glared into the overseer's eyes while pointing to the oarsmen; the overseer's lips moved, but he made no sound.

"Stop them," said Hornblower, and this time he put his hand to the butt of his pistol.

That sufficed. The overseer raised his voice in a high-pitched order, and the oars instantly ceased. Strange what sudden stillness possessed the ship with the cessation of the grinding of the oars in the holes. Now it was easy to hear the bubbling of the water round the galley as her way carried her forward. Hornblower turned back to hail Oldroyd.

"Oldroyd! Where away's the gig?"

"Close on the starboard bow, sir!"

"How close?"

"Two cables' lengths, sir. She's pulling for us now."

"Steer for her while you've steerage way."

"Aye aye, sir."

How long would it take the gig under the oars to cover a quarter of a mile? Hornblower feared anticlimax, feared a sudden revulsion of feeling among the Spaniards at this late moment. Mere waiting might occasion it, and he must not stand merely idle. He could still hear the motion of the galley through the water, and he turned to Jackson.

"This ship carries her way well, Jackson, doesn't she?" he said, and he made himself laugh as he spoke, as if everything in the world were a matter of sublime certainty.

"Aye, sir, I suppose she does, sir," said the startled Jackson; he was fidgeting nervously with his pistols.

"And look at the man there," went on Hornblower, pointing to a galley slave. "Did you ever see such a beard in your life?"

"N-no, sir."

"Speak to me, you fool. Talk naturally."

"I—I dunno what to say, sir."

"You've no sense, damn you, Jackson. See the welt on that fellow's shoulder? He must have caught it from the oversecr's whip not so long ago."

"Mebbe you're right, sir."

Hornblower was repressing his impatience and was about to make another speech when he heard a rasping thump alongside and a moment later the gig's crew was pouring over the bulwarks. The relief was inexpressible. Hornblower was about to relax completely when he remembered appearances. He stiffened himself up.

"Glad to see you aboard, sir," he said, as Lieutenant Chadd swung his legs over and dropped to the maindeck at the break of the forecastle.

"Glad to see *you*," said Chadd, looking about him curiously.

"These men for'rard are prisoners, sir," said Hornblower. "It might be well to secure them. I think that is all that remains to be done."

Now he could not relax; it seemed to him as if he must remain strained and tense for ever. Strained and yet stupid, even when he heard the cheers of the hands in the *Indefatigable* as the galley came alongside her. Stupid and dull, making a stumbling report to Captain Pellew, forcing himself to remember to commend the bravery of Jackson and Oldroyd in the highest terms.

"The admiral will be pleased," said Pellew, looking at Hornblower keenly.

"I'm glad, sir," Hornblower heard himself say.

"Now that we've lost poor Soames," went on Pellew, "we shall need another watch-keeping officer. I have it in mind to give you an order as acting-lieutenant."

"Thank you, sir," said Hornblower, still stupid.

Soames had been a grey-haired officer of vast experience. He had sailed the seven seas, he had fought in a score of actions. But, faced with a new situation, he had not had the quickness of thought to keep his boat from under the ram of the galley. Soames was dead, and Acting-Lieutenant Hornblower would take his place. Fighting madness, sheer insanity, had won him this promise of promotion. Hornblower had never realised the black depths of lunacy in which he could sink. Like Soames, like all the rest of the crew of the *Indefatigable*, he had allowed himself to be carried away by his blind hatred for the galleys, and only good fortune had allowed him to live through it. That was something worth remembering.

VIII

HORNBLOWER
and the Examination for Lieutenant

H.M.S. *Indefatigable* was gliding into Gilbraltar Bay, with Acting-Lieutenant Horatio Hornblower stiff and self-conscious on the quarterdeck beside Captain Pellew. He kept his telescope trained over toward Algeciras; it was a strange situation, this, that major naval bases of two hostile powers should be no more than six miles apart, and while approaching the harbour it was as well to keep close watch on Algeciras, for there was always the possibility that a squadron of Spaniards might push out suddenly to pounce on an unwary frigate coming in.

"Eight ships—nine ships with their yards crossed, sir," reported Hornblower.

"Thank you," answered Pellew. "Hands 'bout ship."

The *Indefatigable* tacked and headed in toward the Mole. Gibraltar Harbour was, as usual, crowded with shipping, for the whole naval effort of England in the Mediterranean was perforce based here. Pellew clewed up his topsails and put his helm over. Then the cable roared out and the *Indefatigable* swung at anchor.

"Call away my gig," ordered Pellew.

Pellew favored dark blue and white as the colour scheme for his boat and its crew—dark blue shirts and white trousers for the men, with white hats with blue ribbons. The boat was of dark blue picked out with white, the oars had white looms and blue blades. The general effect was very smart indeed as the drive of the oars sent the gig skimming over the water to carry Pellew to pay his respects to the port admiral. It was not long after his return that a messenger came scurrying up to Hornblower.

"Captain's compliments, sir, and he'd like to see you in his cabin."

"Examine your conscience well," grinned Midshipman Bracegirdle. "What crimes have you committed?"

"I wish I knew," said Hornblower quite genuinely.

It is always a nervous moment going in to see the captain in reply to his summons. Hornblower swallowed as he approached the cabin door, and he had to brace himself a little to knock and enter. But there was nothing to be alarmed about; Pellew looked up with a smile from his desk.

"Ah, Mr. Hornblower, I hope you will consider this good news. There will be an examination for lieutenant tomorrow, in the *Santa Barbara* there. You are ready to take it, I hope?"

Hornblower was about to say, "I suppose so, sir," but checked himself.

"Yes, sir," he said—Pellew hated slipshod answers.

"Very well, then. You report there at three P.M. with your certificates and journals."

"Aye aye, sir."

That was a very brief conversation for such an important subject. Hornblower had held Pellew's order as acting-lieutenant for two months now. Tomorrow he would take his examination. If he should pass, the admiral would confirm the order next day, and Hornblower would be a lieutenant with two months' seniority already. But if he should fail! That would mean he had been found unfit for lieutenant's rank. He would revert to midshipman, the two months' seniority would be lost, and it would be six months at least before he could try again. Eight months' seniority was a matter of enormous importance. It would affect all his subsequent career.

180

"Tell Mr. Bolton you have my permission to leave the ship tomorrow, and you may use one of the ship's boats."

"Thank you, sir."

"Good luck, Hornblower."

During the next twenty four hours Hornblower had not merely to try to read all through Norie's *Epitome of Navigation* again, and Clarke's *Complete Handbook of Seamanship,* but he had to see that his No. 1 uniform was spick-and-span. It cost his spirit ration to prevail on the warrant cook to allow the gunroom attendant to heat a flatiron in the galley and iron out his neck handkerchief. Bracegirdle lent him a clean shirt, but there was a feverish moment when it was discovered that the gunroom's supply of shoe blacking had dried to a chip. Two midshipmen had to work it soft with lard, and the resultant compound, when applied to Hornblower's buckled shoes, was stubbornly resistant to taking a polish; only much labour with the gunroom's molting shoebrush and then with a soft cloth brought those shoes up to a condition of brightness worthy of an examination for lieutenant. And as for the cocked hat—the life of a cocked hat in the midshipman's berth is hard, and some of the dents could not be entirely eliminated.

"Take it off as soon as you can and keep it under your arm," advised Bracegirdle. "Maybe they won't see you come up the ship's side."

Everybody turned out to see Hornblower leave the ship, with his sword and his white breeches and his buckled shoes, his bundle of journals under his arm and his certificates of sobriety and good conduct in his pocket. The winter afternoon was already far advanced as he was rowed over to the *Santa Barbara* and went up the ship's side to report himself to the officer of the watch.

The *Santa Barbara* was a prison hulk, one of the prizes captured in Rodney's action off Cadiz in 1780 and kept rotting at her moorings, mastless, ever since, a storeship in time of peace and a prison in time of war. Red-coated soldiers, muskets loaded and bayonets fixed, guarded the gangways; on forecastle and quarterdeck were carronades, trained inboard and depressed to sweep the waist, wherein a few prisoners took the air, ragged and unhappy. As Hornblower came up the side he caught a whiff of the stench within, where two thousand prisoners were confined. Hornblower reported himself to the officer of the watch as come on board, and for what purpose.

"Whoever would have guessed it?" said the officer of the watch—an elderly lieutenant with white hair hanging down to his shoulders—running his eye over Hornblower's immaculate uniform and the portfolio under his arm. "Fifteen of your kind have already come on board, and —Holy Gemini, see there!"

Quite a flotilla of small craft was closing in on the *Santa Barbara*. Each boat held at least one cocked-hatted and white-breeched midshipman, and some held four or five.

"Every courtesy young gentlemen in the Mediterranean Fleet is ambitious for an epaulet," said the lieutenant. "Just wait until the examining board sees how many there are of you! I wouldn't be in your shoes, young shaver, for something. Go aft, there, and wait in the port-side cabin."

It was already uncomfortably full; when Hornblower entered, fifteen pairs of eyes measured him up. There were officers of all ages from eighteen to forty, all in their No. 1's, all nervous—one or two of them had Norie's *Epitome* open on their laps and were anxiously reading passages about which they were doubtful. One little group was passing a bottle from hand to hand, presumably in an effort to keep up their courage. But no sooner had Hornblower entered than a stream of newcomers followed him. The cabin began to fill, and soon it was tightly packed. Half the forty men present found seats on the deck, and the others were forced to stand.

"Forty years back," said a loud voice somewhere, "my granddad marched with Clive to revenge the Black Hole of Calcutta. If he could have witnessed the fate of his posterity!"

"Have a drink," said another voice, "and to hell with care."

"Forty of us," commented a tall, thin, clerkly officer, counting heads. "How many of us will they pass, do you think? Five?"

"To hell with care," repeated the bibulous voice in the corner, and lifted itself in song. "Begone, dull care; I prithee be gone from me—"

"Cheese it, you fool!" rasped another voice. "Hark to that!"

The air was filled with the long-drawn twittering of the pipes of the bosun's mates, and someone on deck was shouting an order.

"A captain coming on board," remarked someone.

An officer had his eye at the crack of the door. "It's Dreadnought Foster," he reported.

"He's a tail twister if ever there was one," said a fat young officer seated comfortably with his back to the bulkhead.

Again the pipes twittered.

"Harvey, of the dockyard," reported the lookout.

The third captain followed immediately. "It's Black Charlie Hammond," said the lookout. "Looking as if he'd lost a guinea and found sixpence."

"Black Charlie?" exclaimed someone, scrambling to his feet in haste and pushing to the door. "Let's see! So it is! Then here is one young gentleman who will not stay for an answer. I know too well what that answer would be. 'Six months more at sea, sir, and damn your eyes for your impertinence in presenting yourself for examination in your present state of ignorance.' Black Charlie won't ever forget that I lost his pet poodle overside from the cutter in

Port-o'-Spain when he was First of the *Pegasus*. Goodbye, gentlemen. Give my regards to the examining board."

With that he was gone, and they saw him explaining himself to the officer of the watch and hailing a shore boat to take him back to his ship. "One fewer of us, at least," said the clerkly officer—"What is it, my man?"

"The board's compliments, sir," said the marine messenger, "an' will the first young gentleman please to come along?"

There was a momentary hesitation; no one was anxious to be the first victim.

"The one nearest the door," said an elderly master's mate. "Will you volunteer, sir?"

"I'll be the Daniel," said the erstwhile lookout desperately. "Remember me in your prayers."

He pulled his coat smooth, twitched at his neckcloth and was gone, the remainder waiting in gloomy silence, relieved only by the glug-glug of the bottle as the bibulous midshipman took another swig. A full ten minutes passed before the candidate for promotion returned, making a brave effort to smile.

"Six months more at sea?" asked someone.

"No," was the unexpected answer. "Three!—I was told to send the next man. It had better be you."

"But what did they ask you?"

"They began by asking me to define a rhumb line— But don't keep them waiting, I advise you."

Some thirty officers had their textbooks open on the instant, to re-read about rhumb lines.

"You were there ten minutes," said the clerkly officer, looking at his watch. "Forty of us, ten minutes each— why, it'll be midnight before they reach the last of us. They'll never do it."

"They'll be hungry," said someone.

"Hungry for our blood," said another.

"Perhaps they'll try us in batches," suggested a third, "like the French tribunals."

Listening to them, Hornblower was reminded of French aristocrats jesting at the foot of the scaffold. Candidates departed and candidates returned, some gloomy, some smiling. The cabin was already far less crowded; Hornblower was able to secure sufficient deck space to seat himself, and he stretched out his legs with a nonchalant sigh of relief, and he no sooner emitted the sigh than he realized that it was a stage effect which he had put on for his own benefit. He was as nervous as he could be. The winter night was falling, and some good Samaritan on board sent in a couple of purser's dips to give a feeble illumination to the darkening cabin.

"They are passing one in three," said the clerkly officer, making ready for his turn. "May I be the third."

Hornblower got to his feet again when he left; it would be his turn next. He stepped out under the half-deck into the dark night and breathed the chill fresh air. A gentle breeze was blowing from the southward, cooled, presumably, by the snow-clad Atlas Mountains of Africa across the strait. There was neither moon nor stars. Here came the clerkly officer back again.

"Hurry," he said. "They're impatient."

Hornblower made his way past the sentry to the after cabin; it was brightly lit, so that he blinked as he entered, and stumbled over some obstruction. And it was only then that he remembered that he had not straightened his neckcloth and seen to it that his sword hung correctly at his side. He went on blinking in his nervousness at the three grim faces across the table.

"Well, sir?" said a stern voice. "Report yourself. We have no time to waste."

"H-Hornblower, sir. H-Horatio H-Hornblower. M-Midshipman—I mean Acting-Lieutenant, H.M.S. *Indefatigable*."

"Your certificates, please," said the right-hand face.

Hornblower handed them over, and as he waited for them to be examined, the left-hand face suddenly spoke. "You are close-hauled on the port tack, Mr. Hornblower, beating up-Channel with a nor'easterly wind blowing hard, with Dover bearing north two miles. Is that clear?"

"Yes, sir."

"Now the wind veers four points and takes you flat aback. What do you do, sir? What do you do?"

Hornblower's mind, if it was thinking about anything at all at that moment, was thinking about rhumb lines; this question took him as much aback as the situation it envisaged. His mouth opened and shut, but there was no word he could say.

"By now you're dismasted," said the middle face—a swarthy face; Hornblower was making the deduction that it must belong to Black Charlie Hammond. He could think about that even if he could not force his mind to think at all about his examination.

"Dismasted," said the left-hand face, with a smile like Nero enjoying a Christian's death agony. "With Dover cliffs under your lee. You are in serious trouble, Mr.—ah —Hornblower."

Serious indeed. Hornblower's mouth opened and shut again. His dulled mind heard, without paying special attention to it, the thud of a cannon shot somewhere not too far off. The board passed no remark on it either, but a moment later there came a series of further cannon shots which brought the three captains to their feet. Unceremoniously they rushed out of the cabin, sweeping out of the way the sentry at the door. Hornblower followed them; they arrived in the waist just in time to see a rocket soar up into the night sky and burst in a shower of red stars. It was the general alarm; over the water of the anchorage they could hear the drums rolling as all the ships present beat to quarters. On the port-side gangway the remainder of the candidates were clustered, speaking excitedly.

"See there!" said a voice.

Across half a mile of dark water a yellow light grew until the ship there was wrapped in flame. She had every sail set and was heading straight into the crowded anchorage.

"Fire ships!"

"Officer of the watch! Call my gig!" bellowed Foster.

A line of fire ships was running before the wind, straight at the crowd of anchored ships. The *Santa Barbara* was full of the wildest bustle as the seamen and marines came pouring on deck, and as captains and candidates shouted for boats to take them back to their ships. A line of orange flame lit up the water, followed at once by the roar of a broadside; some ship was firing her guns in the endeavour to sink a fire ship. Let one of those blazing hulls make contact with one of the anchored ships, even for a few seconds, and the fire would be transmitted to the dry, painted timber, to the tarred cordage, to the inflammable sails, so that nothing would put it out. To men in highly combustible ships filled with explosives, fire was the deadliest and most dreaded peril of the sea.

"You shore boat, there!" bellowed Hammond suddenly. "You shore boat! Come alongside! Come alongside, blast you!"

His eye had been quick to sight the pair-oar rowing by.

"Come alongside or I'll fire into you!" supplemented Foster. "Sentry, there, make ready to give them a shot!"

At the threat, the wherry turned and glided toward the mizzen chains.

"Here you are, gentlemen," said Hammond.

The three captains rushed to the mizzen chains and flung themselves down into the boat. Hornblower was at their heels. He knew there was small enough chance of a junior officer getting a boat to take him back to his ship, to which it was his bounden duty to go as soon as possible. After the captains had reached their destinations, he could use this boat to reach the *Indefatigable*. He threw himself off into the sternsheets as she pushed off, knocking the breath out of Captain Harvey, his sword scabbard clattering on the gunwale. But the three captains accepted his uninvited presence there without comment.

"Pull for the *Dreadnought*," said Foster.

"Dammit, I'm the senior!" said Hammond. "Pull for *Calypso*."

"*Calypso* it is," said Harvey. He had his hand on the tiller, heading the boat across the dark water.

"Pull! Oh, pull!" said Foster, in agony. There can be no mental torture like that of a captain whose ship is in peril and he not on board.

"There's one of them," said Harvey.

Just ahead, a small brig was bearing down on them under topsails; they could see the glow of the fire, and as they watched, the fire suddenly burst into roaring fury, wrapping the whole vessel in flames in a moment, like a set piece in a fireworks display. Flames spouted out of the holes in her sides and roared up through her hatchways. The very water around her glowed vivid red. They saw her halt in her career and begin to swing slowly around.

"She's across *Santa Barbara*'s cable," said Foster.

"She's nearly clear," added Hammond. "God help 'em on board there. She'll be alongside her in a minute."

Hornblower thought of two thousand Spanish and French prisoners battened down below decks in the hulk.

"With a man at her wheel, she could be steered clear," said Foster. "We ought to do it!"

Then things happened rapidly. Harvey put the tiller over. "Pull away!" he roared at the boatmen.

The latter displayed an easily understood reluctance to row up to that fiery hull.

"Pull!" said Harvey.

He whipped out his sword from its scabbard, and the blade reflected the red fire as he thrust it menacingly at the stroke oar's throat. With a kind of sob, stroke tugged at his oar and the boat leaped forward.

"Lay us under her counter," said Foster. "I'll jump for it."

At last Hornblower found his tongue. "Let me go, sir. I'll handle her."

"Come with me, if you like," replied Foster. "It may need two of us."

His nickname of Dreadnought Foster may have had its origin in the name of his ship, but it was appropriate enough in all circumstances. Harvey swung the boat under the fire ship's stern; she was before the wind again now, and just gathering way, just heading down upon the *Santa Barbara*.

For a moment Hornblower was the nearest man in the boat to the brig and there was no time to be lost. He stood up on the thwart and jumped; his hands gripped something, and with a kick and a struggle he dragged his ungainly body up onto the deck. With the brig before the wind, the flames were blown forward; right aft here it was merely frightfully hot, but Hornblower's ears were filled with the roar of the flames and the crackling and banging of the burning wood. He stepped forward to the wheel and seized the spokes, the wheel was lashed with a loop of line and, as he cast this off and took hold of the wheel again, he could feel the rudder below him bite into the water. He flung his weight on the spoke and spun the wheel over. The brig was about to collide with the *Santa Barbara,* starboard bow to starboard bow, and the flames lit an anxious gesticulating crowd on the *Santa Barbara*'s forecastle.

"Hard over!" roared Foster's voice in Hornblower's ear.

"Hard over it is!" said Hornblower, and the brig an-

189

swered her wheel at that moment, her bow turned away, avoiding the collision.

An immense fountain of flame poured out from the hatchway abaft the mainmast, setting mast and rigging ablaze and at the same time a flaw of wind blew a wave of flame aft. Some instinct made Hornblower, while holding the wheel with one hand, snatch out his neckcloth with the other and bury his face in it. The flame whirled round him and was gone again. But the distraction had been dangerous; the brig had continued to turn under full helm, and now her stern was swinging in to bump against the *Santa Barbara*'s bow. Hornblower desperately spun the wheel over the other way. The flames had driven Foster aft to the taffrail, but now he returned.

"Hard-a-lee!"

The brig was already responding. Her starboard quarter bumped the *Santa Barbara* in the waist, and then bumped clear.

"Midships!" shouted Foster.

At a distance of only two or three yards the fire ship passed on down the *Santa Barbara*'s side; an anxious group ran along her gangways keeping up with her as she did so. On the quarterdeck another group stood by with a spar to boom the fire ship off; Hornblower saw them out of the tail of his eye as they went by. Now they were clear.

"There's the *Dauntless* on the port bow," said Foster. "Keep her clear."

"Aye aye, sir."

The din of the fire was tremendous; it could hardly be believed that on this little area of deck it was still possible to breathe and live. Hornblower felt the appalling heat on his hands and face. Both masts were immense pyramids of flame.

"Starboard a point," said Foster. "We'll lay her aground on the shoal by the Neutral Ground."

"Starboard a point," responded Hornblower.

He was being borne along on a wave of the highest exaltation; the roar of the fire was intoxicating, and he knew not a moment's fear. Then the whole deck only a yard or two forward of the wheel opened up in flame. Fire spouted out of the gaping seams and the heat was utterly unbearable, and the fire moved rapidly aft as the seams gaped progressively backward.

Hornblower felt for the loop of line to lash the wheel, but before he could do so the wheel spun idly under his hand, presumably as the tiller ropes below him were burned away, and at the same time the deck under his feet heaved and warped in the fire. He staggered back to the taffrail. Foster was there.

"Tiller ropes burned away, sir," reported Hornblower.

Flames roared up beside them. His coat sleeve was smouldering.

"Jump!" said Foster.

Hornblower felt Foster shoving him—everything was insane. He heaved himself over, gasped with fright as he hung in the air, and then felt the breath knocked out of his body as he hit the water. The water closed over him, and he knew panic as he struggled back to the surface. It was cold—the Mediterranean in December is cold. For the moment, the air in his clothes supported him, despite the weight of the sword at his side, but he could see nothing in the darkness, with his eyes still dazzled by the roaring flames. Somebody splashed beside him.

"They were following us in the boat to take us off," said Foster's voice. "Can you swim?"

"Yes, sir. Not very well."

"That might describe me," said Foster, and then he lifted his voice to hail, "Ahoy! Ahoy! Hammond! Harvey! Ahoy!"

He tried to raise himself as well as his voice, fell back with a splash, and splashed and splashed again, the water flowing into his mouth cutting short something he tried to say. Hornblower, beating the water with increasing feebleness, could still spare a thought—such were the vagaries of his wayward mind—for the interesting fact that even captains of much seniority were only mortal men after all. He tried to unbuckle his sword belt, failed, and sank deep with the effort, only just succeeding in struggling back to the surface. He gasped for breath, but in another attempt he managed to draw his sword half out of its scabbard, and as he struggled, it slid out the rest of the way by its own weight; yet he was not conscious of any noticeable relief.

It was then that he heard the splashing and grinding of oars, and loud voices, and he saw the dark shape of the approaching boat, and he uttered a spluttering cry. In a second or two the boat was up to them, and he was clutching the gunwale in panic.

They were lifting Foster in over the stern, and Hornblower knew he must keep still and make no effort to climb in, but it called for all his resolution to make himself hang quietly onto the side of the boat and wait his turn. He was interested in this overmastering fear, while he despised himself for it. It called for a conscious and serious effort of will power to make his hand alternately release their deathlike grip on the gunwale, so that the men in the boat could pass him round to the stern. Then they dragged him in and he fell face downward in the bottom of the boat, on the verge of fainting. Then somebody spoke in the boat, and Hornblower felt a cold shiver pass over his skin, and his feeble muscles tensed themselves, for the words spoken were Spanish—at any rate an unknown tongue, and Spanish presumably.

Somebody else answered in the same language. Hornblower tried to struggle up, and a restraining hand was laid on his shoulder. He rolled over, and with his eyes now accustomed to the darkness, he could see the three swarthy faces with the long black moustaches. These men were not Gibraltarians. On the instant he could guess who they were—the crew of one of the fire ships who had steered their craft in past the Mole, set fire to it, and made their escape in the boat. Foster was sitting doubled up, in the bottom of the boat, and now he lifted his face from his knees and stared round him.

"Who are these fellows?" he asked feebly—his struggle in the water had left him as weak as Hornblower.

"Spanish fire ship's crew, I fancy, sir," said Hornblower. "We're prisoners."

"Are we indeed!"

The knowledge galvanized him into activity just as it had Hornblower. He tried to get to his feet, and the Spaniard at the tiller thrust him down with a hand on his shoulder. Foster tried to put his hand away, and raised his voice in a feeble cry, but the man at the tiller was standing no nonsense. He brought out, in a lightning gesture, a knife from his belt. The light from the fire ship, burning itself harmlessly out on the shoal in the distance, ran redly along the blade, and Foster ceased to struggle. Men might call him Dreadnought Foster, but he could recognize the need for discretion.

"How are we heading?" he asked Hornblower, sufficiently quietly not to irritate their captors.

"North, sir. Maybe they're going to land on the Neutral Ground and make for the Line."

"That's their best chance," agreed Foster.

He turned his neck uncomfortably to look back up the harbour.

"Two other ships burning themselves out up there," he said. "There were three fire ships came in, I fancy."

"I saw three, sir."

"Then there's no damage done. But a bold endeavour. Whoever would have credited the Dons with making such an attempt?"

"They have learned about fire ships from us, perhaps, sir," suggested Hornblower.

"We may have 'nursed the pinion that impelled the steel,' you think?"

"It is possible, sir."

Foster was a cool enough customer, quoting poetry and discussing the naval situation while being carried off into captivity by a Spaniard who guarded him with a drawn knife. Cool might be a too accurate adjective; Hornblower was shivering in his wet clothes as the chill night air blew over him, and he felt weak and feeble after all the excitement and exertions of the day.

"Boat ahoy!" came a hail across the water; there was a dark nucleus in the night over there. The Spaniard in the sternsheets instantly dragged the tiller over, heading the boat directly away from it, while the two at the oars redoubled their exertions.

"Guard boat—" said Foster, but cut his explanation short at a further threat from the knife.

Of course there would be a boat rowing guard at this northern end of the anchorage; they might have thought of it.

"Boat ahoy!" came the hail again. "Lay on your oars or I'll fire into you!"

The Spaniard made no reply, and a second later came the flash and report of a musket shot. They heard nothing of the bullet, but the shot would put the fleet—toward which they were heading again—on the alert. But the Spaniards were going to play the game out to the end. They rowed doggedly on.

"Boat ahoy!"

This was another hail, from a boat right ahead of them. The Spaniards at the oars ceased their efforts in dismay, but a roar from the steersman set them instantly to work again. Hornblower could see the new boat almost directly ahead of them, and heard another hail from it as it rested

194

on its oars. The Spaniard at the tiller shouted an order, and the stroke oar backed water and the boat turned sharply; another order, and both rowers tugged ahead again and the boat surged forward to ram. Should they succeed in overturning the intercepting boat, they might make their escape even now, while the pursuing boat stopped to pick up their friends.

Everything happened at once, with everyone shouting at the full pitch of his lungs, seemingly. There was the crash of the collision, both boats heeling wildly as the bow of the Spanish boat rode up over the British boat, but failed to overturn it. Someone fired a pistol, and the next moment the pursuing guard boat came dashing alongside, its crew leaping madly aboard them. Somebody flung himself on top of Hornblower, crushing the breath out of him and threatening to keep it out permanently with a hand on his throat. Hornblower heard Foster bellowing in protest, and a moment later his assailant released him, so that he could hear the midshipman of the guard boat apologising for this rough treatment of a post captain of the Royal Navy. Someone unmasked the guard boat's lantern, and by its light Foster revealed himself, bedraggled and battered. The light shone on their sullen prisoners.

"Boats ahoy!" came another hail, and yet another boat emerged from the darkness and pulled toward them.

"Cap'n Hammond, I believe!" hailed Foster, with an ominous rasp in his voice.

"Thank God!" they heard Hammond say, and the boat pulled into the faint circle of light.

"But no thanks to you," said Foster bitterly.

"After your fire ship cleared the *Santa Barbara* a puff of wind took you on faster than we could keep up with you," explained Harvey.

"We followed as fast as we could get these rock scorpions to row," added Hammond.

"And yet it called for Spaniards to save us from drowning," sneered Foster. The memory of his struggle in the water rankled, apparently. "I thought I could rely on two brother captains."

"What are you implying, sir?" snapped Hammond.

"I make no implications, but others may read implications into a simple statement of fact."

"I consider that an offensive remark, sir," said Harvey, "addressed to me equally with Captain Hammond."

"I congratulate you on your perspicacity, sir," replied Foster.

"I understand," said Harvey. "This is not a discussion we can pursue with these men present. I shall send a friend to wait on you."

"He will be welcome."

"Then I wish you a very good night, sir."

"And I, too, sir," said Hammond. "Give way there."

The boat pulled out of the circle of light, leaving an audience open-mouthed at this strange freak of human behaviour, that a man saved first from death and then from captivity should wantonly thrust himself into peril again. Foster looked after the boat for some seconds before speaking; perhaps he was already regretting his rather hysterical outburst.

"I shall have much to do before morning," he said, more to himself than to anyone near him, and then addressed himself to the midshipman of the guard boat. "You, sir, will take charge of these prisoners and convey me to my ship."

"Aye aye, sir."

"Is there anyone here who can speak their lingo? I would have it explained to them that I shall send them back to Cartagena under cartel, free without exchange. They saved our lives, and that is the least we can do in return." The final explanatory sentence was addressed to Hornblower.

196

"I think that is just, sir."

"And you, my fire-breathing friend. May I offer you my thanks? You did well. Should I live beyond tomorrow, I shall see that authority is informed of your actions."

"Thank you, sir." A question trembled on Hornblower's lips. It called for a little resolution to thrust it out, "And my examination, sir? My certificate?"

Foster shook his head. "That particular examining board will never reassemble, I fancy. You must wait your opportunity to go before another one."

"Aye aye, sir," said Hornblower, with despondency apparent in his tone.

"Now look'ee here, Mr. Hornblower," said Foster, turning upon him. "To the best of my recollection, you were flat aback, about to lose your spars and with Dover cliffs under your lee. In one more minute you would have been failed—it was the warning gun that saved you. Is not that so?"

"I suppose it is, sir."

"Then be thankful for small mercies. And even more thankful for big ones."

IX

HORNBLOWER
and Noah's Ark

Acting-Lieutenant Hornblower sat in the sternsheets of the longboat beside Mr. Tapling of the diplomatic service, with his feet among bags of gold. About him rose the steep shores of the Gulf of Oran, and ahead of him lay the city, white in the sunshine, like a mass of blocks of marble dumped by a careless hand upon the hillsides where they rose from the water. The oar blades, as the boat's crew pulled away rhythmically over the gentle swell, were biting into the clearest emerald green, and it was only a moment since they had left behind the bluest the Mediterranean could show.

"A pretty sight from here," said Tapling, gazing at the town they were approaching. "But closer inspection will show that the eye is deceived. And as for the nose! The stinks of the true believers have to be smelt to be believed. Lay her alongside the jetty there, Mr. Hornblower, beyond those xebecs."

"Aye aye, sir," said the coxswain, when Hornblower gave the order.

"There's a sentry on the water-front battery here," commented Tapling, looking about him keenly. "Not more than half asleep, either. And notice the guns in the two castles. Thirty-two-pounders, without a doubt. Stone shot piled in readiness. A stone shot flying into fragments on impact effects damage out of proportion to its size. And the walls seem sound enough. To seize Oran by a *coup de main* would not be easy, I am afraid. If His Nibs the Bey should choose to cut our throats and keep our gold it would be long before we were avenged, Mr. Hornblower."

"I don't think I should find any satisfaction in being avenged in any case, sir," said Hornblower.

"There's some truth in that. But doubtless His Nibs will spare us this time. The goose lays golden eggs—a boatload of gold every month must make a dazzling prospect for a pirate Bey in these days of convoys."

"Way'nough," called the coxswain. "Oars!"

The longboat came gliding alongside the jetty and hooked on neatly. A few seated figures in the shade turned eyes at least, and in some cases even their heads as well, to look at the British boat's crew. A number of swarthy Moors appeared on the decks of the xebecs and gazed down at them, and one or two shouted remarks to them.

"No doubt they are describing the ancestry of the infidels," said Tapling. "Sticks and stones may break my bones, but names can never hurt me, especially when I do not understand them. Where's our man?"

He shaded his eyes to look along the water-front.

"No one in sight, sir, that looks like a Christian," said Hornblower.

"Our man's no Christian," said Tapling. "White, but no Christian. White by courtesy at that—a French-Arab-Levantine mixture. His Britannic Majesty's consul at Oran pro tem, and a Mussulman from expediency. Though there are very serious disadvantages about being a true believer. Who would want four wives at any time, especially when one pays for the doubtful privilege by abstaining from wine?"

Tapling stepped up onto the jetty and Hornblower followed him. The gentle swell that rolled up the Gulf broke soothingly below them, and the blinding heat of the noon-

199

day sun was reflected up into their faces from the stone blocks on which they stood. Far down the Gulf lay the two anchored ships—the storeship and H.M.S. *Indefatigable*—lovely on the bluest silver surface.

"And yet I would rather see Drury Lane on a Saturday night," said Tapling.

He turned back to look at the city wall, which guarded the place from seaborne attack. A narrow gate, flanked by bastions, opened onto the water-front. Sentries in red caftans were visible on the summit. In the deep shadow of the gate something was moving, but it was hard with eyes dazzled by the sun to see what it was. Then it emerged from the shadow as a little group coming towards them—a half-naked Negro leading a donkey, and on the back of the donkey, seated sideways far back towards the root of the tail, a vast figure in a blue robe.

"Shall we meet His Britannic Majesty's consul halfway?" asked Tapling. "No. Let him come to us."

The Negro halted the donkey, and the man on the donkey's back slid to the ground and came towards them—a mountainous man, waddling straddle-legged in his robe, his huge clay-coloured face topped by a white turban. A scanty black moustache and beard sprouted from his lips and chin.

"Your servant, Mr. Duras," said Tapling. "And may I present Acting-Lieutenant Horatio Hornblower, of the frigate *Indefatigable?*"

Mr. Duras nodded his perspiring head.

"Have you brought the money?" he asked, in guttural French; it took Hornblower a moment or two to adjust his mind to the language and his ear to Duras' intonation.

"Seven thousand golden guineas," replied Tapling, in reasonably good French.

"Good," said Duras, with a trace of relief. "Is it in the boat?"

"It is in the boat, and it stays in the boat at present,"

200

answered Tapling. "Do you remember the conditions agreed upon? Four hundred fat cattle, fifteen hundred *fanegas* of barley grain. When I see those in the lighters, and the lighters alongside the ships down the bay, then I hand over the money. Have you the stores ready?"

"Soon."

"As I expected. How long?"

"Soon—very soon."

Tapling made a grimace of resignation.

"Then we shall return to the ships. Tomorrow, perhaps, or the day after, we shall come back with the gold."

Alarm appeared on Duras' sweating face.

"No, do not do that," he said, hastily. "You do not know His Highness the Bey. He is changeable. If he knows the gold is here he will give orders for the cattle to be brought. Take the gold away, and he will not stir. And —and—he will be angry with me."

"Ira principis mors est," said Tapling, and in response to Duras' blank look obliged by a translation. "The wrath of the prince means death. Is not that so?"

"Yes," said Duras, and he in turn said something in an unknown language, and stabbed at the air with his fingers in a peculiar gesture; and then translated, "May it not happen."

"Certainly we hope it may not happen," agreed Tapling with disarming cordiality. "The bowstring, the hook, even the bastinado are all unpleasant. It might be better if you went to the Bey and prevailed upon him to give the necessary orders for the grain and the cattle. Or we shall leave at nightfall."

Tapling glanced up at the sun to lay stress on the time limit.

"I shall go," said Duras, spreading his hands in a deprecatory gesture. "I shall go. But I beg of you, do not depart. Perhaps His Highness is busy in his harem. Then no one may disturb him. But I shall try. The grain is here ready—it lies in the Kasbah there. It is only the cattle that have to be brought in. Please be patient. I implore you. His Highness is not accustomed to commerce, as you know, sir. Still less is he accustomed to commerce after the fashion of the Franks."

Duras wiped his streaming face with a corner of his robe.

"Pardon me," he said. "I do not feel well. But I shall go to His Highness. I shall go. Please wait for me."

"Until sunset," said Tapling implacably.

Duras called to his Negro attendant, who had been crouching huddled up under the donkey's belly to take advantage of the shade it cast. With an effort Duras hoisted his ponderous weight onto the donkey's hindquarters. He wiped his face again and looked at them with a trace of bewilderment.

"Wait for me," were the last words he said as the donkey was led away back into the city gate.

"He is afraid of the Bey," said Tapling watching him go. "I would rather face twenty Beys than Admiral Sir John Jervis in a tantrum. What will he do when he hears about this further delay, with the Fleet on short rations already? He'll have my guts for a necktie."

"One cannot expect punctuality of these people," said Hornblower with the easy philosophy of the man who does not bear the responsibility. But he thought of the British navy, without friends, without allies, maintaining desperately the blockade of a hostile Europe, in face of superior numbers, storms, disease, and now famine.

"Look at that!" said Tapling pointing suddenly.

It was a big grey rat which had made its appearance in the dry storm gutter that crossed the water-front here. Regardless of the bright sunshine it sat up and looked round at the world; even when Tapling stamped his foot it showed no great signs of alarm. When he stamped a second time it slowly turned to hide itself again in the drain, missed its footing so that it lay writhing for a moment at the mouth of the drain, and then regained its feet and disappeared into the darkness.

"An old rat, I suppose," said Tapling meditatively. "Senile, possibly. Even blind, it may be."

Hornblower cared nothing about rats, senile or otherwise. He took a step or two back in the direction of the longboat and the civilian officer conformed to his movements.

"Rig that mains'l so that it gives us some shade, Maxwell," said Hornblower. "We're here for the rest of the day."

"A great comfort," said Tapling, seating himself on a stone bollard beside the boat, "to be here in a heathen port. No need to worry in case any men run off. No need to worry about liquor. Only about bullocks and barley. And how to get a spark on this tinder."

He blew through the pipe that he took from his pocket, preparatory to filling it. The boat was shaded by the mainsail now, and the hands sat in the bows yarning in low tones, while the others made themselves as comfortable as possible in the sternsheets; the boat rolled peacefully in the tiny swell, the rhythmic sound as the fendoffs creaked between her gunwale and the jetty having a soothing effect while city and port dozed in the blazing afternoon heat. Yet it was not easy for a young man of Hornblower's active temperament to endure prolonged inaction. He climbed up on the jetty to stretch his legs, and paced up and down; a Moor in a white gown and turban came staggering in the sunshine along the water-front. His gait was unsteady, and he walked with his legs well apart to provide a firmer base for his swaying body.

"What was it you said, sir, about liquor being abhorred by the Moslems?" said Hornblower to Tapling down in the sternsheets.

"Not necessarily abhorred," replied Tapling, guardedly.

203

"But anathematised, illegal, unlawful, and hard to obtain."

"Someone here has contrived to obtain some, sir," said Hornblower.

"Let me see," said Tapling, scrambling up; the hands, bored with waiting and interested as ever in liquor, landed from the bows to stare as well.

"That looks like a man who has drink taken," agreed Tapling.

"Three sheets in the wind, sir," said Maxwell, as the Moor staggered.

"And taken all aback," supplemented Tapling, as the Moor swerved wildly to one side in a semicircle.

At the end of the semicircle he fell with a crash on his face; his brown legs emerged from the robe a couple of times and were drawn in again, and he lay passive, his head on his arms, his turban fallen on the ground to reveal his shaven skull with a tassel of hair on the crown.

"Totally dismasted," said Hornblower.

"And hard aground," said Tapling.

But the Moor now lay oblivious of everything.

"And here's Duras," said Hornblower.

Out through the gate came the massive figure on the little donkey; another donkey bearing another portly figure followed, each donkey being led by a Negro slave, and after them came a dozen swarthy individuals whose muskets, and whose pretence at uniform, indicated that they were soldiers.

"The treasurer of His Highness," said Duras, by way of introduction when he and the other had dismounted. "Come to fetch the gold."

The portly Moor looked loftily upon them; Duras was still streaming with sweat in the hot sun.

"The gold is there," said Tapling, pointing. "In the sternsheets of the longboat. You will have a closer view of it when we have a closer view of the stores we are to buy."

Duras translated this speech into Arabic. There was a

rapid interchange of sentences, before the treasurer apparently yielded. He turned and waved his arms back to the gate in what was evidently a prearranged signal. A dreary procession immediately emerged—a long line of men, all of them almost naked, white, black, and mulatto, each man staggering along under the burden of a sack of grain. Overseers with sticks walked with them.

"The money," said Duras, as a result of something said by the treasurer.

A word from Tapling set the hands to work lifting the heavy bags of gold onto the quay.

"With the corn on the jetty I will put the gold there too," said Tapling to Hornblower. "Keep your eye on it while I look at some of those sacks."

Tapling walked over to the slave gang. Here and there he opened a sack, looked into it, and inspected handfuls of the golden barley grain; other sacks he felt from the outside.

"No hope of looking over every sack in a hundred ton of barley," he remarked, strolling back again to Hornblower. "Much of it is sand, I expect. But that is the way of the heathen. The price is adjusted accordingly. Very well, effendi."

At a sign from Duras, and under the urgings of the overseers, the slaves burst into activity, trotting up to the quayside and dropping their sacks into the lighter which lay there. The first dozen men were organised into a working party to distribute the cargo evenly into the bottom of the lighter, while the others trotted off, their bodies gleaming with sweat, to fetch fresh loads. At the same time a couple of swarthy herdsmen came out through the gate driving a small herd of cattle.

"Scrubby little creatures," said Tapling, looking them over critically. "But that was allowed for in the price, too."

"The gold," said Duras.

In reply Tapling opened one of the bags at his feet, filled his hand with golden guineas, and let them cascade through his fingers into the bag again.

"Five hundred guineas there," he said. "Fourteen bags, as you see. They will be yours when the lighters are loaded and unmoored."

Duras wiped his face with a weary gesture. His knees seemed to be weak, and he leaned upon the patient donkey that stood behind him.

The cattle were being driven down a gangway into another lighter, and a second herd had now appeared and was waiting.

"Things move faster than you feared," said Hornblower.

"See how they drive the poor wretches," replied Tapling sententiously. "See! Things move fast when you have no concern for human flesh and blood."

A coloured slave had fallen to the ground under his burden. He lay there disregarding the blows rained on him by the sticks of the overseers. There was a small movement of his legs. Someone dragged him out of the way at last and the sacks continued to be carried to the lighter. The other lighter was filling fast with cattle, packed into a tight, bellowing mass in which no movement was possible.

"His Nibs is actually keeping his word," marvelled Tapling. "I'd 'a settled for the half, if I had been asked beforehand."

One of the herdsmen on the quay had sat down with his face in his hands; now he fell over limply on his side.

"Sir—" began Hornblower to Tapling, and the two men looked at each other with the same awful thought occurring to them at the same moment.

Duras began to say something; with one hand on the withers of the donkey and the other gesticulating in the air it seemed that he was making something of a speech, but there was no sense in the words he was roaring out in a

hoarse voice. His face was swollen beyond its customa[.]
fatness and his expression was wildly distorted, while h[i]
cheeks were so suffused with blood as to look darker
under his tan. Duras quitted his hold of the donkey and
began to reel about in half circles, under the eyes of
Moors and Englishmen. His voice died away to a whisper,
his legs gave way under him, and he fell to his hands and
knees and then to his face.

"That's the plague!" said Tapling. "The Black Death! I
saw it in Smyrna in '96."

He and the other Englishmen had shrunk back on the
one side, the soldiers and the treasurer on the other, leaving the palpitating body lying in the clear space between
them.

"The plague, by St. Peter!" squealed one of the young
sailors. He would have headed a rush to the longboat.

"Stand still, there!" roared Hornblower, scared of the
plague but with the habits of discipline so deeply en-
grained in him by now that he checked the panic automatically.

"I was a fool not to have thought of it before," said
Tapling. "That dying rat—that fellow over there who we
thought was drunk. I should have known!"

The soldier who appeared to be the sergeant in command of the treasurer's escort was in explosive conversation with the chief of the overseers of the slaves, both of
them staring and pointing at the dying Duras; the treasurer himself was clutching his robe about him and looking
down at the wretched man at his feet in fascinated horror.

"Well, sir?" said Hornblower to Tapling. "What do we
do?"

Hornblower was of the temperament that demands immediate action in face of a crisis.

"Do?" replied Tapling with a bitter smile. "We stay
here and rot."

"Stay *here?*"

207

"The fleet will never have us back. Not until we have
erved three weeks of quarantine. Three weeks after the
last case has occurred. Here in Oran."

"Nonsense!" said Hornblower, with all the respect due
to his senior startled out of him. "No one would order
that."

"Would they not? Have you ever seen an epidemic in a
fleet?"

Hornblower had not, but he had heard enough about
them—fleets where nine out of ten had died of putrid fe-
vers. Crowded ships with twenty-two inches of hammock
space per man were ideal breeding places for epidemics.
He realised that no captain, no admiral, would run that
risk for the sake of a longboat's crew of twenty men.

The two xebecs against the jetty had suddenly cast off,
and were working their way out of the harbour under
sweeps.

"The plague can only have struck today," mused Hornblower, the habit of deduction strong in him despite his
sick fear.

The cattle herders were abandoning their work, giving
a wide berth to that one of their numbers who was lying
on the quay. Up at the town gate it appeared that the
guard was employed in driving people back into the town
—apparently the rumour of plague had spread sufficiently
therein to cause a panic, while the guard had just received
orders not to allow the population to stream out into the
surrounding country. There would be frightful things happening in the town soon. The treasurer was climbing on
his donkey; the crowd of grain-carrying slaves was melt-
ing away as the overseers fled.

"I must report this to the ship," said Hornblower;
Tapling, as a civilian diplomatic officer, held no authority
over him. The whole responsibility was Hornblower's. The
longboat and the longboat's crew were Hornblower's com-

mand, entrusted to him by Captain Pellew whose authori derived from the King.

Amazing, how the panic was spreading. The treasurer was gone; Duras' Negro slave had ridden off on his late master's donkey; the soldiers had hastened off in a single group. The water-front was deserted now except for the dead and dying; along the water-front, presumably, at the foot of the wall, lay the way to the open country which all desired to seek. The Englishmen were standing alone, with the bags of gold at their feet.

"Plague spreads through the air," said Tapling. "Even the rats die of it. We have been here for hours. We were near enough to—that—" he nodded at the dying Duras— "to speak to him, to catch his breath. Which of us will be the first?"

"We'll see when the time comes," said Hornblower. It was his contrary nature to be sanguine in the face of depression; besides, he did not want the men to hear what Tapling was saying.

"And there's the Fleet!" said Tapling bitterly. "This lot—" he nodded at the deserted lighters, one almost full of cattle, the other almost full of grain sacks—"this lot would be a Godsend. The men are on two-thirds rations."

"Damn it, we can do something about it," said Hornblower. "Maxwell, put the gold back in the boat, and get that awning in."

The officer of the watch in H.M.S. *Indefatigable* saw the ship's longboat returning from the town. A slight breeze had swung the frigate and the *Caroline* (the transport brig) to their anchors, and the longboat, instead of running alongside, came up under the *Indefatigable*'s stern to leeward.

"Mr. Christie!" hailed Hornblower, standing up in the bows of the longboat.

The officer of the watch came aft to the taffrail.

"What is it?" he demanded, puzzled.

"I must speak to the captain."

"Then come on board and speak to him. What the devil—?"

"Please ask the captain if I may speak to him."

Pellew appeared at the after cabin window; he could hardly have helped hearing the bellowed conversation.

"Yes, Mr. Hornblower?"

Hornblower told him the news.

"Keep to loo'ard, Mr. Hornblower."

"Yes, sir. But the stores—"

"What about them?"

Hornblower outlined the situation and made his request.

"It's not very regular," mused Pellew. "Besides—"

He did not want to shout aloud his thoughts that perhaps everyone in the longboat would be soon dead of plague.

"We'll be all right, sir. It's a week's rations for the squadron."

That was the point, the vital matter. Pellew had to balance the possible loss of a transport brig against the possible gain of supplies, immeasurably more important, which would enable the squadron to maintain its watch over the outlet to the Mediterranean. Looked at in that light Hornblower's suggestion had added force.

"Oh, very well, Mr. Hornblower. By the time you bring the stores out I'll have the crew transferred. I appoint you to the command of the *Caroline*."

"Thank you, sir."

"Mr. Tapling will continue as passenger with you."

"Very good, sir."

So when the crew of the longboat, toiling and sweating at the sweeps, brought the two lighters down the bay, they found the *Caroline* swinging deserted at her anchors, while a dozen curious telescopes from the *Indefatigable* watched the proceedings. Hornblower went up the brig's side with half a dozen hands.

"She's like a blooming Noah's Ark, sir," said Maxwell.

The comparison was apt; the *Caroline* was flush-decked, and the whole available deck area was divided by partitions into stalls for the cattle, while to enable the ship to be worked light gangways had been laid over the stalls into a practically continuous upper deck.

"An' all the animiles, sir," said another seaman.

"But Noah's animals walked in two by two," said Hornblower. "We're not so lucky. And we've got to get the grain on board first. Get those hatches unbattened."

In ordinary conditions a working party of two or three hundred men from the *Indefatigable* would have made short work of getting in the cargo from the lighters, but now it had to be done by the longboat's complement of eighteen. Luckily Pellew had had the forethought and kindness to have the ballast struck out of the holds, or they would have had to do that weary job first.

"Tail onto those tackles, men," said Hornblower.

Pellew saw the first bundle of grain sacks rise slowly into the air from the lighter, and swung over and down the *Caroline*'s hatchway.

"He'll be all right," he decided. "Man the capstan and get under weigh, if you please, Mr. Bolton."

Hornblower, directing the work on the tackles, heard Pellew's voice come to him through the speaking trumpet.

"Good luck, Mr. Hornblower. Report in three weeks at Gibraltar."

"Very good, sir. Thank you, sir."

Hornblower turned back to find a seaman at his elbow knuckling his forehead.

"Beg pardon, sir. But can you hear those cattle bell-erin', sir? 'Tis mortal hot, an' 'tis water they want, sir."

"Hell," said Hornblower.

He would never get the cattle on board before nightfall.

He left a small party at work transferring cargo, and with the rest of the men he began to extemporise a method of watering the unfortunate cattle in the lighter. Half of *Caroline*'s hold space was filled with water barrels and fodder, but it was an awkward business getting water down to the lighter with pump and hose, and the poor brutes down there surged about uncontrollably at the prospect of water. Hornblower saw the lighter heel and almost capsize; one of his men—luckily one who could swim—went hastily overboard from the lighter to avoid being crushed to death.

"Hell," said Hornblower, again, and that was by no means the last time.

Without any skilled advice he was having to learn the business of managing livestock at sea; each moment brought its lessons. A naval officer on active service indeed found himself engaged on strange duties. It was well after dark before Hornblower called a halt to the labours of his men, and it was before dawn that he roused them up to work again. It was still early in the morning that the last of the grain sacks was stowed away and Hornblower had to face the operation of swaying up the cattle from the lighter. After their night down there, with little water and less food, they were in no mood to be trifled with, but it was easier at first while they were crowded together. A bellyband was slipped round the nearest, the tackle hooked on, and the animal was swayed up, lowered to the deck through an opening in the gangways, and herded into one of the stalls with ease. The seamen, shouting and waving their shirts, thought it was great fun, but they were not sure when the next one, released from its bellyband, went on the rampage and chased them about the deck, threatening death with its horns, until it wandered into its stall where the bar would be promptly dropped to shut it in. Hornblower, looking at the sun rising rapidly in the east, did not think it fun at all.

And the emptier the lighter became, the more room cattle had to rush about in it; to capture each one so a put a bellyband on it was a desperate adventure. Nor we those half-wild bullocks soothed by the sight of their companions being successively hauled bellowing into the air over their heads. Before the day was half done Hornblower's men were as weary as if they had fought a battle, and there was not one of them who would not gladly have quitted this novel employment in exchange for some normal seaman's duty like going aloft to reef topsails on a stormy night. As soon as Hornblower had the notion of dividing the interior of the lighter up into sections with barricades of stout spars the work became easier, but it took time, and before it was done the cattle had already suffered a couple of casualties—weaker members of the herd crushed underfoot in the course of the wild rushes about the lighter.

And there was a distraction when a boat came out from the shore, with swarthy Moors at the oars and the treasurer in the stern. Hornblower left Tapling to negotiate—apparently the Bey at least had not been so frightened of the plague as to forget to ask for his money. All Hornblower insisted upon was that the boat should keep well to leeward, and the money was floated off to it headed up in an empty rum-puncheon. Night found not more than half the cattle in the stalls on board, with Hornblower worrying about feeding and watering them, and snatching at hints diplomatically won from those members of his crew who had had bucolic experience. But the earliest dawn saw him driving his men to work again, and deriving a momentary satisfaction from the sight of Tapling having to leap for his life to the gangway out of reach of a maddened bullock which was charging about the deck and refusing to enter a stall. And by the time the last animal was safely packed in Hornblower was faced with another problem—that of dealing with what one of the men elegantly

213

d "mucking out." Fodder—water—mucking out; deckload of cattle seemed to promise enough work in lf to keep his eighteen men busy, without any thought the needs of handling the ship.

But there were advantages about the men being kept busy, as Hornblower grimly decided; there had not been a single mention of plague since the work began. The anchorage where the *Caroline* lay was exposed to northeasterly winds, and it was necessary that he should take her out to sea before such a wind should blow. He mustered his men to divide them into watches; he was the only navigator, so that he had to appoint the coxswain and the under-coxswain, Jordan, as officers of the watch. Someone volunteered as cook, and Hornblower, running his eye over his assembled company, appointed Tapling as cook's mate. Tapling opened his mouth to protest, but there was that in Hornblower's expression which cut the protest short. There was no bosun, no carpenter—no surgeon either, as Hornblower pointed out to himself gloomily. But on the other hand if the need for a doctor should arise it would, he hoped, be mercifully brief.

"Port watch, loose the jibs and main tops'l," ordered Hornblower. "Starboard watch, man the capstan."

So began that voyage of H.M. transport brig *Caroline* which became legendary (thanks to the highly coloured accounts retailed by the crew during innumerable dogwatches in later commissions) throughout the King's navy. The *Caroline* spent her three weeks of quarantine in homeless wanderings about the western Mediterranean. It was necessary that she should keep close up to the Straits, for fear lest the westerlies and the prevailing inward set of the current should take her out of reach of Gibraltar when the time came, so she beat about between the coasts of Spain and Africa trailing behind her a growing farmyard stench. The *Caroline* was a worn-out ship; with any sort of sea running she leaked like a sieve; and there were always

hands at work on the pumps, either pumping her out
pumping seawater onto her deck to clean it or pumping u̖
fresh water for the cattle.

Her top hamper made her almost unmanageable in a
fresh breeze; her deck seams leaked, of course, when she
worked, allowing a constant drip of unspeakable filth
down below. The one consolation was in the supply of
fresh meat—a commodity some of Hornblower's men had
not tasted for three months. Hornblower recklessly sac-
rificed a bullock a day, for in that Mediterranean climate
meat could not be kept sweet. So his men feasted on
steaks and fresh tongues; there were plenty of men on
board who had never in their whole lives before eaten a
beef steak.

But fresh water was the trouble—it was a greater anxiety to Hornblower than ever it was to the average ship's
captain, for the cattle were always thirsty; twice Hornblower had to land a raiding party at dawn on the coast of
Spain, seize a fishing village, and fill his water casks in
the local stream.

It was a dangerous adventure, and the second landing
revealed the danger, for while the *Caroline* was trying to
claw off the land again a Spanish *guarda-costa* lugger
came gliding round the point with all sail set. Maxwell saw
her first, but Hornblower saw her before he could report
her presence.

"Very well, Maxwell," said Hornblower, trying to
sound composed.

He turned his glass upon her. She was no more than
three miles off, a trifle to windward, and the *Caroline* was
embayed, cut off by the land from all chance of escape.
The lugger could go three feet to her two, while the *Caroline*'s clumsy superstructure prevented her from lying
nearer than eight points to the wind. As Hornblower
gazed, the accumulated irritation of the past seventeen
days boiled over. He was furious with Fate for having

ıst this ridiculous mission on him. He hated the *roline* and her clumsiness and her stinks and her cargo. ıe raged against the destiny which had caught him in this hopeless position.

"Hell!" said Hornblower, actually stamping his feet on the upper gangway in his anger. "Hell *and* damnation!"

He was dancing with rage, he observed with some curiosity. But with his fighting madness at the boil there was no chance of his yielding without a struggle, and his mental convulsions resulted in his producing a scheme for action. How many men of a crew did a Spanish *guarda-costa* carry? Twenty? That would be an outside figure—those luggers were only intended to act against petty smugglers. And with surprise on his side there was still a chance, despite the four eight-pounders that the lugger carried.

"Pistols and cutlasses, men," he said. "Jordan, choose two men and show yourselves up here. But the rest of you keep under cover. Hide yourselves. Yes, Mr. Tapling, you may serve with us. See that you are armed."

No one would expect resistance from a laden cattle transport; the Spaniards would expect to find on board a crew of a dozen at most, and not a disciplined force of twenty. The problem lay in luring the lugger within reach.

"Full and by," called Hornblower down to the helmsman below. "Be ready to jump, men. Maxwell, if a man shows himself before my order shoot him with your own hand. You hear me? That's an order, and you disobey me at your peril."

"Aye aye, sir," said Maxwell.

The lugger was romping up towards them; even in that light air there was a white wave under her sharp bows. Hornblower glanced up to make sure that the *Caroline* was displaying no colours. That made his plan legal under the laws of war. The report of a gun and a puff of smoke came from the lugger as she fired across the *Caroline*'s bows.

"I'm going to heave-to, Jordan," said Hornblower. "Main tops'l braces. Helm-a-lee."

The *Caroline* came to the wind and lay there wallowing, a surrendered and helpless ship apparently, if ever there was one.

"Not a sound, men," said Hornblower.

The cattle bellowed mournfully. Here came the lugger, her crew plainly visible now. Hornblower could see an officer clinging to the mainshrouds ready to board, but no one else seemed to have a care in the world. Everyone seemed to be looking up at the clumsy superstructure and laughing at the farmyard noises issuing from it.

"Wait, men, wait," said Hornblower.

The lugger was coming alongside when Hornblower suddenly realised, with a hot flood of blood under his skin, that he himself was unarmed. He had told his men to take pistols and cutlasses; he had advised Tapling to arm himself, and yet he had clean forgotten about his own need for weapons. But it was too late now to try to remedy that. Someone in the lugger hailed in Spanish, and Hornblower spread his hands in a show of incomprehension. Now they were alongside.

"Come on, men!" shouted Hornblower.

He ran across the superstructure and with a gulp he flung himself across the gap at the officer in the shrouds. He gulped again as he went through the air; he fell with all his weight on the unfortunate man, clasped him round the shoulders, and fell with him to the deck. There were shouts and yells behind him as the *Caroline* spewed up her crew into the lugger. A rush of feet, a clatter and a clash. Hornblower got to his feet empty-handed. Maxwell was just striking down a man with his cutlass. Tapling was heading a rush forward into the bows, waving a cutlass and yelling like a madman. Then it was all over; the astonished Spaniards were unable to lift a hand in their own defence.

217

So it came about that on the twenty-second day of her quarantine the *Caroline* came into Gibraltar Bay with a captured *guarda-costa* lugger under her lee. A thick barnyard stench trailed with her, too, but at least, when Hornblower went on board the *Indefatigable* to make his report, he had a suitable reply ready for Mr. Midshipman Bracegirdle.

"Hullo, Noah, how are Shem and Ham?" asked Mr. Bracegirdle.

"Shem and Ham have taken a prize," said Hornblower. "I regret that Mr. Bracegirdle can't say the same."

But the chief commissary of the squadron, when Hornblower reported to him, had a comment to which even Hornblower was unable to make a reply.

"Do you mean to tell me, Mr. Hornblower," said the chief commissary, "that you allowed your men to eat fresh beef? A bullock a day for your eighteen men? There must have been plenty of ship's provisions on board. That was wanton extravagance, Mr. Hornblower. I'm surprised at you."

X

HORNBLOWER
the Duchess, and the Devil

Acting-Lieutenant Hornblower was bringing the sloop *Le Reve,* prize of H.M.S. *Indefatigable,* to anchor in Gibraltar Bay. He was nervous; if anyone had asked him if he thought that all the telescopes in the Mediterranean Fleet were trained upon him he would have laughed at the fantastic suggestion, but he felt as if they were. Nobody ever gauged more cautiously the strength of the gentle following breeze, or estimated more anxiously the distances between the big anchored ships of the line, or calculated more carefully the space *Le Reve* would need to swing at her anchor. Jackson, his petty officer, was standing forward awaiting the order to take in the jib, and he acted quickly at Hornblower's hail.

"Helm-a-lee," said Hornblower next, and *Le Reve* rounded into the wind. "Brail up!"

Le Reve crept forward, her momentum diminishing as the wind took her way off her.

"Let's go!"

The cable growled a protest as the anchor took it out through the hawsehole—that welcome splash of the anchor, telling of the journey's end. Hornblower watched carefully while *Le Reve* took up on her cable, and then relaxed a little. He had brought the prize safely in, The commodore—Captain Sir Edward Pellew of H.M.S. *Indefatigable*—had clearly not yet returned, so that it was Hornblower's duty to report to the port admiral.

"Get the boat hoisted out," he ordered, and then, remembering his humanitarian duty, "And you can let the prisoners up on deck."

They had been battened down below for the last forty-eight hours, because the fear of a recapture was the nightmare of every prizemaster. But here in the Bay with the Mediterranean fleet all round that danger was at an end. Two hands at the oars of the gig sent her skimming over the water, and in ten minutes Hornblower was reporting his arrival to the admiral.

"You say she shows a fair turn of speed?" said the latter, looking over at the prize.

"Yes, sir. And she's handy enough," said Hornblower.

"I'll purchase her into the service. Never enough despatch vessels," mused the admiral.

Even with that hint it was a pleasant surprise to Hornblower when he received heavily sealed official orders, and opening them, read that "you are hereby requested and required—" to take H.M. sloop *Le Reve* under his command, and to proceed "with the utmost expedition" to Plymouth as soon as the despatches destined for England should be put in his charge. It was an independent command; it was a chance of seeing England again (it was three years since Hornblower had last set foot on the English shore) and it was a high professional compliment. But there was another letter, delivered at the same moment, which Hornblower read with less elation.

"Their Excellencies, Major-General Sir Hew and Lady Dalrymple, request the pleasure of Acting-Lieutenant Horatio Hornblower's company at dinner today, at three o'clock, at Government House."

It might be a pleasure to dine with the governor of Gibraltar and his lady, but it was only a mixed pleasure, at best, for an acting-lieutenant with a single sea chest, faced with the need to dress himself suitably for such a function. Yet it was hardly possible for a young man to walk up to

Government House from the landing slip without a thrill of excitement, especially as his friend Mr. Midshipman Bracegirdle, who came from a wealthy family and had a handsome allowance, had lent him a pair of the finest white stockings of China silk—Bracegirdle's calves were plump, and Hornblower's were skinny, but that difficulty had been artistically circumvented. Two small pads of oakum, some strips of sticking plaster from the surgeon's stores, and Hornblower now had a couple of legs of which no one need be ashamed. He could put his left leg forward to make his bow without any fear of wrinkles in his stockings, and sublimely conscious, as Bracegirdle said, of a leg of which any gentleman would be proud.

At Government House the usual polished and languid aide-de-camp took charge of Hornblower and led him forward. He made his bow to Sir Hew, a red-faced and fussy old gentleman, and to Lady Dalrymple, a red-faced and fussy old lady.

"Mr. Hornblower," said the latter, "I must present you —Your Grace, this is Mr. Hornblower, the new captain of Le Reve. Her Grace the Duchess of Wharfedale."

A duchess, no less! Hornblower poked forward his padded leg, pointed his toe, laid his hand on his heart and bowed with all the depth the tightness of his breeches allowed—he had still been growing when he bought them on joining the Indefatigable. Bold blue eyes, and a once beautiful middle-aged face.

"So this 'ere's the feller in question?" said the Duchess. "Matilda, my dear, are you going to hentrust me to a hinfant in harms?"

The startling vulgarity of the accent took Hornblower's breath away. He had been ready for almost anything except that a superbly dressed duchess should speak in the accent of Seven Dials. He raised his eyes to stare, while forgetting to straighten himself up, standing with his chin poked forward and his hand still on his heart.

"You look like a gander on a green," said the Duchess. "I hexpects you to 'iss hany moment."

She stuck her own chin out and swung it from side to side with her hands on her knees in a perfect imitation of a belligerent goose, apparently with so close a resemblance to Hornblower as well as to excite a roar of laughter from the other guests. Hornblower stood in blushing confusion.

"Don't be 'ard on the young feller," said the Duchess, coming to his defence and patting him on the shoulder. "'E's on'y young, an' thet's nothink to be ashamed of. Somethink to be prard of, for thet metter, to be trusted with a ship at thet hage."

It was lucky that the announcement of dinner came to save Hornblower from the further confusion into which this kindly remark had thrown him. Hornblower naturally found himself with the riff-raff, the tag-rag-and-bobtail of the middle of the table along with the other junior officers —Sir Hew sat at one end with the Duchess while Lady Dalrymple sat with a commodore at the other. Moreover there were not nearly as many women as men; that was only to be expected, as Gibraltar was, technically at least, a beleaguered fortress. So Hornblower had no woman on either side of him; at his right sat the young aide-de-camp who had first taken him in charge.

"Your health, Your Grace," said the commodore, looking down the length of the table and raising his glass.

"Thank'ee," replied the Duchess. "Just in time to save my life. I was wonderin' 'oo'd come to my rescue."

She raised her brimming glass to her lips and when she put it down again it was empty.

"A jolly boon companion you are going to have," said the aide-de-camp to Hornblower.

"How is she going to be my companion?" asked Hornblower, quite bewildered.

The aide-de-camp looked at him pityingly.

"So you have not been informed?" he asked. "As always the man most concerned is the last to know. When you sail with your despatches tomorrow you will have the honour of bearing Her Grace with you to England."

"God bless my soul," said Hornblower.

"Let's hope He does," said the aide-de-camp piously, nosing his wine. "Poor stuff this sweet Malaga is. Old Hare bought a job lot in '95, and every governor since then seems to think it's his duty to use it up."

"But who *is* she?" asked Hornblower.

"Her Grace the Duchess of Wharfedale," replied the aide-de-camp. "Did you not hear Lady Dalrymple's introduction?"

"But she doesn't talk like a duchess," protested Hornblower.

"No. The old Duke was in his dotage when he married her. She was an innkeeper's widow, so her friends say. You can imagine, if you like, what her enemies say."

"But what is she doing here?" went on Hornblower.

"She is on her way back to England. She was at Florence when the French marched in, I understand. She reached Leghorn, and bribed a coaster to bring her here. She asked Sir Hew to find her a passage, and Sir Hew asked the admiral—Sir Hew would ask anyone for anything on behalf of a duchess, even one said by her friends to be an innkeeper's widow."

"I see," said Hornblower.

There was a burst of merriment from the head of the table, and the Duchess was prodding the governor's scarlet-coated ribs with the handle of her knife, as if to make sure he saw the joke.

"Maybe you will not lack for mirth on your homeward voyage," said the aide-de-camp.

Just then a smoking sirloin of beef was put down in front of Hornblower, and all his other worries vanished before the necessity of carving it and remembering his

223

manners. He took the carving knife and fork gingerly in his hands and glanced round at the company.

"May I help you to some of this beef, Your Grace? Madam? Sir? Well done or underdone, sir? A little of the brown fat?"

In the hot room the sweat ran down his face as he wrestled with the joint; he was fortunate that most of the guests desired helpings from the other removes so that he had little carving to do. He put a couple of haggled slices on his own plate as the simplest way of concealing the worst results of his own handiwork.

"Beef from Tetuan," sniffed the aide-de-camp. "Tough and stringly."

That was all very well for a governor's aide-de-camp—he could not guess how delicious was this food to a young naval officer fresh from beating about at sea in an overcrowded frigate. Even the thought of having to act as host to a duchess could not entirely spoil Hornblower's appetite. And the final dishes, the meringues and macaroons, the custards and the fruits, were ecstasy for a young man whose last pudding had been currant duff last Sunday.

"Those sweet things spoil a man's palate," said the aide-de-camp—much Hornblower cared.

They were drinking formal toasts now. Hornblower stood for the King and the royal family, and raised his glass for the Duchess.

"And now for the enemy," said Sir Hew, "may their treasure galleons try to cross the Atlantic."

"A supplement to that, Sir Hew," said the commodore at the other end, "may the Dons make up their minds to leave Cadiz."

There was a growl almost like wild animals from round the table. Most of the naval officers present were from Jervis' Mediterranean squadron which had beaten about in the Atlantic for the past several months hoping to catch the Spaniards should they come out. Jervis had to detach his ships to Gibraltar two at a time to replenish their stores, and these officers were from the two ships of the line present at the moment in Gibraltar.

"Johnny Jervis would say amen to that," said Sir Hew. "A bumper to the Dons then, gentlemen, and may they come out from Cadiz."

The ladies left them then, gathered together by Lady Dalrymple, and as soon as it was decently possible Hornblower made his excuses and slipped away, determined not to be heavy with wine the night before he sailed in independent command.

Maybe the prospect of the coming on board of the Duchess was a useful counter-irritant, and saved Hornblower from worrying too much about his first command. He was up before dawn—before even the brief Mediterranean twilight had begun—to see that his precious ship was in condition to face the sea, and the enemies who swarmed upon the sea. He had four popgun four-pounders to deal with those enemies, which meant that he was safe from no one; his was the weakest vessel at sea, for the smallest trading brig carried a more powerful armament. So that like all weak creatures his only safety lay in flight—Hornblower looked aloft in the half-light, where the sails would be set on which so much might depend. He went over the watch bill with his two watch-keeping officers, Midshipman Hunter and Master's Mate Winyatt, to make sure that every man of his crew of eleven knew his duty. Then all that remained was to put on his smartest seagoing uniform, try to eat breakfast, and wait for the Duchess.

She came early, fortunately; Their Excellencies had had to rise at a most unpleasant hour to see her off. Mr. Hunter reported the approach of the governor's launch with suppressed excitement.

"Thank you, Mr. Hunter," said Hornblower coldly— that was what the service demanded, even though not so

225

many weeks before they had been playing follow-my-leader through the *Indefatigable*'s rigging together.

The launch swirled alongside, and two neatly dressed seamen hooked on the ladder. *Le Reve* had such a small freeboard that boarding her presented no problem even for ladies. The governor stepped on board to the twittering of the only two pipes *Le Reve* could muster, and Lady Dalrymple followed him. Then came the Duchess, and the Duchess's companion; the latter was a younger woman, as beautiful as the Duchess must once have been. A couple of aides-de-camp followed, and by that time the minute deck of *Le Reve* was positively crowded, so that there was no room left to bring up the Duchess's baggage.

"Let us show you your quarters, Your Grace," said the governor.

Lady Dalrymple squawked her sympathy at sight of the minute cabin, which the two cots almost filled, and everyone's head, inevitably, bumped against the deck beam above.

"We shall live through it," said the Duchess, stoically, "an' that's more than many a man makin' a little trip to Tyburn could say."

One of the aides-de-camp produced a last minute packet of despatches and demanded Hornblower's signature on the receipt; the last farewells were said, and Sir Hew and Lady Dalrymple went down the side again to the twittering of the pipes.

"Man the windlass!" bellowed Hornblower the moment the launch's crew bent to their oars.

A few seconds' lusty work brought *Le Reve* up to her anchor.

"Anchor's aweigh, sir," reported Winyatt.

"Jib halliards!" shouted Hornblower. "Mains'l halliards!"

Le Reve came round before the wind as her sails were set and her rudder took a grip on the water. Everyone was so busy catting the anchor and setting sail that it was Hornblower himself who dipped his colours in salute as *Le Reve* crept out beyond the Mole before the gentle southeaster, and dipped her nose to the first of the big Atlantic rollers coming in through the Gut. Through the skylight beside him he heard a clatter and a wail, as something fell in the cabin with that first roll, but he could spare no attention for the woman below. He had the glass to his eye now, training it first on Algeciras and then upon Tarifa—some well-manned privateer or ship of war might easily dash out to snap up such a defenceless prey as *Le Reve*. He could not relax while the forenoon watch wore on. They rounded Cape Marroqui and he set a course for St. Vincent, and then the mountains of southern Spain began to sink below the horizon. Cape Trafalgar was just visible on the starboard bow when at last he shut the telescope and began to wonder about dinner; it was pleasant to be captain of his own ship and to be able to order dinner when he chose. His aching legs told him he had been on his feet too long—eleven continuous hours; if the future brought him many independent commands he could wear himself out by this sort of behaviour.

Down below he relaxed gratefully on the locker, and sent the cook to knock at the Duchess's cabin door to ask with his compliments if all was well; he heard the Duchess's sharp voice saying that they needed nothing, not even dinner. Hornblower philosophically shrugged his shoulders and ate his dinner with a young man's appetite. He went on deck again as night closed in upon them; Winyatt had the watch.

"It's coming up thick, sir," he said.

So it was. The sun was invisible on the horizon, engulfed in watery mist. It was the price he had to pay for a fair wind, he knew; in the winter months in these latitudes there was always likely to be fog where the cool land breeze reached the Atlantic.

"It'll be thicker still by morning," he said, gloomily, and revised his night orders, setting a course due west instead of west by north as he originally intended. He wanted to make certain of keeping clear of Cape St. Vincent in the event of fog.

That was one of those minute trifles which may affect a man's whole after life—Hornblower had plenty of time later to reflect on what might have happened had he not ordered that alteration of course. During the night he was often on deck, peering through the increasing mist, but at the time when the crisis came he was down below snatching a little sleep. What woke him was a seaman shaking his shoulder violently.

"Please, sir. Please, sir. Mr. Hunter sent me. Please, sir, won't you come on deck, he says, sir."

"I'll come," said Hornblower, blinking himself awake and rolling out of his cot.

The faintest beginnings of dawn were imparting some slight luminosity to the mist which was close about them. *Le Reve* was lurching over an ugly sea with barely enough wind behind her to give her steerage way. Hunter was standing with his back to the wheel in an attitude of tense anxiety.

"Listen!" he said, as Hornblower appeared.

He half-whispered the word, and in his excitement he omitted the "sir" which was due to his captain—and in his excitement Hornblower did not notice the omission. Hornblower listened. He heard the shipboard noises he could expect—the clattering of the blocks as *Le Reve* lurched, the sound of the sea at her bows. Then he heard other shipboard noises. There were other blocks clattering; the sea was breaking beneath other bows.

"There's a ship close alongside," said Hornblower.

"Yes, sir," said Hunter. "And after I sent below for you I heard an order given. And it was in Spanish—some foreign tongue, anyway."

The tenseness of fear was all about the little ship like the fog.

"Call all hands. Quietly," said Hornblower.

But as he gave the order he wondered if it would be any use. He could send his men to their stations, he could man and load his four-pounders, but if that ship out there in the fog was of any force greater than a merchant ship he was in deadly peril. Then he tried to comfort himself—perhaps the ship was some fat Spanish galleon bulging with treasure, and were he to board her boldly she would become his prize and make him rich for life.

"A 'appy Valentine's day to you," said a voice beside him, and he nearly jumped out of his skin with surprise. He had actually forgotten the presence of the Duchess on board.

"Stop that row!" he whispered furiously at her, and she pulled up abruptly in astonishment. She was bundled up in a cloak and hood against the damp air, and no further detail could be seen of her in the darkness and fog.

"May I hask—" she began.

"Shut up!" whispered Hornblower.

A harsh voice could be heard through the fog, other voices repeating the order, whistles being blown, much noise and bustle.

"That's Spanish, sir, isn't it?" whispered Hunter.

"Spanish for certain. Calling the watch. Listen!"

The two double-strokes of a ship's bell came to them across the water. Four bells in the morning watch. And instantly from all round them a dozen other bells could be heard, as if echoing the first.

"We're in the middle of a fleet, by God!" whispered Hunter.

"Big ships, too, sir," supplemented Winyatt who had joined them with the calling of all hands. "I could hear half a dozen different pipes when they called the watch."

"The Dons are out, then," said Hunter.

And the course I set has taken us into the midst of them, thought Hornblower bitterly. The coincidence was maddening, heartbreaking. But he forebore to waste breath over it. He even suppressed the frantic gibe that rose to his lips at the memory of Sir Hew's toast about the Spaniards coming out from Cadiz.

"They're setting more sail," was what he said. "Dagoes snug down at night, just like some fat Indiaman. They only set their t'gallants at daybreak."

All round them through the fog could be heard the whine of sheaves in blocks, the stamp-and-go of the men at the halliards, the sound of ropes thrown on decks, the chatter of a myriad voices.

"They make enough noise about it, blast 'em," said Hunter.

The tension under which he laboured was apparent as he stood straining to peer through the mist.

"Please God they're on a different course to us," said Winyatt, more sensibly. "Then we'll soon be through 'em."

"Not likely," said Hornblower.

Le Reve was running almost directly before what little wind there was; if the Spaniards were beating against it or had it on their beam they would be crossing her course at a considerable angle, so that the volume of sound from the nearest ship would have diminished or increased considerably in this time, and there was no indication of that whatever. It was far more likely that Le Reve had overhauled the Spanish fleet under its nightly short canvas and had sailed forward into the middle of it. It was a problem what to do next in that case, to shorten sail, or to heave-to, and let the Spaniards get ahead of them again, or to clap on sail to pass through. But the passage of the minutes brought clear proof that fleet and sloop were on practically the same course, as otherwise they could hardly fail to pass some ship close. As long as the mist held they were safest as they were.

But that was hardly to be expected with the coming of day.

"Can't we alter course, sir?" asked Winyatt.

"Wait," said Hornblower.

In the faint growing light he had seen shreds of denser mist blowing past them—a clear indication that they could not hope for continuous fog. At that moment they ran out of a fog bank into a clear patch of water.

"There she is, by God!" said Hunter.

Both officers and seamen began to move about in sudden panic.

"Stand still, damn you!" rasped Hornblower, his nervous tension releasing itself in the fierce monosyllables.

Less than a cable's length away a three-decked ship of the line was standing along parallel to them on their starboard side. Ahead and on the port side could be seen the outlines, still shadowy, of other battleships. Nothing could save them if they drew attention to themselves; all that could be done was to keep going as if they had as much right there as the ships of the line. It was possible that in the happy-go-lucky Spanish navy the officer of the watch over there did not know that no sloop like *Le Reve* was attached to the fleet—or even possibly by a miracle there *might* be one. *Le Reve* was French built and French rigged, after all. Side by side *Le Reve* and the battleship sailed over the lumpy sea. They were within point-blank range of fifty big guns, when one well aimed shot would sink them. Hunter was uttering filthy curses under his breath, but discipline had asserted itself; a telescope over there on the Spaniard's deck would not discover any suspicious bustle on board the sloop. Another shred of fog drifted past them, and then they were deep in a fresh fog bank.

"Thank God!" said Hunter, indifferent to the contrast between this present piety and his preceding blasphemy.

"Hands wear ship," said Hornblower. "Lay her on the port tack."

There was no need to tell the hands to do it quietly; they were as well aware of their danger as anyone. *Le Reve* silently rounded-to, the sheets were hauled in and coiled down without a sound; and the sloop, as close to the wind as she would lie, heeled to the small wind, meeting the lumpy waves with her port bow.

"We'll be crossing their course now," said Hornblower.

"Please God it'll be under their sterns and not their bows," said Winyatt.

There was the Duchess still in her cloak and hood, standing right aft as much out of the way as possible.

"Don't you think Your Grace had better go below?" asked Hornblower, making use by a great effort of the formal form of address.

"Oh no, *please,*" said the Duchess. "I couldn't bear it."

Hornblower shrugged his shoulders, and promptly forgot the Duchess's presence again as a new anxiety struck him. He dived below and came up again with the two big sealed envelopes of despatches. He took a belaying pin from the rail and began very carefully to tie the envelopes to the pin with a bit of line.

"Please," said the Duchess, "please, Mr. Hornblower, tell me what you are doing?"

"I want to make sure these will sink when I throw them overboard if we're captured," said Hornblower grimly.

"Then they'll be lost for good?"

"Better that than that the Spaniards should read 'em," said Hornblower with all the patience he could muster.

"I could look after them for you," said the Duchess. "Indeed I could."

Hornblower looked keenly at her.

"No," he said, "they might search your baggage. Probably they would."

"Baggage!" said the Duchess. "As if I'd put them in my

baggage! I'll put them next my skin—they won't search *me* in any case. They'll never find 'em, not if I put 'em up my petticoats."

There was a brutal realism about those words that staggered Hornblower a little, but which also brought him to admit to himself that there was something in what the Duchess was saying.

"If they capture us—" said the Duchess, "I pray they won't but if they do—they'll never keep me prisoner. You know that. They'll send me to Lisbon or put me aboard a King's ship as soon as they can. Then the despatches will be delivered eventually. Late, but better late than never."

"That's so," mused Hornblower.

"I'll guard them like my life," said the Duchess. "I swear I'll never part from them. I'll tell no one I have them, not until I hand them to a King's Officer."

She met Hornblower's eyes with transparent honesty in her expression.

"Fog's thinning, sir," said Winyatt.

"Quick!" said the Duchess.

There was no time for further debate. Hornblower slipped the envelopes from their binding of rope and handed them over to her, and replaced the belaying pin in the rail.

"These damned French fashions," said the Duchess. "I was right when I said I'd put these letters up my petticoats. There's no room in my bosom."

Certainly the upper part of her gown was not at all capacious; the waist was close up under the armpits and the rest of the dress hung down from there quite straight in utter defiance of anatomy.

"Give me a yard of that rope, quick!" said the Dutchess.

Winyatt cut her a length of the line with his knife and handed it to her. Already she was hauling at her petticoats; the appalled Hornblower saw a gleam of white thigh

233

above her stocking tops before he tore his glance away. The fog was certainly thinning.

"You can look at me now," said the Duchess, but her petticoats only just fell in time as Hornblower looked round again. "They're inside my shift, next my skin as I promised. With these Directory fashions no one wears stays any more. So I tied the rope round my waist outside my shift. One envelope is flat against my chest and the other against my back. Would you suspect anything?"

She turned round for Hornblower's inspection.

"No, nothing shows," he said. "I must thank Your Grace."

"There is a certain thickening," said the Duchess, "but it does not matter what the Spaniards suspect as long as they do not suspect the truth."

Momentary cessation of the need for action brought some embarrassment to Hornblower. To discuss with a woman her shift and stays—or the absence of them—was a strange thing to do.

A watery sun, still nearly level, was breaking through the mist and shining in his eyes. The mainsail cast a watery shadow on the deck. With every second the sun was growing brighter.

"Here it comes," said Hunter.

The horizon ahead expanded rapidly, from a few yards to a hundred, from a hundred yards to half a mile. The sea was covered with ships. No less than six were in plain sight, four ships of the line and two big frigates, with the red-and-gold of Spain at their mastheads, and, what marked them even more obviously as Spaniards, huge wooden crosses hanging at their peaks.

"Wear ship again, Mr. Hunter," said Hornblower. "Back into the fog."

That was the one chance of safety. Those ships running down towards them were bound to ask questions, and they could not hope to avoid them all. *Le Reve* spun round on

234

her heel, but the fog bank from which she had emerged was already attenuated, sucked up by the thirsty sun. They could see a drifting stretch of it ahead, but it was lazily rolling away from them at the same time as it was dwindling. The heavy sound of a cannon shot reached their ears, and close on their starboard quarter a ball threw up a fountain of water before plunging into the side of a wave just ahead. Hornblower looked round just in time to see the last of the puff of smoke from the bows of the frigate astern pursuing them.

"Starboard two points," he said to the helmsman, trying to gauge at one and the same moment the frigate's course, the direction of the wind, the bearing of the other ships, and that of the thin last nucleus of that wisp of fog.

"Starboard two points," said the helmsman.

"Fore and main sheets!" said Hunter.

Another shot, far astern this time but laid true for line; Hornblower suddenly remembered the Duchess.

"You must go below, Your Grace," he said, curtly.

"Oh, no, no, no!" burst out the Duchess with angry vehemence. "Please let me stay here. I can't go below to where that seasick maid of mine lies hoping to die. Not in that stinking box of a cabin."

There would be no safety in that cabin, Hornblower reflected—*Le Reve*'s scantlings were too fragile to keep out any shot at all. Down below the waterline in the hold the women might be safe, but they would have to lie flat on top of beef barrels.

"Sail ahead!" screamed the lookout.

The mist there was parting and the outline of a ship of the line was emerging from it, less than a mile away and on almost the same course as *Le Reve*'s. Thud—thud from the frigate astern. Those gunshots by now would have warned the whole Spanish fleet that something unusual was happening. The battleship ahead would know that the little sloop was being pursued. A ball tore through the air close by, with its usual terrifying noise. The ship ahead was awaiting their coming; Hornblower saw her top-sails slowly turning.

"Hands to the sheets!" said Hornblower. "Mr. Hunter, jibe her over."

Le Reve came round again, heading for the lessening gap on the port side. The frigate astern turned to intercept. More jets of smoke from her bows. With an appalling noise a shot passed within a few feet of Hornblower, so that the wind of it made him stagger. There was a hole in the mainsail.

"Your Grace," said Hornblower, "those aren't warning shots—"

It was the ship of the line which fired then, having succeeded in clearing away and manning some of her upper deck guns. It was as if the end of the world had come. One shot hit *Le Reve*'s hull, and they felt the deck heave under their feet as a result as if the little ship were disintegrating. But the mast was hit at the same moment, stays and shrouds parting, splinters raining all round. Mast, sails, boom, gaff and all went from above them over the side to windward. The wreckage dragged in the sea and turned the helpless wreck round with the last of her way. The little group aft stood momentarily dazed.

"Anybody hurt?" asked Hornblower, recovering himself.

"On'y a scratch, sir," said one voice.

It seemed a miracle that no one was killed.

"Carpenter's mate, sound the well," said Hornblower and then, recollecting himself, "No, damn it. Belay that order. If the Dons can save the ship, let 'em try."

Already the ship of the line whose salvo had done the damage was filling her topsails again and bearing away from them, while the frigate which had pursued them was running down on them fast. A wailing figure came scrambling out of the after hatchway. It was the Duchess's maid, so mad with terror that her seasickness was forgotten. The Duchess put a protective arm round her and tried to comfort her.

"Your Grace had better look to your baggage," said Hornblower. "No doubt you'll be leaving us shortly for other quarters with the Dons. I hope you will be more comfortable."

He was trying desperately hard to speak in a matter of fact way, as if nothing out of the ordinary were happening, as if he were not soon to be a prisoner of the Spaniards; but the Duchess saw the working of the usually firm mouth, and marked how the hands were tight clenched.

"How can I tell you how sorry I am about this?" asked the Duchess, her voice soft with pity.

"That makes it the harder for me to bear," said Hornblower, and he even forced a smile.

The Spanish frigate was just rounding-to, a cable's length to windward.

"Please, sir," said Hunter.

"Well?"

"We can fight, sir. You give the word. Cold shot to drop in the boats when they try to board. We could beat 'em off once, perhaps."

Hornblower's tortured misery nearly made him snap out, "Don't be a fool," but he checked himself. He contented himself with pointing to the frigate. Twenty guns were glaring at them at far less than point-blank range. The very boat the frigate was hoisting out would be manned by at least twice as many men as *Le Reve* carried —she was no bigger than many a pleasure yacht. It was not odds of ten to one, or a hundred to one, but odds of ten thousand to one.

"I understand, sir," said Hunter.

Now the Spanish frigate's boat was in the water, about to shove off.

"A private word with you, please, Mr. Hornblower," said the Duchess suddenly.

Hunter and Winyatt heard what she said, and withdrew out of earshot.

"Yes, Your Grace?" said Hornblower.

The Duchess stood there, still with her arm round her weeping maid, looking straight at him.

"I'm no more of a Duchess than you are," she said.

"Good God!" said Hornblower. "Who—who are you, then?"

"Kitty Cobham."

The name meant a little to Hornblower, but only a little.

"You're too young for that name to have any memories for you, Mr. Hornblower, I see. It's five years since last I trod the boards."

That was it. Kitty Cobham the actress.

"I can't tell it all now," said the Duchess—the Spanish boat was dancing over the waves towards them. "But when the French marched into Florence that was only the last of my misfortunes. I was penniless when I escaped from them. Who would lift a finger for a onetime actress —one who had been betrayed and deserted? What was I to do? But a duchess—that was another story. Old Dalrymple at Gibraltar could not do enough for the Duchess of Wharfedale."

"Why did you choose that title?" asked Hornblower in spite of himself.

"I knew of her," said the Duchess with a shrug of the shoulders. "I knew her to be what I played her as. That was why I chose her—I always played character parts better than straight comedy. And not nearly so tedious in a long role."

"But my despatches!" said Hornblower in a sudden panic of realisation. "Give them back, quick."

"If you wish me to," said the Duchess. "But I can still

238

be the Duchess when the Spaniards come. They will still set me free as speedily as they can. I'll guard those despatches better than my life—I swear it, I swear it! In less than a month I'll deliver them, if you trust me."

Hornblower looked at the pleading eyes. She might be a spy, ingeniously trying to preserve the despatches from being thrown overboard before the Spaniards took possession. But no spy could have hoped that *Le Reve* would run into the midst of the Spanish fleet.

"I made use of the bottle, I know," said the Duchess. "I drank. Yes, I did. But I stayed sober in Gibraltar, didn't I? And I won't touch a drop, not a drop, until I'm in England. I'll swear that, too. Please, sir—please. I beg of you. Let me do what I can for my country."

It was a strange decision for a man of nineteen to have to make—one who had never exchanged a word with an actress in his life before. A harsh voice overside told him that the Spanish boat was about to hook on.

"Keep them, then," said Hornblower. "Deliver them when you can."

He had not taken his eyes from her face. He was looking for a gleam of triumph in her expression. Had he seen anything of the sort he would have torn the despatches from her body at that moment. But all he saw was the natural look of pleasure, and it was then that he made up his mind to trust her—not before.

"Oh, thank you, sir," said the Duchess.

The Spanish boat had hooked on now, and a Spanish lieutenant was awkwardly trying to climb aboard. He arrived on the deck on his hands and knees, and Hornblower stepped over to receive him as he got to his feet. Captor and captive exchanged bows. Hornblower could not understand what the Spaniard said, but obviously they were formal sentences that he was using. The Spaniard caught sight of the two women aft and halted in surprise;

239

Hornblower, hastily made the presentation in what he hoped was Spanish.

"*Señor el tenente Espanol*," he said. "*Señora la Duquesa de Wharfedale.*"

The title clearly had its effect; the lieutenant bowed profoundly, and his bow was received with the most lofty aloofness by the Duchess. Hornblower could be sure the despatches were safe. That was some alleviation of the misery of standing here on the deck of his water-logged little ship, a prisoner of the Spaniards. As he waited he heard, from far to leeward, roll upon roll of thunder coming up against the wind. No thunder could endure that long. What he could hear must be the broadsides of ships in action—of fleets in action. Somewhere over there by Cape St. Vincent the British fleet must have caught the Spaniards at last. Fiercer and fiercer sounded the roll of the artillery. There was excitement among the Spaniards who had scrambled onto the deck of *Le Reve,* while Hornblower stood bareheaded waiting to be taken into captivity.

Captivity was a dreadful thing. Once the numbness had worn off Hornblower came to realize what a dreadful thing it was. Not even the news of the dreadful battering which the Spanish navy had received at St. Vincent could relieve the misery and despair of being a prisoner. It was not the physical conditions—ten square feet of floor space per man in an empty sail loft at Ferrol along with other captive warrant officers—for they were no worse than what a junior officer often had to put up with at sea. It was the loss of freedom, the fact of being a captive, that was so dreadful.

There was four months of it before the first letter came through to Hornblower; the Spanish government, inefficient in all ways, had the worst postal system in Europe. But here was the letter, addressed and re-addressed, now safely in his hands after he had practically snatched it from a stupid Spanish non-commissioned officer who had been puzzling over the strange name. Hornblower did not know the handwriting, and when he broke the seal and opened the letter the salutation made him think for a moment that he had opened someone else's letter.

"Darling Boy" it began. Now who on earth would call him that? He read on in a dream.

Darling Boy—

I hope it will give you happiness to hear that what you gave me has reached its destination. They told me, when I delivered it, that you are a prisoner, and my heart bleeds for you. And they told me too that they were pleased with you for what you had done. And one of those admirals is a shareholder in Drury Lane. Whoever would have thought of such a thing? But he smiled at me, and I smiled at him. I did not know he was a shareholder then, and I only smiled out of the kindness of my heart. And all that I told him about my dangers and perils with my precious burden were only histrionic exercises, I am afraid. Yet he believed me, and so struck was he by my smile and my adventures, that he demanded a part for me from Sherry, and behold, now I am playing second lead, usually a tragic mother, and receiving the acclaim of the groundlings. There are compensations in growing old, which I am discovering too. And I have not tasted wine since I saw you last, nor shall I ever again. As one more reward my admiral promised me that he would forward this letter to you in the next cartel—an expression which no doubt means more to you than to me. I only hope that it reaches you in good time and brings you comfort in your affliction. I pray nightly for you.

Ever your devoted friend,
Katharine Cobham

241

Comfort in his affliction? A little, perhaps. There was some comfort in knowing that the despatches had been delivered; there was some comfort in a secondhand report that Their Lordships were pleased with him. There was comfort even in knowing that the Duchess was re-established on the stage. But the sum total was nothing compared with his misery.

Here was a guard come to bring him to the Commandant, and beside the Commandant was the Irish renegade who served as interpreter. There were further papers on the Commandant's desk—it looked as if the same cartel which had brought in Kitty Cobham's note had brought in letters for the Commandant.

"Good afternoon, sir," said the Commandant, always polite, offering a chair.

"Good afternoon, sir, and many thanks," said Hornblower. He was learning Spanish slowly and painfully.

"You have been promoted," said the Irishman in English.

"W-what?" said Hornblower.

"Promoted," said the Irishman. "Here is the letter— 'The Spanish authorities are informed that on account of his meritorious service the acting-commission of Mr. Horatio Hornblower, Midshipman and Acting-Lieutenant, has been confirmed. Their Lordships of the Admiralty express their confidence that Horatio Hornblower will be admitted immediately to the privileges of commissioned rank.' There you are, young man."

"My felicitations, sir," said the Commandant.

"Many thanks, sir," said Hornblower.

The Commandant was a kindly old gentleman with a pleasant smile for the awkward young man. He went on to say more, but Hornblower's Spanish was not equal to the technicalities he used, and Hornblower in despair looked at the interpreter.

"Now that you are a commissioned officer," said the latter, "you will be transferred to the quarters for captured officers."

"Thank you," said Hornblower.

"You will receive the half pay of your rank."

"Thank you."

"And your parole will be accepted. You will be at liberty to visit in the town and the neighbourhood for two hours each day on giving your parole."

"Thank you," said Hornblower.

Perhaps, during the long months which followed, it was some mitigation of his unhappiness that for two hours each day his parole gave him freedom; freedom to wander in the streets of the little town, to have a cup of chocolate or a glass of wine—providing he had any money—making polite and laborious conversation with Spanish soldiers or sailors or civilians. But it was better to spend his two hours wandering over the goat paths of the headland in the wind and the sun, in the companionship of the sea, which might alleviate the sick misery of captivity. There was slightly better food, slightly better quarters. And there was the knowledge that now he was a lieutenant, that he held the King's commission, that if ever, ever, the war should end and he should be set free he could starve on half pay—for with the end of the war there would be no employment for junior lieutenants. But he had earned his promotion. He had gained the approval of authority, that was something to think about on his solitary walks.

There came a day of southwesterly gales, with the wind shrieking in from across the Atlantic. Across three thousand miles of water it came, building up its strength unimpeded on its way, and heaping up the sea into racing mountain ridges which came crashing in upon the Spanish coast in thunder and spray. Hornblower stood on the headland above Ferrol Harbour, holding his worn greatcoat about him as he leaned forward into the wind to keep his footing. So powerful was the wind that it was difficult to breathe while facing it. If he turned his back he could breathe more easily, but then the wind blew his wild hair forward over his eyes, almost inverted his greatcoat over his head, and furthermore forced him into little tottering steps down the slope towards Ferrol whither he had no wish to return at present. For two hours he was alone and free, and those two hours were precious. He could breathe the Atlantic air, he could walk, he could do as he liked during that time. He could stare out to sea; it was not unusual to catch sight, from the headland, of some British ship of war which might be working slowly along the coast in the hope of snapping up a coasting vessel while keeping a watchful eye upon the Spanish naval activity. When such a ship went by during Hornblower's two hours of freedom, he would stand and gaze at it, as a man dying of thirst might gaze at a bucket of water held beyond his reach; he would note all the little details, the cut of the topsails and the style of the paint, while misery wrung his bowels. For this was the end of his second year as a prisoner of war. For twenty-two months, for twenty-two hours every day, he had been under lock and key, herded with five other junior lieutenants in a single room in the fortress of Ferrol. And today the wind roared by him, shouting in its outrageous freedom. He was facing into the wind; before him lay Corunna, its white houses resembling pieces of sugar scattered over the slopes. Between him and Corunna was all the open space of Corunna Bay, flogged white by the wind, and on his left hand was the narrow entrance to Ferrol Bay. On his right was the open Atlantic; from the foot of the low cliffs there the long wicked reef of the Dientes del Diablo —the Devil's Teeth—ran out to the northward, square across the path of the racing rollers driven by the wind. At half minute intervals the rollers would crash against the reef with an impact that shook even the solid headland on which Hornblower stood, and each roller dissolved into spray which was instantly whirled away by the wind to reveal again the long black tusks of the rocks.

Hornblower was not alone on the headland; a few yards away from him a Spanish militia artilleryman on lookout duty gazed with watery eyes through a telescope with which he continually swept the seaward horizon. When at war with England it was necessary to be vigilant; a fleet might suddenly appear over the horizon, to land a little army to capture Ferrol, and burn the dockyard installations and the ships. No hope of that today, thought Hornblower—there could be no landing of troops on that raging lee shore.

But all the same the sentry was undoubtedly staring very fixedly through his telescope right to windward; the sentry wiped his streaming eyes with his coat sleeve and stared again. Hornblower peered in the same direction, unable to see what it was that had attracted the sentry's attention. The sentry muttered something to himself, and then turned and ran clumsily down to the little stone guardhouse where sheltered the rest of the militia detachment stationed there to man the guns of the battery on the headland. He returned with the sergeant of the guard, who took the telescope and peered out to windward in the direction pointed out by the sentry. The two of them jabbered in their barbarous Gallego dialect; in two years of steady application Hornblower had mastered Galician as well as Castilian, but in that howling gale he could not intercept a word. Then finally, just as the sergeant nodded in agreement, Hornblower saw with his naked eyes what they were discussing. A pale grey square on the horizon above the grey sea—a ship's topsail. She must be running before the gale making for the shelter of Corunna or Ferrol.

It was a rash thing for a ship to do, because it would be no easy matter for her to round-to into Corunna Bay and anchor, and it would be even harder for her to hit off the narrow entrance to the Ferrol inlet. A cautious captain would claw out to sea and heave-to with a generous amount of sea room until the wind should moderate. These Spanish captains, said Hornblower to himself, with a shrug of his shoulders; but naturally they would always wish to make harbour as quickly as possible when the Royal Navy was sweeping the seas. But the sergeant and the sentry were more excited than the appearance of a single ship would seem to justify. Hornblower could contain himself no longer, and edged up to the chattering pair, mentally framing his sentences in the unfamiliar tongue.

"Please, gentlemen," he said, and then started again, shouting against the wind. "Please, gentlemen, what is it that you see?"

The sergeant gave him a glance, and then, reaching some undiscoverable decision, handed over the telescope —Hornblower could hardly restrain himself from snatching it from his hands. With the telescope to his eye he could see far better; he could see a ship-rigged vessel, under close-reefed topsails (and that was much more sail than it was wise to carry) hurtling wildly towards them. And then a moment later he saw the other square of grey. Another topsail. Another ship. The fore topmast was noticeably shorter than the main topmast, and not only that, but the whole effect was familiar—she was a British ship of war, a British frigate, plunging along in hot pursuit of the other, which seemed most likely to be a Spanish privateer. It was a close chase; it would be a very near thing, whether the Spaniard would reach the protection of the shore batteries before the frigate overhauled her. He lowered the telescope to rest his eye, and instantly the sergeant snatched it from him. He had been watching the Englishman's face, and Hornblower's expression had told him what he wanted to know. Those two ships out there were behaving in such a way as to justify his rousing his officer and giving the alarm. Sergeant and sentry went running back to the guardhouse, and in a few moments the artillerymen were pouring out to man the batteries on the verge of the cliff. Soon enough came a mounted officer urging his horse up the path; a single glance through the telescope sufficed for him. He went clattering down to the battery and the next moment the boom of a gun from there alerted the rest of the defences. The flag of Spain rose up the flagstaff beside the battery, and Hornblower saw an answering flag rise up the flagstaff on San Anton, where another battery guarded Corunna Bay. All the guns of the harbour defences were now manned, and there would be no mercy shown to any English ship that came in range.

Pursuer and pursued had covered quite half the distance already towards Corunna. They were hull-up over the horizon now to Hornblower on the headland, who could see them plunging madly over the grey sea—Hornblower momentarily expected to see them carry away their top-masts or their sails blow from the bolt-ropes. The frigate was half a mile astern still, and she would have to be much closer than that to have any hope of hitting with her guns in that sea. Here came the Commandant and his staff, clattering on horseback up the path to see the climax of the drama; the Commandant caught sight of Hornblower, and doffed his hat with Spanish courtesy, while Hornblower, hatless, tried to bow with equal courtesy. Hornblower walked over to him with an urgent request— he had to lay his hand on the Spaniard's saddlebow and shout up into his face to be understood.

"My parole expires in ten minutes, sir," he yelled. "May I please extend it? May I please stay?"

"Yes, stay, señor," said the Commandant, generously.

Hornblower watched the chase, and at the same time observed closely the preparations for defence. He had given his parole, but no part of the gentlemanly code prevented him from taking note of all he could see. One day he might be free, and one day it might be useful to know all about the defences of Ferrol. Everyone else of the large group on the headland was watching the chase, and excitement rose higher as the ships came racing nearer. The English captain was keeping a hundred yards or more to seaward of the Spaniard, but he was quite unable to overhaul her—in fact it seemed to Hornblower as if the Spaniard were actually increasing his lead. But the English frigate being to seaward meant that escape in that direction was cut off. Any turn away from the land would reduce the Spaniard's lead to a negligible distance. If he did not get into Corunna Bay or Ferrol Inlet he was doomed.

Now he was level with the Corunna headland, and it was time to put his helm hard over and turn into the Bay and hope that his anchors would hold in the lee of the headland. But with a wind of that violence hurtling against cliffs and headlands strange things can happen. A flaw of wind coming out of the Bay must have caught her aback as she tried to round-to. Hornblower saw her stagger, saw her heel as the back-lash died away and the gale caught her again. She was laid over almost on her beam-ends and as she righted herself Hornblower saw a momentary gap open up in her main topsail. It was momentary because from the time the gap appeared the life of the topsail was momentary; the gap appeared and at once the sail vanished, blown into ribbons as soon as its continuity was impaired. With the loss of its balancing pressure the ship became unmanageable; the gale pressing against the fore topsail swung her round again before the wind like a weathervane. If there had been time to spare to set a fragment of sail farther aft she would have been saved, but in those enclosed waters there was no time to spare. At one moment she was about to round the Corunna headland; at the next she had lost the opportunity for ever.

There was still the chance that she might fetch the opening to the Ferrol inlet; the wind was nearly fair for her to do that—nearly. Hornblower on the Ferrol headland was thinking along with the Spanish captain down there on the heaving deck. He saw him try to steady the ship so as to head for the narrow entrance, notorious among seamen for its difficulty. He saw him get her on her course, and for a few seconds as she flew across the mouth of the bay it seemed as if the Spaniard would succeed, against all probability, in exactly hitting off the entrance to the inlet. Then the back-lash hit her again. Had she been quick on the helm she might still have been safe, but with her sail pressure so outbalanced she was bound to be slow in her response to her rudder. The shrieking wind blew her bows round, and it was instantly obvious, too, that she was doomed, but the Spanish captain played the game out to the last. He would not pile his ship up against the foot of the low cliffs. He put his helm hard over; with the aid of the wind rebounding from the cliffs he made a gallant attempt to clear the Ferrol headland altogether and give himself a chance to claw out to sea.

A gallant attempt, but doomed to failure as soon as begun; he actually cleared the headland, but the wind blew his bows round again, and, bows first, the ship plunged right at the long jagged line of the Devil's Teeth. Hornblower, the Commandant, and everyone, hurried across the headland to look down at the final act of the tragedy. With tremendous speed, driving straight before the wind, she raced at the reef. A roller picked her up as she neared it and seemed to increase her speed. Then she struck, and vanished from sight for a second as the roller burst into spray all about her. When the spray cleared she lay there transformed. Her three masts had all gone with the shock, and it was only a black hulk which emerged from the white foam. Her speed and the roller behind her had carried her almost over the reef—doubtless tearing her bottom out—and she hung by her stern, which stood out clear of the water, while her bows were just submerged in the comparatively still water in the lee of the reef.

There were men still alive on her. Hornblower could see them crouching for shelter under the break of her poop. Another Atlantic roller came surging up, and exploded on the Devil's Teeth, wrapping the wreck round with spray. But yet she emerged again, black against the creaming foam. She had cleared the reef sufficiently far to find shelter for most of her length in the lee of the thing that had destroyed her. Hornblower could see those living creatures crouching on her deck. They had a little longer to live— they might live five minutes, perhaps, if they were lucky. Five hours if they were not.

All round him the Spaniards were shouting maledictions. Women were weeping; some of the men were shaking their fists with rage at the British frigate, which, well satisfied with the destruction of her victim, had rounded-to in time and was now clawing out to sea again under storm canvas. It was horrible to see those poor devils down there die. If some larger wave than usual, bursting on the reef, did not lift the stern of the wreck clear so that she sank, she would still break up for the survivors to be whirled away with the fragments. And, if it took a long time for her to break up, the wretched men sheltering there would not be able to endure the constant beating of the cold spray upon them. Something should be done to save them, but no boat could round the headland and weather the Devil's Teeth to reach the wreck. That was so obvious as not to call for a second thought. But—Hornblower's thoughts began to race as he started to work on the alternatives. The Commandant on his horse was speaking vehemently to a Spanish naval officer, clearly on the same subject, and the naval officer was spreading his hands and saying that any attempt would be hopeless. And yet—For two years Hornblower had been a prisoner; all his pent-up restlessness was seeking an outlet, and after two years of the misery of confinement he did not care whether he lived or died. He went up to the Commandant and broke into the argument.

"Sir," he said, "let me try to save them. Perhaps from the little bay there—Perhaps some of the fishermen would come with me."

The Commandant looked at the officer and the officer shrugged his shoulders.

"What do you suggest, sir?" asked the Commandant of Hornblower.

"We might carry a boat across the headland from the dockyard," said Hornblower, struggling to word his ideas in Spanish, "but we must be quick—quick!"

He pointed to the wreck, and force was added to his words by the sight of a roller bursting over the Devil's Teeth.

"How would you carry a boat?" asked the Commandant.

To shout his plan in English against that wind would have been a strain; to do so in Spanish was beyond him.

"I can show you at the dockyard, sir," he yelled. "I cannot explain. But we must hurry!"

"You want to go to the dockyard, then?"

"Yes—oh yes."

"Mount behind me, sir," said the Commandant.

Awkwardly Hornblower scrambled up to a seat astride the horse's haunches and clutched at the Commandant's belt. He bumped frightfully as the animal wheeled round and trotted down the slope. All the idlers of the town and garrison ran beside them.

The dockyard at Ferrol was almost a phantom organization, withered away like a tree deprived of its roots, thanks to the British blockade. Situated as it was at the most distant corner of Spain, connected with the interior by only the roughest of roads, it relied on receiving its supplies by sea, and any such reliance was likely with

251

British cruisers off the coast to be disappointed. The last visit of Spanish ships of war had stripped the place of almost all its stores, and many of the dockyard hands had been pressed as seamen at the same time. But all that Hornblower needed was there, as he knew, thanks to his careful observation. He slid off the horse's hindquarters—miraculously avoiding an instinctive kick from the irritated animal—and collected his thoughts. He pointed to a low dray—a mere platform on wheels—which was used for carrying beef barrels and brandy kegs to the pier.

"Horses," he said, and a dozen willing hands set to work harnessing a team.

Beside the jetty floated half a dozen boats. There were tackle and shears, all the apparatus necessary for swinging heavy weights about. To put slings under a boat and swing her up was the work of only a minute or two. These Spaniards might be dilatory and lazy as a rule, but inspire them with the need for instant action, catch their enthusiasm, present them with a novel plan, and they would work like madmen—and some of them were skilled workmen, too. Oars, mast and sail (not that they would need the sail), rudder, tiller, and balers were all present. A group came running from a store shed with chocks for the boat, and the moment these were set up on the dray the dray was backed under the tackle and the boat lowered onto them.

"Empty barrels," said Hornblower. "Little ones—so."

A swarthy Galician fisherman grasped his intention at once, and amplified Hornblower's halting sentences with voluble explanation. A dozen empty water breakers, with their bungs driven well home, were brought, and the swarthy fishermen climbed on the dray and began to lash them under the thwarts. Properly secured, they would keep the boat afloat even were she filled to the gunwale with water.

"I want six men," shouted Hornblower, standing on the

dray and looking round at the crowd. "Six fishermen who know little boats."

The swarthy fisherman lashing the breakers in the boat looked up from his task.

"I know whom we need, sir," he said.

He shouted a string of names, and half a dozen men came forward; burly, weather-beaten fellows, with the self-reliant look in their faces of men used to meeting difficulties. It was apparent that the swarthy Galician was their captain.

"Let us go, then," said Hornblower, but the Galician checked him.

Hornblower did not hear what he said, but some of the crowd nodded, turned away, and came hastening back staggering under a breaker of fresh water and a box that must contain biscuit. Hornblower was cross with himself for forgetting the possibility of their being blown out to sea. And the Commandant, still sitting his horse and watching these preparations with a keen eye, took note of these stores too.

"Remember, sir, that I have your parole," he said.

"You have my parole, sir," said Hornblower—for a few blessed moments he had actually forgotten that he was a prisoner.

The stores were safely put away into the sternsheets and the fishing boat captain caught Hornblower's eye and got a nod from him.

"Let us go," he roared to the crowd.

The iron-shod hoofs clashed on the cobbles and the dray lurched forward, with men leading the horses, men swarming alongside, and Hornblower and the captain riding on the dray like triumphing generals in a procession. They went through the dockyard gate, along the level main street of the little town, and turned up a steep lane which climbed the ridge constituting the backbone of the headland. The enthusiasm of the crowd was still lively;

when the horses slowed as they breasted the slope a hundred men pushed at the back, strained at the sides, tugged at the traces to run the dray up the hillside. At the crest the lane became a track, but the dray still lurched and rumbled along. From the track diverged an even worse track, winding its way sideways down the slope through arbutus and myrtle towards the sandy cove which Hornblower had first had in mind—on fine days he had seen fishermen working a seine net on that beach, and he himself had taken note of it as a suitable place for a landing party should the Royal Navy ever plan a descent against Ferrol.

The wind was blowing as wildly as ever; it shrieked round Hornblower's ears. The sea as it came in view was chaotic with wave-crests, and then as they turned a shoulder of the slope they could see the line of the Devil's Teeth running out from the shore up there to windward, and still hanging precariously from their jagged fangs was the wreck, black against the seething foam. Somebody raised a shout at the sight, everybody heaved at the dray, so that the horses actually broke into a trot and the dray leaped and bounced over the obstructions in its way.

"Slowly," roared Hornblower. "Slowly!"

If they were to break an axle or smash a wheel at this moment the attempt would end in ludicrous failure. The Commandant on his horse enforced Hornblower's cries with loud orders of his own, and restrained the reckless enthusiasm of his people. More sedately the dray went on down the trail to the edge of the sandy beach. The wind picked up even the damp sand and flung it stinging into their face, but only small waves broke here, for the beach was in a recess in the shoreline, the southwesterly wind was blowing a trifle off shore here, and up to windward the Devil's Teeth broke the force of the rollers as they raced along in a direction nearly parallel to the shoreline. The wheels plunged into the sand and the horses stopped at the water's edge. A score of willing hands unharnessed them and a hundred willing arms thrust the dray out into the water—all these things were easy with such vast manpower available. As the first wave broke over the floor of the dray the crew scrambled up and stood ready. There were rocks here, but mighty heaves by the militiamen and the dockyard workers waist deep in water forced the dray over them. The boat almost floated off its chocks, and the crew forced it clear and scrambled aboard, the wind beginning to swing her immediately. They grabbed for their oars and put their backs into half a dozen fierce strokes which brought her under command; the Galician captain had already laid a steering oar in the notch in the stern, with no attempt at shipping rudder and tiller. As he braced himself to steer he glanced at Hornblower, who tacitly left the job to him.

Hornblower, bent against the wind, was standing in the sternsheets planning a route through the rocks which would lead them to the wreck. The shore and the friendly beach were gone now, incredibly far away, and the boat was struggling out through a welter of water with the wind howling round her. In those jumbled waves her motion was senseless and she lurched in every direction successively. It was well that the boatmen were used to rowing in broken water so that their oars kept the boat under way, giving the captain the means by which, tugging fiercely at the steering oar, he could guide her through that maniacal confusion. Hornblower, planning his course, was able to guide the captain by his gestures, so that the captain could devote all the necessary attention to keeping the boat from being suddenly capsized by an unexpected wave. The wind howled, and the boat heaved and pitched as she met each lumpy wave, but yard by yard they were struggling up to the wreck. If there was any order in the waves at all, they were swinging round the outer end of the Devil's Teeth, so that the boat had to be carefully steered, turning to meet the waves with her bows and then turning back to gain precarious yards against the wind. Hornblower spared a glance for the men at the oars; at every second they were exerting their utmost strength. There could never be a moment's respite—tug and strain, tug and strain, until Hornblower wondered how human hearts and sinews could endure it.

But they were edging up towards the wreck. Hornblower, when the wind and spray allowed, could see the whole extent of her canted deck now. He could see human figures cowering under the break of the poop. He saw somebody there wave an arm to him. Next moment his attention was called away when a jagged monster suddenly leaped out of the sea twenty yards ahead. For a second he could not imagine what it was, and then it leaped clear again and he recognized it—the butt end of a broken mast. The mast was still anchored to the ship by a single surviving shroud attached to the upper end of the mast and to the ship, and the mast drifting down to leeward, was jerking and leaping on the waves as though some sea god below the surface was threatening them with his wrath. Hornblower called the steersman's attention to the menace and received a nod in return; the steersman's shouted *"Nombre de Dios"* was whirled away in the wind. They kept clear of the mast, and as they pulled up along it Hornblower could form a clearer notion of the speed of their progress now that he had a stationary object to help his judgment. He could see the painful inches gained at each frantic tug on the oars, and could see how the boat stopped dead or even went astern when the wilder gusts hit her, the oar blades pulling ineffectively through the water. Every inch of gain was only won at the cost of an infinity of labour.

Now they were past the mast, close to the submerged bows of the ship, and close enough to the Devil's Teeth to be deluged with spray as each wave burst on the farther side of the reef. There were inches of water washing back and forth in the bottom of the boat, but there was neither time nor opportunity to bale it out. This was the trickiest part of the whole effort, to get close enough alongside the wreck to be able to take off the survivors without stoving in the boat; there were wicked fangs of rock all about the after end of the wreck, while forward, although the fore-castle was above the surface at times, the forward part of the waist was submerged. But the ship was canted a little over to port, towards them, which made the approach easier. When the water was at its lowest level, immediately before the next roller broke on the reef, Hornblower, standing up and craning his neck, could see no rocks beside the wreck in the middle part of the waist where the deck came down to water level. It was easy to direct the steersman towards that particular point, and then, as the boat moved in, to wave his arms and demand the attention of the little group under the break of the poop, and to point to the spot to which they were approaching. A wave burst upon the reef, broke over the stern of the wreck, and filled the boat almost full. She swung back and forth in the eddies, but the kegs kept her afloat and quick handling of the steering oar and lusty rowing kept her from being dashed against either the wreck or the rocks.

"Now!" shouted Hornblower—it did not matter that he spoke English at this decisive moment. The boat surged forward, while the survivors, releasing themselves from the lashings which had held them in their shelter, came slithering down the deck towards them. It was a little of a shock to see there were but four of them—twenty or thirty men must have been swept overboard when the ship hit the reef. The bows of the boat moved towards the wreck. At a shouted order from the steersman the oars fell still. One survivor braced himself and flung himself into the bows. A stroke of the oars, a tug at the steering oar, and the boat nosed forward again, and another survivor plunged into the boat. Then Hornblower, who had been watching the sea, saw the next breaker rear up over the reef. At his warning shout the boat backed away to safety —comparative safety—while the remaining survivors went scrambling back up the deck to the shelter of the poop. The wave burst and roared, the foam hissed and the spray rattled, and then they crept up to the wreck again. The third survivor poised himself for his leap, mistimed it, and fell into the sea, and no one ever saw him again. He was gone, sunk like a stone, crippled as he was with cold and exhaustion, but there was no time to spare for lamentation. The fourth survivor was waiting his chance and jumped at once, landing safely in the bows.

"Any more?" shouted Hornblower, and receiving a shake of the head in reply; they had saved three lives at the risk of eight.

"Let us go," said Hornblower, but the steersman needed no telling.

Already he had allowed the wind to drift the boat away from the wreck, away from the rocks—away from the shore. An occasional strong pull at the oars sufficed to keep her bows to wind and wave. Hornblower looked down at the fainting survivors lying in the bottom of the boat with the water washing over them. He bent down and shook them into consciousness; he picked up the balers and forced them into their numb hands. They must keep active or die. It was astounding to find darkness closing about them, and it was urgent that they should decide on their next move immediately. The men at the oars were in no shape for any prolonged further rowing; if they tried to return to the sandy cove whence they had started they might be overtaken both by night and by exhaustion while still among the treacherous rocks off the shore there. Hornblower sat down beside the Galician captain, who laconically gave his views while vigilantly observing the waves racing down upon them.

"It is growing dark," said the captain, glancing round the sky. "Rocks. The men are tired."

"We had better not go back," said Hornblower.

"No."

"Then we must get out to sea."

Years of duty on blockade, of beating about off a lee shore, had ingrained into Hornblower the necessity for seeking sea room.

"Yes," said the captain, and he added something which Hornblower, thanks to the wind and his unfamiliarity with the language, was unable to catch. The captain roared the expression again, and accompanied his words with a vivid bit of pantomime with the one hand he could spare from the steering oar.

"A sea anchor," decided Hornblower to himself. "Quite right."

He looked back at the vanishing shore, and gauged the direction of the wind. It seemed to be backing a little southerly; the coast here trended away from them. They could ride to a sea anchor through the hours of darkness and run no risk of being cast ashore as long as these conditions persisted.

"Good," said Hornblower aloud.

He imitated the other's bit of pantomime and the captain gave him a glance of approval. At a bellow from him the two men forward took in their oars and set to work at constructing a sea anchor—merely a pair of oars attached to a long painter paid out over the bows. With this gale blowing the pressure of the wind on the boat set up enough drag on the float to keep their bows to the sea. Hornblower watched as the sea anchor began to take hold of the water.

"Good," he said again.

"Good," said the captain, taking in his steering oar.

Hornblower realized only now that he had been long exposed to a winter gale while wet to the skin. He was numb with cold, and he was shivering uncontrollably. At his feet one of the three survivors of the wreck was lying helpless; the other two had succeeded in baling out most of the water and as a result of their exertions were conscious and alert. The men who had been rowing sat drooping with weariness on their thwarts. The Galician captain was already down in the bottom of the boat lifting the helpless man in his arms. It was a common impulse of them all to huddle down into the bottom of the boat, beneath the thwarts, away from that shrieking wind.

So the night came down on them. Hornblower found himself welcoming the contact of other human bodies; he felt an arm round him and he put his arm round someone else. Around them a little water still surged about on the floorboards; above them the wind still shrieked and howled. The boat stood first on her head and then on her tail as the waves passed under them, and at the moment of climbing each crest she gave a shuddering jerk as she snubbed herself to the sea anchor. Every few seconds a new spat of spray whirled into the boat upon their shrinking bodies; it did not seem long before the accumulation of spray in the bottom of the boat made it necessary for them to disentangle themselves, and set about, groping in the darkness, the task of baling the water out again. Then they could huddle down again under the thwarts.

It was when they pulled themselves together for the third baling that in the middle of his nightmare of cold and exhaustion Hornblower was conscious that the body across which his arm lay was unnaturally stiff; the man the captain had been trying to revive had died as he lay there between the captain and Hornblower. The captain dragged the body away into the sternsheets in the darkness, and the night went on, cold wind and cold spray, jerk, pitch, and roll, sit up and bale and cower down and shudder. It was hideous torment; Hornblower could not trust himself to believe his eyes when he saw the first signs that the darkness was lessening. And then the grey dawn came gradually over the grey sea, and they were free to wonder what to do next. But as the light increased the problem was solved for them, for one of the fishermen, raising himself up in the boat, gave a hoarse cry, and pointed to the northern horizon, and there, almost hull-up, was a ship, hove-to under storm canvas. The captain took one glance at her—his eyesight must have been marvellous—and identified her.

"The English frigate," he said.

She must have made nearly the same amount of leeway hove-to as the boat did riding to her sea anchor.

"Signal to her," said Hornblower, and no one raised any objections.

The only white object available was Hornblower's shirt, and he took it off, shuddering in the cold, and they tied it to an oar and raised the oar in the mast-step. The captain saw Hornblower putting on his dripping coat over his bare ribs and in a single movement peeled off his thick blue jersey and offered it to him.

"Thank you, no," protested Hornblower, but the captain insisted; with a wide grin he pointed to the stiffened corpse lying in the sternsheets and announced he would replace the jersey with the dead man's clothing.

The argument was interrupted by a further cry from one of the fishermen. The frigate was coming to the wind; with treble-reefed fore and main topsails she was heading for them under the impulse of the lessening gale. Hornblower saw her running down on them; a glance in the other direction showed him the Galician mountains, faint on the southern horizon—warmth, freedom, and friendship on the one hand; solitude and captivity on the other. Under the lee of the frigate the boat bobbed and heaved fantastically; many inquisitive faces looked down on them.

They were cold and cramped; the frigate dropped a boat and a couple of nimble seamen scrambled on board. A line was flung from the frigate, a whip lowered a breeches ring into the boat, and the English seamen helped the Spaniards one by one into the breeches and held them steady as they were swung up to the frigate's deck.

"I go last," said Hornblower when they turned to him. "I am a King's Officer."

"Good Lor' lumme," said the seamen.

"Send the body up, too," said Hornblower. "It can be given decent burial."

The stiff corpse was grotesque as it swayed through the air. The Galician captain tried to dispute with Hornblower the honor of going last, but Hornblower would not be argued with. Then finally the seamen helped him put his legs into the breeches, and secured him with a line round his waist. Up he soared, swaying dizzily with the roll of the ship; then they drew him in to the deck, lowering and shortening, until half a dozen strong arms took his weight and laid him gently on the deck.

"There you are, my hearty, safe and sound," said a bearded seaman.

"I am a King's Officer," said Hornblower. "Where's the officer of the watch?"

Wearing marvellous dry clothing, Hornblower found himself soon drinking hot rum-and-water in the cabin of Captain George Crome, of His Majesty's frigate *Syrtis*. Crome was a thin pale man with a depressed expression, but Hornblower knew of him as a first-rate officer.

"These Galicians make good seamen," said Crome. "I can't press them. But perhaps a few will volunteer sooner than go to a prison hulk."

"Sir," said Hornblower, and hesitated. It is ill for a junior lieutenant to argue with a post captain.

"Well?"

"Those men came to sea to save life. They are not liable to capture."

Crome's cold grey eyes became actively frosty—Hornblower was right about it being ill for a junior lieutenant to argue with a post captain.

"Are you telling me my duty, sir?" he asked.

"Good heavens no, sir," said Hornblower hastily. "It's a long time since I read the Admiralty Instructions and I expect my memory's at fault."

"Admiralty Instructions, eh?" said Crome, in a slightly different tone of voice.

"I expect I'm wrong, sir," said Hornblower, "but I seem to remember the same instruction applied to the other two—the survivors."

Even a post captain could only contravene Admiralty Instructions at his peril.

"I'll consider it," said Crome.

"I had the dead man sent on board, sir," went on Hornblower, "in the hope that perhaps you might give him proper burial. Those Galicians risked their lives to save him, sir, and I expected they'd be gratified."

"A Popish burial? I'll give orders to give 'em a free hand."

"Thank you, sir," said Hornblower.

"And now as regards yourself. You say you hold a commission as lieutenant. You can do duty in this ship until we meet the admiral again. Then he can decide. I haven't heard of the *Indefatigable* paying off, and legally you may still be borne on her books."

And that was when the Devil came to tempt Hornblower, as he took another sip of hot rum-and-water. The joy of being in a King's ship again was so keen as to be almost painful. To taste salt beef and biscuit again, and never again to taste beans and garbanzos. To have a ship's deck under his feet, to talk English. To be free—to be free! There was precious little chance of ever falling again

263

into Spanish hands. Hornblower remembered with agonizing clarity the flat depression of captivity. All he had to do was not to say a word. He had only to keep silence for a day or two. But the Devil did not tempt him long, only until he had taken his next sip of rum-and-water. Then he thrust the Devil behind him and met Crome's eyes again.

"I'm sorry, sir," he said.

"What for?"

"I am here on parole. I gave my word before I left the beach."

"You did? That alters the case. You were within your rights, of course."

The giving of parole by captive British officers was so usual as to excite no comment.

"It was in the usual form, I suppose?" went on Crome. "That you would make no attempt to escape?"

"Yes, sir."

"Then what do you decide as a result?"

Of course Crome could not attempt to influence a gentleman's decision on a matter as personal as a parole.

"I must go back, sir," said Hornblower, "at the first opportunity."

He felt the sway of the ship, he looked round the homely cabin, and his heart was breaking.

"You can at least dine and sleep on board tonight," said Crome. "I'll not venture inshore again until the wind moderates. I'll send you to Corunna under a flag of truce when I can. And I'll see what the Instructions say about those prisoners."

It was a sunny morning when the sentry at Fort San Anton, in the harbour of Corunna, called his officers' attention to the fact that the British cruiser off the headland had hove-to out of gunshot and was lowering a boat. The sentry's responsibility ended there, and he could watch idly as his officer observed that the cutter, running smartly in under sail, was flying a white flag. She hove-to within

264

musket shot, and it was a mild surprise to the sentry when in reply to the officer's hail someone rose up in the boat and replied in unmistakable Gallego dialect. Summoned alongside the landing ship, the cutter put ashore ten men and then headed out again to the frigate. Nine men were laughing and shouting; the tenth, the youngest, walked with a fixed expression on his face with never a sign of emotion—his expression did not change even when the others, with obvious affection, put their arms round his shoulders. No one ever troubled to explain to the sentry who the imperturbable young man was, and he was not very interested. After he had seen the group shipped off across Corunna Bay towards Ferrol he quite forgot the incident.

It was almost spring when a Spanish milita office came into the barracks which served as a prison for officers in Ferrol.

"Señor Hornblower?" he asked—at least Hornblower, in the corner, knew that was what he was trying to say. He was used to the way Spaniards mutilated his name.

"Yes?" he said, rising.

"Would you please come with me? The Commandant has sent me for you, sir."

The Commandant was all smiles. He held a despatch in his hands.

"This, sir," he said, waving it at Hornblower, "is a personal order. It is countersigned by the Duke of Fuentesauco, Minister of Marine, but it is signed by the First Minister, Prince of the Peace and Duke of Alcudia."

"Yes, sir," said Hornblower.

He should have begun to hope at that moment, but there comes a time in a prisoner's life when he ceases to hope. He was more interested, even, in that strange title of Prince of the Peace which was now beginning to be heard in Spain.

"It says—'We, Carlos Leonardo Luis Manuel de Godoy

y Boegas, First Minister of His Most Catholic Majesty, Prince of the Peace, Duke of Alcudia and Grandee of the First Class, Count of Alcudia, Knight of the Most Sacred Order of the Golden Fleece, Knight of the Holy Order of Santiago, Knight of the Most Distinguished Order of Calatrava, Captain General of His Most Catholic Majesty's forces by Land and Sea, Colonel General of the Guardia de Corps, Admiral of the Two Oceans, General of the cavalry, of the infantry, and of the artillery,'—in any event, sir, it is an order to me to take immediate steps to set you at liberty. I am to restore you under flag of truce to your fellow countrymen, in recognition of—'your courage and self-sacrifice in saving life at the peril of your own.' "

"Thank you, sir," said Hornblower.

IT IS A CURIOUS STORY

IT IS A CURIOUS STORY
THE TALE OF SCOTTISH OPERA
1962 TO 1987

CORDELIA OLIVER

SCOTTISH OPERA SILVER JUBILEE

MAINSTREAM
PUBLISHING

First published in 1987
by Mainstream Publishing
7 Albany Street, Edinburgh EH1 3UG

© 1987 Cordelia Oliver
Photographs © 1987 Scottish Opera

British Library Cataloguing in Publication Data
Oliver, Cordelia
    It is a curious story : the tale of Scottish Opera 1962 – 1987.
    1. Scottish Opera——History
    I. Title
    782.1'09414'43   ML1731.8.G52S3

ISBN 1-85158-066-2

Design by James Hutcheson, Artwork by Paul Keir.
Printed in Great Britain by
Butler and Tanner, Frome

Set in 12 point Baskerville by
Pulse Origination, Edinburgh

TABLE OF CONTENTS

DEDICATION

To Sir Alexander Gibson but for whom none
of this would have happened.

PREFACE

The author wishes to record her grateful thanks to all those who so willingly spared time to answer questions, offer information and share memories and anecdotes to help give conviction, credibility and "colour" to this tale of Scottish Opera over twenty-five years. Gratitude, then, to Norman Bailey, Ann Baird, Dame Janet Baker, Anthony Besch, Sheriff Boyle, Evelyn Bryson, John Cox, Jane Davidson, Peter Ebert, Joyce Fieldsend, Sir Alexander Gibson, John Lawson Graham, Leonard Hancock, Claire Livingstone, Ainslie Millar, Bill McCue, Alan Oke, Linda Ormiston, Dr Leonard Paterson, Anthony Phillips, David Pountney, Peter Quilliam-Cain, John Robertson, Ian Rodger, Thomson Smillie, Richard Telfer, Catherine Wilson and Graham Vick. Thanks are also due to Richard Mantle and Roger Witts for giving me the freedom of the Scottish Opera archive of photographs and press cuttings; and especially to the latter who not only planted the idea of using the phrase from Britten's opera as the title of the book, but who also compiled the appendices with the help of work done over the years by the Company's archivist, Richard Telfer. Thanks, also, to the Scottish Opera Endowment Trust and Judy Moir, my editor at Mainstream, whose patience has been exemplary.

Cordelia Oliver

HRH The Duchess of Gloucester,
Patron of Scottish Opera.

photograph by John Swannell

INTRODUCTION

Nobody should become a professional writer of intro-
ductions to books. Your words come back to haunt you,
turning the screw with hardly less inexorability than the
ghosts of Henry James's and Benjamin Britten's masterpiece
from which this book takes its title.

I don't suppose any other organisation has had books written
to celebrate not only its initial ten years but also its Silver
Jubilee, unless it be a business promoting its own image.
Scottish Opera is, I suspect, far too busy to do that, but it
deserves the tributes, and I am honoured to have been asked to
write an introduction both times.

Few artistic bodies in the United Kingdom have so well
harnessed that mixture of attributes which our ambivalent
attitude towards the arts demands its administrators display.
First of all, they need something to sell, and the flair to persuade
the world at large to buy it. Next, the civic sense to make the
enterprise seem worthwhile, even necessary, to a community.
Thirdly, the business acumen to support constant presentation
to the funding bodies, in bad times (with unsympathetic
listeners) as well as in good.

Lastly — and this is the most important attribute — so exact
a sense of equilibrium as to know precisely up to what point to
go too far: artistically, by balancing its artists' need for
adventure with its audience's need for security; financially, by a
nice judgment of how to make slightly too small a subvention
cover slightly more than any accountant would recommend. To
lack this last attribute means taking the worst of all artistic risks:
playing safe.

Nobody has ever buried Scottish Opera and its aspirations
with such an epitaph, and Cordelia Oliver's book explains why.

Lord Harewood

BEGINNINGS

Opera is the amalgam of all the arts — the *gesamtkunstwerk*, covering music, drama, spectacle — and, as such, worth making accessible to as many as might conceivably come to appreciate its ravishments and satisfactions. On the other hand, opera is an outmoded, outdated form of upper-crust entertainment, scornfully labelled elitist by many who, more often than not, are making their judgments at second hand and from a highly prejudiced point of view. Scottish Opera was brought to being by a small group of people who passionately held the first opinion and with equal passion defied the second.

The inauguration of Scottish Opera viewed twenty-five years on, was an incredibly courageous, not to say rash enterprise, for it might easily have failed to take root in this small country with its scattered population (less, overall, than that of greater London) and with no indigenous operatic tradition to boast of. And Glasgow, Scotland's industrial capital, was then just beginning its long, hard, and increasingly successful fight — in which Scottish Opera has played its part — to demolish its bleak reputation as a place notorious for slums, deprivation and gang warfare rather than famed for the love of music and the other arts which has always been part of its make-up.

In the event of failure, Scottish Opera would simply have gone down in history as yet another of those worthy concepts that somehow failed to attract enough support to allow it to survive its infancy. But survive it did and to some purpose, or no book such as this would be written: there would be no twenty-fifth birthday to celebrate and no need for salutation. But Scottish Opera, as everyone knows, not only took root but positively burgeoned in its first half dozen seasons, demonstrating a remarkable surge of energy, fuelled, it has to be said, by expert managerial skill, creative assurance and confident presentation. One knows now that, long before the Company's tenth birthday, opera buffs in the south of England were to be heard asking "Who do these people think they are, up in Scotland, doing *Otello* with Charles Craig, *Boris Godunov* with David Ward, *Die Walküre* with Helga Dernesch, *The Trojans* with Janet Baker?"

What follows is the tale of that conception, birth and early prodigious growth, as well as the later development, with its peaks and valleys, through what might be thought of, perhaps, as a troubled adolescence towards what everyone must surely hope will be a more mature and satisfying future. Much of the matter in the present account is not, cannot be, new. Apart from all the retrospective articles in successive *Scottish Opera Year Books*, there is — only in the libraries now, for it is long out of print — Conrad Wilson's invaluable, detailed account of the Company's euphoric progress towards its tenth birthday in 1972. And for interested researchers there is a long article by Magnus Magnusson in *The New Saltire* (June 1963) which relates in even more microscopic detail, the run-up from the initial conception to that historic first night of *Madama Butterfly* in the Kings Theatre, Glasgow, on June 5th, 1962.

But fifteen years and much controversial water have passed under Scottish Opera's bridge since that golden-haloed tenth birthday; fifteen years in which we have seen a gradual, but surely inevitable, development of what had been, in effect, an annual festival season of opera, into a national opera company with all that that entails. In those years Scottish Opera has given us a rich succession of productions, many new — and some far from predictable, even in the case of the most celebrated classics — but just as many being revivals of popular favourites. And what must have seemed like a pipe-dream in 1972 — the acquisition of a properly equipped opera house as a permanent base for Scottish Opera — became possible within just a few years. A combination of ambition, persuasion and assiduous fund-raising coincided with the great good luck that a suitable theatre became available when Scottish Television, one of Scottish Opera's earliest sponsors, moved out of Glasgow's Theatre Royal to new headquarters nearby.

The fact that possession of Theatre Royal was to create its own serious financial problems for Scottish Opera — a liability which to this day, remains unresolved — is part of what I have called "A Curious Story", after the opening lines of Benjamin Britten's eerie opera, *The Turn of the Screw*. I have done so for more than one reason: the chamber operas of Britten — *Albert Herring*, *The Turn of the Screw*, and *A Midsummer Night's Dream* — are inseparable from the early success of Scottish Opera and

Sir Alexander Gibson in action.

from the well-deserved critical respect accorded the young opera company not just in Scotland but south of the Border and across the Channel. Moreover, *The Turn of the Screw*, in Anthony Besch's magical realisation, seems to me to epitomise that success. The longest-lived production in the repertoire, it is no more dated now and no less magical, as we saw in the 1986 revival, than it was on a certain March evening in 1970 in Aberdeen when the curtain of His Majesty's Theatre first rose on John Stoddart's shimmering, dappled gauze behind which the "curious story" unfolded.

And the second reason for my choice of title? The word "curious", sadly diminished in modern usage, enjoys a wealth of fascinating dictionary meanings. "Skilled as connoisseur or virtuoso" is one, and "made with care or art" another. These and some of the other definitions — for example, "noteworthy", "exquisite", "choice" or "fine" — might well have been applied at times to Scottish Opera over the years; to its founder, directors, designers, performers and even, on occasion, to the audiences. And what of the other meanings, less complimentary in intention — "abstruse", for example, "strange" or "queer"? No doubt there are those who would maintain that in that respect also, though surely less often, the word "curious" is apt enough. Finally, if there is a third reason for linking the title of this book with Britten's opera, it derives from my own feeling that Scottish Opera itself has suffered the turn of the screw more often than need be, and certainly beyond its deserts.

*   *   *

The story begins, of course, with the man of music, Sir Alexander Gibson who, as plain Alex Gibson, was Scottish Opera's founder and who has been involved ever since, bearing the title, Artistic Director. This title has always worried him somewhat since it has never properly described his function which has always been that of Music Director. A musical prodigy, Gibson was a prize-winning student of piano at the Royal Scottish Academy of Music in Glasgow and, after national service in the army, at the Royal College of Music in London. Here his gift for conducting first made itself felt when he organised a student orchestra to underpin the productions of the Opera School, starting well up the mountain range, so to say, with *Cosi fan tutte*.

That was in 1950, by which time there was little doubt that opera would remain central to his career. A year later he entered for an International Conductor's Competition at Besançon where he won the Georges Enescu Prize. After that Alex Gibson went straight to Sadlers Wells as a répétiteur where he was soon entrusted with his first public professional engagement, conducting Smetana's *The Bartered Bride*.

In retrospect, it seems as though Gibson was born with a fine sense of timing — in more than musical terms, that is — an instinct that has served him well. Feeling the need to extend and expand his experience of orchestral work beyond the opera house, he left the Wells and came north again to Glasgow as assistant conductor of the BBC Scottish Symphony Orchestra, under Ian Whyte. But the link with London was by no means broken: Gibson went back to Sadlers Wells on occasion to take up the baton as guest conductor and in 1954 he was to return, full time, as staff conductor. Three years later he was appointed Musical Director, the youngest musician ever trusted with that responsibility.

By the time he made his crucial decision to return once more to Glasgow, as Musical Director of the Scottish National Orchestra, he was already an experienced conductor of opera with a tally of something like thirty productions to his credit. Two of these events had taken place in Glasgow during his spell with the BBC SSO, but oddly enough with the SNO in the pit. The operas in question were Gounod's *Faust* and *The Jewels of the Madonna* by Ermanno Wolf-Ferrari, and they were performed by the Glasgow Grand Opera Society, a notable amateur club with a distinguished history that includes the first British performances of Mozart's *Idomeneo* and two operas by Berlioz, *The Trojans* and *Beatrice and Benedick*. So, after all, maybe it is a mistake to underrate Scotland's operatic potential. The audience was there, waiting; so were the voices — good choirs have always abounded in the central industrial belt and the generous handful of amateur operatic societies in Glasgow alone could each fill the Kings Theatre for a week at a time. All that was lacking was a firmly established structure to promote professional opera on a regular basis; a Company which would also, hopefully, provide a ladder for locally trained singers with operatic potential, of which the first rung would be a full-time chorus. What we were ready for, in fact, was Scottish Opera.

And who more likely than Alex Gibson, with his Glasgow background and Sadlers Wells experience, to realise the possibility of founding such a Company, not least because he had witnessed the great success of Welsh National Opera's annual week at Sadlers Wells. The chorus was the great feature of those performances, Gibson remembers. "All those marvellous Welsh milkmen and so forth singing their hearts out," with Sadlers Wells soloists in the principal roles. WNO had been formed back in the 1940s and "if Wales could do it why not Scotland?" It might be said, then, that Scottish Opera was conceived in the greenroom at Sadlers Wells.

In his last days in London Alex Gibson was strongly encouraged in his notion of forming a Scottish National Opera by some of the Scots expatriates at the Wells, from Staff Producer John Donaldson to already established singers like David Ward, Harold Blackburn and William McAlpine. They all thought him mad to leave the metropolis, but all of them came north in due course to sing with Scottish Opera. The knowledge that he was about to take control of a symphony orchestra of his own with which to underpin the structure of a permanent opera company must have encouraged Alex Gibson to nurse his idea even if only, as he now maintains, at the back of his mind.

"After all, I came up here with another job to do, which was the SNO, and that had to come first" — as indeed it did, for it was Alexander Gibson who, in effect, re-created the former Scottish Orchestra (it had been officially reconstituted a few years earlier as the Scottish National Orchestra but had had no permanent resident conductor) as a notable symphonic instrument.

But the first anomaly that struck the SNO's new, young Musical Director on taking office was a certain blank period in the calendar during late spring and early summer, even though the players were on twelve-month contracts. This, remember, was the very orchestra which had aquitted itself so well under Gibson's baton at Theatre Royal for *Faust* and *The Jewels of the Madonna*. The idea of at least an annual festival season of opera to fill that gap, if not actually a permanent opera company, had finally germinated.

Moral support, however, was crucial; and it was Gibson's good fortune that such enthusiastic backing was forthcoming in good measure. Three men, all avid music lovers, enter the scene at this point, one after another. Richard Telfer, an Edinburgh music teacher and old friend of Alex Gibson's, was the first to make encouraging noises; Ainslie Millar, a Chartered Surveyor in Glasgow who also happened to be a keen amateur opera singer and a member of the Board of Sadlers Wells, was, before long, embroiled in the planning; and the original "gang of four" was finally complete when Millar's family solicitor, Ian Rodger, another ardent opera lover, became involved in putting the scheme on a sound legal footing.

But the going, initially, was far from easy: the four men formed a company so that application might be made to what was then the Scottish Committee of the Arts Council of

Great Britain for what now seems a ludicrously small grant towards a week-long festival of opera in May, 1961. A refusal on the grounds of lack of time ("but really," the joke went "because we didn't have enough eggheads on the letterhead") sent them looking round for more official, more academic weight to impress the guardians of the public purse. Before long, an impressive list of names was put forward as The Scottish Opera Society Ltd., formed in order to ". . . shape the artistic policy, engage the singers . . . the players, the producers and the designers and make all the administrative arrangements for the seasons."

The very substantial and professional-looking combined programme for that first season of two productions, with its expressions of gratitude not only to the Scottish Committee of ACGB (for, clearly, the presence of the "eggheads" had worked the magic and loosened the purse-strings) and to Scottish Television (both contributed £1,000) but also to other anonymous donors and guarantors, includes a list of that first advisory council. It is a list which is surely worth reprinting in the present context if only to emphasise the weight of support and confidence which Gibson and his three colleagues had managed to generate for their project.

Ernest Boden, Vice Chairman, Scottish National Orchestra. W. R. Fell, General Manager, Scottish National Orchestra. Alexander Gibson, Musical Director, Scottish National Orchestra. Dr. Mary Grierson, Lecturer in Music, Edinburgh University. Dr. Henry Havergal, Principal, Royal Scottish Academy of Music. Hugh Marshall, Director, Scottish National Orchestra. J. Ainslie Millar, Scottish Director, Sadlers Wells Opera. Prof. Sydney Newman, Professor of Music, Edinburgh University. Prof. Robin Orr, Professor of Music, Glasgow University (Chairman). Frederick Rimmer, Senior Lecturer in Music, Glasgow University. Ian B. Rodger, Solicitor, Glasgow. H. Noel Stevenson, Managing Director, Scottish Television, Ltd. Richard D. Telfer, Schoolmaster, Edinburgh. J. Graham Wark, Writer to the Signet, Glasgow.

Another name which appears in the first programme, and which has been there in virtually every programme since in one capacity or another, is that of John S. Boyle (now Sheriff Boyle) who acted as publicity officer for the brief initial season. Then not long out of university, John Boyle was Secretary of the Scottish National Orchestra Club at the time of Alex Gibson's appointment. One Sunday morning early in 1962 he lifted the ringing telephone to find Mr. Gibson on the line, asking him round for a drink and a chat. By the time the "chat" was over and the drink imbibed he had become Scottish Opera's first PRO with a press conference to publicise and organise in little more than a week's time. "That, believe me, is no exaggeration; that's exactly what it was like."

Mary Garden, the famous Scots soprano, who created the role of Mélisande in Paris in 1902, and Maggie Teyte who followed her when Debussy's opera was first produced at Covent Garden eight years later, were both invited to grace the occasion of the sixtieth anniversary performance on the second night of

Felicia Weathers as Cio-Cio San, with Chorus in MADAMA BUTTERFLY performed in 1965.

that inaugural season of Scottish Opera. Mary Garden, then very old and somewhat infirm, felt unable to make the journey from her home in the north of Scotland, but Maggie Teyte (Dame Maggie by then) accepted the invitation. Richard Telfer remembers how he met the London train and how almost the first words Dame Maggie uttered were, "Is Mary Garden coming?" "No," replied the ever courteous Mr Telfer, "I'm afraid she doesn't feel up to the journey." "I'll wager you didn't tell her I was coming," said the lady. "If you had done, she'd be here."

Anecdotes there are in plenty about the run-up to that first Scottish Opera season . . . . The publicity-conscious American soprano, Elaine Malbin, arriving at Prestwick Airport, dressed in a miniskirt and promptly commandeering a photocall already in session with the cast of *Pélleas et Mélisande* (Malbin was there to sing the title role in *Madama Butterfly*) to the consternation of the French Mélisande, Micheline Grancher. "There was Malbin," John Boyle remembers, "up on a table, displaying her excellent legs to the cameramen — and to

Pélleas — and there, weeping in a corner, was Grancher, threatening to go home to France immediately. Dennis Arundell, the producer, was prophesying doom, and I remember going out after midnight to buy the morning papers, as you could do in those days, and there it all was in the *Daily Record*, spread over the middle pages, pictures of Malbin flaunting herself and Grancher weeping in her corner. But, you see, it worked. It brought everybody in. What we didn't realise was that to the public this was *real opera*; this was how the real stars behaved. It was wonderful publicity. Was I forgiven? Heavens, yes."

Thomson Smillie, who would in time become Scottish Opera's first official PRO, was then a student on Gilmorehill and running the Glasgow University's Cecilian Society. Prompted by the resourceful Boyle, Smillie set up an all-night camp, with his girlfriend Anne and several of his fellow students, in order to be first in the box office queue for *Madama Butterfly* — a blatant publicity stunt since payment for the exercise was a batch of complimentary tickets. John Boyle then rang up the newspapers and asked, in all innocence, "Why are people camping all night at the Kings Theatre?" and, sure enough, next morning, there were the pictures with a report, splashed across the tabloids. But something much more significant took place on the second night, the civic gala performance of *Pélleas et Mélisande*. Mrs Alexander Gibson made a hasty departure after Act 1 and took a taxi to the hospital where her second son, Philip, was born in time for her husband to be told at the end of the performance.

The auguries could scarcely have been more favourable.

Scottish Opera, then, was away to a fine start: the critics were on its side, by and large, with notices that ranged from benevolent to besotted; the buzz was good; those involved were pleased with the results of their endeavours, and a second season was soon in train for 1963. In fact, however, that first season, achieved on the proverbial shoestring, was really no more than a week-long festival of opera with a volunteer management buying in talent ad hoc for two brief productions. The Scottish National Orchestra was in existence already; Debussy's opera requires only soloists and, for *Madama Butterfly*, the Royal Scottish Academy and Glasgow University could provide the necessary small chorus.

But the second season saw at least the beginning of a new development, with *Otello* as the most powerful element in a short season that also included Mozart's *Seraglio* and a double bill of Ravel and Dallapiccolo. It was already apparent, of course, from the opening season, that Scottish Opera would scorn to play safe with popular favourites only: *Pélleas et Mélisande*, mounted, at the suggestion of the Francophile, Dick Telfer, to mark the sixtieth anniversary of its first performance in Paris, was proof enough of that. It is also a fact that the British premiere of Prokofiev's *The Fiery Angel* was planned for the second season (for which a Gulbenkian Foundation grant was promised) and jettisoned only when it proved too difficult to stage at the Kings Theatre.

In 1963 the season was to be doubled in

KING'S THEATRE, GLASGOW

Proprietors: HOWARD & WYNDHAM LTD.
Manager: EDWARD ASHLEY

Managing Director: STEWART CRUIKSHANK
Telephone: City 5125-7

Week Commencing TUESDAY, 5th JUNE, 1962
Evenings at 7 p.m.   Saturday Matinee at 2 p.m.

THE SCOTTISH OPERA SOCIETY LTD.

in association with

Scottish Television Ltd. and the Scottish Committee
of the Arts Council of Great Britain

presents

A Centenary Production of Debussy's

PELLEAS et MELISANDE

WITH

Micheline Grancher, Emile Belcourt, John Cameron, Joseph Rouleau

and Puccini's

MADAMA BUTTERFLY

WITH

Elaine Malbin, Charles Craig & Laura Sarti

Produced by DENNIS ARUNDELL

Scenery and Costumes by Mark King

Artistic and Musical Director: **ALEXANDER GIBSON**

Associate Conductor: James Lockhart

THE SCOTTISH NATIONAL ORCHESTRA

(Leader: Sam Bor)

Pelleas et Melisande: Wednesday, Friday and Saturday (Matinee)
Madama Butterfly: Tuesday, Thursday and Saturday (Evening)

BOOKING OPENS MONDAY 7th MAY, 1962

Poster for the first season of Scottish Opera in 1962.

extent, with one week, as before, in Glasgow and another in Edinburgh, and for *Otello* a chorus had to be assembled and shaped. The obvious place to look for choral talent was in the operatic societies, in the Glasgow Grand, the Orpheus Society and the Pantheon Club. This, Alex Gibson remembers, took a measure of tact, since the amateur societies were apprehensive that a professional opera company would steal all their best singers. Leon Lovett arrived from Cambridge as the Company's first chorus master and, with John Boyle as his eager secretary, began the process of persuasion. All the amateur societies were consulted and their fears of undue competition allayed. From the start there seems to have been tremendous *esprit de corps*, and by the time *Otello* was staged in Glasgow, the Scottish Opera Chorus was already well into its stride and promising to become one of the best in the country. Ann Baird, then a student chorister from the Royal Scottish Academy, remembers how the great Charles Craig, having sung Otello so magnificently against Peter Glossop's dangerous Iago, turned to the choristers immediately behind him and vowed he had never heard a better soprano line (Norma Goldie was another of the young singers, and Helen McArthur, both of whom went on to greater things). Exaggeration, maybe, in that moment of euphoria, but praise worth hearing nonetheless.

Otello packed the house in both cities, deservedly, and the production by Anthony Besch signalled the start of a close and long-lasting relationship that led to a succession of fine, meticulously created productions (Anthony is the archetypal pursuer of excellence, is how one of the singers has described him). Besch was also, in that second season, responsible for reviving his own New Opera Company production of Ravel's *L'Heure Espagnole*, with Marie Collier, in a double bill with the more esoteric *Volo di Notte* (*Night Flight*) by Dallapiccolo, for which the director was Peter Ebert, son of Glyndebourne's famous Carl Ebert. Peter Ebert, too, was to enjoy a long and close relationship with Scottish Opera, as its first Director of Productions and later as its General administrator. But that was still in the future: meanwhile Ebert's treatment of *Il Sergalio* had a favourable critical reception and a rather poorer attendance than *Otello* and it is remembered as effervescent and enjoyable. At this time two designers appeared on the scene who would set their seal on a variety of Scottish Opera productions for years to come. Ralph Koltai and Peter Rice, each with his own individual style, the one concerned with stripping down, abstracting from reality rather than stylising; and the other with a notable gift for witty, decorative simplification already obvious in his *Seraglio* set, called by one reviewer, "a sort of Turkish portico-cum-patio". Both designers came with international reputations, Koltai in particular having set his seal on the look of productions in opera houses and theatres on both sides of the Atlantic, with design concepts that relate more to symbolic sculpture than to scene painting. Peter Rice, on the other hand was trained as a painter, and even when, as with the Tosca he designed for Scottish Opera in 1980, *verismo* was the order

Scottish Opera Chorus.

of the day, the great Roman church interior for Act 1 was contrived with the emotional accuracy of a good painter's eye.

Even at this early stage in Scottish Opera's history, financial problems loomed, if not yet large enough to worry about unduly. The Company ran at a loss and depended on eventually raising the money to cover the costs. Even so, the cost of that first week in 1962 sounds ludicrously small today, at less than £8,000, some £2,000 more than the original estimate. "We should have learned at the very beginning how costs could run away," Ian Rodger told me, remembering how Dennis Arundell, arriving to direct *Butterfly* and being shown the "hook-up" set being built in a workshop at Garscube Road ("It belonged to an old scene painter who kept a useful supply of props and scenery") just raised his hands in horror and said, this will never do. "So, within seconds our budget was away. We had all the girls rushing up and down Sauchiehall Street looking for Japanese bric-a-brac and artificial flowers to dress the room. And of course he was absolutely right. But that was something that repeated itself again and again — that a director would make an artistic decision at the very last moment that would put everything out in the calculations."

Peter Hemmings entered the story in the autumn of 1962, immediately after the first season; a young, forceful, highly intelligent Cambridge graduate, at that time in charge of repertoire and planning at Sadlers Wells and well known, therefore, to Alex Gibson. Naturally enough, Hemmings had become interested in the fledgling opera company and wasn't altogether surprised to be asked to join it as part-time administrator for the second season, a job that would involve around five weeks in Glasgow during the rehearsal and performance period, since the rest of the administrative work could be done from London. He was seconded "willingly and enthusiastically" by his boss, Norman Tucker, the Sadlers Wells Director, and straight away accepted the job.

"Alex's determination to give Scotland its own opera company excited me greatly. The warmth and friendliness of the Scots, and especially their serious approach to pleasure and leisure, made me want to work with them. And Scottish audiences were loyal as I had found with Sadlers Wells." The amateur Board responsible for organising the first Scottish Opera season immediately and no doubt thankfully, handed things over to Hemmings who ran the show from then on. It was not, however, until 1966, by which time the enterprise had expanded to the point when a full-time General Manager had become necessary, that Peter Hemmings moved to Glasgow with his family, knowing full well, no doubt, that he, himself, was largely responsible for the swift expansion which had made the move necessary.

It was he who organised the modest extension of the second season, with a further week in Edinburgh, and who brought Anthony Besch, with whom he had worked in his days with the New Opera Company at Sadlers Wells, into the scene. Nineteen-sixty-three being the 150th anniversary of the birth of Giuseppe Verdi, *Otello* seemed an admirable choice, an opera not

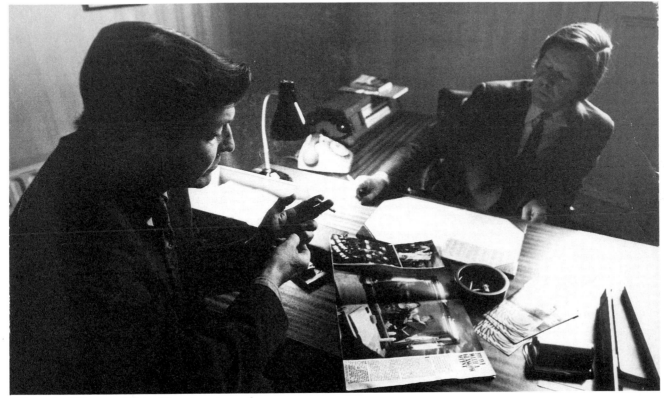

Alexander Gibson and Peter Hemmings in conference.

seen in Scotland for more than a generation and one, moreover, on the grand scale which is always popular. As it happened, 1963 was also the 150th anniversary of the birth of Richard Wagner and another plan to stage *The Flying Dutchman* was dropped only because of casting problems.

How were funds raised for such a season, given that the Company had no capital investment but depended entirely on guarantee and sponsorship? Frankly, with difficulty: *plus ça change, plus c'est la meme chose.* A request to the Arts Council, Scottish Committee, for a grant

of £10,000 was whittled down to £4,500 — exactly one-fifth of what the Welsh Committee awarded the Welsh National Opera in that same season — and another £4,500 came from the Gulbenkian Foundation, originally meant to subsidise *The Fiery Angel* but transferred, by agreement, to help cover the costs of the Dallapiccolo on the double bill. Most of the rest came from Scottish Television which continued in its role of Good Fairy Godmother, and from the Corporations of Edinburgh and Glasgow. There was also one unique donation of £1,000 which represented the total funds of the Edinburgh Opera Foundation.

Since the estimated cost of mounting the second season was £23,000 and, with luck, the box office takings might amount to around £8,000, it was thought safe to go ahead and budget for a modest deficit. And that, in truth, formed the pattern for the years immediately ahead, with each deficiency covered by an increase in the grant. *Otello, Seraglio, Volo di Notte, L'Heure Espagnole*; it was a programme designed to alert audiences to new experiences rather than to lull them with nostalgia-ridden old favourites. The general feeling was that Scottish Opera was steering a sensible, indeed an admirable course between the experimental and the fail-safe. And the fact that *Night Flight*, a contemporary work based on St Exupery's novel *Vol-de-Nuit*, about the hazards of early flight, played to respectable audience numbers, suggests that the experiment was worth the cost.

The programme for 1964 was less adventurous, perhaps because it was felt that audiences unused to modern opera should not be given an overdose before they were ready to accept it. In his book, *Scottish Opera: The First Ten Years*, Conrad Wilson reminds us of a mild controversy in *Music and Musicians* — mild, that is, by comparison with what happens on occasion nowadays — between Nöel Goodwin and the Gibson/Hemmings team; Goodwin gave it as his opinion that for Scottish Opera to present Gounod along with Mozart and Verdi might be compared "with a nascent theatre company putting its faith in Shakespeare, Shaw and East Lynne". *Faust* was the offender, pleasing, Mr Goodwin felt, "only to elderly nostalgics for

whom nothing is ever as good as it used to be. For the sake of its future," he continued, "I hope Scottish Opera will reconsider its policy — and quickly — before too much ground is lost." In their reply Messrs Gibson and Hemmings were at pains to reassure Mr Goodwin that his fears were groundless; that Scottish Opera intended to continue its policy of presenting modern works. But, in defending its choice of *Faust*, they maintained that this opera, in its time the most frequently performed of all, should be shown to each new generation of opera-goers who, at least, deserved an opportunity of endorsing their parents' opinion.

Anthony Besch and Peter Rice were seen in harness once again in *Faust*, the former moving his company with dramatic precision around and through the latter's stylised, simplified, all-purpose Gothic set, with its suggestions of stone arches, and wrought iron blazoned with colourful banners. Joseph Rouleau's sinister Mephistopheles and the Siebel of Laura Sarti are remembered more vividly than anyone else, M. Rouleau making his second appearance with the Company and Miss Sarti her third. "The great thing about Scottish Opera," Anthony Besch told me, "was that, even from the very beginning, they said we will always go for the best singers we can buy, whether they come from Britain or not. They very sensibly carved out that international, perfectionist attitude from the very start: they retained their determination about it and it was their strong working point. But of course, wherever there were wonderful British singers they would use them."

So Peter van der Bilt came from Netherlands Opera in that same season to sing the title role in *Don Giovanni* with Harold Blackburn as Leporello and a formidable Commendatore in David Ward. It was a company that also included Jennifer Vyvyan, Elizabeth Robson and Michael Maurel, and others who would become identified with Scottish Opera over the following years, and none more so than Bill McCue who sang the part of the Commendatore in several performances and who is now perhaps unique in having taken part in every season since 1962 when he sang the Bonze in *Madama Butterfly*.

That *Don Giovanni*, however, was generally considered to be flawed: it failed, most of the critics thought, to measure up to the demands of Mozart's opera either musically or histrionically. However, with the highly popular *Faust* — and Scottish audiences proved that Nöel Goodwin had the wrong end of the stick, at least from their point of view — and with Mozart and Verdi well attended in their turn (for *Otello* was revived with some changes of cast) audience percentages reached the 80s and 90s.

In his foreword to the programme book for the following season, the Chairman strikes an understandable note of self-congratulation. There existed a feeling of satisfaction on the part of all concerned that, in only three years, Scottish Opera had established a reputation for imaginative productions with, at best, exceptional casts, a chorus which was beginning to attract superlatives, and a symphony orchestra good enough to ensure a high musical standard in the pit. Professor Robin Orr now announced a further extension to the season — an extension in geographical terms, what is more, with a further week of performances at His Majesty's Theatre, Aberdeen. Acknowledgments were made to the Corporation and the University of Aberdeen for financial assistance, and to the Scottish Arts Council for an increased grant to make this extension of the season possible. Professor Orr then went on to announce the Company's plans for the future — an increase in the length and scope of the season and even, in due course, a second season at a different time of the year. "There are also long-term plans," he wrote, "for part of the Company, with a smaller orchestra, to present opera in towns which have no theatre capable of accommodating the full Company, but with no reduction of standards or of quality." But he warned that such developments must come gradually, with careful thought for the financial implications. Without subsidy, prices would have to be trebled in Glasgow and Edinburgh and quadrupled in Aberdeen. But the recently published White Paper, *A Policy for the Arts*, with its reference to the need for particular support to be given to the leading arts enterprises in Scotland and Wales, gave reason, he felt, for confidence in Scottish Opera's future.

So, in 1965, the Company made its first appearance at Aberdeen, with some trepidation, it has to be said, since nobody expected the granite city with its modest population (the oil boom was still in the future) and its reputation for parsimoniousness, to flock to His Majesty's Theatre for *Boris Godunov* or *Don Giovanni*,

The Coronation Scene in BORIS GODUNOV performed in 1965.

although *Madama Butterfly* might prove more popular. Bookings, however, averaged 76 per cent with *Boris* reaching the 90s. It may be that the participation of The Gordon Highlanders, as extras for the Coronation Scene, helped to explain the full houses, since all their friends and relatives would no doubt come out of curiosity, and word of mouth would do the rest since the spectacle was known to be extraordinary.

John Boyle, who helped to organise the extras from the barracks, recollects the occasion as though it were yesterday. "The squad were reported for duty at five o'clock sharp on the evening of the first performance of *Boris*, and this young officer who was, I suppose, about my own age, twenty-three, said, 'Ah, Mr Boyle, my sergeant will get the chaps to do anything you want, so do you mind if I just buzz off now?'. And that's just what he did, leaving me with a dozen privates and this wonderful sergeant. And I got them into the splendid Covent Garden costumes, great, long fur-lined coats with fur hats and tremendous halberds. Then I showed them how to march in for the Coronation Scene. They all loved it and it was terrific: they made the most marvellous-looking

Russians. Why did we have to have soldiers? Because Peter Hemmings said we couldn't afford to take the extras up from Glasgow. Just taking the chorus and the orchestra raised the cost of that season alarmingly."

There was, indeed, widespread approval for Scottish Opera's *Boris Godunov*, and not only because Dumbarton-born David Ward, by now an international Wagnerian bass, was singing the title role which he inhabited as to the manner born; but also because Alex Gibson had wisely chosen to sidetrack Rimsky-Korsakov's elaborate adaptation in favour of a return to Mussorgsky's original score. Michael Geliot and Ralph Koltai shared the praise for creating an ambience which Andrew Porter of the *Financial Times* felt matched the Mussorgsky score with its "starker, more urgent, less sophisticated sound than the Rimsky-Korsakov revision. "This," he wrote, "was a *Boris* unlike any other I have seen; a quieter, darker, more lyrical one." And those of us who saw that production will not easily forget it — the power of the spectacle which matched the sound; the former less glamorous and at the same time more impressive than one had visualised.

Don Giovanni and *Madama Butterfly* completed the season, the Mozart being, in effect, a revival with some new casting, but the Puccini completely rethought and redesigned by Peter Ebert and David Wilby. The new *mise-en-scène* was pale, decorative and somewhat uninspired in its faithful Japonaiserie (it remained in the repertoire until 1980, however, which speaks volumes for the popularity of Ebert's production) but the Cio-Cio San was the young black American soprano, Felicia Weathers, singing for the first time in Britain — another Scottish Opera "discovery", whose interpretation was both immensely moving and musically authoritative without an ounce of false sentiment. *Madama Butterfly* was sung in Italian once again, but *Don Giovanni* and *Boris Godunov* were both given in the English versions by E. J. Dent. Whether to present foreign opera in English or in the original language is a subject for ongoing argument, a matter, Sir Alexander Gibson will tell you, for which pragmatism is the only sensible solution.

It is perfectly obvious — and Wagner himself felt this very strongly — that most of his operas should be sung in German. But there are cases where you have to stick to the original language for other reasons. I remember being attacked at a press conference in London by the late Harold Rosenthal who accused us of snobbery in refusing to do something — *Falstaff*, as a matter of fact — in English, because, he said, you are producing opera for a public unfamiliar with the repertoire so why not do it in English? Well, there was a very simple reason. Did we want to hear Geraint Evans singing Falstaff or did we not? Because he said, I'm singing it all over the place in Italian and I can't learn it in English just for Scottish Opera.

It was the same with the *Ring* cycle: somebody then said why not do it in English, especially when so many of the singers are English speakers? But, again, David Ward had an international career singing Wotan in German. It wasn't that he was unwilling to learn it in English for us but, having done that, what happens if he is ill? You won't find anyone else of the right stature to sing it in English but you can always find, from Germany, a serviceable Wotan.

It remains a problem. David Pountney was keen to do *Die Meistersinger* in English and Norman Bailey had actually sung Hans Sachs in English at Sadlers Wells. So it wasn't, again, a question of whether Norman was willing to revert to English for us. It was what do we do for a Sachs if he is ill — which did, in fact, happen on one of the tour performances. In *Rosenkavalier* which, of course, we do in English, Mike Langdon, an international Ochs, learned it for us in English, but on the first night at Aberdeen he sang the first act and most of the second in English and then he suddenly reverted to German. But nobody cared, least of all Janet Baker who sang Oktavian for us — and what an Oktavian that was, although she vowed she would never do it again, and she never has: "What does it matter," she said, "He's such a marvellous Ochs." And, funnily enough, the most intelligible English coming off the stage over that big orchestra was from Helga Dernesch, just because she had to make such an effort to learn it that she enunciated everything absolutely clearly.

Generally speaking, however, English is used wherever it seems most appropriate and always, if possible, for comedy. Pragmatism still rules, of course, but circumstances change. *Die Meistersinger* was revived most successfully in English and clearly many in the Glasgow audience understood the minutiae of Act 1 for the first time.

It was in 1966 that Peter Hemmings became Scottish Opera's first Administrator Director (the title was later altered to General Administrator but the function remained the same) and moved his home to Glasgow. A small office was opened in Holland Street in a four-roomed flat, and, as John Boyle puts it, "Scottish Opera really got into gear". But around this time John Boyle became a member of the Arts Council, Scottish Committee, where he was able to witness the other side of what was to become a gradually worsening relationship between Scottish Opera and the people over in Edinburgh.

I wasn't on the Scottish Opera Board, of course, although in those days nobody at the Arts Council would have made a fuss if I had been: the Chairman of the Scottish National Orchestra was also the Chairman of the Music Committee and the Chairman of the Drama Committee was also the Chairman of Citizens Theatre. So everybody thought I was fair game to be lobbied — and so I was. But it immediately made me see where, right from the beginning, Peter Hemmings, in an attempt to build up the Company, played some astonishing gamesmanship, brinkmanship or whatever you like to call it, with the Arts Council. And I remember, at the time, wondering whether it was quite the right tactic to employ. Peter could simply run rings round all of them and it made them so mad — this arrogance, as they saw it, of Scottish Opera. And I greatly fear it is an attitude and a perception that has persisted at Charlotte Square to the present day.

EARLY DEVELOPMENT

Brinkmanship there was, undoubtedly; arrogance, perhaps; but what mattered above all was Hemmings's determination to succeed in his plan of building up the structure of Scottish Opera and his unshakeable belief that the direction in which he was leading the Company was the right one. These were the qualities, like them or lump them, which not only saw Scottish Opera through the first difficult years common to any infant enterprise which aims high and therefore cannot afford to fail, but which also led Scottish Opera into what many now see as its golden years — the seasons of *Cosi fan tutte*, *The Trojans*, *Fidelo* and *The Ring* in its entirety.

Hemmings, himself, was in no doubt about his aims and the kind of opera company he and Alex Gibson envisaged for Scotland. He was young, keen, able and clearly welcomed the opportunity that had come his way to build something worthwhile and lasting. He was doubly fortunate in that the amateur Board of Scottish Opera was both enthusiastic and knowledgable, and that the times were favourable as never before. The attitude of the Labour government of the day, with Jennie Lee as Arts Minister, and of the Arts Council of Great Britain under the Chairmanship of Lord Goodman, was one of sympathetic understanding that the arts in Britain needed, and deserved, to be properly funded by the state. Inflation was non-existent and grants, Peter Hemmings remembers, went up each year by as much as 25 per cent. "And there was also the fact that the Welsh National Opera, already established for well over ten years, provided a marvellous stick for us all to beat the Arts Council with."

Scottish Opera's early success was based on the belief that public demand must be maintained and stimulated by a catholic choice of repertoire — "everything," as Peter Hemmings says, "from Monteverdi to Henze," and by a mixture of international casting and the creation of a local company. And it was in order to increase the level of government funding that the schedule was expanded to include the whole of Scotland — to make the enterprise Scottish Opera in fact as well as in name, with full-scale, medium-scale and small-scale performances. The decision not to call the Company Scottish National Opera had been taken originally because it was realised that the initials SNO were already applied to the Scottish National Orchestra, and that unacceptable difficulties were bound to arise.

Those were the days before English National Opera North came into existence and Scottish Opera took its productions to a number of theatres south of the Border. This was good for the Company's morale, of course, and for its wider reputation but, according to Peter Hemmings, the Scottish Committee of ACGB always resented this activity, suspecting, quite wrongly, that they were underwriting performances in England. Indeed, Hemmings still believes that if the Scottish Arts Council (as it was soon to become and will be called by me forthwith) had followed the Welsh Arts Council's attitude, a much larger subsidy could have been forthcoming from the Arts Council in London.

But SAC were always suspicious of Scottish Opera, and afraid, almost from the outset, of being overwhelmed by what they saw as an untameable monster. From their Edinburgh base they saw the Glasgow-based institutions, the Scottish National Orchestra, Scottish Opera, Scottish Theatre Ballet, as a soaking up of "their" funds by the rival city in the west. But it is important to point out that, in 1971, more productions of opera were given in Edinburgh than in Glasgow.

In fact, had Edinburgh Corporation gone ahead with its plan to build an opera house on Castle Terrace — actually, it was never quite that but rather a multi-purpose theatre that was envisaged — Scottish Opera would have played a double winter season, annually, whereby each production would have been given four or five performances in each city, leapfrogging between the two theatres. Projected plans for such a season were actually formed, but, as everyone knows, Edinburgh's "opera house" remains a pipe-dream which is unlikely to reach fulfilment in our time.

Meanwhile, *Boris Godunov* had set a new standard for the young Company. The thinking behind Michael Geliot's production was clarified in an anonymous programme note which claimed it was

> ... an attempt to reinstate the objective realism of Mussorgsky's historical music drama by presenting the characters and dramatic situations in as authentic and unexaggerated a light as possible, and by avoiding the customary distraction of spurious theatrical effects and onion-domed Russian trappings. To this end,

Mussorgsky's original score has automatically been preferred to Rimsky Korsakov's more brilliant orchestration, several traditional cuts have been restored, while the production also incorporates the awesome scene outside St Basil's Cathedral in Red Square, which is only to be found in the composer's first version.

Expectations for the next season were running high. Wagner was reputedly on the programme: there was talk, yet again, of *The Flying Dutchman* but, in the event, what we saw at the Kings Theatre, Glasgow, on May 13th 1966, was *Die Walküre*, the first move — though such a thing was never publicly mentioned as a possibility, let alone a certainty — towards the complete *Ring* cycle a few years later on. That season also saw the start of what was to become a close and abiding relationship with the operas of Benjamin Britten. Chosen specifically to fit the modest stage dimensions of the charming little Perth Theatre — visits to that pleasant county town being yet more evidence of Scottish Opera's determination to fulfil the promise held in the title — *Albert Herring* was a success from the start. Anthony Besch was back again to direct and a new, young staff conductor, Roderick Brydon, was in charge of the orchestra, a chamber ensemble culled from the SNO. Brydon, who had worked at Sadlers Wells, was brought into the Scottish Opera team by Alex Gibson, to become an invaluable member of the Company and, eventually, internationally renowned in his own right.

Once again the thinking behind the production was radical in the best sense. Besch and Brydon were of one mind, believing that true comedy must stem from serious roots. Beneath the comic tale of the mother-ridden lad, Albert Herring — who kicks over the traces and hilariously courts disaster in the aftermath of his day as May king, for no girl in the town could be found to equal his good behaviour — is a genuine and pitiable human predicament. The result was both funny and touching, and the company assembled for that production was welded into a true ensemble that would be hard to better. "The extraordinary thing with Albert Herring," Anthony Besch remembers

is that the cast seemed to remain exactly the same for years, except that the little boy and perhaps the two girls would change. But every time I was asked to go back and revive it I would ask, is it the same cast? And Peter would say, gleefully, "Yes". It was certainly one of my favourite productions with Scottish Opera. Britten was so ingenious in exploiting the chamber opera and, of course, for Peter Hemmings and his Company they made wonderfully neat packages to tote around. I imagine him saying to the British Council, "If you want to take British opera abroad, this isn't going to cost you very much." One is always saying to modern composers, for good-ness sake, if you want to have your work performed and even make some money by it, you ought to do one of two things; either write a chamber opera for a small ensemble or write an opera for Christmas — and that would spare us always having to work on *Amahl and the Night Visitors*.

Yet nobody, I think, on that first night in Perth Theatre, by no means full but buzzing with enthusiasm by the time the curtain fell,

Michael Maurel as Sid, adds the rum to Albert's lemonade as Nancy (Catherine Wilson) looks on, from ALBERT HERRING performed in 1966.

could have foreseen that *Albert Herring* would prove to be one of the great success stories in the history of Scottish Opera, revived more often than any other in the next ten years.

It was also the first Scottish Opera production to be seen abroad, at the annual May Festival, the Maggio Musicale, in Florence and later at a number of theatres throughout Germany. On one occasion, also, *Albert Herring* was performed at Reykjavik in Iceland. And many of the singers identified in the memory with this

Sir Geraint Evans as Falstaff with Bardolph (Francis Egerton)
and Pistol (Ian Wallace) in FALSTAFF performed in 1966.

John Shaw as Ford in FALSTAFF performed in 1966.

opera, Gregory Dempsey, Judith Pierce, Francis Egerton, Catherine Wilson, Michael Maurel, Ronald Morrison, Bill McCue, formed the core of what came to be thought of as the Scottish Opera "family" for several years to come.

Falstaff was one of the 1966 productions, with Geraint Evans as Shakespeare's (and Queen Elizabeth's) "fat knight in love". In his autobiography, *A Knight at the Opera*, the rumbustious Welsh baritone, among the most renowned Falstaffs of his day, tells how delighted he was to accept Scottish Opera's invitation because Peter Ebert was to be the director. It was at Glyndebourne, under Carl Ebert, Peter's famous father, that Evans had enjoyed his first success in the role and he was happy that the son's intention was to keep in mind the foundation of the character laid down by the father.

Falstaff, as we have seen, was sung in Italian, and by a cast which could hold its own with any in the world at that time: it was a major triumph for Scottish Opera; a *Falstaff* which, as Conrad Wilson felt he had reason to say, any permanent opera house would have been proud to stage. Once again, the intention was to bring out the humanity of the plot, and the temptation to overdo the comedy by turning it into slapstick was resisted. Behind the scenes there was plenty of comedy, however, as might be expected with two such natural comedians as Ian Wallace and Francis Egerton playing Pistol and Bardolph. Ian Wallace recounts one occasion when Egerton was "nearly knocked flat" by an enraged John Shaw, the formidable Australian baritone whose Ford was so impressive.

> John was the kind of person who, no matter what part he was playing, always looked as though he ought to be playing the sheriff. And one day at rehearsal he gave a really astounding performance of Ford's monologue, better than you would find on many first nights. And afterwards Frank Egerton said, "I really enjoyed that, John. It will be absolutely magnificent when you start singing out." Oh the relief when John Shaw got the message that it was only a joke.

Even in his first plunge into deep Wagnerian waters with *Die Walküre*, Peter Ebert had already begun to crystallise his concept of the *Ring* story as one which could be seen as a ". . . very exciting, but very human drama in spite of all this god-fallen business. Up to then I suddenly realised that I'd always seen the wrong performances. The people on stage seemed always to be trying to echo these immeasurably big sounds coming out of the orchestra — and I mean sounds not in the sense of volume, but in thought and so on."

David Ward, already an experienced and impressive Wotan at Covent Garden, and Anita Valkki as Brunnhilde, were on familiar ground in *Die Walküre*, and although the others (Ann Howard, Donald McIntyre, Elizabeth Fretwell and Charles Craig — the Fricka, Hunding, Sieglinde and Siegmund) were all new to Wagner, the result was impressive enough to earn qualified praise from the critics of the national press. "Already a cut above what one might hear in a German provincial house," the *Financial Times*, might sound grudging but, in retrospect, it was no doubt fair comment on something which promised rather more than it delivered.

The set by Michael Knight was something of a disappointment, not because it was an abstraction (something that could always be depended upon to annoy the reactionaries in the audience) but because, as such, it somehow failed to match the immensities contained in Wagner's theme and music. What the designer had done was to take the idea of a ring, using moveable, slanting segments which were placed in different juxtapositions and only brought together as a complete circle when *Gotterdammerung* was finally staged several years later. The fact, too, that Scottish theatres were still without computerised lighting boards was also a liability, making it difficult, if not impossible, to generate the kind of atmospheric subtlety which was clearly being demanded.

There was an undoubted sense of progress at that time, and a new access of confidence in Scottish Opera's status and importance as a national institution. A supporters' league, the Scottish Opera Club, was founded, with its own magazine, preferential booking scheme, lectures and even occasional organised tours to

European opera houses. Not unnaturally, to those closely involved as well as to Scottish Opera's growing audiences, even to the wider news-reading public, those were heady times; so much so, indeed, that it is difficult to look back with any measure of objectivity.

By now, of course, Scottish Opera was well into the business of publicising itself, with Thomson Smillie — he of the all-night vigil in Bath Street before the first night in 1962 — now officially in charge of the Press and Publicity department. "It was a very personal thing for all of us, the growth and development of Scottish Opera." Thomson, who now runs Kentucky Opera, threatens to become dewy-eyed when he reaches his "anecdotage", remembering his Wordsworth:

> Bliss was it in that dawn to be alive. And to be young was very heaven. Of course, the remarkable thing about those early days of Scottish Opera was the extreme youth of most of us. The grand old man of the Company was a tottering 36-year-old and I was 19. Part of the excitement for me was the fact that it was the most unparochial of organisations even while it drew its strength — all its audience and most of its money, too — from Scotland where it had its roots.

So there was plenty to publicise and with an enthusiastic, energetic youngster like Thomson in the Press Office, critics and journalists in general were kept well in touch with events and developments, one of which was the first invitation to Scottish Opera to participate in the 1967 Edinburgh International Festival with a new production of *The Rake's Progress*

DIE WALKÜRE performed in 1966.

commissioned by the Festival Director, Peter Diamand, for his Stravinsky celebration year.

Since it began in 1947 the Edinburgh Festival had been the main source of international operatic experience for those music lovers in Scotland who lacked the wherewithal to travel abroad, or even to London more than once or twice a year. In the fifteen years between the launching of the first Edinburgh Festival and the founding of Scottish Opera, enthusiasts for music drama might have seen at least fifty productions at Edinburgh. Glyndebourne Opera held sway all through the early years — Carl

DAS RHEINGOLD performed in 1967.

Ebert and Rudolph Bing of Glyndebourne had been instrumental in getting the Festival off the ground in the first place — alternating Mozart with Verdi. Other companies then began to be invited from opera houses all over Europe (The Royal Opera made a surprisingly belated appearance in 1961), bringing productions of works by a far wider range of composers, from Beethoven and Wagner, Strauss and Hindemith to Bellini, Donizetti, Stravinsky, Poulenc and Benjamin Britten.

Peter Diamand's invitation to the Scottish company must be seen as a sign of approval, signifying recognition that the five-year-old company was, indeed, here to stay and demanding not only recognition on its own acount, but also to be judged fairly against its peers from elsewhere. Indeed, having seen Michael Geliot's *Boris Godunov* and Anthony Besch's *Albert Herring* in the same years as several less-than-exhilarating offerings from the Holland Festival, from Stuttgart and from Munich, as well as the English Opera Group's own *Albert Herring* in what seems, in retrospect, a more superficial reading than Scottish Opera's, one cannot help feeling that previous Festival Directors might, with advantage, have erred on the side of adventure and proffered the invitation a few years earlier.

As it happens, 1967 was one season when Scottish Opera was manifestly ready for Edinburgh, when the Company could have furnished the Festival with a full three weeks of first-rate opera. With new productions of *Cosi fan tutte, La Boheme* and *Das Rheingold*, as well as *The Rake's Progress* commissioned for the Festival, this was a vintage season.

In his direction of *Cosi*, Anthony Besch went right to the nerve centre of the plot, and once again, penetrating through the seemingly frivolous surface to the undercurrent of insecurity in the relationship of the central characters, and in particular the two sisters, Fiordiligi and Dorabella. The casting of Elizabeth Harwood and Janet Baker was a positive inspiration. One knows now that Janet Baker needed a great deal of persuasion before she would agree to try conclusions with a role for which she felt herself unsuited. Comedy, she thought, was not her forte and she felt disinclined to plunge into alien waters. Indeed, Alex Gibson tells how he and Peter Hemmings took her out to dinner and set themselves to make her change her mind. But the initial suggestion came from Besch. That they were successful in doing so is now part of operatic history, for her Dorabella went deep into the character of the young woman in the shadow of a beautiful sister, who disguises her own self-doubts with adorably roguish frivolity. This marvellously funny and touching performance killed any notion that this splendid musician, whose instrument happens to be her own exceptional voice, was suited only to the operas of Handel and Purcell and the song cycles of Mahler. "You know you have a comic talent" is what she was told, "and you mustn't let yourself be categorised".

Dame Janet, as she now is, has a very special place in the story of Scottish Opera and in the affections of all who worked with her, and she admits that this warmth of feeling is fully reciprocated.

There are certain times in your life when you know, without doubt, that you are in the right place at the right time, and my relationship with Peter Hemmings and Alex Gibson was one of those occasions. It seemed to me that what they were doing in Glasgow was almost unique in Britain. And yes, it was marvellous to be asked to do a role like Dorabella in *Cosi*; to be taken seriously as someone who would successfully cope with a funny thing. And do you know that Elizabeth Harwood told me recently that she had seen an enlarged photograph in the Mozart House at Salzburg of the two of us in that production — which, I think, shows how highly the profession rates it. That is something of which I am immensely proud.

Cosi fan tutte, in John Stoddart's mainly black and white designs, was charmingly decorative, and musically it reached a state of grace that sent people away from the theatre treading air, as it were. Yet in revival, two years later, it seemed, if anything, even better. In this context it is worth recording the fact that Anthony Besch, unlike some other directors, always returns to supervise revivals of his own productions and that meticulous care inevitably shows in the end result, as was seen in 1986

Janet Baker and Elizabeth Harwood in COSI FAN TUTTE performed in 1967.

with the 17-year-old production of *The Turn of the Screw*. The reason why Janet Baker and Elizabeth Harwood were so perfect as the sisters in *Cosi* is explained, in Besch's opinion, by the fact that they both come from Yorkshire. "It is a strange thing about Yorkshire singers, that they are actually more musical than singers anywhere else in Britain. Other people have good voices; other people may be musical; but singers from Yorkshire have this extraordinary combination of talents, and nobody has ever explained it satisfactorily."

To take on *The Ring of the Nibelungs* must already have been discussed as a possibility between the two men at the head of Scottish Opera once *Die Walküre* had been successfully staged. By 1967, with *Das Rheingold* in the repertoire that possibility had surely become a certainty. But here we are in very different country, theatrically speaking, from *Cosi*. It is not enough to feel one's way, no matter how sensitively, into the demonstrably human inter-relationships of the Nordic gods, goddesses, dwarfs and giants of the Nibelung Saga. All this has to be staged in a way that at least reflects the oceanic nature of the score, encompassing as it does all the immensity of man and nature. Was Wagner asking for the impossible? He was answered at least, in the rising of the curtain on the sun-dappled shimmering gauze during the Rheingold overture, like a great river with the Rhine Maidens floating in its depths, which set the scene in a way that is unforgettable.

Enormous preparation went into those *Ring* productions. Conrad Wilson, with a preview article in view for the *Scotsman*, was given access, unusual for a critic, to the Kings Theatre, Glasgow, in the run-up to the opening performance. Wilson was one of the most consistently supportive of all the critics in Scottish Opera's early years, and in his book he remembers how it felt to be, for once, thus privileged.

For an afternoon I explored the theatre, soaking up sights and sounds, watching first a group of percussionists backstage, practising on a dozen anvils that had been collected for the forging scene (some were real anvils,

Ticho Parly as Siegfried and Francis Egerton as Mime in
SIEGFRIED, which formed part of DER RING DES
NIBELUNGEN performed in 1971.

others were bits of a dismantled railway line)
and though in quantity they were not so
numerous as those in the Decca recording,
they made a fine ringing din . . . more satisfying
than the sound nowadays employed by many
German companies, which is simply to tape
record the sound. Next, two of the stage hands
began thwacking whips in preparation for the
scene in which Mime is thrashed by the
invisible Alberich. The right sound was proving
hard to capture. "Too resonant", called Alex
Gibson from the orchestra pit when they tried
striking a wooden table behind the scenes.
"Why not try skin?" asked Peter Ebert,
cheerfully.

Then Wilson went on to tell how he sighted
the dragon, Hammer-Film style, staring at him
from the wings with its tongue hanging out;
and of the rows of costumes, mesh and glitter
for the Rhine Maidens, a flickering fiery robe
for Loge, dark, thick rubber suits for the giants
Fafner and Fasolt; and of watching Wotan
swinging his spear to determine how much
room he had without driving it right into the
scenery. (There was, in fact, one occasion, in
performance, in the scene where the giants

strike their bargain with Wotan for the gold, when Bill McCue, as Fasolt, pushed his staff into the prepared hole and found it disappearing completely. Whereupon he did what all good actors do when "corpsing", he turned his back until his shoulders stopped heaving.) On Conrad Wilson's peep behind the scenes he did notice that the singers were nervously checking their footholds on the sloping geometric rosta. In all, a vivid picture of the anxious, busy build-up to an important first night.

Perhaps opera-goers should occasionally be allowed a sight of such careful and arduous preparations. This is certainly what Peter Ebert thinks, believing it a pity that the opera world is such a closed society.

> I would like to have had open rehearsals at Scottish Opera and, no, not just dress rehearsals but early rehearsals too. Of course the singers will always say they don't like it, but when they have actually had the experience they have usually found it a good thing. In Germany we set up a kind of seminar, a group of interested people who went through the whole process, preliminary talk, first, middle and late rehearsals, performance, and a final discussion. The audience realised then just how difficult it all was, and they could actually contribute in discussion. I wanted very much to do this in Glasgow, but we were a little too worried and tradition-bound to actually do that kind of thing.

In this respect, albeit more than ten years after the period when Ebert was in charge, it is worth noting that his successor, John Cox, in collaboration with the *Glasgow Herald* as the sponsoring body, opened some rehearsals of his *Marriage of Figaro* to the public in an attempt to show how an opera is prepared. Cox himself directed these rehearsals, with the young singers who were covering (that is understudying) the principal roles, and hosted the discussion-and-question sessions in which singers, conductor, designer and wardrobe mistress also took part. The culmination of the exercise was the final dress rehearsal with the principal artists, in performance conditions.

It was Peter Ebert who staged the final production of the 1967 season, the *La Bohème* which, in spite of an initial coolish response from the critics, has stayed the course remarkably well, pleasing packed houses year after year in numerous revivals, with a succession of Mimis, Rodolphos and Musettas to follow the first trio of Bohemians, Luisa Bosabalian, George Shirley and Barbara Rendell. Peter Rice, once again, contrived the effectively simplified realism of the Paris scene.

But it was *The Rake's Progress* that inevitably found the widest audience at the Festival when, as they say, the world makes tracks for Edinburgh. In the official programme Peter Heyworth of the *Observer* wrote a welcoming article to Scottish Opera in which he traced the flowering of opera in Britain to the foundation of Glyndebourne in 1934 and thence through the first performance of *Peter Grimes* at Sadlers Wells in 1945 to the setting up of a state-subsidised opera at Covent Garden a year later, that being the point where government finally

Patricia Hay as Musetta in LA BOHÈME performed in 1967.

accepted the principle that opera is an art that cannot pay for itself. "These," he wrote, "were all decisive milestones in our belated operatic development. Yet, when the musical history of those years comes to be written, I fancy that an undertaking launched in 1962 by Alexander Gibson on a most modest scale but with the (as it then seemed) immodest title of Scottish Opera, may well come to play an increasing part in solving the Festival's operatic dilemma."

It has to be said however, that, after a first night of *The Rake's Progress* which was not entirely trouble-free, the same Peter Heyworth tempered his praise with criticism, finding the performance, overall, not fully convincing. Ralph Koltai's sets, abstractions as always, created the now predictable doubts in the minds of many, including some music critics, although to others, less prejudiced or merely more aware, visually, they made a strong impact, from the dappled verdure of the first scene to the tortured Bedlam at the end. Everyone, however, seemed to be in agreement about the quality of the Scottish Opera Chorus, not just about its power but also about its intelligent use of expressive vocal colour. Nobody suggested that the invitation to the Festival was undeserved: how could they when the comparison with the other visiting companies that year was so clearly in favour of Scottish Opera.

Opera-in-the-round was a new idea for the Festival, although Tyrone Guthrie, in his inspired and widely influential use of the Assembly Hall of the Church of Scotland had accustomed us all to the theatrical excitement which could be generated in such a space. To continue the Stravinsky theme at the 1967 Festival, Scottish Opera mounted a series of forenoon performances of *The Soldier's Tale* in that same hall during the final week. Wendy Toye was the director and Carl Toms the designer and their production was in sharp contrast to a previous, overly balletic, Festival performance of the work starring Robert Helpman and Moira Shearer. For this Scottish Opera production was given a new relevance that had been lacking in the other. Here was Gordon Jackson as Narrator in casual sweater and slacks; Nicky Henson as the young cockney soldier; Patrick Wymark as a grim, black-uniformed Devil and Una Stubbs, bright-eyed, doll-like and mini-skirted as the Princess. The overt casualness of the event barely disguised the overall precision and control, in everything from the fine orchestral contribution to the silent masked figures who moved the props around and created a whole host of effects by throwing streamers and twirling parasols in a way that owed a great deal to oriental theatre. Sadly, this kind of production in the round, with its studio theatre atmosphere and with the musicians in full view throughout, has never been repeated by an opera company in that particular venue.

THE GOLDEN YEARS

When Alexander Gibson took over as Musical Director of the Scottish National Orchestra it was already obvious that contemporary music would not be ignored. In 1959 the Sinfonia for Two Orchestras, by Iain Hamilton, was commissioned for performance by the SNO at the Edinburgh Festival. To widen people's appreciation and educate the concert-going public to understand and enjoy the work of living composers was taken by him to be an important part of his function. It was Gibson, after all, who gave Glasgow its first festival of modern music, in *Musica Viva*. Who, in that audience, could forget the experience of sitting in the balcony of the late, lamented St Andrews Hall, looking down on the three orchestras and striving to come to terms with Stockhausen's *Gruppen*!

It was only to be expected, then, that the commissioning of a new opera was only a matter of time. In the event it took more than ten years before a scheme went ahead whereby four new operas from Scottish composers were to be commissioned for performance in as many seasons. But earlier still, in 1968, a new one-act opera, *Full Circle*, commissioned by Scottish Television, was staged by Scottish Opera and given its first performance at Perth Theatre. The composer was Robin Orr, the Company's Chairman, whose ambition to write an opera was certainly not new, but up to then still unfulfilled.

Based on a radio play, *The Stick-up*, by the Edinburgh poet Sydney Goodsir Smith, *Full Circle* was set in depressed Clydeside and involved an armed robbery by a seemingly timorous, but desperate, unemployed docker. Melodrama, perhaps, or so some of us thought in those days when the political slogan was "You've never had it so good", but melodrama is the stuff of opera, and the times have seen a tragic turnabout for many people like the central character in *Full Circle*. The score was atmospheric, posing no difficulties for the listener in the way of stylistic extremes. The staging by Michael Geliot — with more than half an eye on the demands of television no doubt — made use of a backdrop of huge screens to accept photographic blowups. But, several months later when *Full Circle* was revived for the Kings Theatre, Edinburgh, in a double bill with a revival of *The Soldier's Tale*, there was a new setting by Bernard Culshaw on a revolving stage which allowed for three different scenes to be changed with a minimum of fuss. It was, wrote Conrad Wilson, in retrospect, ". . . a kind of Glasgow Wozzeck".

Nineteen-sixty-eight was also the year of *Gotterdammerung*, turning the probability of a complete *Ring* cycle into near-certainty. That was the year when *The Marriage of Figaro* was given its first performance, like *Full Circle*, at Perth, with the Besch/Stoddart team in action once again. And, not least important, 1968 saw the Company move into its own headquarters in a rather grand building in Elmbank Crescent which has served the Company as administrative and rehearsal space ever since, as "The Scottish Opera Centre". The building, with its spacious interiors and its solid, typically Glaswegian, architectural presence (for Scotland's industrial

*Catherine Gayer as Susanna in THE MARRIAGE OF
FIGARO performed in 1968.*

capital had a notable architectural flowering
late last century which, in its new state of
cleanliness, has come to be recognised as such,
internationally) had been the property and the
headquarters of the Institution of Engineers
and Shipbuilders in Scotland. But with the
decline of the industry which had put Clydeside
in the world league, the building came on the
market to be saved from the demolishers by
Glasgow Corporation who then leased it to
Scottish Opera, which might, with good reason,
have been called an industry on the move.

Re-christened the "Scottish Opera Centre",
the three-storey, stone-built, generously embellished structure — high quality wood panelling
and artist-designed stained glass are notable in
its interior — offers a top floor rehearsal space
large enough to accommodate in full any
production destined for the largest theatres in
Scotland. For it has to be remembered that,
until the acquisition of the Opera Centre,
rehearsal space posed problems: many rehearsals,
indeed, were held in London since that is where
many of the artists were based. And it is yet
another instance of the "family" nature of
the operation, in which Peter Hemmings
would seem to have been something of a father
figure, albeit somewhat autocratic, that singers
remember, to this day, how Peter, and not an
underling, would often be there at the airport
to welcome them off the London plane.

At Elmbank Crescent there was room for
expansion. The Company's education side
began to be taken seriously, and the small-
scale, piano-accompanied touring section —
the Opera for All group which had been taken
over from the Arts Council in 1966 — continued
to take the experience of opera to the most
distant corners of the country. The administrative
staff required to cope with all this as well
as with the major productions and the day
to day running of the Company, suddenly
found themselves with breathing space after the
cramped quarters of the small office-flat in
Holland Street. And Thomson Smillie, with a
proper Press Room of his own, set his sights
higher than ever in presenting his well burnished
image of Scottish Opera to the world. Indeed,

he had a fine product to publicise.

The *Marriage of Figaro* was admirable, even though it wasn't another *Cosi* — the high expectations roused by that memory served, no doubt, to preclude all-out satisfaction — but *Figaro* brought two young "company" sopranos to the fore; Catherine Wilson, graceful and poignant as the Countess, and Patricia Hay as a bright-faced, nimbly articulate Cherubino; Catherine Gayer made the first of several appearances with the Company as Susanna; and Michael Maurel and Peter van der Bilt, by now another "regular", together created an interesting contrast, cockiness against macho arrogance, in their portrayals of Figaro and Almaviva.

The production that did succeed in catching everyone's imagination that year was *Gotterdammerung* where, above all, Alex Gibson and the SNO seemed absolutely in their element. One is told, moreover, again and again, about Gibson's understanding of singers and the kind of sympathetic support they need from the pit. The visual aspect of Michael Knight's set for the *Ring* was improved, or so it seemed. The lighting was more subtly expressive and the dappled Rheingold gauze came into use again to suggest an elemental flux and also to mask scene changes. Helga Dernesch, in her debut with Scottish Opera, sang Gutrune and made an unforgettable impression on everyone, audiences, critics and fellow artists, with what can only be called her luminosity, both of voice and of presence on the stage.

But there were lighter moments to relieve the emotional high points. Foreign singers some-

Catherine Wilson as Ellen Orford in PETER GRIMES performed in 1968.

times insisted on the fee being paid in hard cash, and Thomson Smillie remembers spending one memorable first night carrying a wad of five-pound notes in a state of nervous agitation all evening in case they were mislaid or stolen before the time came to hand them over to the prima donna in question. After the performance he went round to the lady's dressing room and apologised for having to bring her down to earth so abruptly after her wonderful performance, with the sordid business of money. "Not at all," she said. "Just sit down, my dear,

PETER GRIMES performed in 1968.

and we will count it together." So the notes were duly counted and an elastic band produced from somewhere and snapped efficiently around them: art and finance clearly kept in different pockets, so to speak.

The Hamburg State Opera and the English Opera Group were billed for two weeks at the Kings Theatre during the 1968 Edinburgh Festival, and Scottish Opera were once again invited by Peter Diamand to take part, with four performances of *Peter Grimes* in a new production. That was the Festival's Britten year — Diamand continuing a tradition begun by his immediate predecessor, Lord Harewood,

of focusing, each year, on the work of a different composer. Benjamin Britten himself would be there to give recitals with Peter Pears and Rostropovich, and also to conduct performances of his *Church Parables* by the English Opera Group in St Mary's Cathedral, with Colin Graham as director.

Graham also directed *Peter Grimes* for Scottish Opera with designs by Alix Stone which miniaturised and synthesised the Suffolk fishing village of stone and timber with dramatic chiaroscuro. Surprisingly, Colin Graham, for all his experience of Britten operas, was new, like the Scottish company, to *Peter Grimes*, and the quality of the result suggested that rehearsals must have been, to all concerned, like a voyage of discovery. This was not the first time that *Peter Grimes* had been seen in Scotland but it was generally agreed that the performers, and not least the chorus, so effective not only vocally but also in movement and acting ability, were able to build credible character relations and create tensions in a way that made this opera a perfect vehicle for their talents.

As will be realised by now, Gibson and Hemmings were an extraordinary team, complementary in every way. "They always seemed to me to go together like oil and vinegar" says Thomson Smillie, "or, even more, they remind me, in retrospect, of Gilbert and Sullivan, with Hemmings playing the more aggressive, driving Gilbert and Gibson the gentler, more self-effacing, but fully equal partner." Together, there is no doubt that they were invetcrate scalers of heights; musical mountaineers. To try conclusions with Wagner and Verdi at their most daunting had been irrestistible and now, with the Berlioz centenary in the offing, yet another soaring alp loomed temptingly on the horizon. *The Trojans* was a challenge which, I suspect, simply had to be taken up for more than one reason. Not only was it a major rarity, and the most challenging of all Berlioz works, but it was also a fact that Glasgow, not London, had seen the first British production as long ago as 1935 when Dr Erik Chisholm staged it with the Glasgow Grand Opera Society. This historic production was spread

Interval at a rehearsal of PETER GRIMES. Left to right: Richard Cassilly, William McAlpine and Roderick Brydon.

across both afternoon and evening — I know, because I was taken as a child only to the matinee because the evening performance, *The Trojans in Carthage*, was thought to finish too late for my tender years. All I can remember now is my sense of disappointment when the Trojan Horse turned out to be nothing more impressive than immense two-dimensional legs disappearing upwards out of sight. Scottish Opera's wooden horse was at least complete as well as huge; half barbaric like an archaic war machine and half playful with its wheels and pulleys, like a giant child's Tinkertoy construction.

The decision was made to mount *The Trojans*, uncut in one mammoth evening, with a dinner interval in what would inevitably become a gala atmosphere. As such, it was the first great international event of the Berlioz centenary year. Such occasions always go down in the history books (and now Glasgow had two Berlioz "firsts" to its credit) but *The Trojans*, as presented by Scottish Opera on that May evening (was it as warm and balmy as one remembers?) merits inclusion for more than one reason. Apart from anything else, there was the presence of Janet Baker, one of the world's great musicians, as Dido. Having relished the discovery that it could be important to her development as an artist to be stretched in new directions (as had happened when she sang Dorabella) and knowing that Dido might be — as, indeed, she found to be the case — one of the greatest, most satisfying roles to sing ("You have such a wonderful length of time to develop the character"), she accepted the challenge with a result that has passed into legend. And although the memory of that first night must be illumined by that towering, impassioned performance by a great artist capable of conveying all the tragedy and pathos of Dido's situation, there were other special moments to cherish — the sweet, lyrical tenor voice of John Robertson singing Hylas's song and the long, breath-held scene when Elaine MacDonald, as a sad, sweet-faced Andromache, led her little son, Astyanax, around the stage in a deep silence that spread right through the auditorium.

This was another occasion — there were five performances of *The Trojans* in Glasgow that season — when the SNO and its conductor were wonderfully *en rapport*, with each other and with Berlioz. Criticism was silenced, except where the hideous "Hollywood-Classical" costumes were concerned, not least for poor Ronald Dowd, as Aeneas. Once again the choral work, now under the charge of Arthur Oldham, was magnificent, and said to be so by the critics who, almost to a man, proclaimed the whole event a triumph for singers, players and, not least, for Berlioz.

Later that year the second British production of *The Trojans* was staged at Covent Garden with Josephine Veasey singing Dido and Colin Davis on the podium. One day Josephine Veasey fell ill and, knowing that Janet Baker had sung the role in Glasgow, the Royal Opera management begged her to substitute at short notice. Before the curtain rose, Sir John Tooley came on stage to apologise for the absence of Miss Veasey and to announce that Miss Baker would be singing the role of Dido. A stentorian voice from the upper reaches of the house made itself heard: "And about time, too". Presumably the owner of the voice had been in Glasgow five months earlier.

Elaine MacDonald's impressive, silent, portrayal of the bereaved Andromache, was the work of a ballerina, not an opera singer, and her presence in *The Trojans* — and that of her colleagues in the wonderful running lifts and leaps during the Royal Hunt and Storm —

Janet Baker as Dido in THE TROJANS performed in 1969.

marked the first public appearance in Scotland of what was to become in effect our national ballet company. Western Theatre Ballet, a touring company directed by Peter Darrell with a leaning towards contemporary subject matter, had come, at the invitation of the Scottish Arts Council, to make its base in Glasgow, sharing the Scottish Opera Centre and, to begin with, sharing seasons at Perth, Glasgow and Edinburgh. The original intention was that both companies should build a close and lasting relationship, and the fact that this did not happen precisely as planned is seen by some as unfortunate and by others as inevitable. But, in any case, it lies outwith the scope of the present story.

Somewhat surprisingly, in view of its great success with Berlioz, no invitation came to Scottish Opera from the Edinburgh Festival Director in 1969. Instead, in a programme coloured by things Italian, and especially Florentine, we saw the Teatro Communale from that city, in Donizetti, Verdi, Puccini and Rossini, with its own orchestra, chorus and ballet, sent to Edinburgh at immense cost to the Italian government. It is an old story and a sad fact that because foreign companies are heavily subsidised by their own governments to come to Edinburgh, it is more expensive for the Festival authorities to pay the cost of transporting Scottish Opera from Glasgow, with its sets, stage crew, chorus, orchestra and principals, than to host far larger companies from a thousand miles away in Europe.

Whether or not Scottish Opera was sensible to take part, on its own account, with a new one-act opera by Philip Purser, at the Gateway Theatre, Scottish Television's new studio and headquarters in Edinburgh, is arguable. *The Undertaker* was an STV commission, and performed as a late night double bill with *Full Circle* in revival. It was an interesting effort, more notable, as somebody said, for its hints at what the composer might some day achieve than for its present merits. Not the best protagonists for Tito Gobbi and Gianni Schicci.

The Undertaker has never been revived, nor has Colin Graham's production of Rossini's *Cenerentola* which was mounted as a Christmas offering to Edinburgh at the Kings Theatre, presumably to compensate for the lack of a major presence at the Festival that August. During the summer Edinburgh had also enjoyed a revival of the previous season's dip into comic opera with *The Gondoliers*. It was during that production, on the occasion of a visit by the Royal Family, that The Duke of Plaza Toro, alias the irrepressible Ian Wallace, rewrote the duet, "Small Titles and Orders" . . . and with Johanna Peters as his Duchess, sang the following as an encore:

We're all of a flutter,
Our knees turn to butter
When we're entertaining the Monarch.
We must organise banquets,
Air monogrammed blankets,
And polish the spare room with Ronuk.
I've read books on polo,
And how to fly solo:
I pore over each publication —
Large tomes on race horses
And show-jumping courses,
So I can make bright conversation.

There was laughter in the Royal Box as well as in the audience and next day a copy of the parody (which is considerably longer than the verse I have quoted) was requested from Holyrood. Royal visits to Scottish Opera invariably coincide with the lighter offerings, like *The Merry Widow* and *Don Pasquale*, both of which were attended by Royalty in the years to come. But meanwhile, 1970 saw the Company scaling yet another mountain peak — *Fidelio*, Beethoven's sole venture into the world of opera and, as such, a work which holds a special place in the minds of most musicians. Here the team which made *The Trojans* memorable came together again — Gibson with the SNO, Ebert and Schmuckle in charge of the staging (as before, the nepotism was unfortunate, which left the costume designs to Sylte Busse-Schmuckle). *Fidelio* was mounted to celebrate another anniversary, the Beethoven bicentenary, and Helga Dernesch returned to Scotland to sing her first Leonore. A year later she sang the role again for Karajan at Salzburg.

Apart from the marvellous music, what is unforgettable about that *Fidelio* — and the magic occured again at every revival — was the inspired use of stage lighting, by Charles Bristow, to create wonderful contrasts in a way that somehow seemed to reflect the contrasts in the score; the darkness, not black but disquietingly sombre, of the prison interior and the indescribable, almost painful, blinding radiance when the great door opened and the sunlight flooded in. Almost, the effect on the spirit of Beethoven's finale was matched by the vision on the stage.

Helga Dernesch as Leonore and Charles Craig as Florestan in FIDELIO performed in 1970.

Any experienced drama critic will tell you that such moments in theatre are rare and often unexpected, when everything seems to combine in a kind of creative harmony. In opera it happens even more rarely that everything, so to speak, "jumps together". Either the performance is outstanding, musically, and yet (as with *The Trojans*) leaves something to be desired in terms of what the eye is offered; or the visual imagery is evocative, charming, spectacularly effective, while individual performances, either musically or histrionically, fail to measure up. In that

respect 1970 was a vintage season for Scottish Opera. Not just *Fidelio*, but *Der Rosenkavalier*, *Elegy for Young Lovers*, *The Turn of the Screw* and, on a delightfully whimsical small scale, *The Barber of Seville*, as well as *Traviata* and *The Magic Flute* which was mounted to coincide with the Commonwealth Games. An ambitious programme, with a cost estimated at between £400,000 and £500,000, which did, however, create financial problems for the company. But nobody, looking back and remembering the quality of the product on the stage, could doubt that the money was well spent.

Four, at least, of those new productions remain as memorable as any in Scottish Opera's history. In *The Turn of the Screw* Besch, Stoddart and Bristow brought a blend of intellect and creative imagination to bear yet again on the tensions within a Britten opera, hinting at, rather than spelling out the latent ambiguity — were the ghosts actual emanations of malevolence or figments conjured up in the mind of a neurotic and highly impressionable young woman? Revived again and again with no lessening of its power to grip the imagination — the visual element reflecting the strange, sweet, plaintive power of the score — *The Turn of the Screw* seems likely to stay in the repertoire for some time to come.

The 1970 Edinburgh Festival featured the work of the young German composer Hans Werner Henze, and it was he who directed his

Catherine Gayer as Hilda Mack in ELEGY FOR YOUNG LOVERS performed in 1970. (Director: Hans Werner Henze, designer: Ralph Koltai.)

own *Elegy for Young Lovers* with Scottish Opera at the Kings Theatre. The abstract set, by Koltai, was a gleaming, monumental piece of constructivist sculpture that really did evoke the exhilaration and the menacing nature of a soaring mountain of ice and snow. Henze's opera, a sharp, satirical questioning of the "artist as hero" in the romantic nineteenth century tradition, was mounted, sung and played brilliantly enough to remain, maybe, the definitive production of the work. As such, it allowed Scottish Opera to hold its own, unquestionably, against the other participating companies from Frankfurt and Prague. It is worth mentioning, however, that the latter company, bringing works by Janáček and Smetana (*The Bartered Bride*, *The Cunning Little Vixen* and *The Makropoulos Case*) might be thought to have pointed the way to one direction in which Scottish Opera would go in the future.

Not for some years, however; meanwhile there was a ravishing *Rosenkavalier* with a central trio of stars in the best sense of that much misused expression. Helga Dernesch as the Marschallin, Elizabeth Harwood as Sophie and Janet Baker singing Oktavian for that first and only time. With Anthony Besch again in charge of the action and Gibson with the SNO in the pit, the result is remembered as one of the true highlights in this company's history. *Rosenkavalier* has been revived several times but never again with Janet Baker, a role she found less rewarding than she had hoped it might be. "It is a very strenuous role with a great deal of physical effort involved, and rather less singing

DER ROSENKAVALIER performed in 1971, (Director: Anthony Besch, designer: John Stoddart.)

than I would like. Playing a male involves a different sort of mental energy; changing clothes all the time is terribly exhausting; and I found that being a woman playing a man playing a woman was simply too tiring without the compensation of being musically satisfying." Whether she enjoyed it or not, and whatever she may say about it, says Anthony Besch, Janet Baker was a wonderful Oktavian.

I wonder how many Glaswegians passing the Kings Theatre on their daily business, remember the sight of the poster, early in December 1971, with its stark message, *Der Ring Des Nibelungen*, etched into a blazing, flaming red ground. The

culmination, as it was, of a decade of phenomenal growth, the success of the four performances in that week, for which every seat was booked in spite of what were then extremely high prices (from one pound to seven pounds) is now the stuff of legend. Even the loss of Helga Dernesch through illnesss couldn't lessen the triumphant atmosphere generated by the justifiable sense of achievement.

The overall sense of achievement was not entirely unaccompanied by worries. Peter Hemmings remembers all too well the fact that

Peter van der Bilt as Nick Shadow in THE RAKE'S PROGRESS *performed in 1971. (Director: David Pountney.)*

Robert Tear as Tamino, playing the "Magic Flute" in Pountney's "Midi" production of THE MAGIC FLUTE performed in 1974.

who was then the Music Officer of Northern Arts and who made available a grant for the purpose. The link between Phillips and Scottish Opera was further strengthened when the MacRobert Centre at the new University of Stirling was opened, with Anthony Phillips as its first director. At the core of the MacRobert Centre is a well-equipped, 500-seat theatre which Scottish Opera were invited to open in September 1971 with a new production of *The Rake's Progress* directed by the recently appointed staff producer, David Pountney, newly arrived from Cambridge where the former Chairman of Scottish Opera, Robin Orr, was now Professor of Music.

Not for the first time in his brief but influential involvement with Scottish Opera, this young, brilliantly inventive and ingenious young director — employed, it should be said, by Peter Hemmings, for those very qualities — set the cat among the pigeons by his willingness, if not actual determination at times, to ignore consistency of period in his stagings of certain operas.

The Rake's Progress was a case in point: Koltai's visual abstractions and Pountney's anachronistic elements in production made some members of the audiences uneasy, but I doubt whether, in retrospect, even the dissenters will have managed to blot out of memory the scene in the dark graveyard with its huge central coffin.

Early in 1974 David Pountney was responsible for a totally original and, to my mind entirely delightful, medium-scale version of *The Magic Flute*, designed specifically as the first in what

the *Ring* cycle was seriously threatened by the need to rehearse the Christmas pantomime in the same theatre. "In order to rehearse and properly prepare our productions, more time, and more control over time, was required. The corporation-controlled Kings Theatre was trying to be all things to all men, and that constituted a very real problem." But a possible solution to that problem was almost in sight.

A few years earlier, in 1968, the Company had made its first sortie across the Border, to Newcastle, at the suggestion of Anthony Phillips were to become known as the "Midi Productions". These were fully dressed and set, and accompanied by chamber orchestra, but of a size to fit theatres and other venues too small to accommodate the major productions. Midi productions, however, unlike the piano-accompanied Opera Go Round shows, have usually been designed to give satisfaction even on larger stages and, indeed, that particular *Magic Flute* was seen in some of the full-scale theatres south of the Border as well as in smaller venues all over Scotland.

Indeed, it was after a performance at Theatre Royal, York, that Gerald Larner, reviewing for the *Guardian*, thought that David Pountney had done as valuable a service to opera as any producer in one production could. "He has liberated *The Magic Flute* from its clichés, from the pert and the coy and, above all, from the solemnity which has threatened to submerge the score beneath its ritual for even the most ardent of Mozart lovers."

This scaled-down, economically staged *Magic Flute* was perfect as a Midi Tour production, not least because, as a first experience of opera, it was accessible enough and attractive enough to have made converts galore in places where opera "in the flesh" and performed to this standard, was unfamiliar if not unknown. Somewhere between pure pantomime and Japanese theatre (the trials by fire and water, in particular, were strikingly realised, oriental fashion), it was designed by David Fielding and Maria Bjørnson, with simple cut-out, easily mobile scenery (many Midi Tour venues lack provision for flying) and a colourful, imaginative miscellany of costumes which seemed to relate both to toy theatre and toytown. Sung in English by a cast of young principals and chorus, with the Scottish Chamber Orchestra and Christopher Seaman in the pit, this *Magic Flute* had a fresh vitality that, in Newcastle, tempted one reviewer to write, "Pure magic". Yet there were those, and plenty of them, who felt that Mozart had been trivialised; that the symbols of Freemasonry were far too significant to be so lightly jettisoned. The scene was dismissed as ugly by those who clearly failed to enjoy themselves, but also as "wildly unexpected and eclectic" by one who, just as clearly, did.

Those seasons between Scottish Opera's tenth birthday and that crucial point in its story, three years later, when it took possession of Theatre Royal, saw the Company at the top of its form, taking a wide range and variety of work in its stride. Britten's *Midsummer Night's Dream* was simply and effectively staged for touring by Toby Robertson with a cast of Company principals whose acting ability matched their singing, and that is praise indeed. As an experienced theatre director, of Shakespeare not least, Robertson took farcical liberties that worked brilliantly — and not just with Bottom and company. And in spite of the sensitive treatment of the music by Roderick Brydon and the Scottish Baroque Ensemble, most of the critical reservations were applied to Benjamin Britten's shortcomings in this particular work.

The *Dream* was premiered at Stirling, and indeed, throughout this period the MacRobert Centre with the music-orientated Anthony

Patricia Hay as Hermia and Cynthia as Helena in
A MIDSUMMER NIGHT'S DREAM performed in 1972.
(Director: Toby Robertson.)

Phillips in charge, hosted several of the Midi opera productions, including *The Coronation of Poppea* and the first of the four new works in Scottish Opera's commissioning scheme, *The Catiline Conspiracy* by Iain Hamilton. *Poppea* was a revival by Anthony Besch of a production made several years earlier for the London Opera Centre; an entertainingly naughty romp (it was done in the version made by Raymond Leppard for Glyndebourne in the early 1960s) sung by a cast who were clearly enjoying themselves. Those were the days when almost every artist on the stage seemed to regular opera-goers like an old friend: when Ann Howells as Poppea, David Hillman as Nero, Stafford Dean as Seneca and Patricia Kern as Octavia (like Catherine Wilson, Gregory Dempsey, Michael Maurel, Francis Egerton and Bill McCue in *The Dream*) were part of the Scottish Opera "family" to the appreciative audiences and even, by all accounts, to themselves.

The Catiline Conspiracy by one of Scotland's most advanced composers, was certainly less accessible to the average opera fan who tends to look for a "good night out" from Puccini, Rossini, Bizet or Donizetti; something that *The Merry Widow* had certainly provided in the previous season. And no wonder, for it was gorgeously staged by Besch and Stoddart. Catherine Wilson, too, was brought to the fore, and absolutely in her element as Lehar's charismatic heroine, Hanna Glawari. But *Catiline* was revived in a later season and, as often happens, some of those who had disliked it first time round, came to appreciate its quality.

That was the season, too, of *Tristan and Isolde*, another milestone in Scottish Opera's love-affair with the operas of Wagner. Michael Geliot was the director and, once again, the stark symbolic nature of Koltai's decor worried more than the professional critics. And it is true that the ovoid form that stood for a ship or, when turned over, for a grassy knoll, either "spoke" to you or not according to your sensibility to this kind of meaningful abstraction. Complaints have also been heard at times when principal artists are changed between performances of the same production in different Scottish cities, and Tristan was a case in point. Between Glasgow and Aberdeen Helga Dernesch had replaced the American soprano, Klara Barlow as Isolde, John Shaw had taken over, as Kurwenal, from Norman Bailey, and David Ward, replacing Bill McCue, had brought a more powerful presence to the character of King Mark.

But it was the orchestra that, not for the first time, ran away with most of the praise. Felix Aprahamian, in the *Sunday Times*, recorded his appreciation of, ". . . the passionate expression and glorious sound of the score under Scottish Opera's and The Scottish National Orchestra's own Alexander Gibson," and Ronald Crichton, in the *Financial Times*, likewise singled out the orchestral playing and conducting for his highest praise, saying that whereas the recent performances at Covent Garden, although with orchestral sounds of greater finesse under Colin Davis, ". . . gave us a Tristan from the point of view of an intelligent outsider, Gibson's was more roughly hewn, but it came from nearer

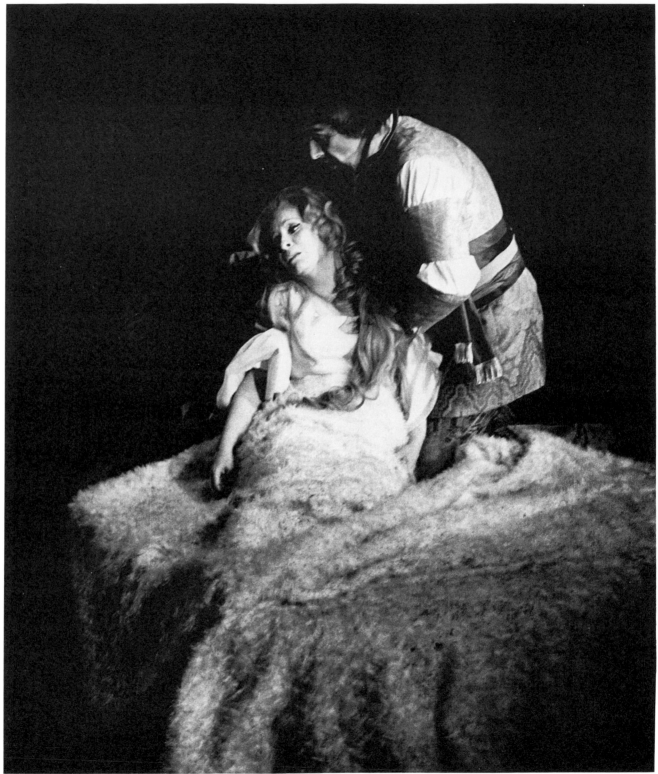

*John Shirley-Quirk as Goland, and Jeanette Pilov as Mélisande
in PÉLLEAS ET MÉLISANDE performed in 1972.*

the heart of the music." Praise of this nature makes it easier to believe the *Glasgow Herald*'s London critic when he declared, "It is some time since I heard such assured and competent playing from a London orchestra pit."

Pélleas et Mélisande was the second Scottish Opera production taken to Sadlers Wells in August 1973 — not the original production of eleven years earlier, but the one prepared by Colin Graham to celebrate the Company's tenth birthday in 1972. It was now that the critical superlatives came out in force. In the *Scotsman*, Conrad Wilson went so far as to say that never had he encountered a *Pélleas* more enthralling, more consistently beautiful to look at (John Fraser was the designer) or more convincingly presented musically, than this. "If I were asked," he wrote, "why Scottish Opera and its policies win all the praise they do, I would say, see this *Pélleas* and find out."

But of course a lot of the praise for Scottish Opera's product was qualified, and in some cases deservedly. And, behind the scenes, money worries were mounting. During the week of *The Ring* cycle in December 1971, chairman Robin Orr made two announcements, one good, one not so good. The birthday would be celebrated with the new *Pélleas et Mélisande*,

but, alas, the fact that the Scottish Arts Council's grant (then in the region of £200,000) would fall short by £60,000 of the Company's needs, meant that, in consequence, the revival of *The Trojans* for the 1972 Edinburgh Festival would not take place. This announcement (plus a subsequent batch of begging letters) had the desired effect. The £60,000 was raised, and Edinburgh saw *The Trojans*, with Janet Baker recreating that remarkable Dido.

When *The Trojans* was performed in Glasgow, sustenance was organised for most of the audience in the nearby Scottish Opera Centre, halfway through the marathon undertaking. In Edinburgh, with no convenient Opera Centre, and no suitable eating place near the Kings Theatre, a different arrangement had to be made. A dozen Edinburgh Corporation buses took the entire audience to George Watson's School to be fed and returned within the hour. "A massive operation which I would not like to tackle nowadays", says Thomson Smillie, "but the whole thing was repaid by the comment overheard from one Edinburgh dowager who, I think, was wearing a tiara. Lifting her long skirt and high-stepping on to the vehicle, she said,"Isn't this splendid fun. Do you know I've never been on a bus before."

THEATRE ROYAL

*Alex Gibson in the pit, with John Currie (Chorus Master) and
Peter Hemmings in the stalls.*

HOME AT LAST

The concept of Theatre Royal was fairly simple and straightforward, according to Peter Hemmings. "In order properly to rehearse and prepare productions, more time was required and, what is just as important, more control over time. Glasgow Corporation owns the King's Theatre which saw itself as being all things to all men. And, don't forget, there was that time in 1971 when we found our *Ring Cycle* seriously threatened by pantomime rehearsals. The other problem was financial. The heady days of the 'sixties were over and grants were falling behind. Major touring was becoming too expensive if standards were to be maintained. So it seemed to me both cheaper and artistically safer to bring people in from a 75-mile radius to Glasgow than to send companies to Ayr, the Borders, even to Edinburgh."

On the face of it this might sound eminently sensible since people are willing to travel even longer distances to London theatres. But Hemmings knows, none better, that his Company's (and his own) ability to bulldoze the Theatre Royal scheme triumphantly through all obstacles, seems permanently to have soured relationships with the Scottish Arts Council, mainly because the whole thing cost more than had been estimated — as, indeed, what major building scheme does not — and because, for that very reason, no endowment fund for Theatre Royal could be created since the extra money raised was needed to cover the inflated cost of converting the theatre.

It has to be said that there exists, in Charlotte Square, an attitude of what seems like resentment of the fact that all the major performing arts organisations are based in Glasgow. Edinburgh, being the capital of Scotland and host city to the largest of the world's arts festivals, has never come to terms with the fact that the city in the west, with its conurbation of more than 2,000,000 people, is the creative powerhouse of Scotland. This undoubted bias has dogged Scottish Opera ever since the company based itself firmly in its own Theatre Royal. It is perhaps worth remembering, in this context, that, in the visual arts Edinburgh alone has the convenience — financial convenience as well as physical since the total cost is borne by the Scottish taxpayer, not the Edinburgh ratepayer — of housing all the National Galleries and Museums which eat up vast amounts of money every year and are housed in buildings which are owned and maintained by the state. There are times, indeed, when, to friends of Scottish Opera, SAC must have seemed like the wicked stepmother in the fairytale, repeating insistently that young Cinderella is becoming far too vain and must be made to stop prinking in the mirror, when, in fact, the stepchild, ambitious for success and determined to fulfil her destiny, is suffering acute impoverishment and in danger of slow starvation.

The vision of Scottish Opera's own Theatre Royal seemed, at the time, like Cinderella's dream come true, a palace of her own, no less. It all began with the private information that the building at the top of Hope Street, which had been used since 1957 as the studio and headquarters of Scottish Television, was due to become vacant when STV moved into new premises nearby. As we have seen, the relationship between STV and Scottish Opera had been warm from the beginning (STV had given what was then a significant contribution of £1,000 to the first season and had since commissioned one new opera and helped to sponsor another) and its directors were anxious that the building, once Glasgow's principal lyric theatre, should pass into safe hands. The price being asked for an "empty, unwanted theatre" was reached, by mutual agreement, at £300,000 — being the value of the site for re-development — a bargain in anyone's terms.

But agreement to purchase, in principle, was only the beginning. A campaign committee of "the great and good and influential" was convened to further the project of purchasing, restoring, re-equipping and endowing Theatre Royal, Glasgow, in order to make it fit to be called Scotland's first national opera house. In April 1974 a press conference was called to make the announcement and to give details both of the theatre itself and of how it was proposed to raise the necessary funds. The press-pack contained a brochure which, as well as some understandable trumpet-flourishing, including quotations from favourable reviews in the national newspapers ("At its best Scottish Opera is unsurpassed by any other opera company in Western Europe" — *Financial Times*; ". . . the best ensemble in the country . . . an unmistakably corporate feeling that one just does not find at the moment in London" — the *Observer*) set forth the story of Scottish Opera from the beginning, its aims for future development and its belief in Theatre Royal as a national investment, along with the projected cost and plans for raising the money.

This makes interesting reading after more than a decade of galloping inflation. It was estimated that £3,000,000 would be needed to cover everything including the purchase price and an endowment fund for the upkeep of the theatre building — a tiny fraction of what had been talked about as the cost of the proposed opera house in Edinburgh. Already, by April 1974, £1,000,000 had been promised from industry and commerce; an approach was being made to government for a like sum, and stage three, now being announced, was a public appeal which listed every possible way in which supporters might contribute. Capital Gift, Deed of Covenant, Short-term Interest-free Loan, Long-term Debenture and, the most valuable contribution of all, the Combined Gift — a way of increasing the value of an outright gift by treating it as a loan annually repayable over ten years, while a covenant for an identical annual amount would give Scottish Opera double use of the money, as capital in the early stages plus the additional value of a covenanted gift.

Two new companies were set up to realise what Campaign Chairman, Gavid Boyd, called, without exaggeration, "this mammoth project". The Scottish Opera Theatre Trust Ltd., would be the recipient of all donations toward the project, and Scottish Opera Theatre Royal Ltd., would be formed to run the opera house. Announcing that Theatre Royal would reopen as a live opera house at 7.30 pm on Wednesday, 15th October 1975, and that, in the following season, ten operas would be given in "fortnightly stagione", Alexander Gibson paid tribute to all those who had worked to realise this huge sum of money "under the most difficult economic and political conditions and Peter Hemmings reiterated the importance of Theatre Royal as a Glasgow institution, not just as the place where Scottish Opera would give four performances of a given opera over two weeks throughout the season, but as the place where national companies from south of the Border would also, hopefully, be seen in the future. "Even if Scottish Opera were to remain homeless" he said, "this complete change in the cultural climate of the city would in itself justify the efforts of the Theatre Royal Campaign Committee."

And who could possibly, at that stage, have disagreed, even if one might suspect that Hemmings spoke with double tongue, since, without Scottish Opera's need for a home, there would have been no Theatre Royal Campaign. Glasgow has benefited from possession of Theatre Royal, reborn as "the finest medium-scale opera house anywhere in the world" in the words of David Pountney who has worked there again and again. With an auditorium both generous and intimate, elegant yet welcoming in its discreet, Victorian renaissance detail, and with, above all, a fine acoustic for opera, Theatre Royal has fulfilled most of what was promised for it.

Many of the questions prudently raised on the final page of that confident 1974 brochure (for nobody can say that Hemmings and Gibson and their loyal supporters on the campaign committee failed to realise that questions would be asked, and doubts raised) have been answered over the years. To the question, why not a permanent home in the new opera house to be built in Edinburgh, the answer was, as indeed it still is, that a multi-purpose theatre of the kind being planned could not offer a suitable home for an opera company resident all the year. And in answer to doubts about the viability of an opera house costing less than £3,000,000 when it was well known that the new Sydney Opera House was to cost over £50,000,000, there was the obvious fact that Theatre Royal needed only renovation and internal reconstruction to bring it up to standard. The question of a possible reduction in Scottish Opera's touring commitment still remains open to doubt and chronic underfunding is the main reason for the Company's staying at home more often than some would like.

But what kind of theatre was causing all the excitement, the sale of which to Scottish Television in 1956 had been seen as a tragedy for the cultural life of Glasgow in taking it out of commission as the main lyric theatre. For the Royal was, and is once again, the one theatre entirely suitable for main-scale productions of opera and ballet. For seventy years prior to its take-over by STV it had provided south-west and central Scotland with the best available touring opera, from the early days of the Moody Manners Company visiting Glasgow in two separate weeks each year with offerings as widely different as *Faust* and *Nabucco*, *Traviata* and *Tristan*, to the regular seasons by the Carl Rosa Opera Company which ceased only when the theatre went out of use, as such. Theatre Royal, indeed, had resounded many times to the sound of Wagner's music, and twice in its history, pre-Scottish Opera, to the great tetralogy, *The Ring*, in its entirety.

On October 1st, 1974 the Theatre Royal was officially handed over to Scottish Opera by Scottish Television. Here, Lewis Hind, (left), Director of STV exchanged the keys with Gavin Boyd, Chairman of the Theatre Royal Campaign Committee, Professor Robin Orr, Chairman of Scottish Opera and Peter Hemmings, General Administrator of Scottish Opera.

The opera company formed in Edinburgh by the Austrian expatriate Ernst Denhof, in the two productive years before his enterprise foundered for lack of financial support, brought to the Theatre Royal not only *The Ring of the Nibelungs* (sung in English) in 1911 but also, a year later, a season of five productions, *The Mastersingers, Tristan and Isolde, The Flying Dutchman, Elektra* and *Orfeo*. In 1917 the Beecham Opera Company played a four-week season at the Royal, with *Otello, Aida, Le Coq d'Or* and *Boris Godunov* in a repertoire that also included *The Magic Flute* and *Tristan*. And the same redoubtable musician/entrepreneur returned a

year later for four weeks with no less than twenty operas. Maybe it was no wonder that Beecham's original venture, like its predecessor, found itself in deep water financially, but continuity was provided when, in 1922, the British National Opera Company rose from the ashes and crossed the Border again to visit the Royal with many of the same singers and a similar repertoire. In turn that company, too, was liquidated but before its demise the British National Opera Company too had brought yet another *Ring* cycle to Theatre Royal, along with *Parsifal*, for which we still await a production by Scottish Opera.

My own first memories of Theatre Royal (like those, I feel sure, of many of my generation) relate not to opera but to the happenings on stage during the annual visits to *Peter Pan*. There were also the Carl Rosa productions, seen over the years, and always in connection with the Royal, and it was there that one saw, in the 1930s, foreign ballet companies of note, not least De Basil's Ballet Russe de Monte Carlo, with some of Diaghilev's dancers, scenery and costumes. So in Theatre Royal one had been able to see revivals of historic ballet productions like *Scheherazade* with the Bakst decor and costumes (in those days one had never heard of Bakst but the effect has proved unforgettable), *Les Sylphides*, *L'Epreuve d'Amour* (with designs by Derain) and the stunning Dances from Prince Igor. Theatre companies, too, presented short seasons in Hope Street: for example, the Macdona Players led by that strange actor, Esmé Percy, provided a memorable Shavian season including *Man and Superman* complete with Act III, and a necessarily long interval for taking sustenance — forerunner of operatic marathons to come, with Scottish Opera's *Die Meistersinger* and *Der Rosenkavalier* in that same theatre forty years on.

Scottish Opera, then, was about to take up permanent residence in a century-old house of considerable charm and personality with a proud history of productions seen and enjoyed by generations of those who live or have lived in Glasgow and its environs. The first Theatre Royal was built in 1867 but totally destroyed by fire twelve years later, when the famous theatre architect Charles John Phipps was asked to rebuild it, which he did in time for the offical opening in October 1880 with a production of Shakespeare's *As You Like It*. Music also entered the scene at an early date with a series of proms featuring two Italian singers, Signore Foli and Runcio and the conductor Tito Mattei. Howard and Wyndham bought the theatre in 1888 and reopened it with Henry Irving and his Lyceum Company in *Faust*. But only a few years later history repeated itself. In those days before electricity, fire again destroyed the building and Phipps, once again, was brought in to reconstruct it more or less as we see it today. More or less, because although extensive reconstruction took place in the modernisation of everything behind the proscenium arch, it was discovered that, in its own previous conversion, Scottish Television had done far less irreversible damage than might have been supposed or indeed expected. Structurally, the main alterations which were necessary were no more than the enlargement of the orchestra pit and the building of a new stage structure, making the pit adaptable for orchestras of anything from 40 to 110 players without disturbing the visual and acoustic properties of the auditorium. Since the grid and the fly-tower were found to be in sound condition, the only other modification was the installation of counterweight flying machinery in place of the old hemp hand-lines. A lighting box was also built into the roof in order to clear away all the clutter of all-too-visible front-of-house lighting.

Important as all these things are for the smooth running of an opera house, it is only the front of house that audiences see. The brown-and-gold auditorium with its elegant horse-shoe tiers and carefully restored and gilded plasterwork makes a pleasant and lasting impression on those who will never penetrate behind the scenes. And that is where the whole operation was managed with extraordinary tact and skill. In an issue of *The Architects Journal*, shortly after the inaugural gala performance of *Die Fledermaus* on October 14th 1975 — a suitably light-hearted occasion before the season proper opened a day after, with *Otello* — William Mann, music critic of *The Times*, wrote that every theatre must have the appearance of a "temple of mysteries". Theatregoers, he said, expect to be treated to a suspension of disbelief and this, he thought, the refurbished Theatre Royal managed to do, in its loving pastiche of 1895 French Renaissance. "Creative pastiche" he called it, involving as it did the building of new areas and a redesigning of the old in ". . . dark, warm, inviting mystery with brown corridors, gentle lighting, brass, mahogany and Victorian paintings of great character" . . . the latter, of course, were borrowed from Glasgow's extraordinarily fine municipal art collection.

Inevitably William Mann also found areas to criticise, in the bars, cloakrooms and so forth, but had he been able to penetrate beyond the pass door to the stage and backstage areas he would have found what is generally agreed to be the finest theatre north of the Border, with much thought given to the quality of general amenities as well as space — to dressing-rooms, offices, greenroom and to the entertainment suite which becomes increasingly necessary in an age where commercial sponsorship is demanded more and more as state subsidy for the arts lags behind.

Would those who think the upkeep of Theatre Royal by Scottish Opera to be a waste of money really like to see yet another giant office block or supermarket at the top of Hope Street? For that is almost certainly what would have happened had Theatre Royal been demolished like the old Alhambra in Waterloo Street, were it not for the tremendous effort in fund-raising carried out by the small committee of enthusiasts who still think of themselves as the Theatre Royal command force. Gavin Boyd, John Boyle, the Hon. James Bruce and, needless to say, Peter Hemmings, had set themselves a target which was to raise £2,000,000 for the theatre and a further £1,000,000 for the endowment fund. Looking back, John Boyle still thinks it was a brilliant operation and relishes the memory of his own involvement.

It really was planned with military precision. I remember how Peter and I flew to London on one occasion, got a taxi, went up in the lift to meet, I think, the deputy chairman of British Petroleum. I then went into my well-rehearsed spiel with Peter backing me up with facts and figures, and this high-powered chap just held up his hand and said, stop, stop, stop! We *know* we have to give you the money — the only question is how much? And it wasn't just BP, but Marks and Spencers, and a whole list of other benefactors. And then there was the great coup of the matching government grant.

Gavin and Peter had set that up initially of course, doing all the preliminary spade work with the Scottish Office in Edinburgh.

Once the excitement of the opening was past and the theatre fully functioning, Scottish Opera felt a new surge of energy, so far as its work was concerned. For the first time the Company could work in a theatre with room in the pit for a full orchestra, with a scene dock and grid capable of accommodating the scenery for two or three full-scale operas besides the one presently on performance. These are facilities that neither of the Kings Theatres can offer, nor even His Majesty's in Aberdeen, in spite of the fact that its front of house can match the best. All three were built as touring houses and would need extensive alterations to bring them up to the standard of the present Theatre Royal.

But even with possession of an opera house there was no question of Scottish Opera engaging a permanent company in the German manner, with a hundred singers on full salary and a permanent chorus and orchestra, so a stagione system was chosen. In the words of Ian Rodger, "It was a matter of all eyes on *Otello*, get it ready, play five times in Glasgow, three in Edinburgh, once in Aberdeen and finish: everybody goes home." Alex Gibson and Peter Hemmings in fact preferred the stagione system because, apart altogether from the fact that Scottish Opera was obviously never going to be able to afford the German type of establishment, the standard at the top would never be so good from a permanent company as when the casting could be done specifically by invitation for the major roles.

Nonetheless, a small group of singers was retained on contract, usually for a given number of performances annually. A nucleus of local artists: Catherine Wilson, Bill McCue, Patricia Hay, Norman White, John Robertson and others were involved in this way over a number of years — and because, as before, certain singers of note, like Norman Bailey and Janet Baker enjoyed the friendliness and the working conditions enough to return to Glasgow again and again, a "company" feeling continued within Scottish Opera and its audiences enjoyed a sense of identification with the personnel on stage.

To coincide with the opening of Theatre Royal the first subscription season was tried out, the idea having been sold to Thomson Smillie by Danny Newman who came from Chicago full of success stories. Somewhat against their natural inclination Hemmings and Gibson allowed themselves to be persuaded and the scheme was presented to the Glasgow public in a relatively hard-selling campaign. In 1975 the first subscription season brochure looked far more brash than it does twelve years on. It is blazoned, in red, yellow, black and white and printed over every inch of its multifold complexity with information, exhortation and postage-stamp pictures of the 70 or so personalities involved in the artistic side of the enterprise, plus a message from Chairman Robin Orr expressing his sense of pride in the whole operation.

Of course there were those who felt that the whole thing was slightly infra dig, but it worked. That first subscription season of ten operas (prices ranged from £3.50 – £45.50 for all ten) was subscribed so fully that it guaranteed a regular audience for a great range of operas. And, what is more, it tended to generate a new social gel in Glasgow, since many friends and acquaintances who found themselves attending Theatre Royal regularly on the same evening once a fortnight, began to arrange after-theatre supper parties in one another's homes where the evening's performance would be discussed at length to everybody's enjoyment and to the general good of Scottish Opera in disseminating interest more widely than ever.

All that was clearly on the credit side: the problem that began to arise, however, and that refused to be ignored, was the sheer cost of owning and running a major theatre without proper endowment. We know that the money which should have gone into a fund for that purpose disappeared in the inflationary spiral of conversion costs, and we know that government had given its £1,000,000 as promised, to match the £1,000,000 from commercial sources. But looking back and realising that, had plans for the "opera house" in Castle Terrace, Edinburgh, gone ahead at a cost of six or seven times the amount Scottish Opera spent on Theatre Royal, the state would almost certainly have contributed six or seven million to the cost (as, indeed, happened at a later date when the Burrell Collection was housed in its new gallery) it does seem that Scottish Opera was less generously treated than it deserved to be, when the interest on a second £1,000,000 would have solved the problem for good. As things were, it was only after Glasgow Corporation offered a large interest-free loan that Theatre Royal managed to open in time for that first performance on the date which had been so confidently announced many months previously. The press release sent out before the first night began, in fact, by saying that Theatre Royal would *not* open as announced on October 15th 1975: instead it would open on October 14th, with a gala performance of *Die Fledermaus*.

Scottish Opera, then, began to carry its burden of a chronic deficiency of over £100,000 a year, caused entirely by the need to maintain Theatre Royal, and that, said Peter Hemmings, in retrospect, was when the Scottish Arts Council decided to change from green to amber because they saw quite clearly that some of the money being allocated for Scottish Opera was in fact carrying the Theatre Royal deficiency which, like a millstone, hung round the company's neck for years, using up money that could have been used for more touring.

David Jackson, the devoted and hard-working manager of Theatre Royal since it became the home of Scottish Opera, has the unenviable task of trying to make the theatre pay its way throughout the months when the opera company is not in residence; unenviable because, frankly, impossible. Scottish Ballet, of course, brings its own audience to Hope Street and, although the relationship between the two companies is less close than some had hoped for, Peter Darrell's company undoubtedly comes next in importance to Scottish Opera in regular occupancy of the theatre.

Even before it belonged to Scottish Opera, Theatre Royal was always thought of as the

Theatre Royal during renovation.

place which housed the touring opera, ballet and serious drama companies, and that is the reputation which still persists even when popular entertainers and the more light-weight dramatic offerings are on the bill. Tradition dies hard and, in Glasgow, tradition dictates that the Kings Theatre, not the Royal, is where you go for "a good night out".

David Jackson has brought some splendid events to the Royal over the years, from the Royal Shakespeare Company's *Henry V*, with Alan Howard as King Henry, and splendid sets by Farrah, to London Contemporary Dance and Ballet Rambert, and the historic production by Tom Fleming, of *Ane Satyre of The Thrie Estaites*, in the week before Sir David Lyndsay's sixteenth century morality play was taken to the 1986 Warsaw Festival where it won a major award.

Initially, Peter Hemmings had an agreement with Glasgow District Council that only opera, ballet and serious drama would be offered at Theatre Royal. This, says David Jackson, was because the Council were worried about potential rivalry with the Kings. Since then, however, a policy has developed of trying to widen the Theatre Royal audience, but always after

consultation with the management of the Kings Theatre in order to avoid simultaneous presentation of the same kind of show. "But it is very important," Jackson insists,

> to spread the word around that the Royal is not the sort of place to be afraid to visit. It is definitely not a theatre which demands that you wear a black tie, though there is no reason why people shouldn't dress up a bit if they want to. Peter Hemmings, I have to say, wanted originally to keep the Theatre Royal sacrosanct, like Covent Garden, and not all the Board disagreed with him. But others felt that we should be presenting a quality house with an altogether wider range.

It is a difficult judgment to make, all the same. I booked in Oscar Peterson and Stefan Grappelli, and Peter immediately said, "Is this the sort of thing we should be doing?" And I had to reassure him that Oscar Peterson is a virtuoso pianist in jazz just as someone like Clifford Curzon is in classical music, and that Stefan Grappelli, too, is an artist in his own field. So he did take my word for it and we began to include people like that. But it certainly isn't easy: nobody can guarantee success. If we had had the endowment fund from the beginning to look after the maintenance of the building, the whole problem would have been eliminated.

TOWARDS A NEW ERA

Those first years at Theatre Royal saw David Pountney really flexing his creative muscles, first of all as Staff Producer and, from 1975 until his departure in 1980, as Director of Productions in succession to Peter Ebert. Pountney, like Hemmings, was a Cambridge man who came to Glasgow in 1970, straight from university where his keen activity in the Opera Society had come to the notice of Robin Orr, now Professor of Music at the English university. David Pountney is now in London, at the English National Opera Company where, as Director of Productions, he is everywhere respected as one of the most imaginative, sensitive and intelligent producers of opera in Britain. But he has no doubt that he owes the training of his formative years to the creative climate he found at Scottish Opera. "It was Peter Hemmings who invited me to Glasgow and who made it possible for me to develop, who gave me a marvellous amount of freedom to travel and work and learn, as well as all the opportunities to do things with the Company." And the things he did were as diverse as they were exciting, from the delightful pantomime-style *Magic Flute* and the spectacular *Golden Cockerel* to the warm, human realism of *Die Meistersinger* and the sombre, bleak and powerful drama of *Macbeth*.

Something which is not widely known but which, in retrospect, I certainly find illuminating, is that, during his first years at Scottish Opera, which were also the early years of Giles Havergal's regime at Glasgow Citizens Theatre, Pountney enjoyed a fairly close relationship with the energetic, innovative team in the Gorbals. A fellow student at Cambridge had been Keith Hack who had gone to the Citizens as trainee director, and Pountney provided the musical direction for some of the latter's productions, notably *In the Jungle of the Cities* by Bertolt Brecht, for which most of the stalls were removed and a huge boxing ring erected in their place, while the audience stood around to watch the action. Pountney also directed a late-night satirical revue on the subject of the critical fraternity and its shortcomings. It was called *Hindsight* because its author, another of Pountney's friends was Archie Hind, the Glasgow novelist. So an element of cross fertilisation seemed to be in process which, had it continued, might have brought benefits to both organisations.

What did happen, however, was that the two young Citizens designers, Sue Blane and Maria Bjornson, were brought into the world of opera. Both had been discovered, as art students, by the eagle eye of Philip Prowse, and it was Bjornson who created the unusual Brechtian *mise-en-scène* in the Gorbals theatre. David Pountney has clearly found himself *en rapport* with her work in particular, for she has teamed with him ever since, most notably in the series of Janáček operas, which have been staged over a number of years as co-productions with Welsh National Opera.

Like myself, David Pountney thinks it a pity that there has never been any kind of collaboration between Scottish Opera and the Citizens Theatre where music, and opera in particular, is deeply understood by all three directors. Giles Havergal is the son of that same

David Pountney and Lawrence Foster at a rehearsal of DON GIOVANNI, 1979.

Dr Henry Havergal who, as Principal of the Royal Scottish Academy of Music and Drama, sat on the first Board of Scottish Opera. And Robert David MacDonald's original training and career was in music, as a student of piano and of conducting, in London and Germany. But all three, Havergal, MacDonald and Philip Prowse, now one of Britain's most admired director/designers, not least in the field of opera and ballet, have been active in recent years as producers of opera. But only MacDonald, with a wonderfully inventive and at times hilarious

production of *The Barber of Seville*, has been offered a chance to direct a work with Scottish Opera. For anyone, says Pountney, who would like to see the audience for opera move into the twentieth century, which is to say, become more open to developments which have taken place in "straight" theatre over the past half-century, such cross-fertilisation would be a godsend.

For it is a vexed question that refuses to go away, this matter of what may, or may not be done to take opera out of the museum. Sir Alex Gibson — and he is, after all, not only the founder and music director, but also the one person who has been present throughout the whole twenty-five years — finds himself rather in the middle ground in this dispute. It is, of course, a complex question, not pertaining to Scottish Opera alone, this shifting emphasis on the elements which go to make up the wonderful bastard art which is opera. Sir Alex explains:

At one time, the prima donna used to hold sway absolutely, no matter how ridiculous the image nor how much the music suffered. Then there was the time when conductors ruled as autocrats — the Toscaninis and the Mahlers — when nothing mattered but the score. Now, almost inevitably, we are in the age of the producer, to use the old-fashioned word. And it really was inevitable because we did want to get away from the old idea of "Just stand and sing and if it sounds good that's lovely, and it doesn't matter what the sets look like, or if you can't create a credible character because the music will win through". Nobody in their right mind would subscribe to that idea today. Even somebody who knows little about opera would pick up the deficiency immediately, and opera lovers in general would refuse to take it because they are used, now, to seeing opera on television, done to a high standard. And that is what they expect to find in the theatre.

There will always be complaints from somewhere about this or that element in a production which fails to fit some private individual's preconception. Many music lovers object strongly when a director chooses to set an opera in a period later than the time when it was written — as with up-dated Mozart — or abstracts the setting in a symbolic manner as has happened with many of Koltai's designs for classics like *Don Giovanni* or *Tristan* (it was interesting to find far fewer complaints about his equally abstract setting for a modern opera, Henze's *Elegy for Young Lovers*). Worse still, in the minds of some, is a director's search for contemporary relevance in a timeless work, as happened with David Alden's *Rigoletto* and, even more clearly, in Graham Vick's striking and highly controversial *Don Giovanni*. But without fail there will be many others in the audience who will relish the stab of surprise, the anachronistic element that can stimulate the imagination and set up associations that, to anyone who brings an open mind to the experience, might even enrich it by shedding new light on the familiar music.

It can, of course, happen that a second visit, or a later revival of the disliked production will reveal attractions of a field of interest, obscured first time round by an audience's expectation of something very different. Dame Janet Baker believes that some of the blame for non-

acceptance of the unusual may have its source in the sudden breaking of a strong personal association with something pleasurable. "I do think that, of all the art forms, opera is the one that people come to with associations that colour the whole experience. Maybe they saw it first on the day they fell in love or got engaged, and it takes an extremely adult, open-minded person to take a new unexpected production at first seeing, that cuts right across those warm associations." It is, she feels, the great responsibility of audiences not to fall into that trap. "Young people, you know, don't get upset when the conventions are set aside. They enjoy a production on its own terms."

Sir Alex, who is no reactionary, also keeps an open mind, but he does, nonetheless, insist that, while the days of the dictators are, or should be, over and that the proper way forward is through teamwork, those who love opera do have a duty to provide the up-and-coming generations of opera-goers — especially in Scotland where young people cannot see the standard repertoire in fairly straightforward productions, as easily as youngsters can in London or in Germany — with some non-experimental stagings of the classics.

It isn't the so-called old guard who write angry letters to the papers, that you need worry about. It is the young people who have no yardstick, no experience of years of *La Bohème, Turandot, Faust* or *Traviata*. Our main problem is that we have a company which is capable of putting on far more opera than we ever do. We could put on performances in Edinburgh and Glasgow every other night,

Peter Glossop as Iago in OTELLO performed in 1975.

since, while it was Pountney's effervescent production of *Die Fledermaus* which baptised the new opera house in musical champagne, the serious business of inaugurating the first Theatre Royal subscription season was left in the hands of Anthony Besch whose well tried and much admired production of Verdi's *Otello* was revived for the occasion, with Charles Craig and Peter Glossop again bringing vocal power and personal charisma to the central roles of the Moor of Venice and Iago. The cast also included many familiar names — David Hillman, John Robertson, Norman White, Claire Livingstone, Bill McCue — some of whom were also seen in Besch's new production which followed, *Ariadne on Naxos* by Richard Strauss. Dame Janet Baker returned to Glasgow to lend lustre to that event, in the breeches role of The Composer, while Norma Burrows and the rising young local soprano, Linda Esther Gray, created what seemed like a contrast of silver and gold in the very different soprano roles of Zerbinetta and the Prima Donna/Ariadne.

But the memorable treatment of *The Golden Cockerel*, mounted that first 1975 season as a colourful offering for the Christmas month, saw David Pountney in his element. Pushkin's fairytale, heightened as it is by the music of Rimsky-Korsakov, gave Maria Bjørnson and Sue Blane endless opportunities for spectacular and sumptuous effects that owed something, surely to the Gontcharova designs for the Diaghilev part-opera, part-ballet production. The singers, from John Angelo Messana (the unearthly sound of the counter tenor lending an apt strangeness to The Astrologer) to Catherine Gayer, as a gorgeously sinuous and sensuous

but we need money to do that. And when your choice is limited to only nine operas a season, you must be very careful to balance the experimental against the familiar. And, in achieving what we call a house style, we must take care that we don't go right over the top and end by thinking that any standard opera we do must be given the treatment, as they say, otherwise it is not worth doing.

David Pountney's versatility must have gone far to reassure and satisfy Sir Alex when it began to become apparent in his work at Theatre Royal. Not immediately, however,

Catherine Gayer as the Queen of Shemakhan in THE GOLDEN COCKEREL performed in 1975. (Director: David Pountney, designer: Maria Bjornson and Sue Blane.)

Queen of Shemakhan, and Don Garrard as the foolish King Dodon (a role that Bill McCue took over in revival and made his own) gave every evidence of enjoying the fantasy which everything conspired to create. There was even, as I remember, a panoramic journey like the one in the first Maryinsky version of the ballet, *La Belle au Bois Dormant*, and there was a high-flying Cockerel (aerialist Inge-Lise in brilliant plumage) with the unseen Patricia Hay providing the glorious high notes off stage.

In the 1976/77 season Pountney was even more prominent in the programme planning, with *Macbeth* at the Edinburgh Festival, *Die Meistersinger* at Theatre Royal, and a revival of the delightful, but somewhat controversially irreverent, *Magic Flute* which had been staged originally as a Midi production. But no less important for David Pountney's own development was the opportunity he was given to direct *Jenufa*, the first in the series of sensitively conceived and gripping productions of operas by Janáček — *Jenufa*, *Katya Kabanova*, the strange *Makropoulos Case*, the enchanting *Cunning Little Vixen* and, lastly, in the 1986/87 season, the composer's final opera, the bleak and powerful *From the House of the Dead* — all of which were shared with Welsh National Opera.

Jenufa was a milestone in the tale of Scottish Opera as well as in Pountney's own career as an exceptionally gifted producer of music drama, because, to the average Scots opera lover, Janáček was unfamiliar ground and therefore gave cause for suspicion. But the music proved so engaging, so emotionally satisfying, and the human drama was made

so riveting by the splendid cast headed by Josephine Barstow as Jenufa and Pauline Tinsley as the Kostelnicka, that the final applause left nobody in doubt that Janáček and Pountney had found many new fans.

For the Janáček cycle we have to thank Peter Hemmings. It was, says David Pountney, "the last piece of constructive planning in Peter's regime at Theatre Royal. He had been looking round for something suitable in the way of a cost-cutting operation and I heard him talking about importing a *Jenufa* from Amsterdam. So I said 'Look here Peter, you know how I feel about Janáček. If you don't let me do it I'm off'. And so we got together with Wales to do *Jenufa* jointly, with me directing, and that is how it all started, all of them as co-productions with Welsh National Opera." *Jenufa* was seen first at Cardiff but some of the others were given their first productions in Scotland — *Katya Kabanova* at Theatre Royal and *Cunning Little Vixen* at the 1980 Edinburgh Festival.

In all these works Pountney's intelligent versatility was as evident in the style of production as Janáček's in the essence of the two very different works, *Katya Kabanova* and *The Cunning Little Vixen*. One, based on a tragic tale of Ostrovsky, was full of storm, stress and guilt, with Josephine Barstow, once again, as the tormented creature at the hub of the action; and the other, based very loosely on a comic serial cartoon about fox-hunting, blended comedy with something less than tragedy in a wonderful pot-pourri of brief, telling episodes in which most of the characters are animals or domestic birds. Maria Bjornson, too, matched her creative

Left to right: Cynthia Buchan, John Robertson, William McCue, Josephine Barstow and Kerstin Meyer in the co-production with Welsh National Opera of KATYA KABANOVA performed in 1979.

vision to the very different demands of each opera, devising a stressful, expressionist *mise-en-scène*, and in the other a charming landscape of green hillocks like an illustration in a child's picture book. In *The Cunning Little Vixen*, too, Pountney and Bjornson had an equally gifted partner in the choreographer Stuart Hopps who managed to control the squads of juvenile extras in a positively remarkable way, so as to bring them into the ensemble as though born to

it. And, just as Barstow had seemed to epitomise everything demanded by the character of the ill-starred Katya, so Helen Field, as the perky, but oddly poignant little mother fox, Sharpears, seemed to give the definitive performance.

These productions, which broke new ground so successfully, took place during the first years of serious financial trouble for Scottish Opera, with any new major productions having to be dependent on commercial sponsorship. The idea of self-help was forced, willy nilly, on arts organisations to the point where an establishment like Scottish Opera found its official grant-in-aid absorbed in the cost of merely keeping the

Gordon Christie (Fox) and Helen Field (Vixen) in THE CUNNING LITTLE VIXEN performed in 1980.

Company afloat. Although some of the most ambitious plans cherished by Peter Ebert — the *Parsifal* for the 1981/82 season, with designs by Philip Prowse was one — had to be abandoned, and the number of operas had to be reduced to six from what had been twelve in 1978/79, the programme through the late 1970s and early 1980s offered much more than a mere miscellany of revivals. Indeed, the revivals themselves — *Falstaff*, (with Sesto Bruscantini) *Cosi fan tutte, Fidelio, A Midsummer Night's Dream* — were not only welcome, but well restored and cast.

Verdi's *Macbeth*, directed by David Pountney at the 1976 Edinburgh Festival, caused disquiet and aroused complaints about directorial perverseness. Ralph Koltai, once again, was the designer, contriving a huge, brutal-looking, revolving structure like a wheel of fate, or torture, to dominate the bleak, but dramatically lit scene. The weird sisters, clad in boiler-suits and fitted out with Struwwel-Peter wigs, caused much of the offence, but the sheer power of the conception, overall, was unmistakable. "A hard, fierce production," wrote Conrad Wilson, "which invites us to regard Verdi's *Macbeth* as a revolutionary work in all senses of the word." Praise for the cast, not least for Norman Bailey and Galina Vishnevskaya, and for the power and sensitivity of Gibson's contribution with the SNO, was not stinted. And Nöel Goodwin, who tended to damn with faint praise, recorded a favourable judgment: "The result is unlikely to please the opera fans but it is welcome evidence that opera can still be made a living art instead of a museum exhibit." When the production was seen at Theatre Royal in the following season, Pauline Tinsley, taking over from Vishnevskaya, brought an even more thrilling dramatic quality to the character of Lady Macbeth.

Then hard on the heels of the controversial *Macbeth* came *Die Meistersinger*, which pleased just about everyone, critics and opera fans alike, with the splendour of Bjornson's settings and the sympathetic treatment of what is, after all, a tremendously rich tapestry in sight and sound, but with a warm, human situation at its centre. And if it is the Hans Sachs of Norman

EGISTO performed in 1982 (right).

BORIS GODUNOV performed in 1965

WOZZECK performed in 1980

THE BARBER OF SEVILLE
performed in 1985

THE GOLDEN COCKEREL performed in 1975

Bailey that one best remembers, maybe that is no wonder, for the warmth of voice and personality that this fine singer/actor can bring to a role that suits him are the very attributes necessary to create a credible Hans Sachs on the opera stage.

This was one production where everything seemed to work together well. The shifts from scene to scene were cleverly brought about by transforming the gothic traceries of Act I into trees thereafter. And the principals (including David Ward, who had also sung a splendid Banquo in *Macbeth*) as Pognor, and Thomas Hemsley as Beckmesser) the chorus and, above all, the SNO under Alex Gibson, gave what Bernard Levin called, in a rave review, ". . . as clear and expressive an account of Wagner's most accomplished score as one is likely to hear in any opera house." One moment, in particular, stands out from that David Pountney production (of which, surely, we have not seen the last); the moment when Sachs, the last of the Mastersingers to leave the trial chamber, passes the slate so heavily filled with Bechmesser's spiteful marks against Walther's song. With a rueful shake of his head, as though to say, "What fools men are," Sachs wipes the slate clean with his sleeve and leaves the stage as the curtain falls. It was with Scottish Opera that Norman Bailey gave his 100th performance as Hans Sachs in *Die Meistersinger*, and that evening, at Theatre Royal, Newcastle, there was a touching little ceremony after the performance when Sir Alex Gibson presented Norman Bailey with a clean slate attached to which was a message that read, "To the best Hans Sachs in the business".

DEATH IN VENICE performed in 1983 (left).

Beckmesser (Thomas Hemsley) and Hans Sachs (Norman Bailey) in DIE MEISTERSINGER performed in 1976.

After *The Catiline Conspiracy* in 1974, each season for the next three years saw another new work by a Scots composer commissioned by Scottish Opera under a scheme masterminded by Professor Frederick Rimmer of the University of Glasgow. *Hermiston*, by Robin Orr, was the second of these, with a libretto by Bill Bryden based on Robert Louis Stevenson's unfinished novel, *Weir of Hermiston*. It was produced by Toby Robertson for the 1975 Edinburgh Festival with a strong cast headed by Michael Langdon and with the American tenor and soprano,

Robin Orr's HERMISTON performed at The Edinburgh
Festival in 1975. (Director: Toby Robertson, designer: Robert Archer.)

Lenus Carlson and Catherine Gayer as the ill-fated lovers, Archie and Christina. Roderick Brydon conducted the Scottish Chamber Orchestra on that occasion. The third of the new operas, *Confessions of a Justified Sinner*, by Thomas Wilson, was premièred at York a year later. This was Wilson's second opera — his first, *The Charcoal Burners*, was commissioned by the BBC in the late 1960s for broadcasting on Radio Three — and he based it on yet another powerful and sombre work of literature, the strange, doppelganger tale, by James Hogg, of a youth who, as one of "God's Elect", feels free from retribution no matter how deeply he wallows in sin and crime. The score was widely associative, from the unmelodic contemporary style to the simple hymn tune sung by an unseen congregation.

The fourth of the new Scottish works and, as a staged opera, arguably the best of all, was Thea Musgrave's *Mary Queen of Scots* to the composer's own libretto based on a play by Amalia Elguera. Colin Graham's production, first seen at the 1977 Edinburgh Festival, highlighted the pleasure-loving, wilful, charismatic personality of the ill-starred Queen of Scots, and gave Catherine Wilson the chance of a lifetime in being allowed to create the role of Mary with Gregory Dempsey and David Hillman as Darnley and Bothwell. It was a role that she badly wanted to play from the time she first heard that the work was planned.

I kept wondering who they would ask to do it and finally — though I'd never done such a thing before — I sat down and wrote a letter to Peter Hemmings saying that I really did feel interested. And then, this is absolutely how it happened — the nearest thing to telepathy I've ever known. I took that letter and I went down to rehearsal meaning to give it to him, but at the Opera Centre I found a note from Peter inviting me to sing the part of Mary.

And sing it she did, superbly, in spite of a bad bout of laryngitis in the weeks beforehand. The whole experience, indeed, is remembered with affection — "working again with Colin Graham and that wonderful company we all looked on as 'family', and wearing those costumes by Alex Reid"; costumes which, as the production photographs show, were beautiful and becoming as well as suggestive of the period in question.

Of the four new Scottish operas only *Mary Queen of Scots* was taken abroad, and that only for one performance at Stuttgart in May 1978. All four were toured widely in Scotland, however, and were also seen at Newcastle where a Scottish Opera subscription series was initiated in 1978. *The Catiline Conspiracy* was performed at Oxford in 1974 and *Hermiston* was taken to the Aldeburgh Festival a year later. Several seasons were to elapse before another full-scale contemporary opera would be presented by the Company. That was *Hedda Gabler*, commissioned by Edward Harper for Scottish Opera by the BBC and directed by Graham Vick at Theatre Royal as part of the 1984/85 season.

David Alden came to the fore as a guest director in 1979 with *Rigoletto* in a production which, up-dated in essence to the turn of the century, was given a punkish gloss to emphasise — as Graham Vick's *Don Giovanni* was to do —

David Hillman as Darnley and Catherine Wilson as Mary in Thea Musgrave's MARY, QUEEN OF SCOTS performed in 1977. (Director: Colin Graham, designers: Robert Ross and Colin Graham, costumes: Alex Reid.)

even more forceably some years later — the moral squalor of the story. It was a production you either enjoyed for its uncompromising view of things plus its immense vitality — not least in the music, both vocal and orchestral with the chorus splendidly on form — or loathed because it cut sharply across all romantic preconceptions, in particular concerning the "nobility" of the Duke of Mantua and his coterie of courtiers. But as a production it

refused to be ignored. That was made clear by the predictable spate of angry and enthusiastic letters to the *Glasgow Herald*. And when it was revived — and, it has to be said, improved, not least in the attention paid to the curse of Monterone on the stairway, which had been all but drowned first time round in the general razzmatazz down below — it was a great success.

Peter Ebert had intended to direct Berg's *Wozzeck* for the 1980 Edinburgh Festival but, after his departure, the production fell to David Alden who created a complete contrast of mood from his *Rigoletto*, as befits the very different essence of the twentieth century German opera based on Buchner's play. Benjamin Luxon, miscast, one would have said, in the title role, gave a stunning performance and David Fielding the designer, who had seemed to glory in the visual extravagance of *Rigoletto*, tempered his vision to the spare, stark setting the plot seemed to demand.

Why Scottish Opera should have wanted to take *The Beggars' Opera* to the Edinburgh Festival in 1981 is hard to understand. Guy Woolfenden and David William were invited to combine in mounting a version of the old ballad opera which everyone thought might be a financial success at least. After the Festival the production was to be taken to London where, at the height of the tourist season, it was expected to prove a prime attraction. But the critics at Edinburgh damned it, by no means without reason, since the orchestration was over-elaborate and some of the action singularly tasteless, with the result that both the tourists

Finale of THE BARTERED BRIDE performed in 1978. (Director: David Pountney, designers: Maria Bjornson and Sue Blane.)

and Londoners stayed away, leaving the Company with a five-figure loss instead of a profit.

Tosca from the previous season would surely have made a splendid Festival offering, in the production by Anthony Besch which was so skilfully and intelligently brought forward in time to around 1940. In consequence, a sinister undercurrent of Fascist cruelty and sadism soured the wonderful verismo of Peter Rice's vast Roman church interior, monumental columns, wrought iron screen, mannerist paintings and all, as well as the scene at dawn on the battlements under a monstrous winged victory.

Alternatively, Festival audiences would have loved the 1978 production of *The Bartered Bride*, with Pountney, Blane and Bjornson extracting

all that Smetana's jovial opera contains of humour and vitality, colour and movement. That particular production had an attractive score and a wonderfully contrived but totally unexpected carnival finale with acrobats and jugglers augmenting the ever versatile Scottish Opera Chorus. (It remains a sore point that Scottish companies are always expected to take brand new productions to the Festival while companies from overseas normally bring well-oiled repertoire works.)

For *The Bartered Bride* Roderick Brydon conducted The Scottish Philharmonia, an orchestra formed in 1973 as a result of Scottish

Opera's need for a full-scale orchestra to replace the SNO which, increasingly, found it difficult to reconcile its own concert work with the longer opera seasons. Touring was a particular problem, and real trouble developed after the opening of Theatre Royal led to an even longer season of opera. The Scottish Philharmonia, managed by the Edinburgh-based Scottish Philharmonic Society, was composed largely of freelance players with a permanent nucleus of members of Leonard Friedman's Scottish Baroque Ensemble which had played for many of Scottish Opera's small-scale productions. In 1974 the Scottish Chamber Orchestra was formed under the same management; a body of between 30 and 40 musicians, suitable for the operas of Mozart and Rossini and contemporary composers like Britten and Henze. Indeed, the SCO was given its first grant by the Scottish Arts Council as the orchestra now principally used by Scottish Opera. But the SCO, in its turn, found an increasing concert programme clashing with its opera commitments. At uncomfortably short notice Scottish Opera was left with little alternative but to form an orchestra of its own. But until then these were the orchestras, with occasional visits by the BBC Scottish Symphony Orchestra, which mainly served Scottish Opera under various conductors besides Gibson and Brydon. The early years at Theatre Royal, for instance, saw Norman del Mar, Gary Bertini, Lawrence Foster and Gyorgy Fischer as regular visitors on the podium.

THE
UNTAMEABLE MONSTER

Sir Alexander Gibson has made no secret of the fact that his ambition, from the beginning, when the Scottish National Orchestra and Scottish Opera were, in a sense, welded together through his own close involvement with both — as Musical Director in the one case and as so-called Artistic Director, (but, in fact, also Musical Director), in the other — was to build the SNO to a numerical strength comparable with the Vienna Philharmonic which serves both the opera house and the concert platform. This means that all the players are given a chance to, as it were, see daylight. For that, according to Sir Alex, is a real problem. "Orchestral players like to be seen: they feel like second-class citizens down there in the pit. I happen to think they are mistaken, but there it is. You can't change human nature."

It is certainly a fact that when Alex Gibson and his SNO were together buoying up the opera productions (and Gibson has conducted around one third of the total, including everything from Verdi, Wagner, Strauss, Mozart and Puccini to Berg, Henze and Benjamin Britten) there was a general feeling that all was well with the music, no matter who the producer might be, or how "curious" his concept of the work in question. That is certainly what comes across in most of the reviews, not least of Alex Gibson's beloved Puccini where, as I have heard it said by more than one participant on the stage, "he lets the music breathe". But there is a feeling in recent years, whether justified or not, that the Scottish Opera Orchestra has never really become Alexander Gibson's own in the same way as the SNO undoubtedly was his instrument. That is in the nature of things, perhaps, and if so it is a pity.

The Scottish Opera Orchestra's potential quality is unmistakable, nonetheless, as we heard when the young Sian Edwards, making her debut at Theatre Royal in 1986, produced some remarkable orchestral playing for *The Rise and Fall of the City of Mahagonny*, and when John Mauceri, in the same season, seemed to inject a different "colour", restrained but sultry, to the score of Bizet's *Carmen*. And when Sir Alex eventually finds it possible, as he almost certainly will, to relinquish all feeling of responsibility for anything but the music in hand — as is bound to happen once he assumes the new relationship with the opera company he founded — a new rapport with the orchestra will doubtless be achieved.

There is one area where Scottish Opera has never come under fire: the chorus continues to rise serenely above all controversy, maintaining its reputation as one of the best in Britain. Since Arthur Oldham took over from Leon Lovett in the third season, and created the first fully professional Scottish Opera Chorus, there have been several gifted chorus masters. Oldham himself was a crucial figure in the enterprise, the marvellous choirmaster who also created the splendid Scottish Festival Chorus for the performance of Mahler's eighth symphony at the 1965 Edinburgh Festival — the body of singers which Karajan was to call, a few years later, "One of the three great choirs of Europe". Oldham was followed by John Currie, whose

The Scottish Opera Orchestra in rehearsal at the SNO Centre, Henry Wood Hall, Glasgow.

work at Scottish Opera, really an expansion of his work as chorus master of the SNO Chorus and his own John Currie Singers, served to bring more lustre than ever to the scene. That is something which still continues, although not only John Currie, but his successor Ian Robertson have departed to carry on the good work across the Atlantic. Ian Robertson, who is also a concert pianist, came to Scottish Opera in 1977 as John Currie's assistant, and by 1983 had become not only Chorus Director in his own right but also Head of Music. The same double responsibility is now about to be shouldered by Robertson's successor, John Pryce-Jones.

Under all three, Oldham, Currie and Robertson, the Scottish Opera Chorus gained and kept its reputation not just for excellence on the musical side, but also for acting ability and expressive movement, attributes which lend credibility to scenes that otherwise might seem forced or stilted. It is this theatrical knowhow that helps to make certain productions memorable. I think, for example, of the immensely impressive stylisation of *The Trojans* and *Fidelio*, the extraordinarily well controlled realism of the crowd scene in *La Bohème* and the final act of *Die Meistersinger*; and of the very different stage

Scottish Opera Chorus.

pictures, alive with human figures, in *The Golden Cockerel*, *The Barber of Seville*, *Rigoletto*, *Mahagonny*, *Carmen* and *The Flying Dutchman*, in all of which the chorus played a very significant part.

To recruit its choristers Scottish Opera holds annual auditions in London and Manchester as well as Glasgow, since the opera schools in all three major music colleges are the most likely sources of talent. Recruiting is not a problem since, unlike companies with many full-time salaried principals — the state opera companies in Germany, for example — Scottish Opera offers a reasonable chance of promotion from the chorus to comprimario roles, or even principal parts when indisposition strikes. And that happens often enough, particularly on tour.

The connection between Scottish Opera and the Royal Scottish Academy of Music is claimed to be entirely informal. Nonetheless, since Leonard Hancock who, until 1980, was Head of Music at Elmbank Crescent, now moves between the two establishments, running the opera school at the Academy and acting as Music Consultant to Scottish Opera (which includes a great amount of coaching, an activity in which his reputation is proverbial) it is a connection that must be close enough to be instrumental in the discovery of potential operatic talent. Nowadays, too, there are various competitions and awards to highlight exceptional ability, three of which are associated with Scottish Opera. The John Noble Bursary was set up in 1973, to be awarded annually after a public concert; the Shell/Scottish Opera International Prize is given each year in competition to a singer under the age of 35; and the John Scott award which is non-competitive, is presented to the young member of the Company who is thought to have shown most promise. Former winners of the John Noble Bursary have, in some cases — as with Isobel Buchanan and Margaret Marshall — gone on to international careers, and prizewinners in more recent years have included singers like Rosa Mannion, Maria Moll and Claire Shearer who are already proving that the judges' confidence was by no means misplaced. As well as several comprimario roles Rosa Mannion has sung Pamina in the 1985 revival of *The Magic Flute*, Maria Moll sang the title role in a recent Opera Go Round production of *Tosca*, and Claire Shearer, who was "covering" Michaela in *Carmen* in 1986, seized her opportunity with great aplomb on the occasion when one of the principals went sick.

One area in which forced savings were made during the critical period to be discussed in the next chapter was the relinquishing of even a small group of singers on contract. This decision has not yet been revised and, more than almost anything else, it has caused disquiet among those who maintain that an establishment lacking a permanent company of salaried principals has no right to the name of opera company. Where in Scottish Opera, they ask, is the natural ladder up which a young aspiring soloist can climb. But the singers themselves are not all of the same opinion in the matter. Catherine Wilson who was part of the Scottish Opera "family" and sang important roles in many productions and on prestigious occasions at that, believes that in the case of the Scottish company, as with most others, it still holds that you have to move away and finish your career elsewhere. "Of course, you will get a chance to start in Scotland, but if you are really ambitious — I mean, if you really want to develop — you will still have to move away. That is true of any company you start in. It's the reason why I left Sadlers Wells and came to Glasgow."

But it is generally agreed that the opportunity to get started is the important thing, and that crucial first rung is still available at Scottish Opera where particularly gifted choristers are chosen to cover (that is to understudy) the principal roles. They are coached in the part, thoroughly rehearsed along with their fellow understudies (paid extra, of course) in what is a very important training process. You may not see them on the stage — although chorus members have been known to step straight into major roles, like Beckmesser in *Die Meistersinger* and The Queen of the Night in *The Magic Flute* — but each emerges from the experience well equipped to take over with assurance and eventually, perhaps, to assume the role in question in his or her own right.

It is too easily forgotten, perhaps, that in the days when there were twelve principals on salary or contract there might be anything up to seventeen productions to keep them busy. Too busy in some cases, for comfort. Patricia Hay, who admits that she owes her own career entirely to Scottish Opera and that she had loved every minute of it, declares that singers today simply wouldn't stand for the amount of work the contract soloists used to do. "I'm not complaining about it," she says,

I loved it all but it couldn't be done nowadays because of the unions, for one thing, and because the singers themselves would feel they simply couldn't do it. There was a time when I sang seventeen Paminas in twenty-two days, and seven Rosinas in ten days. And there are lots of things I could quote, like that. Peter Hemmings worked us terribly hard but we did get wonderful experience, and we managed to stand up to it. And I do have to say that I never felt that I was being abused by Scottish Opera. It was what gave me my career.

Alan Oke is another who freely admits that he owes all his valuable early experience to the Scottish company, and not just as a performer. "Oh, that week of *The Ring*. When I was sixteen that was one of my earliest experiences of opera. I didn't know Wagner except as a vague name, and I would go up to the gods in the Kings Theatre and roll out hours later quite drunk with it all. I didn't quite know why, but it had this physical effect on me, and it was superb. As for David Ward — well, he was a major star by then." Alan Oke, like a number of others, feels sure that nobody can grow to that sort of stature if they stay in the place where they began. "You have to go away and hope to be asked back to sing the parts that suit you." And as for the Scottish Opera tradition of bringing in the best international talent the budget will allow, most of the erstwhile company singers are in agreement. "When you are on the same stage as David Ward or Janet Baker or Charles Craig or Norman Bailey your own standard inevitably rises — you are faced with this level of performance which you then have to strive for on your own account. You can never do it, maybe, but that's not the point. What matters is that your horizon widens."

It is quite true that Gibson and Hemmings in the "golden years" of Scottish Opera, were famed for their ability to persuade exceptional singers into the team for this or that production; famed also for their way of discovering and attracting major singers near the start of their careers when there might be mutual advantage to be gained. We have seen how Dame Janet was persuaded to move from opera seria and recital work into grand opera. Dame Kiri Te Kanawa sang her first Desdemona with Scottish Opera in 1972, and Helga Dernesch made her British debut with the Company as Gutrune in *Götterdammerung* in 1968, returning again and again to sing Leonore, Isolde, Brunnhilde, Cassandra and The Marschallin.

The perception of Scottish Opera from the south of England, in those days, was that it was essentially "a singer house". John Cox, who was then Director of Productions at Glyndebourne, feels sure that that was where the money went.

Productions were safe, often gloriously well sung but, at a time when the Welsh were beginning to become more adventurous, the Scots were, if anything, a bit reactionary. It is

interesting that, at one point, they did engage David Pountney, but he didn't last very long and I think, now, that I know why. It was probably because the resistance to his sort of production was a bit too strong. The critics, too, are a bit behind. They still do, very often, give bad reviews to radical productions — and I don't think, incidentally, that because a production is radical it is necessarily very good in every case. But it is part of the process of educating an audience to take them through these experiences.

Not to present work which is in line with new thinking about opera is like running an art gallery where only the Rembrandts and Turners are shown, but no Picassos, no Henry Moores

Left to right: Kenneth Love, Rosanne Brackenridge, Catherine Wilson and Patricia Kern in THE TURN OF THE SCREW performed in 1970. (Director: Anthony Besch, designer: John Stoddart.)

and certainly no Carl André Bricks.

It is worth remembering, however, that Welsh National Opera was founded more than ten years before Scottish Opera and that it, too, had come through a period of disfavour before regaining its impetus as one of the more forward and outward looking of the British opera companies, regional or otherwise. In recent years WNO has been far more enterprising than Scottish Opera in the matter of inviting gifted foreign directors to work on productions at Cardiff. For example the great Romanian actor/director Liviu Ciulei has been responsible for new productions of *Cosi fan tutte* and *Wozzeck* for the Welsh company, which has also invited Lucian Pintilie and Andre Serban to direct productions of *Rigoletto*, and *I Puritani*. This injection of international creative ideas is now the norm at WNO. In 1986 Peter Stein, Director of the Berlin Schaubuhne, injected a timeless political relevance into Verdi's *Otello*, incidentally giving Donald Maxwell from Perth (an archetypal Scottish Opera singer, and former winner of the John Noble Bursary) an opportunity to demonstrate what a magnificent singer/actor he has grown to be.

Anthony Besch, who was probably the most significant, and certainly the most frequently employed guest director for many years, believes that it is, indeed, possible to excite the "old guard" with something that is challenging, so long as it is both relevant and creative. His own *Tosca*, first seen at Theatre Royal in 1980, was updated by more than a century so that it took on a new meaning for those members of the chorus — and they were many — who were still unborn in the Mussolini era. "But to make it work," he says, "it was absolutely necessary to treat it realistically. Indeed, my real moment of excitement came during our first rehearsal in costume when Marina Krilovici, who was waiting in the wings for her entrance, caught sight of Sarabia in his black Scarpia uniform for the first time and suddenly crossed herself. And I thought, well really, that's exactly what I want to achieve."

But Besch's 1970 production of *The Turn of the Screw*, revived in 1986 as though new minted, was treated not as realism but as impressionism of an eerily effective kind, in a design by John Stoddart based on atmospherically heightened reality. Anthony Besch tells how he took the designer to see an old house in Oxfordshire that he thought might inspire him, and how, later that night, they went to stay with friends in another house with a somewhat overgrown garden. "John was put in a sort of garden room and he woke up during the night and looked out of the window to see a full moon drifting through the tangled thorn bushes. And that, really, was the source of what you saw on the stage in *The Turn of the Screw*."

Scottish Opera is not at present — nor is it likely to become in the foreseeable future — a cradle of advanced ideas and operatic treatments, even though Opera Go Round's *Macbeth* brought surrealism to bear on the supernatural elements, with great effect. An objective observer, nonetheless, would be bound to say that the programme over the past few years has managed to balance the conventional but craftsmanlike against the radical and unexpected in a way that ought to be acceptable to all but the dyed-in-the-wool reactionaries. David Pountney's *Eugene Onegin* was ravishing in the period elegance of set and costume contrived by Roger Butlin and Deirdre Clancy, and Gibson and the SNO were in fine form. The same season saw a revival of *Peter Grimes* with Allen Cathcart in the title role and Catherine Wilson as Ellen Orford, one of the roles she loves best of all. *The Makropoulos Case*, co-produced with WNO (again by David Pountney) and given its Scottish Opera production in 1981 gave Catherine Wilson a

Margaret Marshall as the Countess in CAPRICCIO performed in 1985. (Director: John Cox, designer: Jack Notman.)

chance to take on a role which is absolutely central to the plot, the 300-year-old opera singer, Emilia Marty, kept alive by alchemy and afraid to die.

In 1983 there was a revival of that evergreen favourite, *La Bohème* with Marie Slorach in excellent voice as a charming Mimi and Patricia Hay in her element as Musetta, and of *The Golden Cockerel* with a cast of mostly company singers headed by Bill McCue and Nan Christie with John Robertson and Halcro Johnston as the princely siamese twins. New to Scotland that year was a highly atmospheric *Death in Venice*, directed by Francois Rochaix in a co-production with the Grand Theatre de

Genève. John Cox, now in charge of operations as Scottish Opera's General Administrator gave us a memorable *Idomeneo* (Margaret Marshall and Isobel Buchanan, two Scottish singers with rapidly rising international careers shared the role of Ilia) and a delightful taste of the earlier century in Cavalli's *L'Egisto* in a formal set by Allan Charles Klein that glittered like a gilded orrery, magnified to human scale.

It was in that same season, in the spring of 1984, that *Turandot* became something of a local cause celèbre, rocking Scottish Opera to its very foundations. Staged for the first time in the

Company's history, it was seen in a production by Tony Palmer, previously known only as a film maker, which took as its starting point a belief that Puccini's last, unfinished work was closely connected with his own domestic life: the Liu in the opera was based on the maid harried to the point of suicide by the composer's jealous wife. Stefanos Lazaridis was the designer and while his all-purpose set would have worked well for cinematic purposes it looked extremely cramped on the stage of Theatre Royal. The fact, too, that Palmer's concept corralled both Calaf/Puccini and Liu/maid-servant in a skeletal room to one side of the stage was slightly annoying. But many of the angry complaints, from professional critics and others (the correspondence columns of the *Herald* and the *Scotsman*, sizzled for days with self-righteous wrath) were, frankly, irrelevant. Also, the omission of the Alfano ending was clearly a disappointment to those who wanted to hear the final love duet, and the use of amplified sound was taken to be a deliberate rubbing of salt in the open wound of that thwarted expectation. But in retrospect it all seems like a storm in a teacup. The music was splendid, with Sir Alex on the rostrum, and an excellent cast which should have seen Linda Esther Gray singing her first *Turandot*. The Scots soprano, however, was indisposed, and the fact that her substitute, Ludmilla Andrew in excellent voice, was thought to be visually unsuitable by the director, caused another furore. Tony Palmer wished Miss Gray to mime the role on stage while the invisible Miss Andrew sang the music. "No," said General Administrator Cox, "that is not how we do

things in opera companies." So Mr Palmer took umbrage and left the scene, refusing to appear at the first performance. Marie Slorach sang the part of the slave girl Liu so enchantingly that she ran away with nearly all the plaudits. But the trio, Ping, Pang and Pong (Alan Oke, Gordon Christie and Hugh Hetherington, here dressed like minor civil servants) were also a delight, and Ludmilla Andrew, beautiful or not, sang superbly.

Elegance returned next season with *Capriccio*, that one-act piece by Richard Strauss that, in synopsis, looks so dull — it is, in effect, a long discussion about the relative importance of words and music. In a production by John Cox, in a grand salon designed by Jack Notman, and with a cast that included Margaret Marshall as the Countess Madeleine, Stafford Dean as La Roche, and Maria Moll and Francis Egerton as the two Italian singers, exponents of bel canto at its most extreme, it ravished the eye and was a delight to hear. *Il Barbiere di Siviglia* was likewise a delight, albeit of a very different kind. This was Rossini with knobs on, treated, by the director Robert David MacDonald, to all the hilarious business he will bear — and in truth it is a great deal — but never to the detriment of the music, when that really matters. Sue Blane's pink-washed Spanish warren of domesticity surrounding Dr. Bartolo's menage, was brilliantly conceived, and the singers gave every evidence of enjoyment, from Russell Smyth's personable Figaro of the nimble wit and tongue to Geoffrey Moses' lanky Don Basilio giving full value in his scandal spreading aria, and Ludmilla Andrew's hilariously sluttish Berta.

Graham Vick, newly installed as Director of Productions, was responsible for two operas that season, one of which, the first commissioned work to be staged for several years, was much admired, and the other, a new *Don Giovanni*, which was not. Edward Harper's *Hedda Gabler*, with its stunning pistol-shot opening, its lovely, lyrical score and its powerful undertones of frustrated emotion stayed very close, in essence, to Ibsen, except for the prologue in which the relationship between Hedda and Loevborg was established in a beautiful love-duet. Russell Craig devised an interesting mobile central structure to signify both interior and exterior scenes. And Kathryn Harries, clearly by then a rising star in the operatic firmament, was Ibsen's Hedda to the life.

It was with his attempt to find contemporary relevance in *Don Giovanni* that Graham Vick fell foul of the critics and the local opera fans, though, in truth, a great deal of the criticism had little genuine basis either in intrinsic shortcomings in staging — there were a few hiccups, it's true, but nothing that could not have been resolved in revival — or in conceptual perversion. Where the plot of the music of Mozart was concerned there seemed to be no serious irrelevance. Vick had taken as his starting point the squalid and callous nature of much of the action. With his designer, Russell Craig, he attempted to telescope the centuries, retaining hints of seventeenth century dress in an otherwise abstracted 1980s, graffitti-laden environment for the rape and muggings, murder and retribution with which the plot is manifestly loaded. None of what was seen went counter to the message of the music and the end was as

chilling as might be imagined. Where a more conventional director might have sent his Don Giovanni to a predictable hell, following the dark figure of the Commendatore through that incandescent, coffin-shaped opening upstage, Vicky consigned him to what, for a man like Don Giovanni, was far, far worse — condemned him to remain in the world, invisible, inaudible, untouchable, a watcher in the wings forever.

Graham Vick, who has now left Scottish Opera, bitterly regrets the fact that he will never have an opportunity to work further on this *Don Giovanni*, to sort out, as he says, all the bits that didn't work as well as he hoped they would. It was, after all, a very ambitious production that deserved one revival, at least. What the people wanted, he thinks, who wrote all those virulent letters to the papers and to Scottish Opera, was a Don with a kind of daredevil, Errol Flynn glamour. "But don't they realise that what this man is doing is mocking all the institutions they claim to respect and hold dear? Love and marriage, the family and the Church. That is what *Don Giovanni* is about, and Mozart is telling us so if people would only listen. They hated me, I think, because I actually showed that to be the case."

What affronted the traditionalists more than anything else, no doubt, was the sight — in circumstances that are all too credible today, alas — of the beaten-up Massetto slumped (far upstage, it's true) against a public loo with the penitent Zerlina trying to clean up his wounds. Unfortunately the Scottish Opera management has bowed to the most vociferous section of the audience (for Vick's *Don Giovanni* had plenty of

IDOMENEO performed in 1983 (right).

THE CUNNING LITTLE VIXEN
performed in 1980

THE MARRIAGE OF FIGARO performed in 1986

TOSCA performed in 1980

COSI FAN TUTTE performed in 1967

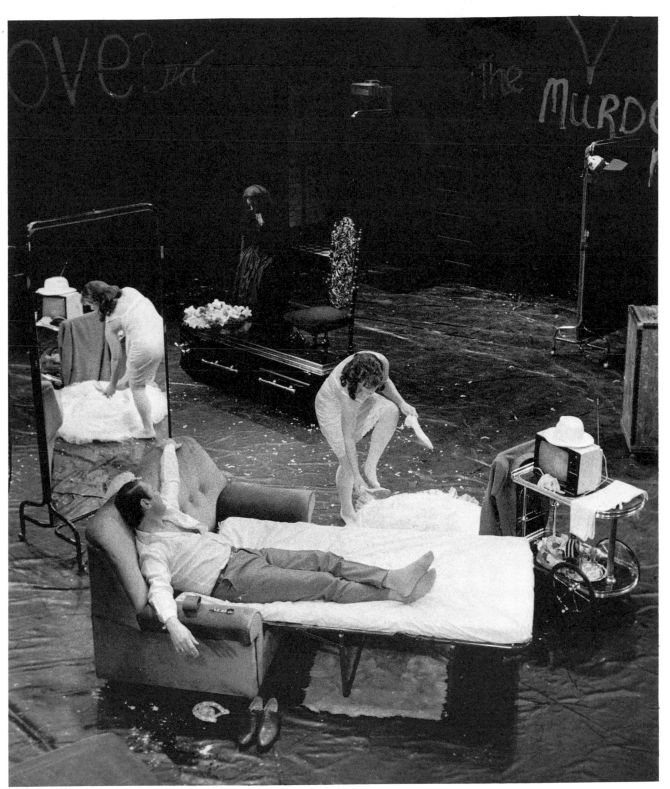

Jonathan Miller's THE MAGIC FLUTE performed in 1983 (left).

Sergei Leiferkus (Don Giovanni) and Faith Elliot (Zerlina) in Graham Vick's production of DON GIOVANNI performed in 1986.

From MAHAGONNY performed in 1986. (Director: David Alden, designer: David Fielding.)

supporters, also) with the result that his production will not be seen again. That, to me, is very sad because, now that the initial shock is over, I believe that more and more people would begin to appreciate the director's intention and come to enjoy the exciting visual aspects of what, for me, has proved an unforgettable event.

When David Alden produced his *Rigoletto* in 1979, also emphasising the moral squalor of a plot that has all too often been heavily romanticised with opulent settings and fancy dress, it, too, was loathed by many at first seeing. But when revived it was found to have made converts and that, I feel sure, would also

have happened with *Don Giovanni*. A more recent David Alden production, *The Rise and Fall of the City of Mahagonny*, gave rise to far less virulent criticism, no doubt because fewer members of the audience came with cherished preconceptions. But that production, too, was staged with a fair degree of deliberate alienation, set in an inimical environment like a disused and half derelict hypermarket, and visually reminiscent of the art of the 1970s conceptualists with a potent injection of the neon-lit creations of Dan Flavin. Alden's sheer inventiveness, ideas sparking off like fireworks, was almost too

Emily Golden as Carmen, with the Chorus in Graham Vick's production of CARMEN performed in 1986. (Designer: Michael Yeargan.)

much to be assimilated at one visit: quirky humour through bleak satire and disgust to downright, chilling alienation. Musically, it was memorable, with the Scottish Opera Chorus in top form, and Sian Edwards, making her professional debut on the rostrum drew a marvellous response from the Scottish Opera Orchestra. She seemed to infect the players with her own obvious relish for the heady mixture of ragtime and full blown operatic sound with which Kurt Weill "coloured" Brecht's sour parable of the city mushrooming on false values of greed and pleasure, and of the chaos that results. That was the production from which the singer originally cast as the lumberjack, Jimmy Mahoney, departed abruptly at the eleventh hour, whereupon Richard Cassily, the American baritone, stepped in and gave a stunning performance. The Widow Begbick was Felicity Palmer and she, too, was well in the spirit of the piece.

The balance was struck, once again, with *The Marriage of Figaro* in a new production by John Cox with set and costumes by the Scots artist/playwright John Byrne, working for the first time in the world of opera. Visually delightful and extremely witty, it offered nothing to offend the traditionalists while delighting the perceptive with associative touches and the perfect, if slightly satirised, period detail. It was a production where director and designer seemed perfectly in accord; the music with Gyorgy Fischer in control, flowed as smoothly as the action. The characterisation was convincing, and for once the underlying sexuality was brought near the surface but still gracefully and without losing the essentially comic aspect of the affair. Margaret Marshall, as the pensive, neglected Countess and Jonathan Summers as Almaviva, arrogant, born to the droit de seigneur, and reluctant to lose it, Diana Montague as the ardent Cherubino, Isobel Buchanan as a witty, charming Susanna, and Roderick Earle as a clever, but unimaginative Figaro — it was a cast and a production that came near to satisfying everyone.

Carmen, too, with Vick again as director and John Mauceri, now Musical Director designate, in the pit, deservedly found favour with most discerning critics and with all but the most reactionary members of the audience. The designer, this time, was Michael Yeargan who made use of a very stark setting based on a huge revolving stage surrounded by a phalanx of simple wooden chairs, and fitted with a rectangular section which rose at certain moments to become a wall pierced by a door. It was against that bleak, blank wall that Emily Golden's Carmen sat alone to sing the Habanera, and through that door that Escamillo entered in all his torero splendour to the cheers of the admiring crowd. The revolve — which, it has to be admitted, caused a little trouble at some performances — gave rise to some highly effective crowd scenes, and at one point the female members of the chorus attempted to transform themselves into fully accoutred flamenco dancers: a valiant, if not entirely convincing effort.

Mauceri slowed the pace more than usual with the effect of intensifying the sultriness and the inner tensions but the musical excitements grew on demand. Emily Golden was a subtle rather than a blatant Carmen with a voice of considerable range that thrilled, especially in its lower register.

After Keith Warner's amusing *Iolanthe*, cleverly set by Marie-Jeanne Lecca against giant red dispatch boxes piled up into a curved wall (the very Victorian fairies, suitably dwarfed by this environment, climbed nimbly up and down and in and out and, on the whole, justice was done to both librettist and composer) came the season's heavyweight, Wagner's *Flying Dutchman*, with Norman Bailey back in Glasgow to sing the role he has made his own. John Cox's production, up-dated to Wagner's own period, was based on the idea that, in the early years of the industrial revolution, a shipmaster like Daland might also, without straining credibility, be the owner of a small family business where his cargoes of cotton would be spun and woven into cloth. Cox's designer was the American Eugene Lee, who found inspiration in authentic Scottish prototypes, like Robert Owen's New Lanark. The initial impact was very powerful, a dark, misty turbulence with Daland's ship, its oilskinned crew crowding under a tall black smokestack, heaving gently as it pulled into the quay. The conductor was Sir Alex Gibson, and the piece was magnificently cast on the whole.

Norman Bailey in THE FLYING DUTCHMAN performed in 1987. (Director: John Cox, designer: Eugene Lee.)

The Chorus in Act I of THE FLYING DUTCHMAN
performed in 1987.

Apart from the sombre, magnetic presence of Bailey's Dutchman, black-coated and booted, in dark leather clothes suggesting a period two centuries earlier, this production could boast a magnificent Senta in one of the finest histrionic sopranos we have seen at Scottish Opera for years. Patrick Power had his great moment in the Steerman's song in Act 1, and Oddbjorn Tennfjord's Daland, conveyed the very essence of nineteenth century materialism (I loved the moment when, stepping ashore, he immediately exchanged his shipmaster's cap for an imposing tall hat).

Here, as in so many of the finest productions over the years, the imaginative vision that creates the lighting effects, made all the difference between success and failure. Nick Chelton was the designer who lit *The Flying Dutchman* as well as many other productions over several previous seasons, including *Turandot* and *Don Giovanni*. But, since the early days when the name of Charles Bristow appeared in the programmes again and again in connection with some of the most famous productions from *Otello* and *Cosi* to *The Golden Cockerel*, other names like Victor Lockwood, Alan Campbell, and several more have become familiar.

PROBLEMS OF MANAGEMENT

Look behind any successful artistic organisation and you will find a system of management that is imaginative, sympathetic to the aims of the enterprise and, above all, capable of tempering the chill winds of administration to the "shorn lambs" who are the creative talents without whom nothing of the sort can exist. It was this combination of attributes that gave the young Scottish Opera its power to grow and sustain itself in the process. The two men at the helm held what hindsight suggests were most of the qualities needed for success. Alex Gibson, the gifted musician, possessed more than enough charisma to attract enthusiastic local support for a popular and much-needed cause, but he is a modest man, lacking the natural aggression which alone would have put his other attributes to best effect; whereas Peter Hemmings, knowledgable, creative in a different way, was capable of bulldozing ideas and plans through seemingly insuperable obstacles; he was an autocrat, but he was also a communicator.

It was this duo, this perfect balance of forces that generated the energy to propel Scottish Opera forward on what seemed to onlookers like a well-lubricated track from the first ad hoc seasons — really no more than gradually extended opera festivals in Scotland — right up to the acquisition of Theatre Royal and the pilot subscription season of ten operas in Glasgow. It has already been said that Alex Gibson was unhappy from the start with his title of Artistic Director but in the early days it didn't seem to matter because, as he himself will tell you, nobody cared too much about titles or what they signified. But as the Company grew and became established it began to worry him more and more.

I was well aware that my title was a false one. There was no question that I wanted to be, or indeed could be, what people think of when they hear that so-and-so is Artistic Director of a company. And when we opened the Theatre Royal and became more obviously a permanent feature on the landscape, I would have liked to change my title then to something more appropriate like Musical Director, but I guessed that people might begin to think I was losing interest. Inside the enterprise, of course, nobody has ever worried much about titles; it is what people do that matters. Peter was the General Manager, and in that sense, *primus inter pares*, but we always worked together as a team and, for me, it has always been the teamwork in this organisation that has got the best results.

Peter Hemmings, as we have seen, has left behind him a legendary reputation for able and sympathetic administration. Autocrat though he was, undoubtedly, he had the gift of attracting loyalty to an unusual degree. Indeed, those who worked under him still wax lyrical about their working relations, notwithstanding memorable stormy passages over this or that vexed question. Ann Baird as Director of Opera Go Round and Opera for Youth, and Evelyn Bryson as Company Manager during Hemmings's regime still talk of his extraordinary intelligence, ". . . which meant that no matter how hard you tried to keep up, Peter was always six steps ahead of you," and of his determination to see that everybody got things right. "He had no time for half-baked ideas and he would make that quite clear to anyone who went to him with a suggestion that wasn't properly thought through. But," says Ann Baird, "the point is that if he thought you had something worth listening to, he would insist that you cost it right down to last detail."

Almost everyone involved with Scottish Opera in those early seasons will tell you that, no matter what the problems were, they cannot remember a time when the attitude wasn't positive, reaching out and extending. It was, they say, a period when the people in middle management felt free to make suggestions, knowing that they would be listened to: not immediately, perhaps, but usually, as Evelyn Bryson then Company Manager recalls, "three days later Peter would call you in and say that he'd been thinking about it and maybe your idea, which he'd tended to dismiss, had something in it after all, so would you go away and work it out."

Nonetheless, all the power was in the hands of the chief executive and he made it abundantly clear who was in charge. "Peter opened all the mail himself," Ann Baird remembers, "so he knew what everybody in the office was doing; he also insisted on seeing a copy of every letter that went out, so he was aware of everything that went on." Peter Hemmings, himself, puts it rather differently.

The most important single element in my time at Scottish Opera was my relationship with Alex Gibson who, as head of the organisation, supported and encouraged my every whim. His public persona, great public following and national and international connections were Scottish Opera's greatest calling card. He was busy with the SNO and a travelling career and left the running of Scottish Opera to me for most of the time. It was, however, my pleasure and my duty to organise my thinking regularly so as to be able to report succinctly to him on all aspects of our Company, and I can never remember any serious disagreement.

At that time, of course, as Hemmings himself admits, inflation was barely perceptible, the spiral was in its very early stage, and those were the heady days of Jennie Lee and Lord Goodman, both major, charismatic fighters for proper state subsidy for the arts they themselves enjoyed. And that was something new to Britain which had lagged far behind some European countries in that field. Scottish Opera was in effect able to go on expanding and developing, safe in the knowledge that any deficit at the end of each year would be met by an increase in grant.

So it was possible to run the enterprise as one might run a festival, with a small permanent organisation and limited overheads, buying in the best talent available, from the directors to the designers, from the principal artists to the amateur chorus, knowing that it was safe enough to budget for a modest deficit.

It is tempting to trace all, or most, of Scottish Opera's now notorious difficulties, in later years, in terms of management and finance, to the acquisition of Theatre Royal without a proper endowment fund to maintain it except by borrowing extra money. Yet hindsight tells us that the time was absolutely right; that even two or three years later, with Theatre Royal still available at the same bargain price, the cost of conversion would have escalated far beyond even Scottish Opera's notable fund-raising ability.

David Ward as Banquo in MACBETH performed in 1976.
(Director: David Pountney, designer: Ralph Koltai.)

MACBETH, performed in 1976 with Pauline Tinsley and Norman Bailey as Lady Macbeth and Macbeth.

The Scottish Arts Council has always insisted that none of Scottish Opera's annual grant must be siphoned off into the maintenance of Theatre Royal. The £150,000 a year which is now the average amount necessary to keep Theatre Royal open throughout the year, equals the whole cost of one main-scale production or two Opera Go Round tours to perhaps 20 venues in small outlying places countrywide.

Having seen Scottish Opera settled into its new home, with a ten-opera season in the first year, including an appearance at the Edinburgh Festival; having brought David Pountney into the team as Staff Producer and encouraged him to develop his own challenging and stimulating ideas in direction (*Macbeth*, *Die Meistersinger*, *The Golden Cockerel* and *Jenufa*) having paved the way for Opera Go Round and Opera for Youth to develop the valuable activity of the old Opera for All and Opera for Schools; Peter Hemmings clearly felt the need to move on. There are still those who continue to harbour a deep sense of deprivation at his departure for Australia in September 1977 and who feel that everything would have been different had he remained at the helm. About that there is no room for argument: Hemmings and his successor Peter Ebert have little in common but their love of opera. But the economic and political climate which allowed Peter Hemmings to supervise the expansion of Scottish Opera between 1966 and 1976 was already changing for the worse before his departure. Even he might have found himself helpless and frustrated in the attempt to keep the Scottish Opera ship on an even keel. Even the legend of Peter Hemmings might have become a little tarnished. And it has to be said that there are those who feel that someone as intelligent as Hemmings must surely have foreseen the lean years ahead as money became scarcer and goodwill towards the arts began to dry up with the increasing shift of politics to the right. True or not, in the autumn of 1977, Peter Hemmings did depart, and Peter Ebert was appointed General Administrator in his place.

Ebert was no stranger to Scottish Opera, having worked there as a freelance producer from the second season and eventually joining

Peter Ebert (left) and Peter Hemmings.

the Company as Director of Productions. Like almost everyone else, Ebert speaks of the "special nature" of the enterprise, and of the community spirit that existed at Scottish Opera particularly in the first ten years or so. And he is careful to emphasise his understanding of the importance of maintaining a sense of continuity, of retaining a company of semi-principals under contract as well as inviting international artists back repeatedly to sing suitable roles so that, over a period of time, they, too, would become identified with Scottish Opera.

Peter Ebert now agrees, however, that in the constant look-out for international talent it was possible to overlook potentially major talent on Scotland's doorstep. "There were a few artists who trained at the Academy here who, I am ashamed to say, had to go to London to make a name, and made it very quickly, and so were missed by Scottish Opera. Margaret Marshall was a case in point: by the time she came to us to sing Euridice and the Countess, she was already an international artist who had been totally ignored at home; Isobel Buchanan was another."

The new General Administrator came to office with admirable intentions of consolidating what his predecessor had built up. Essentially a producer of operas, it was Ebert, of course, who was responsible for some of the most famous Scottish Opera productions: *Falstaff*, *The Trojans*, *The Ring* among them. Peter Ebert was unlike Peter Hemmings who had always maintained that an opera manager, however knowledgable, should have no desire to be a singer, dancer, conductor, director or designer.

In fact, more of Ebert's interest was focused on the artistic side of the operation than should have been the case. And that surely implies that his appointment to that particular post was a misjudgment on the part of Scottish Opera's Board of Directors. Peter Ebert's previous experience in the field of management had been gained in German Opera Houses where the Intendant relies on a cushion of highly experienced and professional senior management which maintains the operation in good financial order. Scottish Opera, having just lost its original, efficient overlord, was in sore need of just such another, particularly in view of the worsening political and economic climate. Instead it was presented with a very different kind of boss, a man of considerable theatrical gifts and commitment whose administrative ability was far from being his strong point, as he, himself, would surely be the first to admit. The result was unfortunate for all concerned, not least for Ebert who became engulfed in a situation for which he was not equipped to cope.

Theoretically, however, his ideas were very sound. It was he who, in 1978, prepared a paper setting out very succinctly the objectives and requirements of Scottish Opera which, from the outset, had aimed at the highest artistic standards. "This goal," he wrote, "has been the cornerstone of the Company's work and of its success, and dictates its line of thought in all other considerations. To present opera of a quality as good as, or better than, what is achieved at most opera houses throughout Europe and elsewhere is the true measure of a national opera company."

Scottish Opera, he went on to say, had created a demand which far exceeded the number of performances the Company was able to give on its present grant. Even with the present level of staffing Scottish Opera could give many more performances than the budget would allow. Basically what was being asked for was an increase in subsidy to allow the Company's strength to be used to best advantage, in giving more performances without any increase in staff. Underutilisation was, in fact, one of Scottish Opera's major inefficiencies.

That, of course, is something which hasn't changed. More recently I heard the same argument put more bluntly. Scottish Opera is still perforce working at three-quarters capacity.

You can't have three-quarters of a Musical Director, a General Administrator, a Director of Productions: you have just got them. Now if you get down to six operas a year you can maybe fire one or two people but with nine operas you can't. And you can do twelve without hiring anyone else. It's what Priestley said in his report on Covent Garden. It's a well-known fact of life that for a little bit more you can do a whole lot more, because you've got your people anyway and most of them are underused. What you need is the money for more nuts and bolts.

Ebert's paper included a list of more or less urgent requirements including a store for bulky scenery, lighting equipment, props, costumes and wigs instead of the accommodation then leased, at an inconvenient distance, and the cramped costume wardrobe at the Opera Centre. The necessity for a proper workshop was emphasised and the staff for the construction and treatment of scenery and stage properties since the cost of construction in London and of long-distance travel and staff transport was not only prohibitive but also unproductive. The need to build up a permanent team of contract singers was also emphasised since part of the Company's policy was to create opportunities for young Scottish singers in all the activities of Opera Go Round and Opera for Youth. And, lastly, it was pointed out that, unlike all the other opera companies in Britain — Covent Garden, English National Opera, Opera North and Welsh National Opera — Scottish Opera was still without an orchestra of its own, but still had to rely on the Scottish National Orchestra, the BBC Scottish Symphony Orchestra and the recently formed Scottish Chamber Orchestra, all of which, inevitably, put their own concert engagements before the needs of the opera company.

Not for the first time, Ebert's paper also pointed out that a major cause of disquiet, even at the present level of funding, was the lack of early and exact information about the size of the grant to be expected for the following financial year; information which, it was justifiably claimed, should be available at least twelve months before the beginning of the

Ian Robertson and John Cox in rehearsal.

new financial year to allow for optimum control of planning and budgeting.

The real crisis with Scottish Opera was something that could not be resolved simply by cutting back on the total annual number of performances — all companies have to do that in times of financial stringency. The problem was that the Company, having reached a level of staffing to enable it to perform throughout the whole year, could not reduce its activity without destroying the very asset which had enabled it to reach that level in the first place — its team of trained and experienced personnel.

Between 1975 and 1977 the income from the local authorities decreased by 14% at a time when the cost of living index had increased by 27%. Scottish Opera found itself caught in a vicious circle. To undertake any major saving, touring — by far the most expensive activity — must be curtailed and that, in turn, provokes local authorities to reduce their contributions further so that the savings thus effected are wiped out by the reduced level of subsidy.

Unfortunately, Peter Ebert's good intentions were not enough to steer Scottish Opera into calmer waters. It is obvious now that both he and his Board of Directors were optimistic to a fault in supposing that funds would be made available for the kind of consolidation they had in mind, and which Ebert had set out in his paper to SAC.

The fact that Peter Ebert was, himself, so closely involved on the artistic side also caused problems since it is a known fact that artists seldom see eye to eye, for reasons which are by no means always objective, with the work of other artists. There are those who will tell you — David Pountney being one of them — that the effect of Peter Ebert's reign was to destroy the mechanics of trust that had been built up in the previous decade. "An opera company needs single-minded leadership," Pountney maintains,

when absolutely everybody feels supported by that person — I mean, of course, all the artistic side. What you, as a director, can do with a subject demands very calm judgment all round. No team can survive on an atmosphere of insecurity, and my own feeling is that the psychological insecurity that resulted from Ebert's regime has never really been resolved.

In the end, of course, realising that the money to pursue the desired programme of development and consolidation was unlikely to be offered in the foreseeable future, Peter Ebert resigned, "owing to a conflict of policy and, in particular, of priorities which it has not been possible to resolve in a way which would ensure the relationship vital to the happiness and continued success of the Company". That was the press statement issued at the time but the blunt facts were that Peter Ebert simply could not come to terms with his Board's demand for restraint. And it was during the mercifully brief interregnum before another General Administrator was appointed that Scottish Opera began to find itself in the middle of a real financial crisis.

Apart from anything else, the Company was caught on the horns of a dilemma — the cost of touring alongside the duty to tour; the cost of maintaining Theatre Royal coupled with what would happen to Scottish Opera if the theatre had to be given up. Together these problems brought about a desperate search for solutions not dependent on the extra funding which everyone now realised would not be forthcoming. By 1981 the situation had become desperate. A separate trust to manage Theatre Royal was one possibility being considered. Indeed, there are those who feel that much trouble might have been avoided had such a trust been set up in the first place instead of a subsidiary company with its own Board of Directors.

The Board of Scottish Opera was faced with a series of unenviable tasks. They had to decide first of all whether to look for a replacement for Peter Ebert at once or to continue operating

Left to right: Don Garrard (Sarastro), Margaret Marshall (Pamina), Gordon Christie (Tamino) and Benjamin Luxon (Papageno) in Jonathan Miller's production of THE MAGIC FLUTE performed in 1983. (Designer: Philip Prowse.)

with senior members of the professional staff taking on the financial and opera planning aspects of the General Administrator's role. With the support of the Company, and on the advice of a detached management consultancy report generously provided by B.P., they opted for the second course of action. They were also faced with the necessity to reduce the programme of performances and also to reduce, in a staged plan over three years, the accumulated deficit caused mostly by the need for borrowing to maintain and run Theatre Royal. But no less important was the need to keep the company intact for better days — a vital element in the plan since, otherwise, the standard of performance would almost certainly have slumped unacceptably. It is to the great credit of everyone concerned that nothing of the sort happened. Instead we were offered some splendid revivals, of *The Mastersingers* (sung in English this time round), *Midsummer Night's Dream* and *Wozzeck*, and several new productions including the memorable, visually exciting *Magic Flute* staged by Jonathan Miller and Philip Prowse.

But the decision worked less well on the non-artistic side of things. As Ian Rodger put it to me.

> The tradition of a non-executive Board depending on the skills of a professional General Administrator as, in effect, a Managing Director and Chief Executive leading the professional opera company, while it worked well in Peter Hemmings's day — who, after all, had all the reins in his hands when everything was new and the atmosphere was euphoric — was not apt in dealing with the intricate mix of several problems: policy, public relations, financial support and opera planning, which emerged in the more troubled days when the fate of the Company itself was in peril. So we had to think very hard about what to do for the best.

So it was not for some time that the Board of Scottish Opera approached John Cox, Director of Glyndebourne and one of the most distinguished figures in the British opera world (Cox had already been booked to produce Cavalli's *L'Egisto* for January 1982) and invited him to join the Company as Peter Ebert's successor. Cox, whose creative ability is matched by a keen intelligence, took some persuasion to accept, if only because he, of all people, could foresee the kind of problem which David Pountney put to me so bluntly. But he saw it as a challenge he might enjoy.

That was in 1981, at the point where the Board were confident that, if the emergency plan proceeded as proposed by a professional team approved by the Scottish Arts Council, Scottish Opera was well on its way to putting its house in order. Cox came to Glasgow believing that he would be the one, before long, to enjoy the benefit of all the hard times and steer Scottish Opera, as he says, "through the last of the shoals and shallows and out into the open sea and prosperity." But to his disquiet he found that the recovery plan had been too ambitious, and the fund-raising requirements too optimistic.

> So I felt that, having had no experience of opera administration, as such, I was going to need all the help I could get from the Boards (there were three by then, to govern Scottish Opera, Theatre Royal, and the Endowment Trust) whose members included lawyers and accountants. I wanted to call on all possible expertise from what I believed should be more than just an honorary body of people who were collectively proud of Scottish Opera.
>
> So it was to the Boards that I turned for a solution. We extracted a "gang of four", and it was that executive committee and myself who would go to Edinburgh and argue the case with the Arts Council and really put up a fight for the existence of the Company. I came to a decision early on that I wanted to make it a very high-profile campaign. I was determined not to keep it all damped down because I thought that only played into the Arts Council's hands. I wanted to make the Scottish Arts Council seen to be answerable to the Scottish public for what they were doing. And then, if the same Scottish public decided that it wanted a national opera company, it would have to play its part in securing that company's future.

One of the things that had to be rectified was the situation that most heads of departments at Scottish Opera were not responsible for their own budgets.

Every head of department had to learn to account for everything, not just the artistic costs, but everything relating to the people in the areas of his or her responsibility. Hardly any of them had training for that and they were already working to capacity. So it was a very hard time for everyone because, of course, we had to do all that and still keep the rehearsal schedule, and the whole organisation afloat.

To begin with, this worried me because I felt that some of the staff might crack under the really tremendous strain but, happily, nobody did and, with unstinting help from the Board members, who could give expert advice, we gradually acquired a really strong management who were clearly never going to let the same thing happen again. In truth, much of the financial muddle had come about because, after Peter Ebert left, and possibly, indeed, during his time, one person alone had been responsible for the finances and he had kept everything very close to his chest. Now all that has changed. From now on whoever is Chief Executive has a lot of people around him who know what is going on. That is new at Scottish Opera and I think it is absolutely necessary and healthy and good.

Ian Rodger was Chairman of the Board in John Cox's first season. "I was merely an interim Chairman," he tells you, having stepped into office at short notice when Sir Patrick Thomas, who had succeeded the first Chairman, Professor Robin Orr, was injured in a motor car accident. No-one, however, could have felt more deeply involved than Ian Rodger who, after all, had been one of the original foursome. He was succeeded, a year later, by the financier J. Raymond Johnstone, who backed John Cox up to the hilt in his fight for the continued existence of Scottish Opera. And one of Johnstone's arguments, over and above the obvious artistic ones, for adequate government funding, is interesting to say the least.

When I am advising an overseas business concern to open a branch in central Scotland one of the first things I am asked — after the obvious interest in a good golf course — is, "Do you have an opera house?" And I can say yes, of course we do. Nobody can fault that as an argument for extra spending, even if there were nothing else — which there clearly is — in favour of sustaining Scottish Opera and Theatre Royal in good health.

Perhaps that was the crucial argument that won a grant of £900,000 from SAC which cleared away the accumulated deficit and transformed the position retrospectively at least. This was given as part of the special grant of £5,000,000 made by government to ACGB to alleviate the troubles of the major arts organisations.

It was Johnstone who led the executive committee which set out to put things right, one member of which was Dr Leonard Paterson who became Chairman of the Board in 1985, and who sees the problem as stemming from even further back than Pete Ebert's regime. Given that he had immense charisma and a crystal clear conception of his own role and his intentions for Scottish Opera, Peter Hemmings, in failing to delegate authority, planted the seeds of future trouble after his own departure at that crucial time when the enterprise had begun to develop into a permanent company with its own chorus, cadre of salaried principals and orchestra. The administrative structure, Dr Paterson maintains, was simply not there to deal with all that.

> If you employ 250 people, whether you are making washers or producing opera, you have a medium-size company in anyone's terms in Scotland, and it is going to have problems of management. And there was simply nobody around who was, in any sense, a manager. Artistically gifted, full of talent, imagination, all those things that are the heart and soul of any opera company; we didn't lack those people. What Scottish Opera lacked was the armature to support them. John Cox most certainly did not create the management problems, as some are inclined to think. He inherited them, and it is greatly to his credit that he faced up to the difficulties and stayed to see us through them.

The cost-cutting continues, of course, sometimes to the detriment — though not often — of what is seen on the stage. There were complaints that the slight wheezing noise from the hydraulic machinery used to cause the heaving of Daland's ship in *The Flying Dutchman*, spoiled the enjoyment of Wagner's music on the first night (someone thought it might be intended to suggest the crying of seagulls but wished that a better recording had been found) but, as Len Paterson explains,

> Five days' rehearsal was all we could have on the stage and for part of that time nobody could get in for the snow. That's the kind of problem you are up against if, as we do, you cut down on stage rehearsals through a re-

scheduling of the amount of time you occupy the theatre because if the opera company is using Theatre Royal the place can't earn its keep.

The continued need for cost-cutting which is forced on Scottish Opera can lead to things which, in ordinary circumstances, would be considered unacceptable, like cutting out stage rehearsal time on tour, so that a production worked out for the stage and auditorium of Theatre Royal will have to take its chance in Edinburgh, Aberdeen or Newcastle because a stage rehearsal there would cost a great deal more than the Company can now afford in subsistence, theatre hire and so forth. The last four or five years, indeed, have seen Scottish Opera fall steadily behind in the purchasing value of the money available to it: maybe as much as 15%. Yet it might well be asked whether any other British opera company does anything like as much — touring its full-scale productions to distant cities; covering the country with Opera Go Round and, to suitable venues, with medium-scale productions; running its exceptionally successful education unit, Opera for Youth — and all from one underfunded resource.

Yet it is an open secret that the Scottish Arts Council harbours a belief that operatic product may be brought in from elsewhere more cheaply than Scottish Opera can supply it at home, and has even put out feelers to companies south of the Border. (There's irony in this when

Marina Krilovici as Floriotosca in TOSCA performed in 1980. (Director: Anthony Besch, designer: Peter Rice.)

it is remembered that the north of England used to depend on the Scottish company for its diet of opera until somebody in London must have decided that national pride was at stake.) SAC appears to be ignoring the fundamental importance of the Company in Scotland, as an institution which any self-respecting nation ought to possess and cherish. You either believe, and back up that belief with adequate funding, that Scotland can justify, and deserves to have, national opera and ballet companies, just as it has national orchestras, art galleries, museums and a national library, or you effectively disable them by forcing them into strait-jackets. How long, I wonder, must we wait to see the major performing companies brought into line with the other institutions and funded directly from the Scottish Office?

Since the setting up of an executive committee of the Board of Scottish Opera in 1983, under the new Chairman of the Board, Raymond Johnstone, to oversee the necessary managerial changes, the current affairs of the Company are so strictly under control that, for the first time in many years, the annual deficit is minimal. Marine metaphors come naturally to the present Chairman whose business is shipping — he will tell you that the management has addressed itself very firmly to all the leaks in the ship which are now more or less sealed. The artistic policy will continue as before, to present a balanced repertoire on different scales of operation to the highest possible — and affordable — standards, with a minimum of nine full-scale operas and two Opera Go Round productions or one medium-scale and one Opera Go Round. In 1986 the full-scale touring

schedule was almost back to normal, with three weeks in Edinburgh, two weeks in Aberdeen, one week at Eden Court Theatre, Inverness, and five weeks in England. The Opera Go Round team was back on the road with a much admired, scaled-down *Tosca*, directed by Keith Warner; and a number of medium-scale venues enjoyed Graham Vick's imaginative production of *Tales of Hoffman* in an ingenious, equally imaginative set by Kenny Miller from the Citizens Theatre.

"We have become more systematic," Dr Paterson says,

about asking for other people's opinions, based on experience, and in gathering and tabulating our own experience about box-office expectations. The trouble has been, to a large extent, that the organisation just "growed like Topsy" with inherent faults that everybody just took for granted, and a lot of hard work had to be done to correct them. Now we are nearly all the way to solving our problems: we have gone through all the hoops demanded of us by the Scottish Arts Council; we have done computer studies, constructed financial models of the Company showing what happens when you do various things; we have educated them into the long-term planning problems of opera — Norman Bailey is singing the Dutchman now only because we booked him two years ago, and there is no way we can find anyone of that stature at six months' notice. So we have done our best to show them just how inflexible is the nature of the operation. We have explained the structure of the Company, about the need to keep us whole so that, if money is not available, we can cut back a little on the

Graham Vick during rehearsals of DON GIOVANNI, 1985.

John Mauceri, Scottish Opera's new Musical Director.

product but we must be ready for better days when they come. Yet, after all that, they don't even seem to recognise that inflation exists.

Is it ineptitude, or politics within the Arts Council about where the money goes? Is it that, outside their own room, members of the music committee are fighting against the other departments for a share of a cake that is far too small in the first place? It seems to me that there is no way, in the present structure, that you are going to get any national, long-term policy for companies that need it, out of throwing money in like pig-swill and watching them all fighting for it. And what are you to think when you hear a very senior member of the Scottish Arts Council staff remark, quite seriously, that the Council feels it is already spending far too much on an art form which deserves to go the way of the dinosaurs?

Lack of money was not the main reason for John Cox's departure at the beginning of 1986. What he saw as even more depressing in the long term was the Scottish Arts Council's entrenched attitude, their insistence on what they called "economies of scale".

In other words, cut yourself down to size. We are constantly being told that what we should be looking at is something like Kent Opera. With one half of their forked tongue they would say, "You must make opera more popular" and with the other half they were saying "you mustn't do such expensive works". But, of course, it is the expensive works that are the popular one, the nineteenth-century blockbusters. They were trying to make us apologise for the fact that Verdi and Wagner and Puccini and Strauss are the ones that bring in the crowds. If we did a festival of Pergolesi we would certainly cut the budget down, but nobody would go. And, really, they are very naïve. Take the suggestion that we should amalgamate with Opera North. Did they really think we were not going to consult with one another and resist it together except in those areas where we were already in co-operation?

There are two things, in my opinion, that are going to secure the future of Scottish Opera. One is that there is a public demand for opera and another is the fact that the Scottish perception of Scottish nationhood includes the major arts organisations. That is how it will survive and, I think, reasonably healthily because, having been through the critical period and survived that, there won't ever again be the same potential for catastrophe.

It is my belief that the Scottish Arts Council was actually waiting for Scottish Opera in its present form to die because it didn't have the courage to kill it. And the thing was set fair to happen. But SAC puts an assessor on the Board of Scottish Opera, a man who has sat in on every meeting since the beginning. Every single paper the Board gets is seen at Charlotte Square and SAC had absolutely no justification for an attitude of self-righteousness about all this because they were in possession of all the facts and they failed, like everyone else, to recognise what was happening.

Cox resigned, reluctantly and with minimum fuss. And, meanwhile, Sir Alexander Gibson had made public a decision which was neither new nor, as some seem to think, forced upon him, to relinquish the formal position he has occupied for the last twenty-five years, although, as he himself insists, his responsibility in caring about Scottish Opera and the quality of its teamwork, will continue as before under the new title, Founder and Conductor Laureate. "I may even do more conducting in the future," he declares, "and certainly I shall feel able to speak out more freely."

In 1985 a new Managing Director, Richard Mantle, was appointed to look after the administration and leave John Cox free for the artistic direction, with Graham Vick as Director of Productions. And John Mauceri will follow in Sir Alex's footsteps as Musical Director at the start of the 1987/88 performing season. Richard Mantle was formerly Deputy to Lord Harewood at English National Opera, and John Mauceri, an American with a distinguished career on the concert platform as well as in the great opera houses of the world — La Scala, Milan, the Metropolitan Opera House, New York, and Covent Garden among them — is no stranger to Scottish Opera, having conducted some performances of *Otello* in 1976, and the much-admired *Carmen* at Theatre Royal ten years

later. Together with the Board and the team already in harness, Mantle and Mauceri will decide the future direction of Scottish Opera.

It has to be said, however, that John Cox is greatly missed, not just for his sympathetic presence and for the stylish power of his own productions — *Manon Lescaut, Idomeneo, Capriccio, The Marriage of Figaro, The Flying Dutchman* and, of course, the delightful *L'Egisto* which introduced his work to the Company — but even more for the breadth of outlook which could recognise great talent in a young director whose uncompromising vision might have been supposed to be in sharp conflict with his own more restrained and elegant style. Graham Vick has also left Scottish Opera, and his exciting, controversial talent will be missed, not least by the younger, more open-minded and progressive element in the Scottish Opera audience who must surely be its hope for the future. That is something the new management team will almost certainly keep in mind.

SCOTTISH OPERA ON THE ROAD

Almost from the beginning, within Scottish Opera, the crucial importance of touring was never questioned; the need to attract new enthusiasts, beyond the main centres, for what was to many an unfamiliar experience; but, equally, the duty to offer both the popular and the less familiar works in main-scale productions wherever possible in Scotland and beyond. Difficulties have only arisen, as we have seen, when the funds available failed to meet the spiralling costs.

The history of touring is almost as old as the Company, going back as it does to the extension of the second season to take a further week of performances in Edinburgh, and only two years after that, with a further extension of the programme to include a week at Aberdeen. Thereafter, Aberdeen became a fixture in the annual itinerary, with visits to His Majesty's Theatre by Scottish Opera becoming part of the social scene in the granite city. His Majesty's is a beautiful playhouse, designed in what might be called Edwardian classical-rococo at its best and most restrained, with its graceful horseshoe balconies and unusually spacious, elaborately embellished stacks of boxes topped by arches and balustrades. But, like most theatres built as touring houses, with no provision for a resident company, His Majesty's, for all its front-of-house opulence and generosity of space, presents difficulties of storage and technical shortcomings for a touring opera company with perhaps three productions on a major scale. Yet, as the principal focus for theatre activity in the north-east of Scotland, His Majesty's might be supposed to offer a ready-made audience for Scottish Opera in what is, after all, a very prosperous city.

The 1966 season was launched, for the first time, at Perth, in the much smaller, more intimate theatre which, like Aladdin's cave, hides its interior wealth behind a nondescript, almost invisible frontage between two shops in the High Street, and is recognised only by the sign on the narrow canopy over the pavement. But climb the short, steep flight of stairs and you find the scene expanding amazingly, for a recent extensive refurbishment and extension programme has given Perth Theatre a well-equipped complex of front-of-house and back-stage spaces. The auditorium, however, remains basically unaltered from the original built by W. Alexander in 1900. Joan Knight, who has run the little playhouse with great aplomb and equal success since the early days of Scottish Opera, once told me that, but for the peccadillos of Oscar Wilde, there would be no Perth Theatre. "George Gibson who built it was Oscar Wilde's manager and when the scandal broke he was so terrified of being implicated that he fled as far as he could out of London, reached Perth, and built this theatre." Perth is fortunate that he did so, for the Edwardian auditorium, intimate as it is with its delicate plasterwork along the balconies and round the narrow boxes that flank the proscenium arch, is a most attractive place to be.

Perth Theatre is, of course, far too small for the major Scottish Opera productions on tour, but perfect for a chamber opera like *Albert Herring*, the first of the Britten operas to be mounted by the Company and the one which went on to enjoy more performances and to be seen in more countries than any other Scottish

Opera production in the first ten years.

In June 1968 Scottish Opera made its first foreign trip, to the Maggio Musicale Fiorentino, taking *Albert Herring* to the Teatro Alla Pergola where the quality of direction and performance was greatly appreciated. The production aroused a genuine interest in Britten's operatic style, as presented by Anthony Besch and the Scottish company, and what followed was a decade of determined missionary work for British Opera and, in particular, for the chamber operas of Benjamin Britten which were taken by Scottish Opera to theatres the length and breadth of Europe. Between June 1968 and July 1981, audiences all over Germany and in Austria, Portugal, France, Switzerland, Poland, Italy, France, Yugoslavia and Iceland had been given a chance of hearing and appreciating not just the Britten operas in a series of highly perceptive and imaginative productions, but also Purcell's *Dido and Aeneas* and one of the new, specially commissioned works, *Mary Queen of Scots* by Thea Musgrave.

But, back in 1967, Perth Theatre once again made history with the first performance of what was to be regarded as legendary in the work of Scottish Opera, Mozart's *Cosi fan tutte*. Anthony Besch's delightful and penetrating production must have come as a revelation in the intimacy of the little theatre where every nuance of the subtly characterised performances by Janet Baker and Elizabeth Hardwood as the two sisters, Dorabella and Fiordiligi, was conveyed superbly.

In 1967, too, as we have seen, the first invitation came to Scottish Opera to participate in Edinburgh's cultural jamboree, with two works by Stravinsky whose turn it was, that year, to be celebrated. That, too, was a notable "first", presaging many further visits to Edinburgh at Festival time. In this context, it seems to me that a judgment made by George Bruce in his book, *A Festival in the North*, is well worth quoting since it comes not from a music critic but from a man with a life-long interest and involvement in the arts, as poet, writer, drama critic and BBC arts producer for many years. "An air of precision and direction over and above the high quality of the singing," he wrote, "has been one of the marks of the company. The purpose of the work is recognised and then the full force of musical intelligence has been bent to the realisation of the given end."

In 1968 Scottish Opera travelled across the Border for the first time, taking the first steps in a long and close relationship with a city and a theatre that, years ago, came to look on the Scottish company as, in part, its own. Theatre Royal, Newcastle, has a monumental classical exterior built in 1837 and an auditorium dating from more than half a century later, the reason for the diversity being, as was so often the case, destruction by fire in 1899. Two years later the theatre reopened with the present Edwardian rococo interior, by Matcham.

From then on — and remember that this was ten years before English National Opera spawned its northern offspring to make its base at Leeds and to tour the theatres around the north of England — Scottish Opera served many theatres across the Border, making regular visits not just to Newcastle, but to The Grand Theatre, Leeds, and the Empire Theatres in

Scottish Opera Pantechnicon at Aix.

Liverpool and Sunderland, all of them splendid touring houses from the great days of theatre and, for the most part, brought up to date under local government management. But by 1986 that touring schedule south of the Border was reduced to only two venues in Newcastle and Liverpool.

Fair enough, it might be said, when there is already an Opera North to serve the population centres across the Pennines. But there are degrees of fairness, particularly when it is remembered that it took Scottish Opera ten years to struggle towards a base in its own theatre, a full chorus and orchestra and a proper administrative back-up with workshop and store, whereas Opera North gained all that within as many months of its birth. It does seem as though the Scottish company has had, by comparison, a very raw deal.

And there it remains: touring is valuable; everyone wants to fulfil obligations in that respect: touring can even be fun and good for morale. But it is hideously expensive. Just to transport a full company including chorus and orchestra to Aberdeen or even to Edinburgh for a week of performances costs as much as to give twice or three times as many performances at Theatre Royal, Glasgow. It takes a powerful effort of imagination for members of an audience used to watching opera from distant seats in large auditoria to visualise the sheer physical effort of continually moving 20-foot flats and other huge items of scenery and props, vast quantities of lighting gear and much else, in and out of theatre dock doors, into pantechnicons and out again, day after day. It is, as somebody said, like continually moving house, but worse, because you are, in effect, dismantling the walls and ceilings and reassembling them with every new move. Co-operation is crucial: without exceptionally smooth teamwork none of this hard, laborious but necessarily skilful process would be possible in the short time available. For this, too, is something that has to be remembered; time is of the essence: the 7.15 deadline is absolute.

With all this to be considered, then, plus the unavoidable cost of transport and subsistence for principals, orchestra, chorus and stage staff, wardrobe staff, electricians and technical crew, it is no wonder that touring costs the earth even when the distance involved is no greater than the 48 miles between Glasgow and Edinburgh. It is, in fact, a sore point with Scottish Opera management that overnight subsistence is demanded as a union right even when those who claim it are able to drive home after the show.

Meanwhile the one area where Scottish Opera has become the acknowledged leader in Britain is in the extent and the quality of its small-scale touring activity. Back in the early 'sixties the Arts Council of Great Britain subsidised three peripatetic Opera For All groups, manned by young musicians who travelled the country with piano-accompanied shows, costumed but without scenery, since most of the small towns and villages visited were without proper facilities. In 1966 Scottish Opera took over responsibility for the Scottish Opera For All group (indeed, that may well have been the original justification for the establishment of the first tiny administration in the historic four-room flat in Holland Street)

Moving the ceiling for THE MARRIAGE OF FIGARO, *1986.*

and set about ensuring that not even the farthest outpost in the Highlands and islands could claim to be ignored or entirely deprived of music drama.

What made the Scottish Opera For All team different from its English counterparts, consisting, as they did, mostly of student singers, was the fact that it was manned by some of the best young singers from the main company, potentially, at least, capable of coping with semi-principal roles in full-scale productions. Patricia Hay, Norman White, John Lawson Graham, Claire Livingstone were some of the young

soloists who would fly out to Shetland or Stornoway with stripped-down productions of *Don Giovanni*, *Madama Butterfly* or *Don Pasquale*. Once arrived at its destination the company of six singers and a pianist would get down to work unloading the scenery, getting it up, unpacking and ironing the costumes ("I always volunteered to do the wigs," says Patricia Hay, "because I loathe ironing") before giving the performance. They would then strike the set and load it again before going to bed. Next morning they would move on to repeat the process somewhere else, possibly many miles away.

But audiences, it seems, could be quite as hardy as the young musicians. This was proved on one occasion in Shetland after a performance of *Don Giovanni* during a tour of three operas with which went a printed programme covering all of them. As usual after the performance the company were busily striking the set and carrying it through the hall when they noticed that two elderly ladies were still in their seats, comfortably chatting to one another. A little later, a chauffeur appeared in search of his charges and one of the company went to tell them so. "Oh," they said, "but aren't you going to do the other two operas?"

Northern journeys in winter weather could produce unforgettable, not to say hazardous moments, as when, on a flight from Shetland to Wick the plane flew through a spectacular storm when static electricity crackled and glittered up one wing, across the body of the aeroplane and down the other wing while the occupants sat glued to their seats in a deathly hush thinking the end had truly come. "But then," John Lawson Graham remembers, "we landed safely at Wick, drove to Thurso and played *Cosi fan tutte* that evening, and it was a great performance. Those were the good old days — and we were all young. But none of us would like to do it now." Nobody is expected — nor would the unions allow them — to do all that in the Opera Go Round of today.

Opera For All, as such, came to an end in 1974 with a tour of *La Boheme*, having outlasted its English counterparts, mainly because of its higher quality overall. It was disbanded in the run-up to the opening of Theatre Royal, no doubt because every ounce of energy had to go towards that end.

In 1977, just before Peter Hemmings left for Australia, a resumption of the Company's small-scale touring arm was planned under the new title, Opera Go Round, which has served it ever since. The prime mover in the first instance was Ann Baird who had been in charge of Scottish Opera's educational activity since that side of the operation was established in its own right as Opera for Schools.

Ann Baird had herself been an opera singer, a soprano who had taken part in the first *Madama Butterfly*, as a member of the student chorus and, a year later, in *Otello*. After a short spell in the chorus of Sadlers Wells Opera she came back to Scottish Opera to sing small roles in *Albert Herring*, *Peter Grimes* and *Cenerentola*; Barbarina in *The Marriage of Figaro* and one of the three spirits in *The Magic Flute*. But when, having come to terms with the fact that her operatic career was likely to be limited, she heard that the Board of Scottish Opera were discussing the possibility of appointing someone to set up an educational unit to strengthen and properly organise what had, up till then, been a largely informal activity, she decided to forget her singing career and applied for the job forthwith. She remembers her nervousness at facing the Board,

> with all those music professors. And the first question they asked me was, "But won't you miss performing?" And, without really having to think, I said this is all about public relations, about selling the idea, surely. And isn't that just another kind of performing? And there they were, all nodding at one another: I'm quite sure that's the moment when I was given the job.

As with so much else in the tale of Scottish Opera, Ann's work in taking music and drama to schools started in a small way. "All done," she tells you, "from my own dining-room, with a part-time secretary. It was I who christened it Opera For Youth and I know that it still continues to develop the good work though I left to join Scottish Ballet shortly after Peter went to Sydney." Opera Go Round also owes its existence to Ann Baird's initiative. An article in a local evening paper caught her eye one day, with a banner headline, "Motherwell gets Free Panto on the State". Reading further she discovered the existence of a new job creation scheme run by the Manpower Services Commission, a scheme which might just have relevance, she thought, for Scottish Opera. On Hemmings's advice she prepared an outline plan, with costings, and "after going through all the hoops with the requisite authorities", was given a grant to sustain Opera Go Round in its first year.

> There were three points in the paper I had prepared: one was to establish a replacement for Opera For All; the second was to take opera into the factories and on to the shop floors; and the third was to expand Opera For Youth which, up till then, had been largely a workshop activity into a performance area where we could marry the young professional singers with an amateur chorus and go beyond the schools into youth and community work with adolescents and young adults. These were the three planks on which the whole thing was constructed. Opera Go Round, in its first life, went to faraway places with opera repertoire in cut-down versions — a continuation, really, of Opera For All. And we really had a splendid, hand-picked team, and some very exciting directors, including, of course, Graham Vick.

Peter Quilliam-Cain, who had previously worked as a freelance on Opera For All, and also on the main company's production team, came in, full time, as Ann Baird's assistant. "Ann was Administrator and I did everything else," is how he puts it. Since Ann's departure Peter Quilliam-Cain has masterminded Opera Go Round, working at first on the Opera For All principle but with the stimulating creative input of a director like Graham Vick who, at the age of only 20 and straight from the college of music at Manchester, had been brought to Scottish Opera by David Pountney. "Graham was obviously keen to make his name," Peter Quilliam-Cain recalls, "and since his interest was in experimental work, it was a glorious opportunity, really, for all of us. It was in 1978 that we began to function: we tried a wide variety of things — factory opera, straight opera-on-the-road, community opera, rock opera — we dabbled in everything that first year. It was a very exciting time." Graham Vick describes things even more fervently: "That first year of Opera Go Round was the happiest, most exciting time of my career, so far. I think, if I could choose just one year to live again, that would be the one. That's why I felt so strongly about the whole Opera Go Round thing, and why I fought to carry on with it and why, when I came back in 1984 as Director of Productions I wanted to develop it, give it value and

Macbeth and the ghost of Banquo (Omar Ebrahim and David Marsh) in Opera Go Round's MACBETH performed in 1987.

weight and make it the home of serious work."

But it wasn't easy. The *Carmen* that saw Opera Go Round come back to life was set up with only two months' warning that money would actually be available — which gives some idea of the precarious nature of the enterprise. Nowadays, it is true, a specific grant is designated for Opera Go Round activity but it still comes out of Scottish Opera's revenue grant.

Somehow a misconception has arisen that, since its revival in 1985, Opera Go Round has perforce ceased to be a permanent company. In fact it never was anything but an ad hoc

organisation with Peter Quilliam-Cain as its single, permanent, full-time manager.

This means that every time a new production is planned, a new team has to be found, though, obviously, I try to keep the good people around me. I try to persuade them, twist their arms, to come back to me, but often they have gone off and got jobs elsewhere. That is the real snag of not being able to afford a permanent company. Obviously, if you have singers and a technical team who work regularly in an ensemble fashion, then you could hone that down and have a really fine performance capability no matter what you did. That's the ideal, of course, but I can't see it ever happening so far as we are concerned. So you must take the next best course which is to think of Opera Go Round as a way of bringing new blood into the profession. That's one of the most exciting elements and it is, I believe, an essential part of Opera Go Round. I find it stimulating, the singers find it stimulating, so do the designers and, I think, the audiences too. Singers coming in through Opera Go Round should be able to go on to semi-principal roles, to provide that nucleus for the main company. They shouldn't remain with us. It is essential that they move on. And that should apply to the directors and designers as well. There are far too many directors and designers whose names you see attached to main-scale productions again and again ad nauseam. This is true not just of Scottish Opera but of all the big companies. Opera has a poor image in that way; a very poor through-put of talent, unlike the rest of theatre.

Opera Go Round has hit the headlines, so to speak, with its two most recent productions, *Jenufa* and *Macbeth*, each having come a very long way from the old idea of the "fit-up" opera. *Jenufa*, directed by Matthew Richardson and designed by Ashley Martin-Davis, was a marvellously well-conceived and tautly structured production where the simplicity of the staging was intrinsic and not self-consciously contrived. In the intimacy of small venues the two central performances by Virginia Kerr (Jenufa) and Linda McLeod (Kostelnicka) must have been extraordinarily powerful. In

Moving Experience.

the small Palace Theatre at Kilmarnock, the effect was of a true medium-scale production, even without orchestral accompaniment. The team is on the road again as I write, with *Macbeth*, not the easiest work to do in these circumstances, being in every sense "grand opera" — Verdi at his best. Richard Jones, the director, has done wonders in adapting it, says Peter. "The old piano operas used to cut all the chorus parts but in *Macbeth* they are all left in. Of course it does mean that the singers have to do three times as much work — all seven are never off the stage, and they have to act all the time, being characters as well as chorus.

One earlier Opera Go Round production, Graham Vick's version of *L'Elisir d'Amore*, actually did end up — somewhat elaborated, it's true — on the stage of Theatre Royal. That may be unusual, but it does serve to illustrate the sort of standard regularly aimed for. So, whether it is Tobermory, Balachulish, Inverurie or Ullapool, Blairgowrie or Dumfries; whether it is seen in school halls, village halls or small purpose-built theatres, Opera Go Round is the purveyor of the real operatic experience to those who live far away from the so-called "centres of excellence" in the big Scottish cities.

To the outsider there would seem to be nothing romantic about these journeys to the outposts of Scotland compared, say, with taking Scottish Opera to European opera houses and festivals. But how romantic, in fact, is the latter exercise? Scottish Opera personnel will tell a different story, of heroic endeavours and funny happenings that are better relished in retrospect than at the time. There are problems of clearing the sets, costumes and props through the customs, even of convincing British customs officials that all this is genuinely re-imported British material. On one such occasion, as Thomson Smillie recalls, Peter Hemmings had just completed an exhausting exercise of this sort when the props master appeared and said "Can I have my bottle of brandy now, please?" And there have been occasions when flights were overbooked, like the time when either Francis Egerton or Michael Maurel had to make do with the "jump-seat" outside the lavatory on the plane. When everyone commiserated with the unfortunate victim on landing, he replied, cheerfully, that he had collected 55 pfennigs on the trip from Hanover to Dortmund.

There is another tale of bad-turned-good, when the company were invited to an official reception after a performance, also in Germany. "Better not say where" my informant warned me,

> but it was one of those British Council occasions which we all tend to dread, when all we want to do is to eat a good meal, put our feet up and watch TV. But there we were, trying to make ourselves presentable — and just think what wearing a wig and heavy make-up does for your appearance — and going along to deal politely with all the usual questions and small talk. We had been led to expect a supper after the reception and so some of us, at least, were politely refusing the canapés and other pick-ups, so as not to spoil our appetites for the real food to come. Then came the shock: no supper, and all of us were starving. By then, of course, it was too late to find a meal anywhere. So back we went to our hotel in desperation and somebody suggested that we pool our resources, gather together all the food we had in our rooms and see what we could make of it. And, wonder of wonders, Ezra Golombok, who was travelling with us, came back with two immense pizzas he'd managed to buy somewhere — great cartwheel things which tasted better than any pizzas before or since. And it turned into a marvellous party.

Ezra Golombok is a Glasgow journalist, as is John Fowler who, some time later, recorded his impressions of a trip to Venice where Scottish Opera were presenting *L'Egisto* at the famous Teatro Fenice. He tells the story of a journey

Francis Egerton as Denia in L'EGISTO performed in 1982.

full of unforeseen problems, on the occasion of an Italian air strike which meant that the plane was forced to land in Yugoslavia and the company then had to travel by bus to Venice. There was a long wait for buses that didn't arrive on time; a five-hour journey through spectacular Adriatic scenery on too little sustenance to allow for unalloyed appreciation; and, finally, overbooking by the hotel management. Another bon mot from the waggish Frank Egerton who played the nurse in *L'Egisto*, is recorded by Fowler. To the young woman who had, unwittingly, taken over his room, Egerton quipped "I hope you enjoy yourself in my bed tonight". All of this plus the unusual difficulties in getting in the scenery next day, with the indefatigable Fowler up at dawn to watch the proceedings, while the Company Manager and the Fenice doorman tried to resolve the final difficulty caused by the low tide that had made a narrow, muddy channel of the canal behind the theatre where the barges were to bring in the scenery and props. A few hours later and all was changed. Fowler, the self-styled Scottish Opera Groupie, was riding happily on one of the loaded barges, "past the raddled splendour of all those peeling palaces — like old ladies of doubtful virtue in decay — while the tourists crowding the vaporettas gaped at our craft, laden with strange timberwork and a gilt sun. It was the only time in a busy week that I managed to see the Grand Canal, but it was worth it. I wouldn't have changed my barge for all the gondolas of Venice."

After all that — exhuberant midnight parties notwithstanding — the performance, in the opinion of the *Scotsman*'s music critic, Conrad Wilson, was "consistently entrancing". One of Scottish Opera's warmest supporters from early on, Wilson was, for many years, something of a fellow-traveller with the Company on its tours at home and away. In the same Scottish Opera Year Book (1982-83) he recorded his impressions of that Venetian visit as the culmination of a tour through several cities in Germany; an activity which he had watched, as it were, from the wings and, most importantly for a critic, savouring

. . . a wonderful opportunity to learn Cavalli's opera and come to terms with it in a series of performances in rapid succession in a way which would have been impossible here at home. I found myself living and breathing *L'Egisto*, almost as if I were a member of the cast. I would wake up in the morning with the words "Clori, Clori" pounding in my brain. Or else, walking along the German streets or across the Venetian piazzas, I would find my feet automatically adopting the rhythms of those catchy songs which Francis Egerton sang in his role of the old nurse. On that occasion, at least, there was no embarrassment, as there can be for the critic guest of an opera company on tour, who is yet under an obligation to send honest dispatches home. Favourable reviews were the order of the day.

EDUCATION AND FRIENDS

I t has already been said that in the range and quality of its small-scale touring activity Scottish Opera has led the field in Britain. Even more so has the Company forged far ahead of all others in its commitment to the value of mission work in schools and community centres. What began in the 1960s as Opera For Schools, with one Board member in particular, Ainslie Millar, in the persuasive forefront, became consolidated and established, as Opera For Youth at the time of that one-off, but crucially important job creation grant offered by the Manpower Services Commission. Since then the education unit has gone from strength to strength though often under severe financial pressure. Indeed, so far ahead of the field is the Opera For Youth of today that organisations in England, Wales and Ireland have been sending observers to watch the group at work and to make use of the same ideas in their own areas. "That, of course, is how the whole thing should work," says Peter Quilliam-Cain,

but I must say that it has taken the other opera companies a long time to cotton-on to what we have been doing here in Scotland for years. So, although we have been well ahead up till now, it is quite another matter whether we shall be able to keep that lead. For that depends on several things and, most of all, money. It depends, too, on how important we are seen to be in the overall concept of opera, and not least it depends on the attitude of Scottish Opera's senior staff.

When Graham Vick was Director of Productions things were very hopeful, but now I have no idea how his successor will feel about it. And that could be crucial. So far we have enjoyed a succession of supportive managements. John Cox was absolutely behind us; so was Peter Ebert and, of course, it was Peter Hemmings who encouraged us right at the start. All I want now is to be able to keep that momentum going and to develop it if possible.

To lead the field and then find the crucial support for development lacking is a not unfamiliar scenario north of the Border. One cannot help remembering the time, back in the 1950s, when James MacTaggart, the young creative genius then enlivening the BBC in Glasgow, was first off the mark in British radio to foresee the potential value of a portable tape-recorder in developing the "Today"-type radio magazine. In this case, too, observers were sent up from London to copy MacTaggart's idea, but the authorities in Scotland tried to clip Jim MacTaggart's wings, whereupon he left for London and a less constricted field of operation. In that case, of course, the trouble was sheer lack of imagination on the part of BBC senior staff. One can only hope with Peter Quilliam-Cain that the new management at Scottish Opera will continue to give the education unit all the support it deserves and needs.

The whole idea of Theatre in Education (TIE) goes back to the 1960s and it was in TIE, not in opera, that Peter Quilliam-Cain began his career. The theatrical rep. companies tended to use TIE as a means of using their excess actors, taking out little shows — often Shakespeare and Shaw suitably adapted — around the schools. It was essentially a performing activity with no participation from the children. When Peter came to Scotland to join Scottish Opera he found a kindred spirit in Ann Baird

Chris Annetts of OPERA FOR YOUTH rehearsing the Garden Dwellers of Willowbank Primary, Glasgow, for the performance of DRAGONFLIGHT.

who, though she came from an operatic background, was an energetic worker in the field, who liked to get things done, and was certainly not averse to experiment.

Ann had very firm ideas abut how Opera for Youth should be run, but she was wonderfully open to experiment. Some things we did were very successful and others were fairly disastrous, but eventually we settled down to a format, in primary school work to begin with, of taking three or four singers/producers, to work with different groups in a school and then bringing them together in a little show. But now it has moved a lot further. Again, we have four producers who go out to primary schools to work on a specially written little show. But the music is now sent out to the teachers four weeks in advance so that the children can learn it. Then, on the day in question, our little party go along and between nine and eleven in the morning they put the children through all the movements, just as you would produce a main-scale opera. There will be three parties of 30 children, that's 90 altogether, and each group will know precisely what they have to do. One group will be the baddies and another will be the goodies and the third will be something else again. That, essentially, has been the pattern. Then, round about 11.30, they bring in the rest of the school to watch what everybody thought was going to be a final rehearsal. But just at the last moment we put them all into costume and give them all props which, of course, transforms the whole thing. It gives the children that extra lift so that, despite themselves, what they give is a real performance.

But then, alas, the Opera for Youth team will have to pack up and go, leaving a legend behind them of three splendid hours of magic for the 90 participants and half an hour for the audience at the performance. The sad thing is that the team cannot develop what they have begun; can never go back to the same school again. And that is a source of real annoyance to Peter Quilliam-Cain.

When Opera Go Round was established in 1978, Graham Vick and Peter were able to develop the participatory idea further, using similar techniques — somewhat expanded — in secondary schools, with the 16-18 age group.

We used four producers once again, Graham with three helpers, and three or four groups of youngsters, so that there would be about 120 on the stage at one time. But instead of just working over two hours on one morning we would be there over two complete days. The first day would be spent just getting to know everybody; getting to know the school, the staff and the children. Then the second day was spent rehearsing the production all morning and all afternoon, but instead of giving the children that last minute "lift" by

producing the costumes and props, we did it in another way. Around four in the afternoon of the show we would produce some of the Opera Go Round principals, like Alan Oke and Harry Nichols, and they would sing the main roles with the youngsters providing the chorus. So that, just about the time when they were all tired out, having worked terribly hard, they would hear those splendid new voices and, again, they'd be lifted right over the top. Then we'd put them into costumes and run the evening show before they'd had time to think. And all the parents and other members of the public would come and say how wonderful they all were.

Money, Peter feels, should be poured into that sort of activity, for these are often schools in deprived areas, "And yet the things the children can produce are sometimes unbelievable. We discovered that those 16-18-year-olds can sometimes give a superb, even a magnetic performance, heightened and greatly helped, of course, by the singers from Scottish Opera. But, once again, that was it: we could never go back and build on what we'd begun."

As an activity it was truly exhausting — not just physically but also psychologically.

Besides having to be planned in the minutest detail — I had to know each minute of the day what we were doing — it was very intense because, that first day the school didn't know us and there we were disrupting all the schedules, turning the place upside down, upsetting the head teacher, the music teachers and all the other teachers. And Graham and his assistants had, in a way, to fight the children, weld them into a team on that first day. Then after they'd all gone home we

Opera Go Round's first public performance of PEACE by Carl Davis and John Wells in 1978.

would work through most of the night to light the show and bring the thing together technically speaking — the lighting came from Scottish Opera and my full Opera Go Round technical team came up. Then, on the second day, with all the rehearsing and the performance at night, we all ended up in a state of utter exhaustion. We were never able to do more than two of those events in any one week and never for more than three weeks at a time. We did two shows at that time, in that way. *Peace* was one, with music by Carl Davis, and another was *Quest of the Hidden Moon* which used a pot-pourri of songs from the operas mixed with dialogue. Ian Robertson arranged the music and Graham Vick wrote the story which was quite an exciting tale about a struggle between good and evil forces.

Not surprisingly, Opera For Youth has no trouble at all in filling up its diary, so quickly does the word get around that here is an extraordinarily rich experience for youngsters who, without realising it, are learning a lot about how opera is produced and presented, and getting a taste of the exhaustion and the excitement that follows all the hard work.

If to some of those hundreds of children the experience may just act as a spur to eventual enjoyment of *Tosca* or *Figaro* or *Tristan* in the opera house, then that is a bonus, but the *raison d'etre* of the exercise is to expand and enrich the immediate experience of young people.

With a more generous budget much more could be done: some of the most promising schools could be revisited and the work developed further; and, of course, all the schools still on the waiting list could be satisfied. As things are, without the co-operation of the education departments, particularly of Strathclyde and Tayside, Opera For Youth may have to close down. Even so, there are new developments. Jane Davidson is now Scottish Opera's Education Officer, working closely with Peter Quilliam-Cain and the Opera Go Round team, servicing schools from Tayside to North Wales, wherever the education authorities are willing to support the activity. But of these Strathclyde Region is by far the most instrumental in making it possible for Opera For Youth to survive.

The work in primary schools has reached a point where it functions so well that to try to change the format would be foolish. But it is with the older, secondary school age group that new thinking has brought interesting results. Jane Davidson, a local girl with a background and training in theatre, not opera, has begun to work, with freelance assistance, in community centres, focusing on adolescents and young adults in the 16-22 age group, encouraging them to create their own operas. "Actually, of course, we do give them a story line, although they are free to make changes, which they often do. We also have the bones of the music already

written, but we don't tell them that." What transpires is true "live theatre" which sometimes works extremely well and at other times doesn't quite come off as planned. But that is really immaterial because the whole point of the exercise is to draw something out of the youngsters themselves, and it is the drawing out that matters. "They are the ones who are sparking it off," says Jane, "and to make that happen is precisely our role."

Sadly, the school teachers' industrial action in the past two seasons means that Scottish Opera's work in secondary schools has suffered badly: no advance preparation is now possible. And that is really why, in what Jane Davidson calls "our desperate need to extend the work and to lift the kids out of the school disciplines", the team worked out a different approach and a different attitude. And, again, the education authorities have been helpful.

For example, Dumbarton helped us to get youngsters together from six schools, busing them in to one venue; and on the island of Tiree we had 54 youngsters from three schools — the whole of the island's juvenile population — with some of the staff.

The most valuable thing that we have done in terms of community involvement is to go in as so-called "skilled enablers" and to set up something which really needs a balance of skills and local knowledge to bring it up to complete fruition. We bring a loose story line and a musical structure which is flexible enough to accommodate anything of value the kids themselves can bring. And the edge is that everybody has a voice of some kind — not always of the best, it's true, but everybody can sing, and a lot of our stuff is chorus anyway. What we do is rock music, not famous pop music but tunes which they can learn quickly and easily, and often with a good deal of humour. We work with two musicians, one trained in classical music but with an interest in jazz, and the other a rock musician. And our choreographers are trained in modern dance rather than ballet.

Opera For Youth works on a five-month season from October to March, but a mere £10,000 extra in the kitty would allow for an extension of around 50%. Yet, despite the fact that the unit's reputation grows with each new project (a recent invitation to the Wexford Festival saw Opera For Youth doing ten workshops in one week followed by the rock opera, *Strange Happenings*, with singing from the Irish children which was "absolutely superb. We gave our very best to them and they certainly gave their best in return") the basic funding for this immensely valuable activity still has to be drawn from the hard-pressed parent body, Scottish Opera. In view of the Scottish Arts Council's current, much bruited benevolent attitude to "community arts", in areas that might well be considered less valuable than the activity of Opera For Youth, this looks to an outsider like nothing more than yet another "turn of the screw".

What is really encouraging is that the outworn old system of schools matinées, with those potted-opera performances which are neither fish nor flesh nor good red herring, have now given way to a much better system wherein three operas will be chosen from a Theatre Royal season, and a pack prepared which will cut right across the curriculum, with interest for Geography, History and English as well as Music departments. Talks will be arranged beforehand, aimed at senior school children, and the project will wind up with visits to full evening peformances.

Opera For Youth is in no sense a narrow attempt to persuade everyone to come to Theatre Royal, although, in a respectable number of cases, that is the result. Rather it is intended to act as self-stimulation, not least in the case of youngsters who often lack confidence because they are pushed into the despised "non-academic" stream. Not that academics are ignored: at one end of the scale the Opera For Youth team might be developing ideas for involving the handicapped but, at the other, the Drama Department of Glasgow University is now enjoying the benefit of comprehensive study packs that may well lead to a widening of horizons that tend to be too narrowly concentrated.

If Scottish Opera For Youth's first consideration is for the stimulation and education (in the true sense of "drawing out") of young people rather than, as a direct result at least, to provide audiences for the operatic product at Theatre Royal, the Kings Theatre, Edinburgh, or His Majesty's, Aberdeen, the formation of a Scottish Opera Club came about because a number of those who were already enthused by the work of the Company on the stage felt a wish to extend the interest by organising ancillary méetings, preferential booking schemes, even tours to foreign opera houses. The first of these was as early as 1968, two years after the Club's formation, to Rome and Verona. The Scottish Opera Magazine which members auto-

Wexford Opera Festival 1986, Mark Robertson from OPERA FOR YOUTH with the Gremlins of Kennedy Park School, Wexford.

matically received, helped to keep all interested parties au fait with events and developments. In a sense the old Scottish Opera Club had been run mainly for the benefit of its members. But in 1984, at a very low point in the Company's history, both financially and in morale, when, between the departure of Peter Ebert and the arrival of John Cox, there was a lack of able, purposeful direction, there gathered a sort of groundswell, among Scottish Opera's well-wishers, of determination that something had to be done to restore confidence, and to counter the rumours that were damaging the Company's image. This was the first stirring of what became the Friends of Scottish Opera, with its own constitution making it independent of the main Company, and so allowing it to be in a position to give friendly advice and render assistance when necessary. Inevitably, of course, the most welcome kind of assistance would almost certainly be financial.

So the Friends of Scottish Opera was set up at a time when it was badly needed. For, whereas the old Scottish Opera Club had tended to keep a low profile, as an unambitious organisation without any lobbying function, the new Friends saw a large part of their function in raising funds and proselytising in general. Since its formation in 1984 Friends' branches have ramified throughout Britain, from the Highlands down to London and with an American branch of the Friends of Scottish Opera whose chairman is none other than the same Gavin Boyd who was the stalwart Chairman of the Theatre Royal Campaign Committee.

The Chairman of the Friends is automatically made a Director of Scottish Opera and, indeed, there are some influential Friends who see a far greater participation in the affairs of Scottish Opera as an admirable end in itself. This, no doubt, could happen in time, were some future British government to follow the American example and allow major tax relief on substantial arts sponsorship by private individuals. But, at present, friendly advice, whether accepted or not, is the extent of the Friends' influence on affairs at Elmbank Cresent and Theatre Royal.

To be a Friend, however, is to avail onself of a wide variety of pleasure and enjoyment, both educational and purely social, from the ongoing Lunch and Listen series of informal interviews — which help to put human faces and personalities on some of those who otherwise tend to remain remote figures on the stage, and the opera fore-talks for first-timers and others, which are aimed at giving greater insight into productions, not least in the case of unusual or rarely seen works — to all the social events which are even more popular. There have been concerts in famous country houses like Drumlanrig and Kinross; recitals, gala concerts, (in 1985 two such concerts, with Dame Kiri te Kanawa, raised £34,000 for Scottish Opera) as well as the now famous Scottish Opera Ball in 1983 for which the Theatre Royal auditorium underwent an effective transformation under Jack Notman's direction, and which raised no less than £60,000.

In the five years of their existence the Friends have raised enough money to sponsor a new opera, *Hedda Gabler* by Edward Harper, and contribute towards a Midi tour of *The Tales of Hoffmann*. Sponsorship also extends to Opera Go Round performances in various parts of the country, with funding of each event by the local branch. So strongly entrenched is the organisation, and so wide and complex is its network countrywide, that a full-time manager has been appointed with an office at the Opera Centre in Elmbank Crescent. But the man who has been the prime mover of the organisation for many years, since the days, in fact, of the old Scottish Opera Club, the man who travels the country and masterminds events, is the indefatigable Norman White. How he finds time for all he does is a mystery: Norman, a baritone and a talented performer on his own account, has been involved with Scottish Opera since the days of Opera For All, and he is still in constant demand for comprimario roles in main house productions. In his unique position as go-between he owns one of the best-known faces in the Company.

CRITICAL INTERLUDE

From time to time behind the iron curtain of any theatre you will hear the cry "Who Needs Critics?". The answer is, of course, that critics are not actually needed; they just exist. Critics enjoy what they do for a living, whatever they may say to the contrary, and people enjoy reading them, whether to agree or disagree, as may be seen when any unusually controversial production has the effect of flooding the correspondence columns of the daily newspapers with letters pro and con.

As one of the breed for many years past I know what I am talking about. I have sat in my stall or circle seat in theatres all over the country (for critics are given good seats in order to placate them) on innumerable occasions, scribbling in the dark in early days until I discovered that I need not verbalise in situ, but could dig the golden nuggets out of the mind's eye and ear when the time came to put words on paper. But I have always been uncomfortably aware that, try as one may, it is very, very difficult to discard preconceptions in the face of the unexpected on any stage, not least when the work in question is a standard classic and, indeed, over-familiar — like *Hamlet*, say, or *Don Giovanni*.

Maybe that is why Mozart's blackest of black tragi-comedies comes right at the top — well nearly at the top — of Scottish Opera's most controversial productions over many years. Not so much, perhaps, when it was done early on under Peter Ebert's direction, although even then the abstract sets by Ralph Koltai came in for disparagement. But when David Pountney revived the production with considerable alter-ations, treating it rather like Jacobean drama, the fat was in the fire well and truly.

In order to write this chapter I have rummaged at length through the boxes of press cuttings at the Scottish Opera Centre, and I have found many interesting anomalies which show that no director, performer, designer or conductor need lose too much sleep over a clutch of bad reviews: there will always be at least one appreciative notice to weigh in the balance — and in most cases more than one.

Whereas, for one critic reviewing that *Don Giovanni*, "the eerie menace of the piece, which is never far from the surface, was stunningly caught," and another spoke of "Maria Bjornson's sumptuous costumes and subtle sets", a third reviewer saw merely ". . . a production style that had abandoned the once typical Scottish Opera virtues of good sense and plain speaking in favour of modish claptrap". The production, it seemed, exhibited "several of the noxious tendencies peculiar to that dangerous species, the Modern Thinking Producer" (*Financial Times*). This was the same production which had yet another critic enthusing about "the potent presence of the Don . . . a glittering figure with a mocking hypnotic smile", and calling it a highly romantic interpretation (*Sunday Times*). But what is the would-be opera goer to think when, having read a review like that, he or she opens another newspaper to be told that Pountney's production of *Don Giovanni* is really no more than "a desperate (if understandable) attempt to be different" (*Yorkshire Post*)? Irrelevance was the word that featured in more than one review of that production, reviews which, however, certainly failed to

*The Blessed Spirits (choreography by Peter Darrell) in ORFEO
ED EURIDICE performed in 1979.*

agree in other areas. There were serious and unaccountable differences of opinion even over individual performances: Felicity Palmer's Elvira was "loud and squawking" or, if you read a different paper, "Elvira's sufferings were expressed with painful intensity", while, in yet another, "Felicity Palmer sang everyone else off the stage". Even the orchestral contribution fell between two different opinions: on the one hand, "half-hearted conducting, often out of phase with the singers" (*Guardian*) and "lack-lustre, curiously subdued approach to the score", (*Illustrated London News*) and on the other, "The best flow of all came from the orchestra and the singers — but that would have been the same, and even preferable, in a concert performance" (*Yorkshire Post*).

But so far as that particular Mozart opera is concerned, much worse was to come when Graham Vick directed his new production in the 1985 spring season at Theatre Royal. The professional critics, to a man (there was one woman reviewer at Newcastle who made her appreciation clear) found the whole thing deplorable. From the *Glasgow Herald*, "Graham Vick has, incredibly, succeeded in exorcising from this perpetration any semblance of the *Don Giovanni* of Mozart and da Ponte as we know it", a comment that was typical of many. Some opted for sarcasm, the critic's security blanket, with, for example, "A more pretentious producer might have tried to invent some kind of laborious interpretation which would make a meaningful feature of the bare stage and unconcealed lighting rig" (the *Guardian*) as a deceptively soft prelude to a list of the various

ways in which the young director had indulged his immature imagination.

Letters to the *Glasgow Herald* and the *Scotsman* were even more heated, if not more outspoken, than the professional reviews, but interestingly the virulence was refreshingly tempered with praise from those who had not only understood the director's intention, but had actually enjoyed themselves and been given food for thought. Fiona R McKinlay, of Glasgow, remembered how often, on previous occasions, she had watched members of the Scottish Opera audience nodding off before the end of the first scene, "only to be jolted into consciousness by sporadic applause. But no-one," she wrote, "slept through *Don Giovanni*. Controversial though his methods may be, Graham Vick held the audience in rapt attention from overture to finale. I understood the approach and appreciated the up-dated element of black comedy, particularly as much of the original humour was intended for audiences two centuries younger. Must an art form remain static simply to please its sponsors?"

At the moment it may seem as though the recently departed Director of Productions, Graham Vick, and his predecessor, David Pountney, the "young turks" of the profession as I have heard them called, have aroused more criticism than any before them at Scottish Opera. But adverse reviews are, in fact, no new development. When Peter Ebert directed Gluck's *Orfeo ed Eurydice* in 1979 it was resoundingly rejected as unworthy of the Company, not least when it was taken to London. "Those travelling critics who witter on about the marvellous work being done by the regional opera companies will be keeping a low profile after Scottish Opera's season at Sadlers Wells," wrote one tetchy reviewer, while Stanley Sadie in *The Times* complained that Ebert was ". . . treating poor Orfeo as stuff for a producer's sport". His demand for more naturalness, more emphasis on human emotion might have been taken more seriously had Janet Baker not been cast as Orfeo. Her portrayal, in the opinion of Conrad Wilson, who had certainly got his priorities right on that occasion,

> was bound to make its effect with much eloquence; but not the valour she brought to her bravura aria in Act 1, not the beauty of her "Che puro ciel", nor the mounting intensity of her "Che faro" fully prepared us for the ferocity with which, at the climax of the work, she railed against Amor after Eurydice's second death. This was Dame Janet in a rage, and it gave the opera a dramatic truth which Gluck, even in his most revolutionary moments, could hardly have visualised.

In general, Ebert's production, Wilson thought, was treated "quite imaginatively". But the Dance of the Blessed Spirits (they were portrayed as Sisters of Mercy in white robes and starched white headgear) seemed to *The Times* critic "like a ballet of ludicrously posturing nuns" but, on the other hand, to Noel Goodwin, writing in *Music and Musicians*, "They moved around the sleeping Eurydice with gestures of piety, the choreographer combining stylisation with a smooth, flowing movement." Once again satire was invoked for a description of the white, tent-like setting as ". . . a marquee such

Willard White and Leporello and Anthony Roden as Don Ottavio with the coffin at the funeral of the Commendatore in DON GIOVANNI performed in 1986.

as might house a prizegiving or a garden party, with a little platform at one end on which, sure enough, the prizes (posies for the principals) are duly placed in the vaudeville finale". But it was Tom Sutcliffe of the *Guardian* who delivered the nastiest kick where it hurts when he finished by saying that the one virtue of Ebert's production was that the bright lighting in which he bathed the white gauze tent "enabled one to study the other members of the audience. There we all soporifically sat, our eyes half-closed . . .".

Even something as light, elegant and enjoyable as Cavalli's *L'Egisto*, in the hands of John Cox whose intelligence and taste are seldom in question, was damned with faint praise in some quarters. "The best thing about it is the Allan Charles Klein setting" — it was a glittering astrolabe with revolving planets — "a beautiful metaphor and spectacle of light and colour which is to rank as Scottish Opera's best conceived set for quite some time." (*Evening Chronicle*, Newcastle) had to be set against the voice of the *Guardian*'s Tom Sutcliffe, who, once again, made it clear that he found himself bored, this time by Cavalli. He thought the staging "straightforward . . . but Roderick Brydon obviously likes driving this luxury vehicle, which is easy listening".

But others were more enthusiastic. The Newcastle *Evening Chronicle* recommended everyone to go and see "this 17th century *Dallas* of operas — a tale of passion, powers, infidelities and jealousies, but solved by supernatural intervention rather than J.R.'s oil dollars".

The Spectator's Rodney Miles, who clearly enjoyed the event, had even more fun describing the naughty costumes with their simulated semi-nudity ("Charles Klein's costumes are just the job: lots of leg, dizzily plunging necklines . . . and that's on the chaps!") and he finished up by asking, "Am I taking this opera seriously enough? I think so: Cavalli was a good second-rate composer; the fun quotient is half the battle." Those who took the evening paper headline, "Naughty Night at the Opera", seriously, however, were in for a disappointment. It was, in the words of yet another enthusiastic critic, "A production of rare beauty and imagination".

In my opinion Scottish Opera has suffered the fate of any enterprise which aims high from the start and maybe finds itself over-praised initially and therefore increasingly unable to measure up to impossible expectations. "Glittering start", "Superb", "Could hardly be improved upon", all written of the first *Otello* in 1963, would be hard to follow, no matter what. After the Edinburgh first night Christopher Grier admitted that he found difficulty in writing temperately. "It would have been a poor return for the evening's musical splendours had the audience streamed out of the theatre shouting 'Viva Verdi', and forgot to add 'Viva l'Opera dell Scozia'." And of *Boris Godunov* in the Company's first visit to Aberdeen, Robin Millar wrote, "Never have I seen stage crowds so thrilling as in these pictures of half-barbaric Russians," while he felt that "David Ward's death scene was gigantic, worthy of Chaliapin's memory".

It is only fair to say that, over the years, there have been wonderfully perceptive reviews of Scottish Opera productions, but the past four or five seasons, it seems to me, have seen something very like a critical ganging up, not least on Graham Vick whose *L'Elisir d'Amore*, even as far back as 1980, was pretty thoroughly scourged for its up-dated setting and supposed triviality. Seen in Glasgow by Conrad Wilson, "It lacked sparkle, the decor was dull, the conducting heavy footed, the chorus imprecise, and the evening steadily lost pace as it proceeded." The self-same production in

Liverpool was recommended without reserve in the *Liverpool Echo*. "Re-staged in an Italy of 1950-ish vintage to excellent effect . . . Russell Craig's settings are a delight to the eye and, indeed, Graham Vick's production moves with a sprightly pace from start to finish."

But oh, the furore that greeted the same director's interesting attempt to give some consistency and relevance, however fantastical, to the far-fetched story line by Planché on which Weber's last opera was composed. A new libretto for *Oberon* had been commissioned from Anthony Burgess as part of an ongoing concern to provide literate translations when English is to be used, and the opera was given a new setting in the 1930s neverland of Hollywood as the one place in modern times where anything might be imagined to take place, whether in real life or on the movie screen. It was a good idea which worked for some and not for others. "Almost unbelievably, the producer, Graham Vick and his designer, Russell Craig have gratuitously chosen to drag in Hollywood . . ." (*Sunday Telegraph*). "The screen at the back of the stage is flooded with old films, from silent cinema drama to Busby Berkley dance routines and new film in the old style," wrote Gerald Larner in the *Guardian*: "It goes beyond entertainment and alienation to distraction and from there to send-up." As for the new libretto: "Cheap, trite and unfunny Americanese" (the *Glasgow Herald*); "Burgess should perhaps have written his own opera rather than overpainting someone else's, especially since his command of metre is unfailingly inept and uningratiating" (*Times Literary Supplement*). But to a different ear, on

the self-same evening, "Burgess's sung and spoken words are always ingenious and often quite felicitous as well" (*Classical Music*).

More surprising, perhaps, was the lack of agreement over the orchestral contribution. The critic of the *Telegraph* thought that "things might have seemed more satisfactory musically had not the orchestra, under Sir Alexander Gibson, played so abysmally," and the *Guardian* suggested that "Sir Alexander Gibson who conducts the overture with the kind of anticipation you feel in the dentist's waiting room, finds only occasionally the true lyrical impulse". Both were written at the same hearing as that which drew an admiring comment from the music critic of the *Times Literary Supplement*: "If one person was aware of Weber's standing, it was Sir Alexander Gibson who gave the score a truly Wagnerian ebb and flow."

Not even Graham Vick, however, caused anything like the scandal that ensued when Tony Palmer was given an opportunity to direct his first opera at Theatre Royal — though he has declared that he will never attempt another after his experience in Glasgow which hit the headlines with a vengeance. *Turandot* was the focus of the row which still reverberates, but faintly now, whenever opposing opinions meet socially and engage in argument. Palmer, the film-maker, clearly saw the production in terms of that medium. One critic decided that it was a film he wished he were making — indeed, Tony Palmer used the Scottish Opera *Turandot* rehearsals for a Channel 4 film about Puccini, and nobody knows which was the chicken and which the egg. The idea behind the staging of the

OBERON performed in 1985. (Director: Graham Vick; designer: Russell Craig.)

opera was the possible connection between the unfinished *Turandot* and Puccini's own troubled domestic relations, and that, in itself, caused disquiet since it was seen to risk "the banality of converting art back into experience" (*The Times*). Almost everything, on and off stage, caused exasperation in some quarter, from anachronistic costumes — "Turandot in bridal attire and her father dressed like a European constitutional monarch" to the fact that there was scarcely a bit of chinoiserie in sight, and, worse still, the use of amplified sound.

Indeed, the listing of a "sound designer" in the programme was like a red rag to a bull.

"The most embarrassing experience so far in the life of a once intelligent opera company" (the *Guardian*); "A massive bout of producer's ego-tripping weakly disguised as a profound and innovative attempt to get to grips with the creator as well as the creation . . . apart from anything else, a terribly boring *Turandot*" (*Financial Times*). The weight of professional opinion was decidedly negative. But the production had its champions, among them Michael Tumelty of the *Glasgow Herald* who declared it to be "a magnificent production . . . a sustained assault on just about every convention of operatic presentation. The very foundations of 19th century grand opera are challenged." But the *Herald*'s correspondence columns again seethed with righteous wrath, disgust, outrage and vilifaction. "Vandalism", "Malignant", "Squalid", "Trite": Sir Alex Gibson was blamed for not putting a stop to the nonsense before it had a chance to reach the stage. One professional music critic, Michael Kennedy of the *Daily Telegraph*, who clearly felt distaste and was inclined to place the ultimate blame on the same shoulders, did at least have the honesty to record the generous applause, "showing that there's no accounting for taste and nowt so queer as folk".

But *Turandot* had its defenders, typified by one of a number of enthusiastic letters in the *Glasgow Herald*. Mr Ian Syzmanski of Helensburgh declared himself encouraged, "More, I am delighted. Scottish Opera is once again the subject of controversy because of its productions rather than its financial state. This is a welcome sign of health and vigour. I am reminded," he went on, "of similar protests on your letters page after productions of *Macbeth* and *Rigoletto* . . . perhaps the spirit of Pountney and Hemmings is not dead but only resting".

The same newspaper's Arts Editor, John Fowler, was in no doubt where he stood in the matter and he wrote an article to make his position clear. "Blandness is all in the minds of the orthodox and anything that disturbs the calm surface of tradition is to be feared and scorned." But in the long run, he felt, audience reaction is proof of success. "Booing on a first night is a hoary old tradition among opera-goers, but there was no doubt about the feelings of the audience at the next performance (grey-haired ladies as many of the Saturday matinee ticket holders tend to be). They were buzzing with excitement."

TWENTY-FIVE YEARS ON

When you have spoken, as I have done in the course of writing this "tale of Scottish Opera", to many of the individuals who have been closely involved in some aspect of the remarkable enterprise over the twenty-five years since it came to being, you find it increasingly necessary to steer a careful course through the contrary winds of powerful prejudice on the one hand and blind devotion on the other. I have to admit that I, myself, find it difficult to maintain a completely objective view of Scottish Opera but I know that both attitudes at their most extreme, are equally false and must be avoided in any attempt to assess the value and the place of Scotland's national opera company in the life and culture of the country.

As has been said already, the founding of Scottish Opera all those years ago was little short of miraculous. It happened not only because a number of people wished for it, but because they were also willing to put their energy and their expertise into making it happen. The rare combination of talents and the now legendary rapport which made the Gibson/Hemmings duo seemingly invincible, found itself in the right place at the right time as a marvellously cohesive force. And given the continuation of the stable financial scene and the climate of optimism which together helped Scottish Opera to become airborne, so to speak, even the departure of Peter Hemmings might have had a less drastic effect on morale than now seems to have been the case.

At the very least, we might have witnessed a steadier consolidation of the Company's structure than actually happened, given the unfortunate accumulation of adverse circumstances already recounted. But crying over spilled milk gets nobody anywhere, as the saying goes. And the truth is that the chill wind of change was already perceptible in 1977 before Peter Hemmings left the job which, he admits, gave him "the happiest and most exciting years of my life, up till now when, once again, in Los Angeles I feel the same tingle of excitement and challenge".

The loss of Peter Hemmings, whether or not his famed talent for successful brinkmanship would, or could have continued to function in the colder economic climate that was already perceptible at the time of his departure, must have been felt by Alex Gibson like the loss of a limb. His successor, Peter Ebert, for all his talent as a producer of operas, and despite the affection in which he is still held by many of the Scottish Opera singers who worked with him in the rehearsal room and on the stage, could never have filled the gap left by Hemmings if only because, as we have seen, his abilities and his main interest lay elsewhere than in administration, and what the Company needed more than anything else at that time was a clear-minded, hard-headed chargé d'affiares to keep the house firmly in order and to avoid, at all costs, getting into a position of weakness vis à vis a Scottish Arts Council who were already making it clear that the "untameable monster" could expect no special treatment but must cut itself down to size and live within its income, come what may.

I have been very critical of the Scottish Arts Council's attitude to Scottish Opera and, in my opinion, justifiably so, if for no other reason

Yoko Watanabe (left), as Cio-Cio San in MADAMA BUTTERFLY performed in 1987, with Nuria Espert (director).

than their persistence in maintaining a negative attitude towards an enterprise of which they ought to have been proud and supportive. We know that the arts in Britain are seriously underfunded by an essentially philistine government, and that the Scottish arm of the Arts Council of Great Britain finds itself without enough funds to allow it to be generous to all comers. But it is noticeable that, even when extra money has been made available from London to cover inflation, as happened in 1986, SAC refused to pass on more than half the inflationary increase to Scottish Opera.

Is grand opera, or for that matter, opera of any sort, really an élitist entertainment, or even, as has been said, a theatrical dinosaur worthy only of murder by starvation? The crowded foyer at Theatre Royal, Glasgow, and all the other theatres, large and small, where the Company takes its wares, would seem to prove otherwise. Regular opera-goers come in all varieties, from the elderly in dinner jackets and furs (fewer and fewer of those as time goes by) to the youngsters in jeans and sweatshirts discovering, for the first time, the attraction of full-scale Verdi and Wagner and Puccini which will hold them in its grip for the rest of their lives — always supposing that Scotland is allowed to sustain an opera company of its own.

A country without its national art galleries is inconceivable; likewise a country which can boast no symphony orchestra (Scotland has no less than three of those): why, then, should the national opera be forced into a different category, as though it were a provincial theatre company which could expand and contract to suit the financial climate. But such expansion and contraction is not possible where opera companies are concerned: whereas theatre companies can plan a season with small-cast plays (though for good health such a thing ought not to happen ad infinitum) and economic sets, an opera company, besides having to maintain an orchestra and chorus as well as the artistic and administrative staff, must regularly stage the popular "blockbusters" if audiences are to be satisfied and their experience of grand opera is to be properly fulfilled.

It is not the fault of Scottish Opera that the great period of popular opera was the 19th century and that the composers of that era had grand ideas. It is, of course possible, as Opera Go Round has shown us with its production of Verdi's *Macbeth*, to reduce a masterpiece to fit village halls in out-of-the-way places, and that is precisely what Scottish Opera has been providing thoughout much of its history. But piano-accompanied Opera-Go-Round is only possible because the hub is there, in the structure of the main company, without which the standard would fall below an acceptable level, which is what happened, in fact, to the old Opera-For-All companies south of the Border.

I have suggested that Scotland compares unfavourably with its neighbour countries in the matter of subsidy for opera. The fact that *The Trojans* at Scottish Opera in 1969 cost around £8,000 compared with £80,000 for the same opera at Covent Garden only a few months later, speaks for itself. And, except for the difference in money values, things have not greatly altered in that respect. Scottish Opera has had cause to be grateful for generous commercial sponsorship, as well as innumerable private donations, but sponsorship, especially in a small country like Scotland, is unlikely ever to do more than keep the ship painted and rust-free above the water line. But that, of course, is all the public sees of any ship. Without the interest of the insurance companies, like Standard Life, Scottish Amicable and Scottish Mutual; the banks and oil companies (the Royal Bank of Scotland and the National Westminster with Amoco and Britoil, in particular) productions like *Die Meistersinger*, *The Bartered Bride*, *Rigoletto*, *The Cunning Little Vixen*, *Tosca*, *La Traviata*, *The Magic Flute*, *Mahagonny*, *Carmen* and several others would not have been possible. But, on the other hand, only an opera company of Scottish Opera's weight and stature would be able to put them on in the first place. It is a problem that will not simply disappear by wishing it so.

There is an element still, then, of dicing with death at the Opera Centre in Elmbank Crescent, but there is no denying that, at Board level, as at management level, the determination to survive is undiminished. What does continue to worry the more progressive spirits in the team, however, is the number of people around,

Act III of TOSCA performed in 1980.

both outside and within the Company, who seem to feel that nothing must change and that, somehow, "we must all try to get back to what it was at the beginning"; people, in other words, who see everything that happened in those days, good, bad and indifferent, through a rosy glow of nostalgia.

"Of course it was marvellous," says Chairman Len Paterson. "It was new and it was ours. There were people like Charles Craig and Janet Baker coming to sing in Glasgow. We didn't have to go to London to see and hear top quality opera; we didn't have to listen to the gramophone because we could have it on our own doorstep. But everything now is second-time round and people are used to it. Change is necessary — change, and surprise."

There is a strong feeling among opera lovers who live beyond easy commuting distance from Glasgow that we in the west of Scotland have an unfair advantage in being able to enjoy more Scottish Opera productions, evenly spaced out over a long annual season, than any other area in the country. It is felt by some as a slight that, whereas Edinburgh and Aberdeen must be content with a brief feast and a long hunger, Glasgow's opera-goers are able to plan months of social activity to coincide with nine or ten operas from early October to the end of May.

Iain Hamilton's THE CATILINE CONSPIRACY performed in 1974. (Director: Anthony Besch, designer: Luciano.)

For, indeed, it is true that, for many people, opera nights have become an excuse for further socialising at which the production of the evening tends to become the main topic of conversation.

But there is another side to the argument; the fact, for example, that, given a suitable opera house in Edinburgh, built when the time was ripe — plus, of course, an increase in grant to help cover the considerable extra cost involved — Peter Hemmings's original plan to leapfrog each production between the two cities would have gone ahead. Edinburgh would then have enjoyed a season more or less identical with Glasgow's. Another point to be considered is that roughly one-third of the population is to be found within a twenty-five mile radius of the country's largest city — a mere stone's throw in metropolitan terms. That fact, too, weighed strongly with Hemmings (as an Englishman he might be thought unprejudiced) in his vigorous support for basing Scottish Opera at Theatre Royal. And lastly, should anyone still stubbornly insist on harbouring doubts about Glasgow's right to be the home of the national opera company, there is the indisputable fact that Glasgow is where Scottish Opera came to being. To clinch matters still further, one need only turn to the index of most books on opera, where the name of Glasgow appears, on its own account, (for Edinburgh is there, too, but only as host to the International Festival) as the place where several important British premières took place during the 1930s, *The Trojans* among them, in performance by one of no less than six amateur opera companies sustained by the city of the west. The interest in opera, then, is not new, but legendary.

For twenty-five years, then, Glasgow has been the home of professional opera in Scotland — a long time in the history of an organisation, and yet not so long for a company like Scottish Opera which has had to fight unduly hard, at times, for acceptance on its own terms as a national institution. Not so long in which to try and reconcile opposing camps of expectation where its creative work is concerned, at least without the level of funding which would allow it to increase the number of productions to the point where both factions might be satisfied and more employment given to local singers, whether aspirant or established.

In its very first season, Scottish Opera seemed to be proclaiming that the popular would always be balanced by the esoteric and so it must remain, otherwise stagnation is inevitable. There has been an unfortunate tendency, among some of his most fervent admirers who ought to know better, to propagate the notion that Sir Alexander Gibson is a pillar of reaction. Alexander Gibson, who brought that uncompromising work of Stockhausen, *Gruppen*, to Glasgow almost thirty years ago; who gave us experiences of Ligeti, Poulenc, Boulez and other contemporary composers in

weeks of Music Viva and Musica Nova; whose first new work at the Edinburgh Festival was the Sinfonia for Two Orchestras by the same Iain Hamilton who wrote *The Catiline Conspiracy* for Scottish Opera some fifteen years later.

Nothing could be further from the truth, like that other myth of his forced retiral from the Scottish Opera scene. On the contrary, although Gibson would be the first to admit that not everything that happens on the Scottish Opera stage has his complete approval in every aspect, he does enjoy innovative direction; enjoys, too, the teamwork which presuppoes compromise. "In the course of five weeks rehearsal there are bound to be constant adjustments," he will tell you,

and the musical side is just the same as the production side. At the planning stage, of course, I will sometimes decide that I don't like this, or that that won't work, and there have been plenty of instances of things being omitted or changed around in some way. What I have always liked doing is working as a team and if certain aspects of that teamwork mean being involved with the kind of work which is in the air, especially around Europe, I just see it as my job to make sure that the music is as good as I can make it. As for all the controversy — for everybody who writes to a newspaper saying they don't like it, there may well be five or six who have actually enjoyed it but can't be bothered writing to say so.

This book has been published to celebrate Scottish Opera's Silver Jubilee, and rather like a constitutional monarch, Sir Alexander Gibson occupies the central role in that celebration. As anyone with intimate knowledge of the

Yoko Watanabe as Cio-Cio-San in MADAMA BUTTERFLY.

Company will tell you, however, he has never been known to steal the show — except through the music he makes, and that, when he is truly on form, can be superb. The critic who wrote of *Die Meistersinger* that, "Alexander Gibson, conducting a brilliant cast and devoted orchestra paced the work with majesty, breadth and countless moments of sheer, lyrical beauty" was not alone in his admiration, either on that occasion or on many others.

When Sir Alex Gibson raises the same baton once again on the overture to Puccini's *Madama Butterfly* on June 5th 1987, as he did twenty-five years ago, to the very day, at Scottish Opera's debut, the music will be the same, and the lyrical intensity of the orchestral performance will be just as likely to raise the emotional temperature of the audience then present. But the scene on the stage will be vastly different. Times and attitudes have changed, after all, and the traditional Japanese neverland of cherry blossom and pretty, doll-like Geisha girls will no longer serve. The producer on this occasion is the world-famous Spanish actress and director of plays, Nuria Espert, making her debut in the world of opera. The new credibility, if not absolute realism, of the set, by Ezio Frigerio, and the acting by all concerned, is as powerful as the singing. Here is a rickety, populous, towering tenement, hung with bedding

as well as banners and graced only by a twisting wisteria tree in blossom for Act I and bare thereafter. Here, too, is Norman Bailey's utterly convincing picture of a world-weary, disillusioned American consul in a thankless oriental outpost; Seppo Ruohnen's less than young and somewhat seedy Lieutenant Pinkerton for whom affection is as thoughtless as it is easy; and, for once, in a splendid performance by the young Japanese soprano, Yoko Watanabe, a Cio-Cio San who moves us all the more by the very strength of character that so clearly underlies the graceful and yielding exterior. This is, indeed, a *Madama Butterfly* for the nineteen eighties, and, for those who have doubts, it is worth remembering that Puccini, himself, sets his opera "in the present day".

And now Sir Alexander Gibson is about to retire, to abdicate responsibility for the Company he founded. But no, he maintains that this is not retiral but a willing relinquishing of the position which carried the misnomer of a title, "Artistic Director", in favour of another, honorary, status and title, "Founder and Conductor Laureate". The link will certainly not be broken, however. As a conductor he will be there in the pit, as often as ever. And as for responsibility, "I have always seen my responsibility as lying in caring for the Company and I still do."

APPENDICES

Scottish Opera's First Nights

Compiled by two of the Company's founder board members — Richard Telfer, Archivist for Scottish Opera throughout its twenty-five years, and Ian Rodger, Chairman of the Company from 1980 to 1983. Both Richard Telfer and Ian Rodger retired from the Board of Scottish Opera in 1983.

c=conductor; dir=director; des=designer; cho=choreographer; l=lighting

1962

June 5 — **Madama Butterfly** Puccini — 3 performances / Italian
King's Theatre, Glasgow
c Alexander Gibson
dir Denis Arundell
des Mark King
l Charles Bristow

June 6 — **Pelléas et Mélisande** Debussy — 3 performances / French
King's Theatre, Glasgow
c Alexander Gibson
dir Denis Arundell
des Mark King
l Charles Bristow

Total 6 performances

May 29 — **Double Bill** — 4 performances
Volo di Notte Dallapiccola
King's Theatre, Glasgow
c Alexander Gibson
dir Peter Ebert
des Ralph Koltai
l Charles Bristow

L'Heure Espagnole Ravel
King's Theatre, Glasgow
c Brian Priestman
dir Anthony Besch
des Peter Rice
l Charles Bristow

Total 13 performances

1963

May 27 — **Otello** Verdi — 4 performances / Italian
King's Theatre, Glasgow
c Alexander Gibson
dir Anthony Besch
des Ralph Koltai
l Charles Bristow

May 28 — **Die Entführung aus dem Serail** Mozart — 5 performances / English
King's Theatre, Glasgow
c Leon Lovett
dir Peter Ebert
des Peter Rice
l Charles Bristow

1964

May 14 — **Faust** Gounod — 5 performances / French
King's Theatre, Glasgow
c Alexander Gibson
dir Anthony Besch
des Peter Rice
l Charles Bristow

May 16 — **Don Giovanni** Mozart — 6 performances / English
King's Theatre, Glasgow
c Leon Lovett
dir Peter Ebert
des Ralph Koltai
l Charles Bristow

Revival — **Otello** — 5 performances

Total 16 performances

David Ward as Boris in BORIS GODUNOV performed in 1965.

1965

May 14   **Boris Godunov**   6 performances
Mussorgsky   English
King's Theatre,
Glasgow
c Alexander Gibson
dir Michael Geliot
des Ralph Koltai
l Charles Bristow

May 15   **Madama**   8 performances
Butterfly   Italian
Puccini
King's Theatre,
Glasgow
c Norman Del Mar

dir Peter Ebert
des David Wilby
l Charles Bristow

Revival   **Don Giovanni**   5 performances
Total 19 performances

1966

April 11   **Albert Herring**   9 performances
Britten   English
Perth Theatre
c Roderick Brydon
dir Anthony Besch
des Adam Pollock
l Charles Bristow

May 6   **Falstaff** Verdi   7 performances
King's Theatre,   Italian
Glasgow
c Alexander Gibson
dir Peter Ebert
des Peter Rice
cho Shelah Wells
l Charles Bristow

May 13   **Die Walküre**   8 performances
Wagner   German
King's Theatre,
Glasgow
c Alexander Gibson
dir Peter Ebert
des Michael Knight
l Charles Bristow

Revival   **Faust**   5 performances
Total 29 performances

1967

April 12   **Così fan tutte**   9 performances
Mozart   English
Perth Theatre
c Alexander Gibson
dir Anthony Besch
des John Stoddart
l Charles Bristow

May 6   **Das Rheingold**   5 performances
Wagner   German
King's Theatre,

Glasgow
c Alexander Gibson
dir Peter Ebert
des Michael Knight
l Charles Bristow

May 11	**La Bohème** Puccini King's Theatre, Glasgow *c* Roderick Brydon *dir* Peter Ebert *des* Peter Rice *l* Charles Bristow	7 performances Italian
August 22	**The Rake's Progress** Stravinsky King's Theatre, Edinburgh (Edinburgh International Festival) *c* Alexander Gibson *dir* Peter Ebert *des* Ralph Koltai *l* Charles Bristow	4 performances English
September 4	**The Soldier's Tale** Stravinsky King's Theatre, Edinburgh (Edinburgh International Festival) *c* Alexander Gibson *dir* Wendy Toye *des* Carl Toms *l* Charles Bristow	6 performances English
Revivals	**Albert Herring** **Otello**	4 performances 5 performances Total 40 performances

1968

April 9	**The Marriage of Figaro** Mozart Perth Theatre *c* Alexander Gibson	16 performances English

Left to right: Count Almaviva (John Shirley-Quirk), Antonio the Gardener (John Lawson Graham) and Figaro (Stafford Dean) in THE MARRIAGE OF FIGARO performed in 1968.

dir Anthony Besch
des John Stoddart
l Charles Bristow

April 10	**Full Circle** Orr Perth Theatre *c* Alexander Gibson *dir* Michael Geliot *des* Neil Parkinson	3 performances English
May 15	**Götterdäm- merung** Wagner King's Theatre, Glasgow *c* Alexander Gibson *dir* Peter Ebert	5 performances German

	des Michael Knight *l* Charles Bristow	
August 19	**Peter Grimes** Britten King's Theatre, Edinburgh (Edinburgh International Festival) *c* Alexander Gibson *dir* Colin Graham *des* Alix Stone *l* Charles Bristow	6 performances English
August 26 Sponsored by the Scottish Gas Board	**Il Ballo delle Ingrate** Monteverdi Adam Rooms, Edinburgh (Edinburgh International Festival *c* Roderick Brydon *dir* Peter Ebert *des* Jack Notman *l* Alexander Bennett	5 performances
December 12	**The Gondoliers** Gilbert and Sullivan King's Theatre, Edinburgh *c* James Loughran *dir* Joan Cross *des* Jack Notman *cho* Clover Roope	6 performances
December 16	**Full Circle** Orr King's Theatre, Edinburgh *c* Alexander Gibson *dir* Ian Watt-Smith *des* Bernard Culshaw (*Second Production*)	2 performances

Revivals	**The Soldiers Tale** (as part of a double bill with **Full Circle**) **Boris Godunov** **Madama Butterfly** **Albert Herring**	2 performances 6 performances 6 performances 2 performances Total 57 performances
1969 May 3	**The Trojans** Berlioz King's Theatre, Glasgow *c* Alexander Gibson *dir* Peter Ebert *cho* Laverne Meyer *des* Hans Ulrich Schmückle (*set*) Sylta Busse Schmückle (*costumes*) *l* Charles Bristow	5 performances English
May 22	**The Gondoliers** King's Theatre, Edinburgh – First visit of the Queen and Duke of Edinburgh to Scottish Opera. (Royal family staying at Holyrood for the Queen to act as Lord High Commissioner for the General Assembly.)	8 performances Total 53 performances
September 1	**The Undertaker** Purser Gateway Theatre, Edinburgh (Edinburgh	10 performances English

International
Festival)
c Alexander Gibson
dir Ian Watt-Smith
des Ken Wheatley (*set*)
      Alex Reid (*costumes*)

December 5	**Cinderella**	4 performances
	Rossini	English
	King's Theatre, Edinburgh	
	c Bryden Thomson	
	dir Colin Graham	
	des Emanuele Luzzati	
	l Colin Graham	
Revivals	**Cosi fan tutte**	11 performances
	Full Circle	7 performances (+ 10 performances as double bill with **The Undertaker**)
	Albert Herring	8 performances

1970

March 26	**The Turn of the Screw** Britten	12 performances English
	His Majesty's Theatre, Aberdeen	
	c Roderick Brydon	
	dir Anthony Besch	
	des John Stoddart	
	l Charles Bristow	
May 1	**Fidelio** Beethoven	12 performances
	King's Theatre, Glasgow	German
	c Alexander Gibson	
	dir Peter Ebert	
	des Hans Ulrich Schmückle (*set*)	
	Sylta Busse Schmückle (*costumes*)	
	l Charles Bristow	

Anthony Besch giving advice to Elizabeth Harwood during rehearsals of DER ROSENKAVALIER.

July 20	**The Magic Flute**	16 performances
	Mozart	English
	Royal Lyceum Theatre, Edinburgh (Commonwealth Games, 1970)	
	c Alexander Gibson	
	dir Peter Ebert	
	des Geoffrey Scott (*set*) Alex Reid (*costumes*)	
	l André Tammes	
August 25	**Elegy for Young Lovers** Henze	5 performances English

Janet Baker as Oktavian and Noel Mangis as Baron Ochs auf
Leichenau in DER ROSENKAVALIER performed in 1971.

King's Theatre,
Edinburgh
(Edinburgh
International
Festival)
c Alexander Gibson
dir Hans Werner
Henze
des Ralph Koltai
(*set*) Fausti Moroni
(*costumes*)
l Charles Bristow

December 12	**La traviata** Verdi	3 performances
	Royal Lyceum	Italian
	Theatre,	
	Edinburgh	

c James Loughran
dir Ian Watt-Smith
des Bernard
Culshaw (*set*)
Alex Reid (*costumes*)
l Charles Bristow

Revivals	**Cinderella**	13 performances
	Don Giovanni	10 performances
	Albert Herring	4 performances
		Total 75 performances

1971

May 8	**Siegfried** Wagner	5 performances
	King's Theatre,	German
	Glasgow	

c Alexander Gibson
dir Peter Ebert
des Michael Knight
l Charles Bristow

May 20	**Der**	7 performances
	Rosenkavalier	English
	Strauss	
	King's Theatre,	
	Glasgow	

c Alexander Gibson
dir Anthony Besch
des John Stoddart
l Charles Bristow

July 26	**The Barber of**	15 performances
	Seville Rossini	English
	Royal Lyceum	
	Theatre,	
	Edinburgh	

c Gary Bertini
dir Ian Watt-Smith
des Bernard
Culshaw (*set*)
Alex Reid (*costumes*)
l Roger Jackson

September 29	**The Rake's**	6 performances
	Progress	English
	Stravinsky	
	MacRobert Centre,	
	University of	
	Stirling	

c Alexander Gibson
dir David Pountney
des Ralph Koltai
l Roger Jackson

December 13/ 14/16/18	**The Ring Cycle**	4 performances
	Wagner	
	King's Theatre, Glasgow	
	c Alexander Gibson	
	dir Peter Ebert	
	des Michael Knight	
	l Charles Bristow	

Revivals	**Albert Herring**	4 performances
	The Turn of the Screw	4 performances
	La traviata	15 performances
	Das Rheingold	9 performances
	The Magic Flute	8 performances
	Die Walküre	3 performances
	Don Giovanni	8 performances
	Götterdämmerung	1 performance
		Total 89 performances

1972

March 24	**A Midsummer Night's Dream**	18 performances English
Sponsored by Scottish Television	Britten MacRobert Centre, University of Stirling	
	c Roderick Brydon	
	dir Toby Robertson	
	des Robin Archer	
	cho Eleanor Fazan	
	l Michael Outhwaite	

May 18	**Pelléas et Mélisande**	5 performances French
	Debussy King's Theatre, Glasgow	
	c Alexander Gibson	
	dir Colin Graham,	
	des John Fraser	
	l Charles Bristow	

Can-can dancers at Maxim's in THE MERRY WIDOW performed in 1973. (Director: Anthony Besch, designer: John Stoddart.)

September 12	**Don Pasquale**	12 performances English
	Donizetti King's Theatre, Glasgow	
	c Alexander Gibson	
	dir Peter Ebert	
	des Peter Rice	
	l Charles Bristow	

Revivals	**Così fan tutte**	16 performances
	The Barber of Seville	14 performances
	Die Walküre	3 performances
	Otello	7 performances
	The Marriage of Figaro	16 performances
	The Trojans	6 performances
		Total 97 performances

Gordon Sandison as Papageno in David Pountney's "Midi" production of THE MAGIC FLUTE performed in 1974.

1973

March 12	**The Coronation of Poppea** Monteverdi MacRobert Centre, University of Stirling *c* Raymond Leppard *dir* Anthony Besch *des* Roger Butlin (*set*) Joyce Conwy Evans (*costumes*) *l* Howard Eldridge	11 performances English
April 28	**Tristan und Isolde** Wagner King's Theatre, Glasgow *c* Alexander Gibson *dir* Michael Geliot *des* Ralph Koltai (*set*) Maria Bjørnson (*costumes*) *l* Robert Ornbo	14 performances German
June 19	**The Merry Widow** Lehar King's Theatre, Glasgow (Clyde Fair 1973) *c* Alexander Gibson *dir* Anthony Besch *des* John Stoddart *cho* Virginia Mason *l* Charles Bristow	28 performances English
September 20	**The Donkey** Oliver Opera for Schools MacRobert Centre, University of Stirling *c* David Frame *dir* David Pountney *piano* Joyce Fieldsend	5 performances

Revivals		
	The Turn of the Screw	8 performances
	Don Pasquale	14 performances
	The Marriage of Figaro	13 performances
	Peter Grimes	6 performances
	Pelléas et Méllisande	6 performances
	Madama Butterfly	9 performances
	La traviata	3 performances
	A Midsummer Night's Dream	3 performances

Total 120 performances

1974

February 8   **The Magic Flute**   37 performances
Mozart   English
King's Theatre,
Glasgow
c Christopher
Seaman
dir David Pountney
des David Fielding
(*set*) Maria
Bjørnson (*costumes*)
l Victor Lockwood

March 16   **The Catiline**   10 performances
Conspiracy   English
Hamilton
MacRobert Centre,
University of
Stirling
Scottish Opera
Commission
c Alexander Gibson
dir Anthony Besch
des Luciana Arrighi
l Charles Bristow

August 19   **Alceste** Gluck   6 performances
King's Theatre,   French
Edinburgh
(Edinburgh
International
Festival)
c Alexander Gibson
dir Anthony Besch
des John Stoddart
cho Peter Darrell
l Charles Bristow

September 27   **Lucia di**   8 performances
Lammermoor   Italian
Donizetti
Theatre Royal,
Newcastle upon
Tyne
c Roderick Brydon
dir John Copley
des Henry Bardon (*set*)
   Alim Stone (*costumes*)

Josephine Barstow as Leonore in FIDELIO performed in 1975.

cho Jim Hastie
l Charles Bristow

October 3   **The Lion, the**   3 performances
Witch and the   English
Wardrobe
McCabe
Opera for Schools
c David Frame
dir Jeremy Sutcliffe
des David Burrows
piano Joyce
Fieldsend

Revivals   **A Midsummer**
Night's Dream   6 performances
The Merry
Widow   10 performances
La traviata   10 performances

David Pountney's production of DON GIOVANNI performed in 1975.

Fidelio	10 performances	
Boris Godunov	7 performances	
Elegy for Young Lovers	7 performances	
Der Rosenkavalier	9 performances	
The Barber of Seville	7 performances	
La Bohème	3 performances	
	Total 133 performances	

1975

April 25   **Un Ballo in Maschera** Verdi
King's Theatre,
Glasgow
c Alexander Gibson
dir John Copley
des Carl Toms
cho Jim Hastie
l Charles Bristow

10 performances
Italian

June 14   **Die Fledermaus**
J Strauss
King's Theatre,
Edinburgh

16 performances
English

c David Frame
dir David Pountney
des David Fielding
(*set*) Alex Reid
(*costumes*)
cho Jim Hastie
l Charles Bristow

August 27   **Hermiston** Orr
King's Theatre,
Edinburgh
(Edinburgh
International
Festival)
Scottish Opera
Commission
c Roderick Brydon
dir Toby Robertson
des Robin Archer
l Robert Ornbo

10 performances
English

October 27   **Don Giovanni**
Mozart
Gaiety Theatre,
Ayr
c David Frame
dir Jeremy Sutcliffe
des Ralph Koltai
l Victor Lockwood

5 performances
English

November 12   **Ariadne on Naxos**
R Strauss
King's Theatre,
Glasgow
c Norman Del Mar
dir Anthony Besch
des Peter Rice
cho Jim Hastie
l John B Read

4 performances
English

December 10   **The Golden Cockerel** Rimsky-Korsakov
Theatre Royal,
Glasgow
c Alexander Gibson
dir David Pountney
des Sue Blane (*set*)
Maria Bjørnson
(*costumes*)
l Charles Bristow

5 performances
English

Revivals **The Turn of the Screw** 5 performances
Elegy for Young Lovers 7 performances
The Barber of Seville 32 performances
Lucia di Lammermoor 16 performances
La Bohème 14 performances
Pelléas et Mélisande 6 performances
Don Giovanni 8 performances
Otello 4 performances
Così fan tutte 4 performances
A Midsummer Night's Dream 2 performances
Total 148 performances

1976
April 16 **The Rape of Lucretia** Britten 7 performances English
MacRobert Centre, University of Stirling
c Roderick Brydon
dir Anthony Besch
des John Stoddart
l Victor Lockwood

June 15 **Confessions of a Justified Sinner** Wilson 16 performances English
Theatre Royal, York
Scottish Opera Commission
c Norman Del Mar
dir Michael Geliot
des Alexander McPherson
l Victor Lockwood

August 23 **Macbeth** Verdi 15 performances Italian
King's Theatre, Edinburgh (Edinburgh International Festival)

Thea Musgrave conducting a rehearsal of her own opera, MARY QUEEN OF SCOTS.

c Alexander Gibson
dir David Pountney
des Ralph Koltai
l Nick Chelton

December 1 **Die Meistersinger** 4 performances
Sponsored by Standard Life Wagner German
Theatre Royal, Glasgow
c Alexander Gibson
dir David Pountney
des Maria Bjørnson
cho Jim Hastie
l Charles Bristow
and Victor Lockwood

Revivals	**Die Fledermaus**	8 performances
	A Midsummer Night's Dream	11 performances
	Don Giovanni (*Ebert*)	11 performances
	Madama Butterfly	5 performances
	Falstaff	11 performances
	Don Giovanni (*Sutcliffe*)	18 performances
	Die Fledermaus	6 performances
	Ariadne on Naxos	7 performances
	The Golden Cockerel	4 performances
	Otello	4 performances
	The Merry Widow	11 performances
	The Magic Flute	13 performances
	La Bohème	5 performances
	Don Pasquale	5 performances
	plus	
	Hansel and Gretel (*Puppets*)	4 performances

Total 165 performances

1977

February 16 — **Jenufa** Janáček — 9 performances / English
Theatre Royal, Glasgow
c Richard Armstrong
dir David Pountney
des Maria Bjørnson
cho Terry Gilbert
l Victor Lockwood

February 28 — **The Marriage of Figaro** Mozart — 29 performances / English
MacRobert Centre, University of Stirling
c Roderick Brydon
dir Toby Robertson
des Alan Barrett
cho Jim Hastie
l Victor Lockwood

September 6 — **Mary Queen of Scots** Musgrave — 8 performances / English
King's Theatre, Edinburgh (Edinburgh International Festival)
Scottish Opera Commission
c Thea Musgrave
dir Colin Graham
des Robin Don *and* Colin Graham (*set*)
Alex Reid (*costumes*)
l Charles Bristow

Revivals	**The Merry Widow**	19 performances
	Fidelio	17 performances
	The Rape of Lucretia	8 performances
	The Magic Flute (*Pountney*)	16 performances
	Macbeth	12 performances
	The Turn of the Screw	7 performances
	Don Pasquale	10 performances
	Die Meistersingers	9 performances
	Otello	5 performances
	Ariadne on Naxos	4 performances
	The Golden Cockerel	7 performances
	Falstaff	2 performances
	Hansel and Gretel (*Puppets*)	4 performances

Total 166 performances

1978

February 8

Sponsored by Scottish Amicable

The Bartered Bride Smetana — 14 performances / English
Theatre Royal, Glasgow
c Roderick Brydon
dir David Pountney
des Sue Blane (*set*)
Maria Bjørnson (*costumes*)

cho Peter Darrell
l Victor Lockwood

March 1 **Seraglio** Mozart   25 performances
Theatre Royal,   English
Glasgow
c Gary Bertini
dir David Pountney
des David Fielding
(*set*) Maria
Bjørnson (*costumes*)
l Victor Lockwood

March 12 **L'Elisir D'Amore**   11 performances
Donizetti   English
(Orchestra-
accompanied
Opera Go Round)
Gardyne Theatre,
Dundee
c Stewart
Robertson
dir Graham Vick
des Russell Craig
l Victor Lockwood

June 20 **Hansel and Gretel** 15 performances
Humperdinck   English
Theatre Royal,
Glasgow
c Sir Alexander
Gibson
dir Peter Ebert
des Sue Blane (*set*)
Maria Bjørnson
(*costumes*)
l Victor Lockwood

July 20 **Dido and Aeneas**   9 performances
Purcell   English
(1978 Aix-en-
Provence Festival)
c Sir Charles
Mackerras
dir John Copley
des Stephanos
Laziridis
cho Jim Hastie

October 4 **Simon**   5 performances
Boccanegra Verdi Italian
Theatre Royal,
Glasgow
c Henry Lewis
Mackerras
dir Peter Ebert
des Peter Rice (*set*)
Mario Vanarelli
(*costumes*)
l Victor Lockwood

November 15 **Savitri** Holst   4 performances
Theatre Royal,   English
Glasgow
c Sir Charles
Mackerras
dir Graham Vick
des Russell Craig
l Victor Lockwood

November 15 **Fanny Robin**   5 performances
Harper   English
Theatre Royal,
Glasgow
c Edward Harper
dir Graham Vick
des Russell Craig
l Victor Lockwood

Revivals **Falstaff**   4 performances
The Marriage of
Figaro   2 performances
The Rape of
Lucretia   9 performances
Madama
Butterfly   7 performances
Der
Rosenkavalier   8 performances
The Turn of the
Screw   5 performances
Die Meistersinger 2 performances
A Midsummer
Night's Dream   6 performances
Mary Queen of
Scots   1 performance

Pelléas et Mélisande 3 performances
La Bohème 5 performances
Jenufa 5 performances
The Catiline Conspiracy 4 performances
plus
Magical Musical Wardrobe 6 performances
Total 165 performances

1979

April 4 **Katya Kabanova** 8 performances
Janáček English
Theatre Royal,
Glasgow
c Richard
Armstrong
dir David Pountney
des Maria Bjørnson
l Victor Lockwood

April 18 **Rigoletto** Verdi 13 performances
Sponsored by Theatre Royal, Italian
Commercial Glasgow
Union c Sir Alexander
Gibson
dir David Alden
des David Fielding
(set) Alex Reid
(costumes)

May 21 **The Two Widows** 2 performances
Smetana English
Perth Theatre
(1979 Perth
Festival)
c Albert Rosen
dir David Pountney
des Sue Blane
l Victor Lockwood

June 21st **Fiddler on the Roof** Bock 34 performances
Theatre Royal, English
Glasgow
c Guy Woolfenden
dir Peter Ebert
des Michael Knight (set)
Mark Negim (costumes)

cho Royston Maldoom
l Victor Lockwood

September 1 **Eugene Onegin** 6 performances
Tchaikovsky English
King's Theatre,
Edinburgh
(Edinburgh
International
Festival)
c Sir Alexander
Gibson
dir David Pountney
des Roger Butlin
(sets) Deirdre
Clancy (costumes)
cho Terry Gilbert
l Nick Chelton

October 17 **Orfeo ed** 9 performances
Eurydice Gluck Italian
Theatre Royal,
Glasgow
c Sir Alexander
Gibson
dir Peter Ebert
des Ingrid Rosell
cho Peter Darrell
l Charles Bristow

November 14 **Don Giovanni** 11 performances
Sponsored by Mozart Italian
National Theatre Royal,
Westminster Glasgow
Bank c Sir Alexander
Gibson
dir David Pountney
des Maria Bjørnson
l Nick Chelton

Revivals **Der Rosenkavalier** 2 performances
Die Fledermaus 6 performances
A Midsummer Night's Dream 4 performances
La Bohème 10 performances
Simon Boccanegra 8 performances
Hansel and Gretel 1 performance

**The Golden
Cockerel**   7 performances

**The Turn of the
Screw**   3 performances

**Pelléas et
Mélisande**   5 performances
                    Total 131 performances

1980
August 27   **The Cunning**   3 performances
             Little Vixen   English
             Janáček
             King's Theatre,
             Edinburgh
             (Edinburgh
             International
             Festival)
             c Richard
             Armstrong
             dir David Pountney
             des Maria Bjørnson
             cho Stuart Hopps
             l Nick Chelton

August 28   **Wozzeck** Berg   9 performances
             King's Theatre,   German
Sponsored by Edinburgh
Amoco   (Edinburgh
             International
             Festival)
             c Sir Alexander
             Gibson
             dir David Alden
             des David Fielding
             cho Stuart Hopps
             l Charles Bristow

October 15   **Tosca** Puccini   16 performances
             Theatre Royal,   Italian
Sponsored by Glasgow
Scottish   c Sir Alexander
Amicable   Gibson
             dir Anthony Besch
             des Peter Rice
             l Mark Henderson

November 4   **The Barber of**   4 performances
             Seville Rossini English

*Anne-Marie Owens as the actress, Poppy Teane in LA VIE
PARISIENNE performed in 1985.*

MacRobert Centre,
University of
Stirling
c Ian Robertson
dir John Lawson
Graham
des Alex Reid
l Victor Lockwood

Revivals   **Eugene Onegin**   3 performances
              The Two Widows   6 performances
              **The Bartered
              Bride**   15 performances
              Rigoletto   11 performances
              **Mary Queen of
              Scots**   4 performances

Peter Grimes	8 performances	
L'Elisir d'Amore	15 performances	
A Midsummer Night's Dream	4 performances	
Orfeo and Eurydice	2 performances	
Madama Butterfly	2 performances	
Fiddler on the Roof	3 performances	
The Marriage of Figaro	12 performances	
La Bohème	2 performances	
	Total 119 performances	

1981
March 11

Sponsored by Commercial Union

La traviata Verdi
Theatre Royal,
Glasgow
c Sir Alexander
Gibson
dir David William
des Michael Annals
(*set*) Alex Reid
(*costumes*)
cho Stuart Hopps
l Victor Lockwood

17 performances
Italian

April 15

The Makropoulos Case Janáček
Theatre Royal,
Glasgow
c Richard
Armstrong
dir David Pountney
des Maria Bjørnson
l Nick Chelton

9 performances
Enlgish

September 1

The Beggar's Opera Gay
King's Theatre,
Edinburgh
(Edinburgh
International
Festival)
c Guy Woolfenden
dir David William

21 performances
English

des Michael Annals
(*set*) Alex Reid
(*costumes*)
cho Geraldine
Stephenson
l Spike Gaden

September 9

The Pearl Fishers
Bizet
Theatre Royal,
Newcastle upon
Tyne
c Ian Robertson
dir Steven Pimlott
des Stefan Lazardis
cho Eleanor Fazan
l Mark Henderson

11 performances
French

Revivals

La Bohème	12 performances
Lucia di Lammermoor	17 performances
The Barber of Seville	12 performances
Eugene Onegin	14 performances
A Midsummer Night's Dream	3 performances
The Rape of Lucretia	2 performances
Die Fledermaus	13 performances
Così fan tutte	5 performances
	Total 136 performances

1982
January 13

L'Egisto Cavalli
Theatre Royal,
Glasgow
c Roderick Brydon
dir John Cox
des and l Allen
Charles Klein

23 performances
Italian

August 22

Manon Lescaut
Puccini
King's Theatre,
Edinburgh
(Edinburgh
International

15 performances
Italian

Festival)
c Sir Alexander
Gibson
dir John Cox
des Allen Charles
Klein (*set*) Alix
Stone (*costumes*)
cho Nigel Nicholson
l Robert Bryan

Revivals	**The Pearl Fishers**	26 performances
	Così fan tutte	5 performances
	Tosca	15 performances
	The Cunning	
	Little Vixen	7 performances
	Seraglio	15 performances
	A Midsummer	
	Night's Dream	9 performances
		Total 115 performances

1983
January 12   **The Magic Flute**   19 performances
Mozart   English
Theatre Royal,
Glasgow
c Sir Alexander
Gibson
dir Jonathan Miller
des Philip Prowse
l Robert Bryan

April 27   **Werther** Massenet   10 performances
Theatre Royal,   French
Glasgow
c Roderick Brydon
dir Rhoda Levine
des John Conklin
l Robert Bryan

August 20   **Death in Venice**   9 performances
Britten   English
Theatre Royal,
Glasgow
c Roderick Brydon
dir Francois
Rochaix
des Jean-Claude
Maret
l Jean Philippe Roy

October 19   **Idomeneo** Mozart   8 performances
Theatre Royal,   English
Glasgow
c Gyørgy Fischer
dir John Cox
des Roger Butlin
l Robert Bryan

December 17   **My Fair Lady**   14 performances
Theatre Royal,   English
Glasgow
c Ian Robertson
dir Peter Lichtenfels
des Adrian Vaux
(*set*) Tim
Goodchild
(*costumes*)
cho Kedzie Penfield
l Alan Campbell

Revivals	**A Midsummer**	
	Night's Dream	2 performances
	Seraglio	2 performances
	Pearl Fishers	4 performances
	Manon Lescaut	1 performance
	The	
	Mastersingers	11 performances
	Wozzeck	5 performances
	The Golden	
	Cockerel	12 performances
	Hansel and Gretel	8 performances
		Total 105 performances

1984
April 18   **Turandot** Puccini   11 performances
Theatre Royal,   Italian
Glasgow
c Sir Alexander
Gibson
dir Tony Palmer
des Kenneth Carey
(*sets*) Barbara Lane
(*costumes*)
l Nick Chelton
sound Derrick Zieba

May 22   **The Marriage**   9 performances
Contract Rossini   English

Escamillo in CARMEN performed in 1986.

	Perth Theatre (1984 Perth Festival) *c* Richard Honner *dir* Graham Vick *des* Russell Craig *l* Ian Sommerville	
May 22	**The Silken Ladder** Rossini Perth Theatre (1984 Perth Festival) *c* Richard Honner *dir* Graham Vick *des* Russell Craig *l* Ian Somerville	9 performances English

August 21	**Orion** Cavalli King's Theatre, Edinburgh (Edinburgh International Festival) *c* Raymond Leppard *dir* Peter Wood, *des* John Bury *l* Robert Bryan *archery coach* Beryl Shaw	13 performances English
Revivals	**L'Elisir d'Amore**	11 performances
	La Bohème	11 performances
	L'Egisto	9 performances
	Fidelio	15 performances
	Rigoletto	15 performances
		Total 103 performances

1985

January 9	**Capriccio** R Strauss Theatre Royal, Glasgow *c* Norman Del Mar *dir* Jon Cox *des* Jack Notman *cho* Peter Darrell *l* Alan Campbell	7 performances English
February 13	**The Barber of Seville** Rossini Theatre Royal, Glasgow *c* Sir Alexander Gibson *dir* Robert David MacDonald *des* Sue Blane *l* Gerry Jenkinson	17 performances Italian
April 17	**Don Giovanni** Mozart Theatre Royal, Glasgow	7 performances Italian

c Sir Alexander
Gibson
dir Graham Vick
des Stefanos
Lazardis *and* Clare
Mitchell
cho Terry Gilbert
l Nick Chelton

May 8	**Orlando** Handel Theatre Royal, Glasgow *c* Richard Hickox *dir* Christopher Fettes *des* Antony McDonald *cho* Ian Spink *l* Paul Pyant	11 performances English	

June 5	**Hedda Gabler** Harper Theatre Royal, Glasgow (Commissioned by the BBC) *c* Diego Masson *dir* Graham Vick *des* Russell Craig *l* Matthew Richardson	5 performances English

September 4

Sponsored by
Citbank and
Cognac
Courvoisier

La Vie Parisienne 16 performances
Offenbach   English
Theatre Royal,
Glasgow
c Sir Alexander
Gibson
dir Graham Vick
des Richard Hudson
cho Bruno Tonioli
l Bruno Boyer

October 23   **Oberon** Weber   12 performances
Theatre Royal,
Glasgow
c Sir Alexander
Gibson

dir Graham Vick
des Russell Craig
l Nick Chelton

Revivals   **The Bartered
Bride**   15 performances
**The Marriage
Contract**   4 performances
**The Silken
Ladder**   4 performances
The Magic Flute   9 performances
                 Total 107 performances

1986

January 22   **Il trovatore** Verdi 11 performances
Theatre Royal,   English
Sponsored by   Glasgow
Britoil   *c* Graeme Jenkins
                dir Graham Vick
                des Michael
                Yeargan
                l John Waterhouse

March 5   **The Rise and Fall** 11 performances
                of the City of   English
Sponsored by   **Mahagonny** Weill
Standard Life   Theatre Royal,
                Glasgow
                c Sian Edwards
                dir David Alden
                des David Fielding
                l Alan Campbell

March 20   **The Tales of**   11 performances
                Hoffmann   English
                Offenbach
                Gardyne Theatre,
                Dundee
                c Simon Halsey
                dir and l Matthew
                Richardson
                des Kenny Miller

April 30   **The Marriage of**   11 performances
                Figaro Mozart   Italian
                Theatre Royal,
                Glasgow
                c Gyørgy Fischer

	dir John Cox *des* John Byrne *cho* Ian Spink *l* Paul Pyant	
September 30	**Carmen** Bizet Theatre Royal, Glasgow *c* John Mauceri *dir* Graham Vick *des* Michael Yeargan *cho* Sean Walsh *l* Nick Chelton	14 performances English
October 10	**Intermezzo** R Strauss Theatre Royal, Glasgow *c* Stephen Barlow *dir* John Cox *des* Martin Battersby *cho* Imogen Claire *l* Alan Campbell	8 performances English
October 21	**Iolanthe** Gilbert and Sullivan Theatre Royal, Glasgow *c* Wyn Davies *dir* Keith Warner *des* Marie-Jeanne Lecca *l* Nick Chelton	14 performances English
Revivals	**Werther** **The Turn of the** **Screw** **Tosca**	8 performances 8 performances 13 performances Total 109 performances

**1987
(to June 1987)**

January 27	**The Flying** **Dutchman**	12 performances German

	Wagner Theatre Royal, Glasgow *c* Sir Alexander Gibson *dir* John Cox *des* Eugene Lee *cho* Imogen Claire *l* Nick Chelton	
February 25	**From the House** **of the Dead** Janáček Theatre Royal, Glasgow *c* Richard Armstrong *dir* David Pountney *des* Maria Bjørnson *l* Chris Ellis	7 performances English
April 28	**Madama Butterfly** Puccini Theatre Royal, Glasgow *c* Sir Alexander Gibson *dir* Nuria Espert *des* Ezio Frigerio (*set*) Franca Squarciapino (*costumes*) *l* Bruno Boyer	13 performances Italian
May 21	**Billy Budd** Britten Theatre Royal, Glasgow *c* John Mauceri *dir* Graham Vick *des* Chris Dyer *l* Nick Chelton	8 performances English
Revivals	**The Marriage of** **Figaro** **The Barber of** **Seville**	11 performances 10 performances Total 61 performances

Opera Go Round

Piano-accompanied small-scale productions presented by Scottish Opera.

1978

The Elixir of Love Donizetti 36 performances
piano John M Querns
conductor Stewart Robertson
dir Graham Vick
des Russell Craig
l Victor Lockwood
(This production was later expanded into a mainscale production).

Così fan tutte Mozart 18 performances
harpsichord John M Querns
conductor Stewart Robertson
dir John Lawson Graham
des Alex Reid (*costumes*) Emma Purdy (*set*)
l Victor Lockwood

Peace Carl Davies 16 performances
piano John M Querns
conductor Stewart Robertson
dir Graham Vick
des Russell Craig
l Victor Lockwood

Candide Bernstein 10 performances
piano John M Querns
conductor Stewart Robertson
dir Graham Vick

1979

Curtain Calls 33 performances
based on Offenbach
piano John M Querns
devised and directed by Graham Vick

La traviata Verdi 30 performances
piano John Querns
dir Graham Vick
des Russell Craig
l Victor Lockwood

1979-1980

The Telephone Menotti 19 performances
piano John M Querns
conductor Ian Robertson
dir Graham Vick
des Alan Hutton *and* Graham Vick
l Peter Bentley

1979-1982

The Quest of the Hidden Moon Ian Robertson 39 performances
piano John M Querns/Joyce Fieldsend/Lesley Anne Sammons
conductors Ian Robertson/Simon Halsey
dir Graham Vick
des Alan Hatton *and* Graham Vick
l Peter Bentley

1980

Susanna's Secret Wolf Ferrari 17 performances
piano Lesley Anne Sammons/John Querns
dir and des Graham Vick
l Peter Bentley

1981-1983

Cinderella Rossini 48 performances
piano Lesley-Anne Sammons/Peter Lockwood/Christopher Middleton
dir Graham Vick
(*Revival by* Alexis Leighton)

des Alex Reid
l Alan Campbell

1981   **The Marriage of**   35 performances
Figaro Mozart
piano Lesley Anne
Sammons
dir Rebecca Meitlis
des Emma Purdy
(*set*) Sue
Wilmington
(*costumes*)
cho Jim Hastie
l Peter Bentley

1982-1983   **Madam Butterfly**   24 performances
Puccini
piano Peter
Lockwood
dir John Lawson
Graham
des Tony Whelan
l Alan Campbell

1983   **Don Giovanni**   10 performances
Mozart
piano Peter
Lockwood/Chris-
topher Middleton
dir Declan
Donnellan
des Nick Ormerod

1985   **Carmen** Bizet   20 performances
supported by   *piano* Gerald Moore
Scottish   *dir and des* Keith
Post Office   Warner
Board   *l* Peter Bentley

supported by   **Tosca** Puccini   23 performances
the Scottish   *piano* Lesley Anne
Post Office   Sammons
Board   *dir* Keith Warner
    des Marie-Jeanne
    Lecca
    l Victor Lockwood

1986   **Jenufa** Janáček   19 performances
supported by   *piano* Brenda
the Scottish   Hurley
Post Office   *dir and l* Matthew
Board   Richardson
    des Ashley-Martin
    Davies
    cho Steven Goff

1987   **Macbeth** Verdi   20 performances
Sponsored by   *piano* Brenda
the Scottish   Hurley
Post Office   *dir* Richard Jones
Board   *des* Nigel Lowery
Supported by
Wintun
Weather Beaters

Conductors of Scottish Opera 1962-1987

Norman Del Mar conducting CAPRICCIO performed in 1985.

Stephen Barlow
Stuart Bedford
Gary Bertini
Roderick Brydon

James Conlon
John Currie

Meredith Davies
Wyn Davies
Norman Del Mar
Jacques Delacote
Neil Dodd

Sian Edwards
Alberto Erede

Gyørgy Fischer
Lawrence Foster
David Frame
Janos Furst

Sir Alexander Gibson
Sir Charles Groves

Simon Halsey
Leonard Hancock
Edward Harper
Richard Hickox
Richard Honner
Anthony Hose

Graeme Jenkins

Raymond Leppard
Henry Lewis
James Lockhart

James Loughran
Leon Lovett

Sir Charles Mackerras
Diego Masson
John Mauceri
Kenneth Montgomery

Brian Priestman

Ian Robertson
Stewart Robertson

Lesley-Anne Sammons
Christopher Seaman
Peter Stanger
Robin Stapleton

Bryden Thomson

Walter Weller
Guy Woolfenden

Ronald Zollman

Principal Performers with Scottish Opera 1962-1987

Ian Adam
Christopher Adams
Donald Adams
Malcolm Aitken
Konuhen Akauny
Robert Alderson
David Aldred
Lewis Allan
Malcolm Allen
Thomas Allen
Graham Allum
Stacey Almond
Eduardo Alvares
Jon Andrew
Ludmilla Andrew
Richard Angas
Elder Anton
Simon Doro Antonioli
Paul Anwyl
Curt Appelgren
Colin Arbuckle
Margaret Aronson
Sheila Armstrong
Judith Ashman
John Austin

Gary Bachlund
Norman Bailey
Elizabeth Bainbridge
Ann Baird
Dame Janet Baker
Marco Bakker
Anthony Baldwin
Enid Ballantyne
Brian Bannatyne-Scott
Yvonne Barclay
Sergio Barlotinni
Klara Barlow
Barbara Barnes
Una Barry
Josephine Barstow

Jill Bartlam
David Bartleet
Frederick Bateman
Riaz Beg
Charles Begbie
Heather Begg
Emile Belcourt
Donald Bell
Eleanor Bennett
Sharon Bennett
Hugh Beresford
Leon Berger
Richard Berkeley-Steele
Jennifer Bermingham
Noreen Berry
Jonathan Best
Lola Biagioni
Julia Birch
Harold Blackburn
Joyce Blackham
Derek Blackwell
Gerald Blakely
Jonny Blanc
Peter Bodenham
Franco Bonanome
Franco Bonisolli
Luisa Bosabalian
Christine Botes
Bonaventura Bottone
James Bowman
Lesley Boyd
John Brackenridge
Rosanne Brackenridge
Adrian Brady
Dennis Brandt
Jacqueline Bremar
Patricia Brigenshaw
Keith Brookes
Rhonda Bruce
Joanna Bruno
Sesto Bruscantini

Andrew Bryce
Elaine Bryce
Delme Bryn-Jones
Cynthia Buchan
Isobel Buchanan
Sandy Buchanan
Una Buchanan
Bruce Budd
Paula Bukovac
Brian Burrowes
Norma Burrowes
Reginald Byers

Ian Caddy
Teresa Cahill
Janice Cairns
Ian Caley
John Cameron
Damian Campbell
Phyllis Cannan
Joan Carden
Lenus Carlson
Joan Carlyle
Frances Carroll
Frank Carroll
Clarice Carson
Kathleen Carson
Jessica Cash
Richard Cassilly
Allen Cathcart
Gabriela Cegolea
Sona Cervena
Janice Chapman
Shirley Chapman
David Christie
Gordon Christie
Nan Christie
Kristine Ciesinski
Barry Clark
Bruce Clark
Graham Clark

Left to right: Oktavian (Janet Baker), Sophie (Elizabeth Harwood) and Marshcallin (Helga Dernesch) in DER ROSENKAVALIER performed in 1971.

Patricia Clark
Josephte Clement
Joan Colledge
Marie Collier
Ian Comboy
Billy Connolly
Ann Conoley
David Conyers
Russell Cooper
Janet Coster
Philip Cox
Charles Craig
Rosanne Creffield
Jim Croon
Robert Crowe
Rita Cullis
Carol Anne Curry
Tim Curry
Phyllis Curtin
Mark Curtis
Iain Cuthbertson

Andrew Dalton
Graeme Danby
Marion Darby
Frederico Davia
Arthur Davies
Joan Davies
Menai Davies
Ryland Davies
Anthony Davis
Robert Dean
Stafford Dean
Iris Dell'Acqua
Ann Dempsey
Gregory Dempsey
William Dempsey
Gita Denise
Adrian De Peyer
Jan Derksen
Helga Dernesch
Cristina Deutekom

Emily Golden as Carmen and Gary Bachlund as Don José in CARMEN performed in 1986.

Bernard Dickenson
Alison Doig
Geoffrey Dolton
Frederick Donaldson
Alex Donnan
Malcolm Donnelly
Helena Dose
Nigel Douglas
Ronald Dowd
Meryl Drower
Sandra Dugdale
Ray Dunsire

Roderick Earle
John Eastham
Omar Ebrahim
Jenifer Eddy
Francis Egerton

Rosalind Elias
Alasdair Elliott
Faith Elliott
Brent Ellis
William Elvin
Sally Erskine
Elfego Esparza
Hermin Esser
Paul Esswood
Simon Estes
Sir Geraint Evans

Anthony Feltham
Robert Ferguson
Pier Miranda Ferraro
Helen Field
David Fieldsend
Wendy Fine

Left to right: The Horn (Frank Jones), Rezia (Janice Cairns), Hugh MacLaren (Dennis Bailey), Geoffrey Cabot (Geoffrey Dolton) and Selina (Beverley Mills) in OBERON performed in 1986.

Linda Finnie
Kate Flowers
Michael Follis
Nicholas Folwell
Garrick Forbes
Glenys Fowles
Rupert Frazer
Elizabeth Fretwell
Yvonne Fuller

Zehava Gal
Elizabeth Gale
Jake Gardner

Stuart Gardner
Don Garrard
Eric Garrett
Catherine Gayer
Rachel Gettler
Peter Glossop
Howell Glynne
Victor Godfrey
Emily Golden
Norma Goldie
Jill Gomez
Otoneil Gonzanga
Catriona Gordon

Nancy Gottschalk
John Lawson Graham
Micheline Grancher
Clifford Grant
Linda Esther Gray
Richard Greager
Bernadette Greevy
Patricia Greig
Gwyn Griffiths
Elizabeth Gronow
Andrea Guiot
Iwan Guy
Jane Guy
Ingrid Gwyther
Julien Haas
Hăken Hagegărd
Margaret Haggart

Mark Hamilton
Nigel Hamilton-Shaw
Winifred Hanworth
Glenville Hargreaves
Stuart Harling
Eiddwen Harrhy
Paul Harrhy
Kathryn Harries
Elizabeth Harwood
John Hart-Dyke
Enid Hartle
Jim Hastie
Jonathan Hawkins
Patricia Hay
Raymond Hayter
Marie Hayward
Ann Heggie
Janet Henderson
Gerald Henderson
Fiona Hendley
Louis Hendrikx
Nicky Henson
Thomas Hemsley
Raimund Herincx
Hugh Hetherington
Marie-Anne Hetherington
Angela Hickey
Martyn Hill
David Hillman
Grace Hislop
Richard Holm
Ann Howard
Anne Howells
Heather Howson
Campbell Hughes
Clifford Hughes
David Hughes
Janet Hughes
Jonathan Hyde
Alice Hynd

Inga-Lise
Thom Irvine

Harry Ireland

Arthur Jackson
Ellen Jackson
Gordon Jackson
Maria Jagusz
Oscar James
Peter Jeffes
Neil Jenkins
Halcro Johnston
Philip Joll
Della Jones
Ava June

Galina Kalinina
Miriam Karlin
David Kelly
Moultrie Kelsall
Brian Kemp
Roderick Kennedy
Jonathan Kenny
Yvonne Kenny
Thora Ker
Patricia Kern
Virginia Kerr
Fiona Kimm
Malcolm King
Robert King
Margaret Kingsley

Leonore Kirschstein
John Kitchiner
Victoria Klasicki
Peter Knapp
Gillian Knight
Beryl Korman
Ursula Koszut
Ude Krekow
Werner Krenn
Marina Krilovici
Kathleen Kuhlman

Martin Lane

Michael Langdon
Philip Langridge
Erica Laurentius
Keith Latham
Louis Lebherz
Louise Lebrun
Robin Leggate
Sergei Leiferkus
Margaret Leigh-Hamilton
John Leishman
Moira Leitch
Sally Le Sage
Michael Lewis
William Lewis
Berit Lindholm
Peter Lindroos
Graham Lister
Gyula Littay
Claire Livingstone
Laureen Livingstone
Mary Lloyd-Davies
Robert Lloyd
Nicole L'Orange
Felicity Lott
Kenneth Love
Benjamin Luxon
Norman Lumsden
Peter Lyon

Anna Macciarti
Elaine MacDonald
Morag Mackay
Jane Leslie Mackenzie
William Mackie
Elaine Mackillop
John Macurdy
Elaine Malbin
Catherine Malfitano
Noel Mangin
Werner Mann
Jane Manning
Rosa Mannion
Doreen Mantle

Omar Ebrahim and Mary Lloyd-Davis in Opera Go Round's MACBETH performed in 1987.

Pamela Myers
Raymond Myers

Thomas McAllister
William McAlpine
Kathleen McCarney
Patricia McCarry
Moira McCorkindale
Joyce McCrindle
William McCue
Declan McCusker
Tom McDonnell
Gillian McDougall
Ian McGregor
Sheila McGrow
Donald McIntyre
James McJannett
Ian McKinven
Marie McLaughlin
Libby McLean
Una McLean
Anne McLellan-Scott
Hector McLeod
Linda McLeod
Marjory McMichael
Josephine McQueen

William Neill
Paul Neemer
Margaret Neville
Henry Newman
Hyacinth Nicholls
Evelyn Nicholson
Nigel Nicholson
Harry Nicholl
Raymond Nilsson
Birgit Nordin
Pekka Nuotio

Jane Oakland
John Oakman
Alan Oke
Timothy Oldham

Tom Marandola
Angelo Marenzi
David Marsh
Margaret Marshall
Adrian Martin
Bruce Martin
Anne Mason
Rachel Mathes
Karita Mattila
Michael Maurel
Louis Maurin
Ermanno Mauro
Donald Maxwell
Vahan Merankian
Morley Meredith
John Angelo Messana
Kerstin Meyer
Dorothy Miller
Jenny Miller

Kevin Miller
Lajos Miller
Beverley Mills
Nelly Miricioiou
John Mitchinson
Pamela Molcher
Claire Moll
Maria Moll
Diana Montague
Eleanor Moore
Barry Mora
Beverley Morgan
Gerwyn Morgan
Alexander Morrison
David Morrison
Ronald Morrison
Geoffrey Moses
Conelius Murgo
Michael Myers

Alexander Oliver
Dennis O'Neill
Doreen O'Neill
Patricia O'Neill
Alan Opie
Linda Ormiston
Anne-Marie Owens

Felicity Palmer
Moises Parker
Ticho Parly
Anne Pashley
James Paterson
Joseph Pathmanathan
Ian Patrick
Moyra Patterson
Patricia Payne
Maria Pellegrini
Richard Perrett
Margaret Perry
Carol Anne Petherick
Joanna Peters
Norman Philips
Judith Pierce
Donald Pilley
Jeanette Pilou
Geoffrey Pogson
Shirley Power
Patrick Power
Margaret Preece
Patricia Price
Patricia Purcell
Ashley Putnam
Forrester Pyke

Gino Quilico

Gillian Ramsden
John Rath
Gaetano Rea
Patricia Reakes
Arley Reece
Deborah Rees

Walter Reid
David Rendall
Barbara Rendell
Alberto Remedios
Anna Reynolds
Marco Riato
Lawrence Richard
Grant Richards
Stephen Richardson
Peter Richfield
Michael Rippon
Elizabeth Ritchie
Eric Roberts
Dorothy Robertson
Duncan Robertson
John Robertson
Forbes Robinson
Elizabeth Robson
Anthony Roden
Peter Rodenham
Anne Rodger-Bowen
Joan Rodgers
Janine Roebuck
Anthony Rolfe-Johnston
Natalia Rom
Clover Roope
Carole Rosen
Neil Rosenshein
Elise Ross
Marjory Ross
Suzanna Ross
Joseph Rouleau
Carol Rowlands
Eryl Royle
Michael Royle
Peter-Christoph Runge
Seppo Ruohonen
Karen Russell

Regina Sarfaty
Gordon Sandison
Guillermo Sarabia
Laura Sarti

Sylvia Sass
Robert Savoie
Paula Scalera
Manfred Schenk
Vida Schepens
George Scott
David Scrivens
Rita Shane
Norma Sharp
Terence Sharpe
John Shaw
Clare Shearer
Neil Shicoff
John Shiels
William Shimell
George Shirley
John Shirley-Quirk
Andrew Shore
Geoffrey Shovelton
Marie Slorach
Alison Smith
Russell Smythe
Angela Sorrigan
Zurab Sotkilava
Ingrid Steger
Donald Stephenson
Debra Stuart-Roberts
Una Stubbs
Marion Studholme
Paul Strathearn
Jacek Strauch
Lilian Sukis
Joan Summers
Jonathan Summers

Gillian Taylor
Robert Tear
Kiri Te Kanawa
Oddbjørn Tennfjord
Pierre Thau
Robert Thomas
Shirley Thomas
Adrian Thompson

OTELLO, performed in 1975 with Charles Craig as Otello.

Winton Thomson
Mark Tinkler
Pauline Tinsley
Alan Titus
José Todaro
John Tomlinson
John Tranter
John Treleaven
Llyndall Trottman
Inia Te Wiata
Robert Carpenter Turner
André Turp
Paul Tyers
Marilyn Tyler

Anita Valkki
Richard Van Allan
Pieter Van der Berg
Peter Van der Bilt
Jef Van Wersch
Alceste Varady
Stephen Varcoe
Elizabeth Vaughan
Lee Verona
Galina Vishnevskaya

John Wakefield
Barbara Walker
Patricia Walker
Ian Wallace
Delia Wallis
David Ward
Joseph Ward
Derek Waring
Colin Watson
Lillian Watson
Yoko Watanabe
Alan Watt
Helen Watts
Felicia Weathers
Patricia Wells
Norman Welsby
Jon Frederick West
Kurt Westi
Ian Westrip
Norman White
Willand White
Tom Emlyn Williams
Marjory Williamson
Nuala Willis
Catherine Wilson

Timothy Wilson
John Winfield
Simon Withers
James Witts
Rae Woodland
Kenneth Woolam
Patrick Wymark

John York-Skinner
Alexander Young
Margaret Gatner Young

Mira Zaki

This list of principal peformers with Scottish Opera from 1962 to June 1987, including chorus members taking substantial roles, children with written parts, actors and dancers, has been compiled from programmes, stage management reports and YearBooks in Scottish Opera's archives. To any performer inadvertently omitted, Scottish Opera extends sincere apologies.